'The first edition of this book was a welcome and timely contribution to a fast-moving subject in an omnichannel world. Four years later, this fully revised edition makes for fascinating reading, drawing as it does from a greater variety of new international and sectoral examples and experiences. Once again, Professor Ziliani and her team at the Università di Parma's Loyalty Observatory demonstrate an authoritative command of this important topic.'

Professor Jonathan Reynolds, Academic Director, Oxford Institute of Retail Management, University of Oxford

'Does incorporating sustainable, behavior-inducing practices into loyalty programs pay off? How can brands balance commercial and ethical goals to achieve the best long-term results? What loyalty strategies can address the psychological aspects underlying shopping behavior? In this new edition, Ziliani and Ieva review 25 years of loyalty program evolution, CRM and CX management, and delve into state-of-the-art questions that brands are facing today.'

Stefano Piazzolla, Analytics & Business Intelligence Manager, Esselunga

'The book *Loyalty Management* by Professor Cristina Ziliani and Professor Marco Ieva is a valuable resource for anyone wanting to build a solid understanding of customer loyalty management. Drawing from the authors' research and years of experience in the loyalty space, the book combines rigorous research insights with practical examples and industry trends to cover comprehensive topics in loyalty management. This updated edition includes new timely materials such as a thorough review of sustainability practices in loyalty and case studies of real-world loyalty programs. Whether you are new to the loyalty industry or a seasoned professional, the book's mixture of informative content and personal reflections will make for a rewarding read.'

Professor Yuping Liu-Thompkins, Ph.D., Director of Loyalty Science Lab, Strome College of Business, Old Dominion University, USA

LOYALTY MANAGEMENT

In this insightful text, Cristina Ziliani and Marco Ieva trace the evolution of thinking, contemporary themes and practice in loyalty management.

Loyalty management is increasingly identified with the design and management of a quality customer experience in the journey across the many touchpoints that connect the customer with the brand. Evaluating the research on best practice and offering concrete examples from industry, including seven international case studies, the authors present a fresh take on the tools, strategies and skills – from loyalty programs to CRM to CX – that underpin loyalty's key significance in marketing. New to this 2nd edition, readers will find:

- A new chapter exploring the strategic relevance of loyalty management for company long-term profitability.
- A new chapter on loyalty and sustainability, based on research on 90 case studies of loyalty initiatives worldwide, supporting organizations as they strive to meet their ESG requirements and demonstrating how they can use their loyalty programs to do so.
- Coverage of the role of touchpoints in developing loyalty, from physical stores to voice assistants, drawing from state-of-the-art international scientific research.
- Discussion of metrics and KPIs for measuring loyalty management, as well as further exploration of the role of emerging technologies, in particular the application of predictive and generative artificial intelligence to loyalty strategies.
- New case studies and examples from a broader range of industries and geographical regions.

Celebrating 25 years of experience in research, consulting and teaching within the Osservatorio Fedeltà UniPR (Loyalty Observatory), the authors have compiled a unique research-based, practice-oriented text.

It will guide marketers, business leaders and postgraduate students through the changes in marketing thought and practice of loyalty management – including omnichannel, AI and sustainability – as well as offering practical guidance on the skills and capabilities that companies need if they want to be successful at delivering essential, loyalty-driving customer experiences.

Cristina Ziliani, PhD, is Professor of Marketing at the University of Parma, Italy and the scientific director of the Osservatorio Fedeltà UniPR. She lectures at leading universities and business events around the world.

Marco Ieva is Associate Professor in Marketing at the University of Parma, Italy. His research interests are retailing, loyalty management and marketing innovation.

LOYALTY MANAGEMENT

Driving Engagement with Loyalty
Programs and Customer Experience

Second Edition

Cristina Ziliani and Marco Ieva

Routledge
Taylor & Francis Group

LONDON AND NEW YORK

Designed cover image: cnythzl / Getty Images

Second edition published 2025
by Routledge
4 Park Square, Milton Park, Abingdon, Oxon, OX14 4RN

and by Routledge
605 Third Avenue, New York, NY 10158

Routledge is an imprint of the Taylor & Francis Group, an informa business

First edition published by Routledge 2019

British Library Cataloguing-in-Publication Data
A catalogue record for this book is available from the British Library

ISBN: 978-1-032-51036-1 (hbk)
ISBN: 978-1-032-51035-4 (pbk)
ISBN: 978-1-003-40078-3 (ebk)

DOI: 10.4324/9781003400783

Typeset in Galliard
by SPi Technologies India Pvt Ltd (Straive)

To the memory of my beloved parents, to Alessandra – the discovery of trustful sisterhood, and to Francesco – the construction of long-lasting, loyal love
                                                      Cristina Ziliani

To my parents, to Stefania, who has supported me tirelessly in all circumstances, and to my colleague and friend Giada, who has devoted great effort to this book
                                                      Marco Ieva

CONTENTS

ILLUSTRATIONS

Tables

PREFACE

When Routledge called us and told us that our book *Loyalty Management* had been doing very well, and asked if we were interested in doing a second edition, we could not simply do some updating and reprint. And not simply because we are celebrating 25 years of activity in 2025 and something special was in order!

In fact, a lot has happened since the first edition in 2020 – think of Covid-19 and artificial intelligence. The world is not the same nor is loyalty management. Here is what we decided to do:

- Academic research is now abundant to prove that having a customer management orientation – be it with the aid of a formalized loyalty program or through customer relationship management (CRM) and customer experience (CX) – is the way the world goes, and it provides superior profitability: we introduced Chapter 1 to discuss such research, to support the case for steering firms' strategies towards loyalty.
- Best in class of loyalty management have emerged in the five continents, so we reached out to creators and leaders of successful loyalty programs and packed Chapter 10 with seven case studies, full of insights: Club Matas, Dialog Star Points, Dotz, Picard et Nous, VeryMe Rewards by Vodafone, XPLR Pass, yuu Rewards Club.
- Sustainability has emerged as a big topic for corporate executives and marketing teams, so we have done an extensive research project on sustainability in loyalty programs and introduced Chapter 3 to present its results.
- Technology has been modifying the environment more than we could imagine back in 2020, with omnichannel and generative AI – not only predictive AI – transforming customer experiences and company practice: the implications for loyalty are discussed in Chapters 2 and 5.

- Engagement has emerged as the antecedent of loyalty, so we called fellow researcher and expert Giada Salvietti to write about this and about gamification's role to cultivate it in Chapter 6.
- Since managers from an increasing number of sectors and countries call us in search of benchmarks for their loyalty activities and results, we created Chapter 8 to share the surveys we have done of Italian companies and consumers over the past five years on various aspects of loyalty, CRM and CX management, to provide benchmarks and examples of research to replicate in your own markets.

These are the new features we have worked on from 2020 to 2025 that you will find in the book that is in your hands. The passion for research, for telling and for sharing that we put into it ... they are the same as in the past 25 years (or in the case of Marco, 13 years)!

INTRODUCTION

A central proposition frames the rationale and content of the book currently in your hands: securing customer loyalty is a priority for businesses. In today's world, marketing is largely based on the goal of earning long-term loyal customers, and long-standing loyalty tools – transformed by the information revolution into data-rich, interactive touchpoints – have become the enablers of loyalty-oriented and customer-centred omnichannel strategies that are shaping the consumer world. This book discusses the changes in society and markets that have made and will continue to make the goal of loyalty so central and examines how this has been reflected in the evolution of marketing paradigms and business practices throughout the world.

In both the academic and business worlds, loyalty management has grown in stature. What makes and how to make customers loyal has been debated in lecture halls, discussed at conferences, designed in boardrooms and played out on shop floors and e-stores. The rise of digital has added a new online dynamic and along with it, inevitable challenges and opportunities, amplified today by artificial intelligence. At the same time, firms' need to find purpose and to ensure and prove their environmental and social sustainability through ESG practices has requested loyalty management to find the most appropriate way to embrace new values and remain engaging and effective. Over more than a century, a variety of loyalty tools and practices have arisen and diffused across industries and countries. The paraphernalia of loyalty management has taken manifold forms from tickets, tokens and stamps of the early days to plastic cards, vouchers and coupons to digital wallets, wish lists and personalized journeys. And it's not only aimed at customers – ensuring the loyalty of channel partners and strengthening business-to-business (B2B) relationships is just as essential in today's interconnected business environment. The journey of loyalty management traces a path that leads from Green Stamps to the Tesco Clubcard to Amazon Prime and the Starbucks wallet. Managing both customer and partner loyalty has shifted from running programs to managing relationships to curating experiences.

Over the past three decades loyalty management has undergone three phases. From 1980 to the end of the twentieth century, it meant running a loyalty program. Since 2000, companies have shifted their focus towards harnessing the 'invisible' advantages of such programs: the insight they offer into the world of their customers, the opportunity this gives them to develop and manage positive relationships with those customers, and the value created by being able to use scheme data to inform decision-making and shape targeted marketing efforts to retain, upsell, cross-sell or reactivate their customer base. That was the CRM phase. In 2020 we entered a new phase. Loyalty management now is increasingly being identified with the design and management of a quality customer experience across the various touchpoints that connect the customer and the brand and through which the customer journey evolves.

Overall, loyalty management is, and has always been, a continuous effort to create and expand a space of *free circulation* for the customer, in which she is identified as an individual with unique characteristics derived from data collected at various touchpoints, and to provide superior value based on individual preferences and needs in doing so. The advances made in recent years in technology have only accelerated and expanded this process. Tools and methods derived from data science and artificial intelligence have improved the ways in which customers can be identified and tracked across an ever-increasing variety of touchpoints and have given brands the means to reach new heights of sophistication in the personalizing of interactions, offers, conversations and environments. The recent developments in retailer media networks are a testimony to this. The information revolution made it possible for companies to collect, analyse and use vast amounts of individual customer data upon which more accurate marketing decisions could be made, thus helping to bring about the shift in emphasis towards customer relationship management (CRM) techniques. Customer-centric measures of success, such as share of wallet, retention rates and customer lifetime value, soon entered the boardroom and are today valued very highly by business leaders and investors, as the chapter by Michela Giacomini and Miriam Panìco (formerly with dunnhumby) on customer-based decision-making illustrates.

The impact of ubiquitous digital technology was profound. Not only is print media like coupons, flyers, cards and direct mail delivered to your mobile phone screen, traditional one-size-fits-all price cuts and special offers are now personalized to individuals and sequenced to nudge the customer towards brand and store loyalty. New business models have emerged centred on price or loyalty promotion: mobile rewards platforms, curated subscription models and wallets, to mention but a few. The environments in which we consume products, services and experiences have become intelligent, mixed realities, simultaneously operating offline and online, where identified customers can move freely and interact with humans and artificial agents. Digital services such as click and collect, persistent shopping baskets, wish lists, in-store virtual catalogues and chatbots interweave touchpoints and bridge channels, providing the customers with a unified and seamless experience with the end goal of retaining them, making them loyal. We now live in an omnichannel, increasingly responsive and intelligent environment.

The customer experience management (CEM) and omnichannel management frameworks that have emerged in this environment help managers eliminate barriers across channels so that customers might have a seamless experience in which they are recognized and served based on their individual preferences, needs and loyalties. Central to this is understanding and managing how they perceive their interaction with all the different touchpoints they encounter in offline and online channels. The two frameworks share a common goal: achieving customer loyalty. Companies are now wrestling with how to organize resources to provide such loyalty-building omnichannel experiences. This book provides some empirical responses to this challenge and demonstrates that the means exist within most companies. Companies that already have loyalty programs and/or CRM models, and thus the people and skills required to execute them, already have in place the building blocks of omnichannel CEM. They may also already believe in the principles and philosophy that drives it. In any case, an overhaul is not generally necessary – existing loyalty programs and CRM systems are optimal starting points. An understanding of the critical role of engagement, and of gamification and personalization to develop it, as discussed by Giada Salvietti in her valuable chapters, will contribute to success.

The aims of this book are twofold. First, to assist the reader in navigating the changes that have shaped marketing thought and practice on loyalty management. Second, to offer guidance on the skills and capabilities that companies will require if they want to be successful at delivering omnichannel, sustainable, intelligent customer experiences that drive loyalty. We believe there is something here for everyone, whether you are a marketer, business leader or student, or simply someone curious about how loyalty works in a consumer setting. We have plenty of novelties for those who liked to first edition too, as we draw on 25 years of scientific research, consultancy and education to try to bring a fresh take on concepts seen by some as buzzwords and by others as irrelevant outside of a marketing department. We believe they are neither. Rather, loyalty program, CRM, CEM, omnichannel and sustainability are steps in the evolutionary process of any successful, value-creating organization. They are lived by every customer and business partner. And each provides the foundation for the next. Nothing is lost, but everything is transformed: to take the first steps towards needed transformation, companies need to look no further than their 'old' loyalty scheme. It starts from there.

THE LOYALTY OBSERVATORY

The Osservatorio Fedeltà (Loyalty Observatory) was created in 1999 at the University of Parma, Italy, with the goal of studying the adoption of loyalty management and the use of customer data in European retailing and overseas. Tracking of the loyalty practices of over 130 retail groups had begun in 1997 and provided the foundation for our understanding of the loyalty management phenomenon between 1980 and 2000, when we expanded the monitoring to loyalty activities in other industries.

The Loyalty Observatory is a research centre based within the Department of Economics and Management of the university, where it draws on over 40 years of research in the fields of marketing, retail management, channel relationships and trade marketing. From the beginning, our goal has always been to contribute to the development of a customer loyalty culture among Italian managers across all industries and support managers, researchers and students interested in developing research projects, strategy redesign, training or simply knowing more about loyalty management and customer relationship management (CRM). At our annual workshop, where more than 400 managers, marketing practitioners and academics gather together in Parma, the Observatory's research is disseminated among companies in the consumer goods manufacturing, retailing and services sectors.

The Observatory develops research and training projects for companies on loyalty, CRM and customer experience management. We also promote theses and dissertations that result from close cooperation between firms and students. In 2015 we celebrated 15 years of our annual workshop and its related activities and by 2025, our reach has grown significantly. As this book goes to press, we are preparing to celebrate our twenty-fifth anniversary, and the Conference's record makes for impressive reading: nearly 4,000 delegates (representing more than 1,500 companies), over 180 speakers, 40 sponsors, and more than 500 student organizers. We are proud of the work that has been achieved: over 120 master's theses on loyalty, more than 60 academic papers and six books.

Our partners and sponsors

The Observatory Steering Committee is formed of managers from companies that aim to support the Observatory in its research and dissemination activity. Dialogue is established with the Observatory team to exchange ideas, develop projects, create events and recruit talented graduates and professionals in the fields of loyalty and CRM. Our partners help shape the Observatory research agenda and are visible at our events, on our website and in our publications. Over the years, we have partnered with distinguished players in the fields of marketing intelligence, customer data, loyalty, CRM, promotion platforms, consulting and services. dunnhumby, who contribute a chapter to this book, has been a sponsor and close partner for several years. We continue to enjoy long-time partnerships with Advice Group, Kettydo+, *Promotion Magazine*, and NielsenIQ has partnered with us on consumer studies for fifteen years. Internationally, we have developed a network of collaborations with other research centres, associations and experts who are devoted to contributing to the development of a loyalty management culture in the business world: l'Observatoire de la Fidélité at the University of Bordeaux (France), the Loyalty Science Lab at Old Dominion University (USA), the Australian Loyalty Association, TheWiseMarketer, the International Loyalty Awards, and other agreements are on the way.

The annual conference

Since 1999 the Observatory has showcased its research at its annual Conference in Parma. The format has been established over the years as a full day of research presentations, successful case histories, international keynote speakers, industry roundtable discussions and a networking lunch. The theme of the workshop differs each year:

2024 Loyalty Redesign
2023 Loyalty and Growth Strategies
2022 Loyalty Has New Boundaries
2021 Digital Loyalty Revolution
2020 Restarting from Loyalty
2019 Data, Value and Loyalty
2018 Loyalty in the Age of Experience
2017 Loyalty Marketing Evolution: International Stories and Leaders
2016 Loyalty Disruption? Emotions, Big Data and New Players
2015 15 Years of Loyalty Marketing: What's Next?
2014 From Print to Digital: What Happens to Loyalty?
2013 Growing Through loyalty in Times of Economic Crisis
2012 Brand Loyalty Strategies: From Macro to Micro Approaches
2011 The Value of Loyalty in the Choice Overload Age
2010 The Future of Loyalty Marketing: New Models and Technologies
2009 Ten Years of Loyalty Marketing in European Retailing
2008 Channel Loyalty: Making Channel Partners Loyal
2007 Innovation in Promotions
2006 Partnerships for Value Creation
2005 Creating Value with Customer Information
2004 Measuring Promotion Effectiveness
2003 Data Mining for Value Creation and Loyalty
2001 Creating Relationships in the Internet Age
1999 Value from Customer Relationships

The academy

In 2022, after running the Conference online for two years, we decided we wanted more moments to keep in touch with our loyal audience during the year; moreover, we wanted to respond to requests that we received continuously of in-depth training on specific loyalty topics, by junior and senior management alike. We therefore developed a unique format of 2-hour-long webinars dedicated to a specific topic where we share the state of the art of academic research on the subject, we invite the speech of an international expert and two of the members of our steering committee discuss with brands their successful case studies on the subject. We have been blessed with an incredibly positive response so far, with over 250 attendees at every episode. Here are the subjects of our webinars (content available to registered attendees only):

2024 'Loyalty Redesign' and 'Engagement Redesign'
2023 'Effective Gamification', 'Data Quality for Omnichannel' and 'Measuring the Impact of Touchpoints on Customers'
2022 'Loyalty and Sustainability' and 'Engagement and Loyalty'

Our research projects

2023   Generations and Loyalty Programs
2022   The New Frontiers of Loyalty
2021   Loyalty Touchpoints in the Italian Grocery Retail Sector During Covid-19
2020   Customer Loyalty in Italy: Between Loyalty Programs and Personalization of the Customer Experience
2019   Overview of Loyalty Management in Italy
2018   The Market for Loyalty Services and Products
2017   Omnichannel Loyalty Management
2016   Touchpoint Management Approaches for Customer Experience and Loyalty Management
2015   Promotion Intermediaries
2014   The Role of Medium in Loyalty and Price Communication
2013   Planned or Impulse? Consumer Behaviour in Time of Crisis
2012   Loyalty Card Data for Promotional Flyer Improvement
2011   Loyalty and Multichannel Behaviour in Retailing
2010   Beyond Loyalty Cards: Making Retail Customer Loyal with Targeted and Untargeted Tools
2009   Supermarket Industry Loyalty Practices
2008   Channel Loyalty: Loyalty in the B2B context
2007   Cross-industry Analysis of Loyalty Marketing Practices
2006   Loyalty Promotion in Italy: Gift Catalogues
2004   Loyalty Marketing Trends in Europe
2001   Loyalty Card Insight-sharing Between Retailers and Suppliers
1999   Information-sharing Between Retailers and FMCG Manufacturers

Selected scientific publications

Flacandji, M., Passebois Ducros, J. and Ieva, M. (2023) 'Redesigning loyalty marketing for a better world: the impact of green loyalty programs on perceived value'. *Journal of Service Theory and Practice*, 33(4), pp. 465–487.

Frasquet, M., Ieva, M. and Ziliani, C. (2021) 'Online channel adoption in supermarket retailing'. *Journal of Retailing and Consumer Services*, 59, 102374, pp. 1–9.

Ieva, M., De Canio, F. and Ziliani, C. (2018) 'Daily deal shoppers: what drives social couponing?'. *Journal of Retailing and Consumer Services*, 40, pp. 299–303.

Ieva, M. and Ziliani, C. (2017) 'Towards digital loyalty programs: insights from customer medium preference segmentation'. *International Journal of Retail & Distribution Management*, 45(2), pp. 195–210.

Ieva, M. and Ziliani, C. (2018a) 'The role of customer experience touchpoints in driving loyalty intentions in services'. *The TQM Journal*, 30(5), pp. 444–457.

Ieva, M. and Ziliani, C. (2018b) 'Mapping touchpoint exposure in retailing: implications for developing an omnichannel customer experience'. *International Journal of Retail & Distribution Management*, 46(3), pp. 304–322.

Ieva, M., Ziliani, C., Gàzquez-Abad, J. C. and D'Attoma, I. (2017) 'Online versus offline promotional communication: evaluating the effect of medium on customer response'. *Journal of Advertising Research*, 58(3), pp. 338–348.

Lugli, G. and Ziliani, C. (2004) *Micromarketing: Creare valore con le informazioni di cliente*. Turin: UTET.

Salvietti, G., Ziliani, C., Teller, C., Ieva, M. and Ranfagni, S. (2022) 'Omnichannel retailing and post-pandemic recovery: building a research agenda'. *International Journal of Retail & Distribution Management*, 50(8/9), pp. 1156–1181.

Ziliani, C. (2008a) *Loyalty marketing: Creare valore con le relazioni*. Milan: EGEA.

Ziliani, C. (2008b) 'Making the point: the challenge of loyalty program effectiveness measurement'. *Mercati & Competitività*, 4, pp. 127–150.

Ziliani, C. (2015) *Promotion revolution: Nuove strategie e nuovi protagonisti della promozione 2.0*. Milan: EGEA.

Ziliani, C. and Bellini, S. (2004) 'From loyalty cards to micro-marketing strategies: where is Europe's retail industry heading?' *Journal of Targeting, Measurement and Analysis for Marketing*, 12(3), pp. 281–289.

Ziliani, C. and Ieva, M. (2015) 'Retail shopper marketing: the future of promotional flyers'. *International Journal of Retail & Distribution Management*, 43(6), pp. 488–502.

Ziliani, C. and Ieva, M. (2016) 'Customer relationship management in a digital world: profiling best in class companies'. Paper presented at the Italian Management Conference 'Management in a digital world: decisions, production, communication', 9–10 June.

White papers (in Italian)

2023   Generations and loyalty programs
2022   The new frontiers of loyalty
2021   Retail loyalty touchpoints in times of Covid-19
2020   Loyalty Management in Italy between loyalty programs and CX
2019   The market for loyalty management products and services in Italy
2018   Customer Experience Management in Italy
2017   Managing Touchpoints for Customer Experience and Loyalty
2016   Loyalty Management and CRM in Italy

ACKNOWLEDGEMENTS

This book is testament to 25 years of work conducted at the Loyalty Observatory and we would like to thank the people and organizations that have supported, advised, worked with and inspired us throughout this period. Our first thought goes to Jonathan Reynolds and Richard Cuthbertson at the Saïd Business School, University of Oxford. It was there in 1998, while Cristina was completing her doctorate, that she first became interested in research on loyalty programs. Back in Parma, Professor Gianpiero Lugli saw how promising this research stream was, especially for retailers, and pushed her to delve into it. In the same year, John Dawson at University of Edinburgh started supporting Cristina in her research efforts, providing advice, contacts and research opportunities. John has become a very dear friend.

We thank Oracle, WincorNixdorf, ICTeam and Buongiorno, who supported the early editions of the Observatory Conference and our first website www.partnership4loyalty.com, and Seri Group for creating the CRM Award, which was assigned to distinguished CRM campaigns during the Observatory Conference from 2005 to 2008. We'd also like to acknowledge our current partners (Advice Group, Fingroove, Kettydo+, Promotica, dunnhumby, Edenred, E-fidelity, Konvergence, PwC, Omnio Europe, Promotion Magazine) and former partners of the last three years (Amilon, Catalina Marketing, Comarch, Epipoli, GoGift, Loyal Guru, Reloy, Royalty Maps Group) for sponsoring the Observatory and enriching our work through precious dialogue. A special mention goes to Filippo Genzini whose advice and friendship has been as indispensable to us as his work on coordinating sponsors and partnerships.

We are grateful to have made many friends in the field of loyalty research, consulting and training around the world: Mike Capizzi, Aaron Dauphinee,

Michael Flacandji, Bill Hanifin, Charlie Hills, Zsuzsa Kecsmar, Eileen McGuinness, Annich Mcintosh, Phil Mooney, Yuping Liu-Thompkins, Juliette Passebois-Ducros, Sarah Richardson, Paula Thomas and Phil Rubin.

Special thanks go to our many friends working in the field of market research who are always ready to collaborate and share their expertise: Maria Grazia Bolognesi, Christian Centonze, Debora Costi, Maria Francesca Cuomo, Chiara De Maio, Lorenzo Facchinotti, Gabriella Bergaglio and Cristina Colombo, Roberto Borghini, Enrico Billi and Stefano Di Palma.

We have benefitted from the contribution of over 180 speakers at conferences held by the Loyalty Observatory and at lectures on loyalty marketing and CRM hosted by the University of Parma. The conference has seen almost 4000 attendees from more than 1,500 companies, some of whom have been with us since the first iteration in 1999. Their input has been immensely helpful as have the hundreds of managers and experts who responded to our surveys, dedicated their time and shared their ideas with us.

Special thoughts go to: Bruno Aceto, Maurizio Alberti, Odoardo Ambroso, Chiara Angeli, Augusta Angelino, Gianluca Annoni, Nicola Antonelli, Stefano Araldi, Filippo Arroni, Massimo Baggi, Mario Bagliani, Stephane Baizeau, Flavio Baldes, Michael Ballings, Alessandro Barbieri, Enrico Barboglio, Christopher Barth, Lorenza Bassetti, Marc Battailler, Elena Bernardelli, Giuseppe Belvisi, Rossana Bianco, Chiara Bignazzi, Desirée Bison, Claudio Bonetti, Maurizio Bonfante, Graham Bradley, Lorenzo Bracco, Els Breugelmans, Alessandro Bucich, Giuseppe Calabrini, Mirko Calamante, Caterina Camerini, Furio Camillo, Giuseppe Cantone, Mike Capizzi, Fausto Caprini, Carlo Caranza, Rosa Carbone, Carlo Carmagnola, Alessandra Carnelli, Marco Carola, Valentina Carnevali, Daniele Carraro, Gianluca Carrera, Mara Cassinari, Sergio Cassingena, Roberto Catanzaro, Luciano Cavazzana, Daniele Cazzani, Andrea Cerioli, Manuel Chinchio, David Ciancio, Patrizia Cicognani, Stefano Cini, Felice Ciniglio, Daniela Colombara, Ruggero Colombo, Carola Conti, Francesco Cordani, Claudio Corti, Lorenza Cortivo, Debora Costi, Davide Cozzarolo, Maria Francesca Cuomo, Donnino Dalla Turca, Marta Dall'Arche, Francesco Daveri, John Dawson, Romolo De Camillis, Francesca De Canio, Chiara De Maio, Daniele De Sano, Siro Descrovi, Gianfranco Delfini, Antonio De Martini, Andrea Demodena, Alessandra Del Corso, Barbara Del Neri, Anna Del Piccolo, Francesco Del Porto, Pietro De Nardis, Matteo De Tomasi, Federico Dezi, Gabriele Dorfmann, Andrea Duilio, Roberto Falcinelli, Javi Férnandez, Maurizio Ferraris, Claudia Filippini, Marco Filipponi, Stefano Fiorentino, Michele Fioroni, Anthony Finiguerra, Maura Franchi, Valeria Freschi, Paolo Frignani, Marco Formisano, Valentina Francot, Alberto Frau, Fulvio Furbatto, Monica Gagliardi, Ludovico Galimberti, Vittorio Gallese, Marco Gandolfi, Armando Garosci, Francesco Gasca, Marcello Genovese, Agostino Ghebbioni, Michela Giacomini, Chiara Gianaroli, Gaetano Giannetto, Sharon Glass, Claudia Golinelli, Enzo Grassi, Angelo Grisolia, Alberto Gualtieri, Michele Guerra,

Rasmus Houlind, Paolo Iabichino, Mirko Iacona, Giulia Ietto, Ines Joao, Luca Lanza, Laura Lavizzari, Flora Leoni, Luca Leoni, Carla Leveratto, Roberto Liscia, Edoardo Loasses, Simon Lonsdale, Giacomo Lovati, Paolo Lucci, Luca Luminoso, Irene Lunelli, Maria Luppi, Valeria Maniscalco, Luigi Mansani, Giovanna Manzi, Michele Marchigiani, Gianluca Marchio, Stefano Masi, Natalia Massi, Stefano Mazza, Katia Mazzoni, Annich Mcintosh, Patrizia Meneghini, Marco Metti, Paolo Michelis, Roberta Mincione, Marcello Molinari, Sara Molteni, Chiara Monteleone, Sergio Muller, Federico Mussetto, Bianca Mutti, Anja Nachtwey, Michela Natale, Francesca Negri, Stefano Notturno, Pedro Ortega Poblete, Lucia Palmerini, Paolo Palomba, Mara Panajia, Silvio Panetta, Miriam Panìco, Federica Paterno, Giles Pavey, Fabrizio Pavone, Ambra Pazzagli, Bryan Pearson, Simone Pescatore, Davide Pellegrini, Alessandro Petazzi, Giuliano Pezzano, Laura Pezzotta, Ferruccio Piazzoni, Andrea Piccirelli, Enrico Piccirilli, Jeroen Pietryga, Marco Pisani, Arturo Pisapia, Mauro Poli, Stefano Poli, Osvaldo Ponchia, Stefano Portu, Stefano Quartullo, Massimo Rabuffo, Eleonora Radici, Deva Rangarajan, Stefania Ranieri, Umberto Rapetto, Marco Ravagnan, Ornella Raveane, Fabio Regazzoni, Jonathan Reynolds, Alexander Rittweger, Sergio Rizzato, Federico Rocco, Valentina Rocco, Samuele Ronchin, Diego Rosso, Luigi Rubinelli, Dimitrios Salampasis, Giorgio Santambrogio, Marco Santambrogio, Massimo Schembri, Ansgar Schneider, Joan Schwoerer, Phil Shelper, Henry Sichel, Vincenzo Sinibaldi, Giancarlo Spina, Giuseppe Staglianò, Roberto Stanco, Bart Steenken, Mirco Stefanoni, Giusy Strippoli, Davide Surace, Tiziano Tassi, Luca Tateo, Christoph Teller, Daniele Tirelli, Susi Tondini, Stefano Tonella, Leandro Torres, Diego Toscani, Alessandra Tosi, Melissa Tosi, Angelo Tosoni, Gabriele Traversi, Yves Van Vaerenbergh, Davide Vegetti, Laura Ventura, Giulia Venturini, Pooja Venugopal, Andrea Verri, Walter Afonso Vieira, Marino Vignati, Barbara Vignola, Lucio Volponi, Antonio Votino, Alvise Zanardi, Sergio Zani, Francesca Zecca, Matteo Zenoni, Filippo Zuffada, Giuseppe 'Pino' Zuliani, and to all fellow members of the scientific committees of *Promotion Magazine*, the DMA Italia Awards, the Promotion Awards and the International Loyalty Awards. We would also like to specifically thank our friend Andrea Demodena for his ongoing support and valuable advice throughout the years.

Thank you to our friends and colleagues at the Academy of Marketing Science, the EAERCD, the NBPL and the CERR conferences, and of the Italian SIM and SIMA, for consistently stimulating our thoughts about loyalty over the years. We are grateful to the Hartman Center for Sales, Advertising and Marketing at the Duke University in North Carolina for seeing the value in the study of sales promotions and awarding Cristina with a research grant to work on B2B loyalty programs. We are grateful too to Professor Dirk Van den Poel at the University of Ghent for his availability and support throughout the years. Marco gained invaluable knowledge and experience during his time there, where he had the opportunity to learn state-of-the-art techniques in customer relationship management (CRM) and market research from Prof. Van den Poel, Prof. Michael Ballings, Prof. Dauwe Vercamer, Prof. Andrey Volkov, Prof. Mario Pandelaere and Prof. Jeroen D'Haen. We thank them all. We are especially grateful because in 2020 a promising Ph. D student crossed our path and stayed with us, to become a talented researcher, critical thinker and extraordinary blessing for the Observatory: Giada Salvietti, who authored two chapters of this book. We also thank our colleagues at the Department of Economics and Management at the University of Parma, with whom we share a passion for research and teaching. We are especially grateful to our friends and colleagues, Maura Franchi and Alberto Guenzi, with whom Cristina shares a love for sociology and the history of marketing.

We also acknowledge the hard work of the junior researchers who spent periods with the Observatory, long and short: Chiara D'Onofrio, Annalisa Guarnieri, Francesco Termite, Elena Mosca, Alberto Frau, Chiara Bonaretti Alessandri, Virginia Bonaretti, Nicola Pizzolato, Roberto Boniburini, Davide Bessi, Elisabetta Mariano, Rita Giulia Rizzitello, Jessica Borsi, Greta Pescarossa, Marcello Fantuzzi, Fabio Fichera, Gabriele Longo, Valentina Spinozzi, Claudia Fasano, Dario Consoli, Mattia Casotti, Deborah Inzerillo, Ketty Ilacqua, Martina Colombano, Simona Galioto, Nicola Canevari, Giorgio Tucci, Elisa Pini, Matteo Corti, Giulia Provitera, Elena Baldiserri, Irene Santalucia, Chiara Pasculli, Grazia Palandra, Costanza Olivieri, Valentina Patuzzo, Elisa Conti, Mariacaterina Lunardo, Silvia Chessa, Clelia Galvano, Nicole Baldassa, Ilenia Cavaliere and indeed our students, who make the Loyalty Observatory annual conference possible every year, organizing each and every aspect of it with ceaseless commitment and enthusiasm. Special thanks must go to those who work more closely with us on loyalty and marketing research: Silvia Bellini, Maria Grazia Cardinali, Ida D'Attoma, Marta Frasquet, Juan Carlos Gàzquez-Abad, Chieko Minami, Christoph Teller and Yuping Liu-Thompkins. As teachers, our students help make our work meaningful and Cristina has been the proud director of the Trade and Consumer Marketing Master's course at the University of Parma since 2012. More than a 120 of you have graduated with theses on aspects of loyalty, CRM and customer experience and for many of you it was the beginning of a sparkling career. We are very proud of you.

In bringing this new edition of the book to the world, we are indebted to Jacqueline Curthoys and to Sophia Levin and her team at Routledge who took on our manuscript and helped see it into print. We'd also like to thank Jon Wilcox who worked with us on our original pitch and the early drafts of the first edition of this book, helping us to clarify our ideas and improve our expression. His efforts have been invaluable and we could not have accomplished this without his expertise, acumen and patience. Several anonymous reviewers helped us fine-tune our proposition and we are grateful for all the feedback we received in preparing the manuscript for publication.

We reserve a special thanks to Michela Giacomini and Miriam Panìco, who were at dunnhumby when they wrote a chapter for the first edition of this book and we are grateful to dunnhumby for approving its reprint in the present edition and for continuing to share ideas and give their time and effort to collaborating with us on developing an understanding of loyalty.

Finally, we are deeply grateful to the authors of the case studies in Chapter 10: Peter Anders Franch, David Gosse, Erica Hood, Isuru Madhushanka, Jacky Mak, Jonathas Mendes, Leandro Torres and Michelle Williams for the time and effort they put in writing them and sharing valuable insights. And to Charlie Hills, Rasmus Houlind, Michael Flacandji, Sarah Richardson, Phil Shelper, Paula Thomas, and Pooja Venugopal for creating the connections with the case studies authors.

Genuine progress is made when academia and business work together and common efforts are made to advance both theoretical insight and practical application. Our final thanks go to our families and partners whose encouragement and patience gave us the time and the strength to accomplish this book.

Cristina Ziliani and Marco Ieva

LIST OF ABBREVIATIONS

AI	artificial intelligence
AMA	American Marketing Association
B2B	business-to-business
B2C	business-to-consumer
CEM	customer experience management
CHAID	chi-square automation interaction detector
CRM	customer relationship management
CSR	corporate social responsibility
CX	customer experience
DEM	direct emailing
EDLP	everyday low price
EDV	everyday value
EPOS	electronic point-of-scale
ESG	environmental, societal and governance
EXQ	customer experience quality
FMCG	fast-moving consumer goods
GDPR	General Data Protection Regulation
IAT	intelligent agent technology
KPI	key performance indicator
LMPS	loyalty management products and services
LMUK	Loyalty Management UK
MSR	My Starbucks Rewards
NDL	National Demographics & Lifestyles
RFM	recency, frequency, monetary
ROI	return on investment

SERVQUAL	service quality measure
SKU	stock keeping unit
POP	point-of-purchase
WER	word error rate

AUTHOR BIOGRAPHIES

Cristina Ziliani, PhD, is full professor of marketing at the University of Parma, Italy. She lectures on loyalty management at leading universities and business events around the world, including Australia, Brasil, Japan, the US, UK, France, Belgium, Spain and Thailand. Her research focuses on loyalty marketing, customer relationship management, promotions and customer experience. She is the author of over 50 scientific papers on loyalty and six books, and is the scientific director of the Osservatorio Fedeltà UniPR (Loyalty Observatory) since 1999.

Cristina is also the director of the master's course in trade and consumer marketing at the University of Parma, growing talents for marketing, CRM and loyalty positions in Italy and abroad.

Marco Ieva, PhD, is associate professor in marketing at the University of Parma where he lectures in customer relationship management, e-commerce and digital analytics and services marketing. His research spans retailing, loyalty marketing, customer experience and marketing innovation. He has published papers in multiple academic outlets, such as *Journal of Advertising Research, Industrial Marketing Management, Journal of Cleaner Production, Journal of Retailing and Consumer Services* and *International Journal of Retail and Distribution Management.*

Contributors

Michela Giacomini has more than 20 years of experience in the customer data world, having worked for 12 years with dunnhumby and 10 years with SAS before that. Michela used to lead a team of client managers who runs projects with all new dunnhumby partners in Europe. She run strategic pricing, category management, CRM and loyalty projects. Michela has a solid statistical and analytical background, having previously worked as an insight director and analytical consultant. Currently, she is retail customer strategy and insights expert at PwC Italy.

Miriam Panico was customer engagement manager EMEA at dunnhumby when she coauthored Chapter 7 in this book. With over 10 years of loyalty and CRM experience in the retail business, she has worked with European clients such as Tesco, Gruppo Pam, CRAI and other retailers, as well as FMCG companies. She previously worked as a communications manager at ENIT, the Agenzia Nazionale del Turismo (Italian Government Tourist Board). She is now client director at Loyal Guru.

Giada Salvietti, PhD, is post-doctoral research fellow and adjunct professor in marketing at the University of Parma, Italy, where she lectures in loyalty management and sustainability marketing. She is also a member of the Loyalty Observatory. Her main research interest is the Omnichannel phenomenon and its influence on consumer behaviour and management strategies, with a specific focus on loyalty-related outcomes. Her work has been published in international and national journals, such as *Psychology and Marketing* and *International Journal of Retail and Distribution Management*.

1

LOYALTY MANAGEMENT

Strategy for profitable growth

Cristina Ziliani

Loyalty-centred strategies today: the way to go (profitably)

The year 2023 was one of robust growth for Alibaba, posting double digit figures for their e-commerce websites Taobao and Tmall. As I was reading through the transcript of the earning call to shareholders of June 2023, I was struck by what Trudy Dai, Taobao and Tmall Group CEO, attributed the growth to: 'the members of our 88VIP loyalty program [who have been] growing double digit, and so their average order value ... We will continue to invest in program members to grow their average order value, and hereby grow the company' (Alibaba Group, 2023). As part of the activity of the Loyalty Observatory at the University of Parma, we track loyalty programs across numerous sectors around the world: I knew, therefore, that in 2017 Alibaba had merged its Tmall and Taobao loyalty programs into a single membership club, the '88 Membership' program (88, a number considered lucky in China, is pronounced 'baba'), to offer members greater discounts and benefits than the preceding loyalty clubs and track members' behaviours more seamlessly across the group's properties, and in 2018 even added a fee-based VIP tier not dissimilar from Amazon Prime. However, it struck me that one of the largest corporations in the world would mention their loyalty program and program members as the prominent drivers of growth, while speaking to the financial world. It echoed what I had read a few months earlier, from Expedia Group's earning call for the first quarter: 'Our strategy is to attract and retain high value customers, get them into the loyalty program and make them use the app, as program members and app users show higher profits per transaction and higher repurchase rates, that

DOI: 10.4324/9781003400783-1

translates into higher lifetime value. Growing this type of customers is the way to grow the business faster and more profitably' (MFT, 2023). Expedia Group had just merged the three loyalty programs of their brands Expedia, Hotels.com and Vrbo into one single club, named OneKey, with a total base of 168 million members, and again the company was explicitly drawing the causal link 'loyalty program – growth strategy'. 'Well,' I thought, 'after all we are talking of e-commerce companies: they are well aware that profit in this business is rooted in retention and customer lifetime value.' I became curious, however, to find examples of companies in other industries, touting loyalty as the way to grow. I expected that in more 'traditional' sectors such as store-based retail and consumer goods there would be none, as I felt those to still be the realm of acquisition and brand-based strategies, where customer-based metrics such as average order value are seldom seen and where loyalty has made its appearance, but rather as a marketing tactic.

I am certainly aware of the long way customer retention had come over the past thirty years. In 1996 Frederick Reichheld, founder of Bain & Co., author of *The Loyalty Effect* and a pioneer in loyalty research, wrote that companies considered loyalty 'a problem for the marketing department' (Reichheld, 1996, p. 2), nothing that top management and investors should be concerned with. However, in recent years financial analysts and authoritative news sources have started signalling that a lot has changed.

In 2016, in the wake of a change in Starbucks's loyalty program aimed at rewarding only the high spenders among its customer base (see Chapter 9), *Fortune* magazine published an article with the headline 'This is why Starbucks might not be the best stock to buy right now', implying a link between delusional customers and a plunge in future returns on the company's stock (Shen, 2016). Around the same time, as Dunkin' Brands (owner of several consumer brands such as Dunkin' Donuts) announced that it had reached a milestone in its loyalty scheme, a special report on the US network CNBC TV pointed out that shares in Dunkin' Brands rose nearly 2% after the company's announcement (Whitten, 2016). To consecrate Wall Street's 'love affair' with customer loyalty, *Forbes* magazine published a global study of retail and publishing executives in September 2016 entitled 'Retentionomics: the path to profitable growth'. Loyalty had finally left the marketing department and taken over the boardroom. And, as another task of the Loyalty Observatory at the University of Parma is to keep abreast with academic research that appears in scientific journals regarding loyalty, loyalty programs, customer relationship management (CRM) and customer experience (CX), I recalled the 2021 study of Faramarzi and Bhattacharya, who investigated whether loyalty program introduction affects firm value. The conducted a study of 260 announcements which cover 110 firms in the United States across different industries for 18 years from 2000 to 2017. They found that the introduction of loyalty programs, on average, positively influences firm value, as measured by abnormal stock returns. Still, I was intrigued by the idea of tracing down how loyalty was the intentional choice of strategic goal for the companies in pursuit of growth. I started collecting statements appearing in earning call transcripts and press releases, and soon found other evidence. Sephora, the beauty retail chain, for example, had routinely updated its Beauty Insider loyalty program since 2018, when it introduced more redeemable products, altered its points system and increased reward options. The program has 34 million members, a 30% increase since 2020.

Levi's Jeans CEO Chip Bergh revealed in 2023 that 'members' transactions and average order value continue to grow, as a consequence of our strategy that is all focussed on growing program membership' (Parisi, 2023). The program has reached 26 million members, a 40% increase over 2022.

So, retention was openly seen as a strategic option for corporate growth in the mentioned statements. But how widespread was this? A handful of sentences, although interesting, were not significant proof. That's when I came across an online seminar given at the Marketing Science Institute of the USA by Prof. Werner Reinartz, on firms' focus on brand versus customer management. In his study, he analysed 80,800 earning call transcriptions and financial documents of 2085 companies in 10 sectors for 16 years, from 2003 to 2019 (Reinartz, 2024). Beyond merely reporting performance results, quarterly earnings statements serve as communication tools between the firm's management and the public, and provide a picture of top management's mental model (Han et al., 2021). By carefully recording the employed wording whenever referring to results and their causes, they aimed at identifying each firm's orientation towards brand management, as opposed to customer management, as the two main approaches to a firm's organic growth. They recalled that brand management is the strategic process of developing and sustaining the value of a firm's brands. It identifies and differentiates firm's offerings from competitors to create distinct market value (Chernev, 2017), and measure success with brand equity, brand awareness, and market share. Customer management, on the other hand, is the strategic process of increasing the value of a firm's customer base. It identifies the most profitable customers, and aligns the firm's products with their needs (Kumar, 2015). The success measures here are retention rate, customer profitability and lifetime value. By mapping the prevalence of words and sentences in the brand or customer management domains, the study clearly found that there is no correlation between the two, i.e. practising brand management seems to be an independent activity/choice vis-à-vis practising customer management, and the customer management approach is dominant today, having displayed a +35%

growth since 2003, versus a more modest growth of +4% of the brand management approach. As far as sectors, all industry sectors exhibit a higher customer management focus in 2019 than in 2003, and it is most interesting to
note that customer management dominates 9 out of 10 industries, with the
sole exception of consumer staples, where brand management still predomi-
nates. Last, but not least, the study looked at the correlation between having
a customer management (or brand management) focus and profitability: a
positive correlation exists between a customer management focus and superior results, while no correlation exists in the case of brand management and
finally, a negative correlation is found when there is no clear orientation: having no clear compass for growth definitely leads to inferior growth. In this
book we look at customer management approaches for growth, that pursue
retention and the growing of customer lifetime value (Figure 1.1). They can
take two forms: they may adopt loyalty programs, i.e. formal rules to sustain
customers' desired behaviours and attitudes by means of rewards, or employ
other approaches, such as CRM and CX management, without a formal loyalty program in place.

The adoption of retention strategies over the past forty years has gone
through phases, notably, the early days, the era of the loyalty program, the age
of CRM and the current age of CX. We will discuss this timeline of the evolution of loyalty management later in this chapter. First, we look at the factors
that make it so important today to focus on the current customer base, and we
track down the origin of loyalty and CRM in the history of marketing.

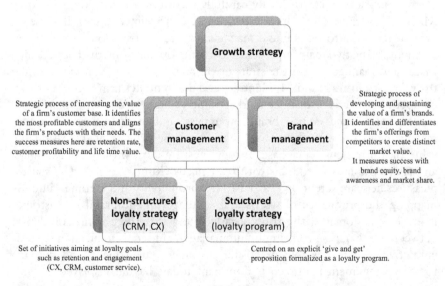

FIGURE 1.1 Customer management and brand management approaches to growth.

Why loyalty matters today

Why are companies now paying so much attention to a concept that – we will see – is a century old and has been neglected for so long – at least in mainstream marketing literature? Several factors are at play. Companies today must tackle significant changes in consumer behaviour and the marketplace. In terms of changing consumer behaviour, it is necessary to deal with several things, such as consumers' time scarcity, multitasking, reduced attention spans, the need for convenience, and the growing appetite for products and services to be provided on demand. Consumers are more demanding and expectations are ever increasing. They have access to information at reduced or no cost and they can share information at the click of a button thanks to social media. As the previous sentence implies, many of these consumer changes are a consequence of the information revolution (see Chapter 2). And the result is a continued threat to or actual reduction of customer loyalty to specific brands and stores.

And there are other factors. Changes in the marketplace have occurred too. Markets have become globalized, competition has increased, substitute products and services are now ubiquitously available, and it has become increasingly difficult to differentiate products based on intrinsic quality. At the same time, the service industries, and the related centrality and empowerment of the customer, have become increasingly relevant, if not dominant: companies turn to the building of service relationships with customers as key differentiators. The information revolution has enabled the introduction of new channels and touchpoints in the customer journey, thus making company strategies multichannel and omnichannel. It has ushered in a range of new technological tools for customer contact, data collection, analysis and personalization. Decades of direct and database marketing knowledge and, more recently, customer relationship management (CRM) knowledge, and of academic research into the economic effects of customer retention have provided the conceptual frameworks for adopting both technological and marketing tools, such as loyalty programs. Imitation, as companies seek not to be left behind in the ever-increasing pace of technological and marketing innovation, has done the rest.

The interplay of these trends in consumer behaviour and the marketplace has led to closer scrutiny of the impact of customer loyalty on company results – that is, sales and profits – and to the adoption of retention approaches in a number of industries, so much so that it is tempting to say that loyalty has 'disrupted' marketing. In this book we argue, however, that the emergence of loyalty at the forefront of marketing and in the boardroom was more an evolution than a disruption. There is no doubt that the increasing emphasis on loyalty has brought about major changes in marketing and business theory and practice. Specifically, we have seen a shift from acquisition orientation to retention orientation, the adoption of customer-based metrics to measure company performance, the systematic collection of individual customers' information and the establishment of interactive, tracking customer databases, the widespread adoption of CRM approaches and large-scale CRM systems, and the diffusion of loyalty programs. The rest of this chapter is devoted to discussing these changes, starting with the growing relevance of loyalty across marketing paradigms in academic literature and moving to marketing practice, where we will focus on customer-based success measures.

Evolution of marketing paradigms and the role of relationships

Marketing is both an activity, or set of activities, performed by organizations in the market, and a field of study and research. The term was first employed in 1910, in universities in the American Midwest, by agricultural economists in their studies of how commodity markets worked. The dominance of the farm sector made it relevant to explore and make sense of how crops were brought to market and prices determined. According to these scholars, marketing was 'a set of social and economic processes', that made it possible for goods to move from production to consumption (Webster, 1992, p. 2). In his analysis of the intellectual and pragmatic roots of marketing as a body of knowledge, theory and practice, Frederick Webster (1992, p. 2) identified three schools that evolved within this tradition that 'focused on the *commodities* themselves, on the marketing *institutions* through which products were brought to market, especially brokers, wholesalers, and retailers in their many forms ... and finally on the *functions* performed by these institutions'. This last 'functionalist' approach had the most success and became the conceptual framework for the marketing discipline. In their description of the various aspects they privileged, those early approaches shared a view of marketing as a set of *social*, not only economic, processes.

In 1948 the American Marketing Association (AMA) defined marketing as the 'performance of business activities that direct the flow of goods and services from producers to consumers' (Keefe, 2004, cited in Ringold and Weitz, 2007, p. 256). This marked an important shift in emphasis. Marketing activities were defined as business activities rather than as social or economic processes. The flow of goods and services towards the final users was considered 'manageable', that is plannable and controllable. During the 1950s and 1960s several textbooks appeared – in the US, it must be noted – which adopted this marketing management perspective and focused on problem-solving, planning, implementation and control as the essence of marketing.

These early managerial authors borrowed analytical frameworks from economics, psychology, sociology and statistics. The adoption of the behavioural and quantitative sciences gave important legitimacy to marketing as a separate academic discipline in an era in which rigour in management education was strongly advocated. The main tenets of this marketing management paradigm were:

- marketing takes the form of scientific solutions to specific decision-making problems
- attention is paid to problem-solving, planning and control
- the company's goal is to maximize profit
- success is measured by sales volume
- the relevant viewpoint is the 'transaction' (i.e. the individual sale).

At the root of most of the research literature on marketing in those days was the basic microeconomic paradigm, with its emphasis on profit maximization (Anderson, 1982, cited in Webster, 1992, p. 3). Companies such as Procter & Gamble, Colgate-Palmolive, General Foods, General Mills and Gillette hired specialists who could apply rigorous methods to solve problems in sales, distribution, advertising and promotion and marketing research, and organized them into marketing departments. The new marketing departments were a good fit in the large, hierarchical organization that was the American corporation in the 1950s and 1960s. The companies that were the cornerstone of the US economy were characterized by multiple layers of management and functional specialization. They organized and managed internally all the necessary operations (production, pricing, distribution, sales and advertising) for *taking the goods and the services from the producer to the consumer/user*. In this framework, the tasks of the marketing function were:

1 to develop an exhaustive understanding of the marketplace to ensure that the firm was producing goods and services required and desired by the consumer
2 to generate demand for these standardized products
3 to create consumer preference through mass and personal communications
4 to manage the channel of distribution through which products flowed to the consumer.

(Webster, 1992, p. 4)

Marketing practice and theory inevitably draws from the historical and social context in which it emerges, and so it was in the 1970s as the world was transformed by the advent of flexible technologies and advances in transport and communication – in a word, globalization. The oil crises of the early 1970s marked the 'end of predictability' and companies realized the world was becoming a global marketplace. What happened in one country directly affected what would happen in others. The inputs of managerial decision-making processes were no longer easy to forecast. Just as the price of crude oil was no longer predictable, so were other costs on the supply side. And neither was the disposable income and growth rates that drive demand.

This new environment was unfavourable to the large, fully integrated US corporations. Their enormous size and carefully planned processes were cumbersome and not easy to change in order to adapt to the new circumstances. For the first time the structure of the big corporations was questioned: high fixed costs and slow decision-making made them unfit to thrive in the new era of unpredictability. Companies had to look for new ways to be successful. New forms of business organization and relationships developed among companies: partnerships, joint ventures, alliances and networks. These partnerships were characterized by flexibility, specialization, and an emphasis on relationship management instead of market transactions. Within these new types of organizations, traditional ways of organizing the marketing function and of thinking about the purpose of marketing activity were re-examined, with a new focus on long-term customer relationships, partnerships and strategic alliances.

Marketers began to see the necessity of moving away from a focus on the individual sale towards an understanding of the need to develop long-term, mutually supportive relationships with their customers. The *keiretsu*, a Japanese institution, provided inspiration for this new organizational thinking and turned managers' attention towards the importance of relationships. The *keiretsu* are 'complex groupings of firms with interlinked ownership and trading relationships' (Webster, 1992, p. 8). They are not formal organizations with clearly defined hierarchical structures. Nor are they impersonal, decentralized markets. Rather, they are bound together in long-term relationships based on reciprocity.

National economies all over the world in the late 1970s and 1980s set into recession and stagnation, frequently accompanied by serious deteriorations in labour and social conditions. Yet a few localities stood out as exhibiting a remarkable resilience and even growth: the industrial districts in Italy, England and Germany. These districts were geographically defined, productive systems, characterized by a large number of small firms that are involved at various stages, and in various ways, in the production of a homogeneous product. A characteristic of the industrial district is that it should be conceived as a social and economic whole. That is to say, there are close interrelationships between the different social, political and economic spheres, and the functioning of one is shaped by the functioning and organization of the others. Their success lied not just in the realm of the 'economic': broader social and institutional aspects were just as important. In his review of the literature on districts, Jesús M. Zaratiegui (2004) argued that the essence of a district is that the different members of it trust one other. Alfred Marshall argued that 'districts offer certain advantages when compared to more traditional types of organisation, which are the result of the spatial proximity of producers and the specific atmosphere beneficial to the exchange/emulation of knowledge, to learning effects and trust' (cited in Zaratiegui, 2004, p. 93). In his transaction cost analysis, Oliver Williamson (1975) drew from the same perspective when he argued that the 'atmosphere' of a transaction comprises, on the one hand, the social, legal and technological framework of the transaction and, on the other, factors like trust and the sharing of common values of the involved parties.

In Europe, and specifically in the works of academics active in the Nordic countries in the 1980s, a new view of how companies should operate to be successful was being developed. The economies of these countries were characterized by strong business-to-business (B2B) industries and service sectors: in such contexts, companies pursuing success ought to develop relationships with customers, distributors and suppliers. No wonder that to observers such as local academics the relevance of relationships, trust and loyalty was evident, and reflected in their work.

The importance of establishing, strengthening and developing long-term and enduring customer relations was stressed in a new theory of industrial marketing and purchasing that emerged in the 1980s and 1990s called the network theory (see Takala and Uusitalo, 1996). In this view, marketing is defined as all the activities of a firm to build, maintain, and develop customer relations. Thus, marketing is not primarily concerned with the manipulation of the 4Ps (product, place, promotion, price) of consumer goods marketing. Rather, it is aimed at reaching a critical mass of relationships with customers, distributors, suppliers, public institutions and individuals (Gummesson, 1987). Grönroos, an advocate of the Nordic view of marketing, stated:

> Marketing is to establish, maintain and enhance (usually, but not necessarily, long-term) relationships with customers and other partners, at a profit, so that the objectives of the parties involved are met. This is achieved by a mutual exchange and fulfilment of promises.
>
> *(Grönroos, 1990, p. 138)*

'Relationship marketing' thus differs from traditional marketing since

> it does not seek a temporary increase in sales but attempts to create involvement and product loyalty by building a permanent bond with the customer. While it may be used to facilitate product repositioning, gain competitors' customers or help to launch new products, the ultimate goal is to increase sales in the long term.
>
> *(Takala and Uusitalo, 1996, p. 46)*

The relationship marketing paradigm criticizes the overarching goal of profit maximization, the rigidity of the 'marketing mix', the marketing department and the transactional focus. Instead, its core ideas are:

1 Marketing is responsible not only for sales and profits but also for making sure that every aspect of the business is focused on delivering superior value to customers in the competitive marketplace.
2 The business is likely to be a network of strategic partnerships.
3 Marketing as a distinct management function is responsible for being the expert on the customer and for keeping the rest of the network organization informed about the customer.
4 Everyone in the organization is a 'part-time marketer'.

The relationship marketing paradigm was pioneering in so far as it foresaw the roles both information technology and loyalty were going to play in marketing.

Technological progress brought about sophisticated data management applications, ranging from electronic data interchange, spreadsheets, sales forecasting tools, inventory management tools, and content management systems. These tools made it possible for managers to access customer and product inventories and market intelligence data. This, in turn, enabled a more tailored response to customers. In B2B industries, account managers focused on creating long-term relationships, rather than increasing sales transactions, quickly recognized the value of these tools in enabling customer profiling, customer acquisition and retention strategies, customized marketing messages, upsell and cross-sell communications, and marketing promotions. Technological advancements enabled managers to make decisions regarding customer behaviour and company actions more easily. The first academic studies appeared that heralded the transition from product/brand management to customer management, and from product portfolio management to customer portfolio management (Johnson and Seines, 2004; Sheth, 2005).

In 2005 the *Journal of Marketing*, the world's most influential academic marketing publication, devoted a special section to CRM. The same year, AMA put forward a definition of marketing as 'an organizational function and a set of processes for creating, communicating and delivering value to customers and for managing customer relationships in ways that benefit the organization and its stakeholders' (Grönroos, 2006, p. 397). It appears from this definition that the paradigms of marketing management (using scientific methods to solve problems; transactional focus) and relationship marketing (retaining customers; relational focus) have been synthesized and coexist today. It is worth noting, however, that the verb 'manage' is still employed when referring to customer relationships, implying that these are under the control of the firm.

However, any idea of control would soon to be challenged, in the US and Europe alike. With the advent of Web 2.0 tools, and social media in particular, in the context of the information revolution (see Chapter 2) individuals were now constantly connected with their social groups of interest. The discourse about brands was no longer controlled by brands or by the traditional media: companies could no longer control what people said about them. The power of the social media revolution has been further amplified by the massive worldwide adoption of portable devices, smartphones in particular. People carry the Internet in their pockets at all times, and the view of two separate 'times' and 'contexts' – online and offline – has rapidly morphed into a new hybrid, mixed reality that is enriched every day with the latest development in augmented reality.

The Italian scholars Mandelli and Accoto (2014) have suggested that with the emergence of ubiquitous social media, 'social mobile marketing' is a new marketing paradigm. We agree, and argue that loyalty will play a major role in it. Certainly, new media and touchpoints that cannot be controlled by the company – but, at best, listened to – confirm every day that loyalty cannot be bought but must be earned. In the new era of social mobile marketing, managing loyalty for businesses means building customer identification mechanisms for tracking them, analysing their rich data profiles – not only behaviours but attitudes and lifestyles – and deriving insights to create value through a proposition that is delivered across touchpoints in a consistent, responsive and individual way. The opening of channels for individual customer data collection brings with it a responsibility to measure changes in their loyalty (whatever metrics we employ for it) and to listen to what they have to say, take it into account and react accordingly. After all, loyalty management is, in the era of the social, a promise that the company will behave like a human being: talk, listen, reply, remember what was said and proceed from there. And with the advances of big data and artificial intelligence (AI) these are not mere figures of speech; they are reality. Some argue that we are now in the era of another marketing paradigm: that of big data marketing. Following Mandelli (2018) we see instead a continuum in the evolution of marketing stimulated by the information revolution and we discuss the impact of big data and AI on marketing in Chapter 2.

Evolution of CRM from direct and database marketing

To support retention efforts, the adoption of CRM approaches on the on hand, and formal loyalty programs on the other have become commonplace over the past 30 years (Figure 1.1). Since we see the adoption of CRM as one of the phases in the evolution of loyalty management from tactical tool to company strategy (Figure 1.2), it would be useful here to recall the origin of CRM and how it relates to, and stems not only from relationship marketing, as discussed above, but also from direct marketing and database marketing.

We start with the history of direct marketing, borrowing from the fascinating account made by Petrison, Blattberg and Wang (1993). In its early days, direct marketing was a synonym of catalogue sales. Commercial catalogues existed in Europe as early as the fifteenth century, when the invention of the

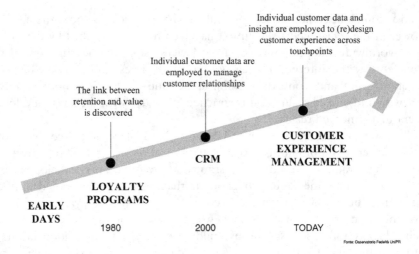

The link between
retention and value
is discovered

Individual customer data are
employed to manage
customer relationships

Individual customer data and
insight are employed to (re)design
customer experience across
touchpoints

**CUSTOMER
EXPERIENCE
MANAGEMENT**

CRM

**LOYALTY
PROGRAMS**

**EARLY
DAYS**

1980

2000

TODAY

Fonte: Osservatorio Fedeltà UniPR

FIGURE 1.2   The evolution of loyalty management.

printing press made reproducing documents relatively inexpensive. At first it was books and surgical instruments that were sold through catalogues, followed after that by luxury goods for the home such as china, furniture and wine. From the fifteenth to the nineteenth century, catalogue customers largely belonged to the elite in society – the few who could read, write and purchase luxury goods. The Industrial Revolution opened up mass markets and impacted direct marketing. In Europe, high population density and short distances enabled the proliferation of retail stores. In the US, by contrast, with the frontier constantly pushed westward, people moved to territories where the goods they were used to were not available: to procure them it made more sense to move the goods rather than having people travel long distances.

The first variety merchandise catalogues, Montgomery Ward and Sears, date back to the nineteenth century. The Sears catalogue had grown in its first ten years from listing 700 products to listing 6000. In 1927 Sears mailed 10 million letters annually, 15 million catalogues and 23 million special catalogues. During the 1920s, catalogue companies were calculating costs, revenues and profits at the level of the individual customer – as individual customer records were kept for shipping and for managing payments. They soon managed to reduce costs by saving on those customers who generated higher costs than profits, and invested in retaining profitable ones. During the 1950s a virtuous circle stimulated the expansion of direct marketing, driven by a sharp increase in the demand for goods following the end of World War II and the availability of high-quality mailing lists, such as the Polk & Donnelley, comprising names and addresses of any American who owned a car, driving licence and telephone. The 1960s marked the progressive adoption of information technology by direct marketers. From this moment onwards, the costs and possibilities of list management, mailings, segmentation, statistical testing, modelling and customized communication would be determined by the various technologies through which they were executed.

Computer power was employed to manage the problem of duplications. Merge/purge programs were the first computer software adopted in the industry, the precursors to the database. De-duplication was crucial in that it improved both the efficiency and effectiveness of direct marketing efforts, and this made it attractive to a wider variety of industries and company sizes. Computers also supported the production of personalized communication. Mass mailings targeting all American citizens with the surname Smith had been pioneered by *Time* magazine since the late 1940s and enjoyed response rates six times as high as untargeted mailings, which made up for higher printing costs.

During the following decade, several factors contributed to the growth and increased scientific vigour of the direct marketing business. To paraphrase Petrison, Blattberg and Wang (1993), they were as follows:

- There was a sharp increase in postage costs, which required mailings to yield higher returns. Efforts multiplied to reduce the cost per response by improving list quality and testing.
- Credit cards changed consumer habits and the perception of the costs and benefits of distance selling.
- Toll-free numbers played the same role and attracted consumer goods manufacturers' attention onto direct marketing tools to get in touch with customers and prospects.
- A reduction in consumers' – especially working women' – time devoted to purchase activities made distance ordering more attractive.
- Technological developments, growing interest from statisticians and mathematicians in direct marketing issues, and the development of data analysis software packages such as SAS and SPSS enabled direct marketers to tackle the above challenges and seize opportunities. In the 1970s predictive techniques based on regression, CHAID, factor, discriminant and multivariate analysis were developed. By the end of the decade any given direct marketing company had its own proprietary models to forecast customer loyalty and determine the maximum allowable spend for acquisition and retention.
- New mail-order companies selling niche products emerged, making the identification of highly targeted prospects crucial.

The 1980s saw the consolidation of direct marketing practices and their diffusion to other industries. The new analytical techniques ceased to be experimental and became rules of business. Advances in technology, notably in processing power and decreasing costs of data storage (see Chapter 2), made it possible to process growing amounts of data for organizations of all sizes. IBM launched DB2, one of the first ever database software programs that, thanks to its SQL operating language, became one of the most successful tools to aggregate and analyse customer data, even from multiple sources.

Database marketing practices started to appear in several industries. Airlines were first. Following pricing deregulation, companies had flooded the market with discount coupons to make frequent flyers loyal. To fight fraud related to the birth of an illicit coupon market, airlines built customer databases and begun the systematic management of discounts and incentives through mailings and loyalty cards. American Airlines' AAdvantage card launched in 1981, the first 'modern' loyalty program, using a plastic card to identify its members and match their details on a customer database. Credit card companies followed suit, with American Express a forerunner, then telephone companies, car manufacturers and consumer goods manufacturers – especially cigarette manufacturers, who were denied access to mass advertising on TV. Every direct marketing effort was based on databases: direct marketing practices begun to be known as 'database marketing'.

During the 1990s customer databases and loyalty programs were established, transaction records were parsed to model prospect customer behaviours, and customer magazines were printed using selective binding in order to target consumers based on their individual interests. As all this was taking place, a powerful new catalyst emerged that accelerated the spread of database marketing approaches, tools and techniques – the Web, that made it possible for any business to organize and operate as direct marketers. Indeed, nascent e-commerce companies shared with established catalogue companies and direct marketers several traits and practices: (1) direct channels to market (no intermediaries); (2) no physical stores; (3) distribution and delivery as a major cost, when they sold physical goods; (4) evidence of the relevance of customer retention to sustain the business; (5) relevance of technologies both as customer touchpoints and as data collection tools; (6) availability of individual customer data; (7) opportunities to track individual customer costs and revenues, and marketing efforts return on investment (ROI). This is still the case today and the success of e-commerce we are witnessing in the twenty-first century – aiming to be half of the total modern retail sales worldwide by 2030 – can rightly be considered a triumph of the principles that have guided the direct marketing industry for a century.

Direct/database marketing was defined by Alan Tapp in 1998 as a way of acquiring and retaining customer by providing a framework for three activities: analysis of individual customer information, the definition of strategies and their implementation in order to obtain a direct response from them (Tapp, 1998). A few years later, Payne and Frow offered the following comprehensive definition of CRM:

CRM is a strategic approach concerned with creating improved shareholder value through the development of appropriate relationships with key customers and customer segments. CRM unites the potential of relationship marketing strategies and IT to create profitable, long-term relationships with customers and other key stakeholders. CRM provides enhanced opportunities to use data and information to both understand customers and co-create value with them.

(Payne and Frow, 2005, p. 168)

When we recall the definition of relationship marketing given in the previous section, it becomes evident that CRM is the fusion of the relational focus on the one hand, and the use of individual information available in databases for marketing purposes on the other.

With the diffusion of formal loyalty programs, CRM studies and applications were developed to support their design and management. Such studies flourished in the 2000s and addressed challenges such as cross-selling and upselling, reducing churn, enhancing loyalty and making the best use of multiple channels (Winer and Neslin, 2014). Key metrics in CRM studies and applications have followed the shift from campaign management to customer management, which in turn reflects the general marketing trend from focusing on the short term to focusing on the long term and on relationships. Metrics in fact have moved from immediate-term profit, ROI and response rates of short-term actions such as direct mail campaigns to customer lifetime value and its submetrics such as retention rate, migration probability and more, as shall be discussed in the following section of this chapter.

A brief history of customer loyalty metrics

The growing attention towards customer relationships in marketing has brought about the adoption of customer-based measures of company success. Among these, a series of loyalty measures have emerged and gained ground in academic literature and business practice over time.

As far as the marketing literature is concerned, the rich early history of customer loyalty research allowed Jacoby and Chestnut to cite as early as 1978 more than 50 definitions of loyalty. At a workshop on customer retention, however, some of the most distinguished scholars in the field (Ascarza et al., 2018) made the point that despite the plethora of contributions, research on loyalty has failed to completely align with managerial needs. We choose therefore to concentrate in this section on the loyalty metrics that have found favour among marketers and become common practice in business. Table 1.1 marks out some key dates in the history of approaches to measuring customer loyalty.

TABLE 1.1 Timeline of measuring customer loyalty

Year	Key event
1923	Copeland introduces the concept of brand loyalty
1950s	Relative measures of loyalty emerge (share of requirements and share of wallet)
1969	Day distinguishes between behavioural loyalty and attitudinal loyalty
1988	Parasuraman, Zeithaml and Berry introduce the Servqual model and attract managers' attention to the relevance of customer satisfaction to obtain customer loyalty
1990s	Reichheld introduces the retention rate as the litmus test of a company's value creation capability
2001	Keiningham and Vavra introduce 'customer delight', thus stressing the fact that only high satisfaction turns into loyalty
2003	Reichheld introduces the net promoter score, an easy to compute, highly successful measure of customers' intention to spread positive word of mouth

It was in 1923 that a marketer named Melvin Copeland gave the deceptively simple definition that a brand-loyal person was 'anyone in a market who buys your brand 100% of the time'. From then on, a view of the market developed as being composed of 'loyals' and 'switchers'. It is easy to understand that such a definition was rooted in the times. This was a period where few substitute products were available and the reassuring role of brands amid unbranded, generic products was evident. As markets and consumer behaviour matured, the degree of a person's loyalty to a brand started to be measured by looking at what 'share' of that person's requirements in a category were fulfilled by that brand. In the 1950s the concept of 'share of requirements' (known as 'share of wallet' when retail stores, instead of brands, are considered) emerged in marketing literature and practice. The share of requirements is calculated solely among buyers of a specific brand. Within this group it represents the percentage of purchases within the relevant category accounted for by the brand in question.

Identifying who is loyal is then a matter of agreeing on how many times a person should buy a brand to be classified as loyal. If a person buys Levi's seven out of ten times when buying jeans, then Levi's has a 70% share of that person requirements when it comes to jeans. In many industries it became practical and common to use the standard of 67% share, i.e. two times out of three, as the threshold for considering a customer 'loyal'. But what if a customer buys a brand because it is the only one available? People can buy a brand 'loyally' but still not be attached to it. We cannot deduct how a consumer feels from observing her behaviour: she may be buying the same brand again because she is unaware of alternatives, or because that type of purchase has minimal relevance to her. Thus a distinction needed to be made. Buying a brand repeatedly without attachment is 'behavioural loyalty'. Buying a brand repeatedly because it is preferred to others is 'attitudinal loyalty'.

Although there is no consensus definition of loyalty, current theories most often delineate attitudinal loyalty and behavioural loyalty as the primary elements of customer loyalty (Chaudhuri and Holbrook, 2001). Today, research generally agrees that loyalty 'represents a mix of attitudes and behaviors that benefit one firm relative to its competitors' (Day, 1969; Dick and Basu, 1994; Melnyk et al., 2009; Liu-Thompkins et al., 2022). Day was the first, in 1969, to define attitudinal loyalty as 'a biased behavioural response over time in favour of a brand as a result of a psychological evaluative process' (Melnyk et al., 2009, p. 32). Attitudinal loyalty has been shown to derive from various components, such as: satisfaction with the brand, perception of the alternatives (even if dissatisfied, the customer doesn't switch); importance of brand choice (if brand choice is unimportant, she is 'uninvolved'); degree of ambivalence (the greater the ambivalence, the more likely that brand choice will be delayed until the last moment – market variables become important). Satisfaction with the brand, though not the only driver of customer loyalty, plays an important role.

Customer satisfaction is the extent to which a product's perceived performance matches expectations. If the product's performance falls short of expectations, the buyer is dissatisfied, but if performance matches or exceeds expectations, the buyer is satisfied. Starting from the late 1980s, many approaches have been introduced to measure and foster customer satisfaction. Before long, customer satisfaction programs started putting emphasis on customer retention (Bolton, 1998). For many companies, it was not enough to have high satisfaction scores. Rather, customer satisfaction scores needed to be demonstrably linked to key outcomes such as customer retention. Typically using techniques such as correlation or regression analysis, firms calculated the relationship between satisfaction and repurchase intention. For instance, using such a model, it was estimated that for a service industry, a one-unit change in overall satisfaction produces a 6% change in likelihood of continued use, the so-called repurchase intention.

In 1990 Reichheld and Sasser published a seminal paper entitled 'Zero defections: quality comes to services' which disseminated the idea that loyal customers generate more revenues and profits thanks to a combination of the following:

- repeat purchases
- lower service costs
- low remarketing costs
- cross-category purchases

- purchases on and off promotion
- premium charges
- lower dissatisfaction costs
- employee satisfaction
- higher percentage of acquisition costs covered
- more referrals thanks to word-of-mouth advertising
- reduced company need for acquisition.

In the paper, and his subsequent book *The Loyalty Effect*, Reichheld employs 'loyal' as a synonym of a 'retained' customer, focusing on the value that a company derives from customers who remain (i.e. continue transacting) with the company. The early 1990s were the years in which the total quality management – or 'zero defects' – philosophy swept across the corporate world and attracted management attention to the idea that prevention (of defects) is more economical than treatment or fixing afterwards. Hence the analogy drawn in the title of the article by Reichheld and Sasser, the former of which later revised his original thesis that companies should strive to retain all customers to retaining the 'right' customers. The attention on retention, however, stuck, and retention rate started being employed as a popular measure of loyalty and a company's health.

The retention rate is the ratio of the number of retained customers to the number of customers at risk. The retention rate expresses the average likelihood that a customer purchases from the firm in a period (t), given that this customer has also purchased in the period before ($t - 1$). In contractual situations, it makes sense to talk about the number of customers currently under contract and the percentage retained when the contract period runs out.

In 2000 Anderson and Mittal introduced the satisfaction–loyalty–profit chain to illustrate the intuitive connections at play: customer satisfaction driven by product, service and employee performance results in retention/loyalty and company revenue/profit. According to their analyses, firms that manage to create superior customer satisfaction should enjoy commensurate profits: research at the aggregate level showed a positive correlation between aggregate satisfaction scores for the firm and overall profitability measures. However intuitive that may seem, the links are far from straightforward. One cannot assume that a 1% increase at one end of the chain drives an x% increase in one of the other nodes, especially towards the other end of the chain.

Anderson and Mittal (2000) explained two important characteristics of the links in the satisfaction–loyalty–profit chain. First, the links are often asymmetric. That is, the impact of an increase is different from the impact of an equivalent decrease, not only in terms of direction but also in terms of size. Second, the links can also be non-linear. At certain points in the chain, non-linearity appears in the form of diminishing returns. That is, each additional one-unit increase in an input has a smaller impact than the preceding one-unit increase.

For the links between performance and satisfaction, consecutive performance increases in certain types of product attributes (e.g. speed) will have less of an impact on satisfaction. At other points in the chain, there are increasing returns. Focusing on the satisfaction-retention link, the shape of the relationship, and especially the 'elbows' or points at which customers cross the threshold and become either 'customers for life' or 'customers never more,' varies enormously across industries. The aggressiveness of competition, the degree of switching barriers, the ability of customers to accurately assess quality, and their level of risk aversion in the face of such uncertainty are some of the key factors influencing the shape of the link between satisfaction and repurchase intent.

The relationship between retention and revenue/profits is also non-linear. In fact, not all customers are as attractive in terms of revenue generation (Zeithaml, 2000). Furthermore, the successive acquisition of customers is also likely to be more expensive. As a firm keeps acquiring more and more customers, the quality of customers acquired may decline, resulting in higher maintenance costs and lower revenue. Thus, the diminishing returns to acquiring new customers. The idea is that a firm should focus on acquiring and keeping the 'right' customers, rather than just blindly expanding its customer base. Central to this aim is the calculation of customer lifetime value discussed earlier. This is regarded as 'today's foremost CRM metric' (Winer and Neslin, 2014). Customer lifetime value is the total amount of value derived by a company from a customer over the full lifetime of her engagement with the company or product.

In the early 2000s, another measure of satisfaction and repurchase intention was introduced, one that has proven very successful in terms of the number of companies adopting it: the net promoter score. It is calculated based on responses to a single question: how likely is it that you would recommend our company/product/service to a friend or colleague?[1] Its straightforwardness has made it popular in several industries and with e-commerce sites, although it has been shown to be no more superior to other approaches to forecasting retention or future profits (Keiningham et al., 2008).

In our more than 20 years of experience with loyalty projects for business, as well as research, we have noticed that what a company defines as 'loyalty', and therefore sets as the target for their loyalty strategy, varies across companies and industries.

Our surveys of Italian companies from a range of industries with the aim of understanding (1) how companies defined a customer as loyal to their brand and (2) what measures of loyalty did they employ show that the most common conceptualizations of a loyal customer are:

- one who repeats purchase ('frequency' perspective)
- one who chooses our brand most or all the times for need x ('share' perspective)

- one who has an emotional bond with our brand ('attitude' perspective)
- one who does not cede to competitors' promotions and offers ('switching barrier' perspective).

Respondents in retail tended to cite frequency as the proof of loyalty, while manufacturers preferred a share-of-requirement/share-in-handlers perspective. Behaviours, rather than attitudes, tended to be 'working definitions' of loyalty for companies. The most cited metrics were behavioural measures: frequency and spending for retailers, frequency and share of requirement for manufacturers. We also found that engagement has gained attention, so much so that we treat the topic in Chapter 6. The current status of loyalty metrics – as far as Italy is concerned – is further discussed in Chapter 8.

The evolution of loyalty management: the four phases

In this section we tell the story of the tools and techniques that have enabled marketers to encourage customers to return and repurchase, with the aim of shaping their habits in favour of the brand or store. It is a story in four phases (so far!) that begins two centuries ago with premiums and tokens, and, passing through loyalty programs and plastic cards, lands today in our email boxes and smartphone screens with CRM activities and engaging experiences.

The early days: premiums promotions and trading stamps

If we read the fascinating guidebooks of Henry Bunting (1913) and Frank Waggoner (1939) we learn about the prominent role of 'premium promotions' in the economy of the early twentieth century. Premium promotions were promotions that did not reduce the price of a product but instead employed premiums that the customer received immediately with her purchase – direct premiums – or, after several purchases, through the redemption of coupons:

> The latter imply the diligent collection of proofs of purchase (like wrappers, box tops, stamps, coupons or tokens) by the customer to be given the right of receiving the item offered, and are to be employed *where sustained series of purchases from loyal customers are the objective.*
> (*Waggoner, 1939, p. 35: my emphasis*)

The link between non-price-incentive-based promotions and the goal of repeat patronage by loyal customers was quite clear. It is worth clarifying that premiums are different from prizes, as the latter are awarded by chance to some customers and not to others (and are consequently treated like lotteries), whereas premiums are available to all customers.

The marketing and competitive effects of premium promotions were already well known to business at the beginning of the twentieth century. By reading Bunting (1913) we can clearly understand that premium promotions increased sales, as was tested with controlled experiments, and supported the differentiation of new entrants in a crowded retail market. They were significant in helping small retailers fight established department stores and helped create profit for stores in unfavourable locations.

For practitioners in those years, premiums appealed to the heart, to the emotions and to sentiment, and not to reason and intellect as space advertising does (Woloson, 2012). Premium promotions were ignored in academia, probably because all the mentioned authors were practitioners themselves. They would be 'rediscovered' by academic research more than half a century later when studies of the effects of loyalty programs began.

Meredith (1962) outlined three phases in the development of premium promotions in the US. The first phase (1851–1900) involved illustrated cards and lithographs, the second (1900–1930) saw the growth of token redemption, and the third phase (1930–1950) was that of direct premiums. The collection of tokens – that is, promotions employing premiums deferred in time – is most relevant to our history of loyalty management tools. We therefore focus on these below.

The early days of token-based premium promotions can be then traced to the late eighteenth century, although there are accounts of a New Hampshire merchant who, back in 1793, gave customers small copper tokens that could be used, once a certain number was collected, to get goods for free at his store (Lonto, 2000/2013). In 1851 the B. A. Babbitt Company began putting certificates in packages of Sweet Home laundry soap. When a specified number of certificates were collected, they could be exchanged for colour lithographs. In 1872 the Grand Union Tea Company introduced the use of issuing cardboard tickets to customers in its stores, which were later redeemed for merchandise in a company catalogue (Lonto, 2000/2013). It was, however, a department store in Milwaukee that first issued trading stamps to the public in 1891. One stamp was handed out for every dime spent and customers pasted them in booklets provided, which were redeemed for merchandise in the same store. The requirement that the stamps be affixed in books not only gave the customer a convenient place to put them, but it also helped prevent fraudulent misuse. Independently, trading stamps had first appeared in the UK in 1851 (Beard, 2016).

The trading stamp 'is essentially the retailer's system for accomplishing the same result as the coupon for the manufacturer ... [however,] while the coupon is centred on producing loyal customers for specified products and those only, the stamp or other retailer token embraces store-wide sales. The retailer's aim is to create loyal customers for the store and all the merchandise it handles' (Waggoner, 1939, p. 131). What would be a distinctive feature of token schemes was already in place in the last years of the nineteenth century. It was not individual retail companies that launched the token scheme – although some did, and in some cities large department stores issuing their own stamps even permitted smaller retailers or traders in non-competing lines to use the same stamps, in a sort of 'loyalty coalition' – but third parties, sort of 'loyalty intermediaries' that performed all necessary activities to promote the scheme, affiliate retailers and supply them with sheets of stamps and booklets for their customers.

These third-party companies developed premium catalogues and even managed dedicated premium stores, the so-called 'redemption centres', where the items featured in the catalogue could be seen, touched and purchased – with stamps only. The history of these token schemes in the US develops alongside that of the most famous of those intermediaries, the Sperry & Hutchinson Company, founded in 1896, whose 'S&H' logo identified the most popular brand of stamps, the Green Stamps. A few years later, Green Stamps were handed out to customers by department stores, grocers and supermarkets, while many entrepreneurs started their own stamp companies.

In 1910 the Kroger Grocery & Baking Company – a leader in loyalty today – started building its retail empire 'with a chain of a few small retail stores organised on the premium system' (Bunting, 1913, p. 81). It would give a premium coupon with every purchase, from a nickel's worth of soap upwards. Mr Kroger himself supervised the program, preaching the following principle: 'See that the customer gets the premium, push the premium on the customer diplomatically, whether he cares for it or not … Get the customer into the habit of wanting his premium, and of saving his coupons for that specific purpose. In a word, get your customer into the premium habit' (Bunting, 1913, p. 82). The Kroger company was not a price-cutter, nor a big advertiser, and was entering a territory ridden with competitors: nevertheless, in less than a decade it went from distributing $3000 worth of premiums a year to $300,000.

Despite the fact premium offers became popular in Europe in the 1920s, much later than in the US (Guenzi, 2015), both continents experienced similar waves of 'trading stamp fever' during the twentieth century – that is, periods of five to ten years during which stamp schemes proliferated. It became a social phenomenon, attracting the intervention of regulators, until interest faded due to significant economic changes or dramatic events such as the two world wars.

Premium promotions and stamp or token schemes enjoyed a great revival after World War II as consumer markets boomed and welcomed any novelty. In 1951 King Soopers, a major US supermarket chain, relaunched Green Stamps, soon followed by competitors, all resorting to stamp companies. Consumers witnessed a real 'stamp war' as supermarkets offered double, triple and quadruple stamps on designated days, then every day, to attract customers, until stamp companies forbade the practice. Industries other than department stores, supermarkets and fast-moving consumer goods (FMCG) manufacturers adopted stamp schemes: petrol stations, chemists, laundrettes, cinemas and independent grocers and retailers started offering them, opening up new markets for 'loyalty intermediaries', while bigger players such as the national chains looked at stamp schemes more as a necessary evil to stay in business.

In 1965, 83% of American families were collecting points, but the downward trend had begun: modern, low-priced retail chains such as Kmart and Target were flourishing across the US, and the oil shock and subsequent spike in consumer goods prices and plunge in consumer confidence swept stamps away for more than a decade. Later they would be subsumed into another extremely successful promotional tool – the card-based loyalty program.

The age of the loyalty program (1980–2000)

As Figure 1.2 shows, after trading stamp schemes held the stage for decades, the next step in the history of loyalty management tools was the birth of modern loyalty programs in the 1980s. Traditionally, 1981 is seen as the start of the loyalty program era since it was that year that American Airlines launched its AAdvantage frequent flyer club.

So, what *is* a loyalty program? According to Butscher:

> a loyalty program or customer club is a union of people or organisations, initiated and operated by an organisation in order to contact these members directly on a regular basis and offer them a benefit package with a high perceived value, with the goal of activating them and increasing their loyalty by creating an emotional relationship.
>
> *(Butscher, 1993, p. 20)*

To be considered as such, loyalty programs ought to have means for individual member identification, and for collection and retrieval of individual member data. Typically, in the 1980s – and the forty years since – this has been done by means of a plastic card – the loyalty card – and a customer database. Remember that the 1980s was the decade of database marketing.

Plastic cards and customer data

Several industries and companies began to adopt database marketing coupled with some form of loyalty program, as defined above. Commercial aviation was the first industry to adopt data-based, card-based loyalty schemes. In the US, following deregulation of pricing in 1978, airlines flooded the market with discount coupons to attract frequent flyers. To fight fraud related to the birth of an illicit coupon market, airlines built customer databases and started the systematic management of discounts and incentives through mailings and loyalty cards.

The AAdvantage club launched the first modern loyalty program, based on a plastic card to identify its members and a customer database. It also introduced a loyalty program 'currency' – air miles – which corresponded to how many miles a member had flown. Members could accumulate points (equivalent to miles of free air travel) by buying airline tickets and other products and these points would be redeemable against the cost of air travel with that particular airline. AAdvantage was soon followed by similar schemes from United Airlines, Trans World Airlines and Delta Airlines – and other airlines around the world quickly replicated the practice (see Table 1.2). In 1987, Southwest Airlines launched a program which rewarded members with points for trips flown, irrespective of the number of miles, starting a debate that has not ceased today on whether loyalty program rewards should be based on spending or frequency (as shown by the Starbucks case study in Chapter 9). Soon after the launch of these airline loyalty programs, hotel and car rental companies began partnering with airlines to offer miles or points as a way to grow their share of the lucrative world of business and high-value leisure travel. Thus, the first cross-industry loyalty alliances were created.

TABLE 1.2 Timeline of the rise of modern loyalty programs

Year	Key event
1981	American Airlines launches AAdvantage
1983	Holiday Inn becomes the first hotel to launch a loyalty program; shortly followed by Marriott
1986	Discover launches cashback; Canadian retailer Zellers launches the Club Z rewards program
1987	National Car Rental launches the Emerald Club; Ukrop's introduces the Valued Customer Card program
1988	Air Miles begins operating in the UK, managed by the Loyalty Management Group
1990	AMC Theatres launches MovieWatcher, thought to be the entertainment industry's first loyalty program
1991	Nordstrom launches Fashion Rewards
1993	Programs follow worldwide, launched by Superquinn (Ireland), Delhaize Le Lion (Belgium), Morgan Tuckerbag (Australia)
1994	Launch of flybuys in Australia; Air Miles introduced in the Netherlands; loyalty programs launched in Italy by supermarket retailer Esselunga and department store Rinascente
1995	Tesco introduces its loyalty card Tesco Clubcard in the UK
1996	Sainsbury's follow with its Reward card (forerunner to the Nectar Card)
1997	Boots, the UK's leading chemist, launches its Advantage Card
2000	Payback, Germany's first coalition loyalty program, is launched
2002	The Nectar scheme, run by Loyalty Management Group, is launched, merging several existing loyalty programs
2006	The Malina coalition loyalty program is launched in Russia

During the 1990s loyalty programs were adopted in several industries. The Loyalty Observatory was born in those years with the original goal of studying the adoption of loyalty management and use of customer data in European retailing, and overseas. For this reason, the tracking of loyalty practices of over 130 retail groups began in 1997 and provides the foundation for our understanding of the loyalty management phenomenon between 1980 and 2000, when we expanded the monitoring to loyalty programs in other industries.

Below we share some insights gained from this work of the Loyalty Observatory. Rather than going into detail about how individual loyalty programs worked, it is more interesting, and critical to this book, to outline how they developed specific characteristics in different countries and different industries. This is no mere historical curiosity: as more industries and companies adopt new loyalty management tools, there are lessons to be learned on how market and country-specific factors may impact success. Think, for example, of the influence market structure may play in avoiding dangerous price competition in the UK, of the role of consumers' readiness to accept new payment methods in France or that of legislation that forbids targeted direct communication in Germany.

In Europe it was the supermarket industry that led the adoption and advancement of loyalty programs. Retail in Europe was, in the 1980–2000 period, a collection of very diverse markets: some were concentrated, competitive, and the territory dense with modern retail formats operated by large, managerial, publicly traded companies (Ziliani, 1999). Others counted tens of thousands of mom-and-pop stores organized in local or regional distribution groups, where a 'buy cheap to sell cheap', rather than a customer-oriented mentality prevailed. Such structural differences played a role in the adoption of loyalty programs. In countries where the supermarket industry was most concentrated, such as the UK, Finland, Norway and Sweden, where three to four groups held 60% or more of the market, two to three large-scale loyalty programs emerged and quickly dominated the landscape. Awareness of these programs was high among consumers, and their strategic valence was clear to the management that ran them.

The cycle of loyalty programs in Britain

In the UK, the concentrated, oligopolistic market and the prevalence of the chain store strategic group, as opposed to small-scale organized distribution, certainly played a role in determining a very fast 'launch–imitation–diffusion–shake out' cycle for loyalty programs. A saturated market – the average Briton could find all top three supermarkets within ten minutes of their home, largely offering very similar ranges – made it very difficult to grow by opening new stores, as good locations were already taken, or by buying competitors' stores – which antitrust law disallowed on the grounds of obstructing competition. Growth by acquiring competitors' customers by means of price offers yielded diminishing results, as consumers would move back and forth among their two or three stores of reference to take advantage of temporary price cuts, in a zero-sum (and zero profit) game that in the end left each retailer with the same, but increasingly price-sensitive, customer base.

In such a scenario, non-price promotion looked to Tesco like a promising approach. Several advantages accrued from offering to regular customers rewards that were different from immediate price reductions and which grew progressively over time with the customer's spending. First, the shelf price remained untouched, so the manoeuvre could not be easily imitated in the short term like a classical price cut and did not ignite immediate competitor response. Second, the delayed benefits stimulated repeat patronage and consolidation of customers' share of wallet with Tesco in a virtuous circle. It is to be noted that Tesco rewarded customers with vouchers worth 1% of their total spent over the preceding quarter, that could be spent in the store. Third, Tesco would be the first to offer such a program in the UK and would thus enjoy a certain visibility and the first-mover advantage (Lugli and Ziliani, 2004). It is interesting to note that collecting customer transaction data to improve marketing and operational decision-making was not among the company goals at the beginning: it would take a few years, and the intuition of Tesco's consultants – dunnhumby – to turn management attention to the non-visible advantage of a loyalty program: customer insight.

In 1995, Tesco Clubcard was launched. One might wonder why, given the UK market situation, it was Tesco, and not one of the other prominent players, to take this step. This is no idle question since, in our opinion, it helps shed light on the relevance of internal, company-specific, not only external factors, in determining a business's adoption of loyalty management. At the time, Tesco was a follower, second-in-command in the UK supermarket industry to Sainsbury's. However, it saw the opportunity to gain leadership by consolidating a few points of individual share of wallet, multiplied by ten million loyalty cardholders, into the few points of national market share that separated it from Sainsbury's. The latter had been the leader for decades and, possibly suffering from 'marketing myopia' (Levitt, 1960), did not deem a retention investment necessary – after all, loyalty programs cost 1.5–2% of annual turnover, which, for a large group, meant tens of millions of pounds. Asda, on the other hand, had a cost leadership orientation that kept it away from extra marketing costs such as those of loyalty programs: in other words, it preferred to put a discount on the final price, rather than through a card.

In oligopolistic markets it seems that once a first player introduces a loyalty program or some sort of loyalty management approach, this becomes a requirement for staying in business for all major competitors. At least, they need to 'take a stand' – that is, incorporate in their positioning a clear proposition regarding what they offer as far as customer retention strategy is concerned. Consumers become familiar with the nationally advertised scheme and start evaluating retailers also along their loyalty propositions. Sainsbury's is a case in point. After dismissing Tesco's Clubcard as nothing more than 'the electronic version of trading stamps' and initially refusing to do the same, it rushed to introduce its own Reward Card a year later, after realizing that Clubcard holders were spending 28% more at Tesco and 16% less at Sainsbury's (Shabi, 2003).

The imitation phase had begun. Safeway introduced its version, the ABC (Added Bonus Card) loyalty scheme, in 1995 but ditched it in 2000, after it failed to be distinctive and have any impact on customer behaviour. Boots rolled out the Advantage Card in 1997 and scores of other operators in other retail industries developed similar schemes, including Barclaycard, BP, Shell and WHSmith. Card adoption rates were high during this phase, reaching 20–30% growth per year. National advertising and communication supported the effort. When a scheme introduced a successful perk, the others followed, trying to differentiate it at the same time.

When the number of loyalty programs increase but existing loyalty program member bases grow at a slower pace, we enter into the diffusion phase. In 1999 the penetration of loyalty cards among the UK population was growing at a 3% rate, against the 25% growth rate of 1997. In this phase, businesses such as petrol suppliers, restaurants and telecommunication companies that had familiarized themselves with loyalty programs by partnering with super-market schemes – for points earning or points burning (redeeming points) or both – began to launch their own loyalty programs. In attempts to attract more customers, points earning thresholds were lowered, point conversion rates were doubled, and ever more aggressive moves took place, such as when Asda began accepting vouchers issued by competing schemes or when Tesco converted the points balances of Safeway customers to the Clubcard after the closure of the ABC program.

The fourth and final phase of the cycle – shake out – soon starts. Out of a total of 150 loyalty programs recorded in the UK by Marketing Week in 2004, more than half would disappear within ten years. According to Euromonitor, in 2000 the UK had the highest card-to-person ratio in Europe (2.2), fol-lowed by the Scandinavian countries. France's was 1.6, Italy's 1.3 and Germany only 0.6 (Lugli and Ziliani, 2004).

Loyalty schemes go global

In Sweden, Norway and Finland the highly concentrated market situation was coupled with a peculiar feature: the strong tradition of cooperatives. The customer-member is by definition at the centre of the company's attention: he is the actual owner of the cooperative, he pays a membership fee when he joins, and he is rewarded at the end of the year with a rebate that is calculated thanks to the tracking of his purchase history facilitated by the membership card. It is easy to see that the main conditions for a loyalty program were already in place in these markets. Swedish cooperative Ica had launched its own card in 1990 in three versions: credit, debit and points only. The payment cards were developed completely independently of the banking system, based on the typical expertise and strength of cooperatives in savings collection and management. S-Group in Finland offered the same proposition of credit, debit and membership/rewards only cards. The dominant position of the cooperatives' loyalty programs in both Sweden and Finland forced competitors to follow suit and even join efforts to bridge the gap.

Payment cards paved the way for loyalty programs in France too. Here, hypermarkets dominated retail and had been offering credit and debit cards for years: Carrefour launched Pass in 1981, Auchan introduced Accord in 1983, and Castorama, Darty, Conforama and Picard Banners shared Aurore since 1985. In 1993 there were twenty-five million active retail payment cards in circulation (Ziliani, 1999). Hypermarkets, though, were slow to add loyalty features to their payment cards: it was supermarkets, struggling to compete, that saw the opportunity. Spurred on by their second-best position relative to hypermarkets, they embraced loyalty programs to provide consumers added reasons for repeat patronage. They introduced points-based schemes that rewarded customers with vouchers entitling them to reduced prices on selected items in store or with premiums from a catalogue.

France was also home to the longest running scheme in Europe – that of Galeries Lafayette, which is said to have started in 1965. Department stores introduced loyalty management activities well before the supermarket industry: Dutch group KBB and British store Debenhams in the mid-1970s, Zellers in Canada and Coin in Italy in 1986. When the grocery industry was still dominated by independent, traditional, family-run stores, the department store format was in a much more advanced stage of development. Many department stores originate from a trading company of the nineteenth century, involved in importing luxury goods from overseas to supply the leisure class of European capital cities. The type and value of the goods sold may explain why these companies developed payment cards first, and only a decade or so later, following the loyalty program trend, added a loyalty card or loyalty functionalities to the original payment card. Possibly due to lower penetration rates of payment cards compared to ordinary loyalty cards (30% against 80% of the average customer base), department stores were slow in leveraging insights and develop targeted communication, even if they did make use of direct mailing, if for no other reason but to send customers payment balance information.

Italy saw the first wave of payment cards introduced by selected retail groups in the late 1980s. However, in a country where cash was the dominant means of payment, and use of debit and credit cards lagged behind most markets, consumers were not ready to adopt retailers' cards and all projects failed. Those early failures probably contributed to making retailers cautious if not sceptical of card-related projects for some time. The Italian retail market was, and still is, fragmented into dozens of regional organized distribution networks, and two major groups, Conad and Coop, are consortia of independent cooperatives with complex decision-making processes. Individual companies lacked the culture and critical mass to develop and communicate marketing innovations effectively. Moreover, retailers in Italy depended strongly on suppliers' contributions for advertising and promotion, a situation that hindered the development of an autonomous marketing orientation and played in favour of preserving long-established practices. Even by the time loyalty programs became common practice – the end of the 1990s – suppliers were only modestly interested in paying contributions for targeted promotions by means of loyalty card data since the small scale of retail companies made the numbers very small and to have an impact would require signing multiple agreements with many retailers – provided there were enough who not only had a loyalty program but the necessary human resources and actionable databases too (Ziliani, 2008). By contrast, suppliers in the UK were keen to invest in Tesco's targeted promotions since they knew doing so would mean reaching 30% of British consumers through Tesco's mailing activities.

There were exceptions, of course. Some cooperatives had excellent information systems and so soon experimented with CRM as well as e-commerce. Esselunga became the 'best in class' example of loyalty management and is still regarded today as a benchmark. Its intuition was, among others, that loyalty management is a long-term strategy and thus should be treated as a brand: it needs an image, positioning and consistency so that it can 'envelop' activities and promotions that evolve over time.

In Belgium, planning and commercial laws had hindered the modernization of the retail trade and the landscape was polarized between three large, modern retail chains and a plethora of traditional grocers organized into buying groups and voluntary chains. The two market leaders – Delhaize and GB – both offered loyalty programs, with distinct flavours. Delhaize, in alignment with its EDLP strategy, geared its program towards lower prices for members, while GB opted for a point collection scheme for direct and differed premiums from a catalogue.

Switzerland had an extraordinarily concentrated retail trade, where Migros dominated not only the supermarket business but also others such a petrol stations, DIY hardware stores and bookshops. Despite the reluctance of market leaders to innovate, around the time that Sainsbury's declared its indifference to loyalty programs, Migros's unsatisfactory financial results and poor customer satisfaction is recognized as being the reason for their launch of its M-Cumulus card in 1997.

Spain is the home of an early experiment with targeted loyalty promotions in the grocery industry. The discounter Dia – owned by Carrefour – ran a very successful card-based program that rewarded cardholders with reduced prices and special offers printed on till receipts to stimulate repeat visits. While the Spanish hypermarket sector was dominated by French groups (that 'exported' the payment-card approach described above), it was smaller supermarket chains that developed loyalty programs: Caprabo, for example.

Legislation in Austria and Denmark banned the collection and use of customer transaction data: this kept loyalty programs at bay for years in those countries. A similar legal ban was in force in Germany until 2000. That, coupled with Germans' reluctance to disclose personal information and a checkout scanner penetration rate that was lower than the European average, contributed to a delay in the adoption of loyalty programs.

What was happening outside Europe, during the same period, between 1980 and 2000? While Japan, China and India would only see loyalty programs develop from 2000 onwards, one would reasonably assume that US loyalty programs would be the most advanced, given the pioneering experiences of the airline industry and the legacy of the direct marketing industry. As far as the retail industry is concerned, however, this was not the case. Again, market factors provide some background for understanding this.

According to *Supermarket News*, 60% of US grocery retailers had a loyalty program in place in 1996. However, this represented 'very low cost, low technology investment in some kind of short-term incentive programme' (Reynolds, 1995, p. 34). Typically, US supermarket loyalty programs provided benefits in the form of reduced shelf prices for cardholders (so-called 'two-tier pricing'). One of the reasons that lured US retailers to loyalty programs was to get rid of the cumbersome burden of managing the billions of print coupons that manufacturers pushed to consumers, and that stores had to manage. In other countries the coupon phenomenon was totally marginal compared to the US, where one of the most popular slogans to advertise the launch of a loyalty card was 'The Clipless Coupon'. Retailers declared to industry press that the reason for the launch was to 'improve customer service and convenience by eliminating coupons, to reduce the high costs of the Hi-Lo price model, and to improve image by adopting a modern tool' (Ziliani, 2004). Immediate discounts were communicated with two-tier pricing, that is shelf labels showing two prices: the regular price and a discounted price for cardholders only. Customers had to show their card at the till to be entitled to the reduced prices. Such immediate price reductions made US supermarkets 'essentially no more than glorified sales promotions exercises with a dose of technology thrown in' (Reynolds, 1995, p. 35). The US technological advancement, the tradition of co-marketing with FMCG manufacturers, notably through coupons, the absence of a national leader in loyalty management – for historical reasons, the US market had been dominated by regional, not national chains – played in favour of a formidable spread of instant reward systems, be it supermarket loyalty programs or checkout couponing networks such as Catalina's. It would take a full ten years before Kroger embraced loyalty management, significantly under the guidance of dunnhumby, the authors of the Tesco Clubcard success.

Features of the loyalty program phase of loyalty management

The 1980–2000 period of loyalty management can be broadly summarized as follows:

1 Loyalty programs were the main tool for loyalty management. They adopted plastic cards to identify customers at every transaction.
2 They operated a basic segmentation of the customer base into two groups: cardholders and non-holders. Subgroups, such a 'life stage' or 'lifestyle' clubs, where they existed, were mass advertised to the whole customer base who were invited to join by opting in (self-segmentation).
3 Rewards took the form of points, premiums, services and statuses. Table 1.3 classifies the benefits to members identified by the Loyalty Observatory in its cross-industry analysis of loyalty programs in those times.
4 There was very little or no use of data to generate customer insight. One US supermarket retailer admitted to having 'thrown away' the first five years of transaction data before realizing it could be put to use. Tesco itself focused initially on rewarding customers for their loyalty, not on the insight it could derive from loyalty program data.
5 The first entrant advantage was real.
6 The simplistic idea that it is sufficient to distribute a card for customers to spend more was common in the early days. Little was known about the impact of the loyalty program on customer behaviour (see Chapter 4). Overconfidence in loyalty program impact on behaviour led to poor planning of program costs. Underestimation of some loyalty program costs, such as the need to revamp the program periodically to maintain engagement or the costs associated with database maintenance, hindered results. Moreover, companies that knew little about the economics of retention – such as the need to wait in order to see customer lifetime value grow in a loyalty program after the initial erosion of profits – and expected immediate results from loyalty programs were soon disappointed, and when projects lacked strong internal support, they were simply closed.
7 Exits were numerous. Many loyalty programs were opened and then closed within a year or a few, such as the case of Safeway, that folded the ABC scheme notwithstanding its 6.5 million active users.

TABLE 1.3 Price and non-price benefits of loyalty programs in the 1980–2000 period

Price	Non-price		
	Premium/prize/game	*Services*	*Self-segmentation*
Immediate discounts	Direct premiums	Payment (debit)	'Life stage' clubs:
Deferred discounts (points or spending or time threshold)	• single • piece a week Deferred premiums • catalogue • self-liquidating	Payment (credit) Financial services Insurance ISP (email box)	• mother and child • families with children • Students
Vouchers (to spend in store/to spend with partners)	Sweepstake Instant win	Home delivery Shopping evenings Free parking Self-scanning Remote ordering Partners for points earning and burning Private sales Tastings/ demonstrations Customer magazine	• Seniors 'Lifestyle' clubs: • Gourmet • World of wine • Healthy living • Quit smoking • Me time • Free time

CRM and the information revolution (2000 to 2020)

With the dawn of the twenty-first century, loyalty management ceases to be identified with a single promotional tool (loyalty programs) and broadens its boundaries to encompass an ever-increasing variety of instruments and processes. This is the consequence, on the one hand, of opportunities generated by what has become known as the information revolution, in the form of new data collection and analytical instruments, statistical techniques, new digital media and new devices (see Chapter 2). Figure 1.3 provides a glimpse into the rise of loyalty tools on the foundation of evolving information and communication technologies.

On the other hand, it is the consequence of companies' search for differentiation in a market increasingly crowded with 'traditional' loyalty programs. One powerful catalyst of this evolution in loyalty management was the global economic crisis of 2008–2013 which forced companies to invest in innovative promotions to sustain slumping sales. The economics of retention and its benefits were well known by then, so marketers set out to innovate not only price promotion but also loyalty promotion. An increasingly sophisticated digital world allowed new hybrid forms of promotion to be born and for the rise of entirely new players in the promotional arena.

This phase of the story of loyalty management starts with the increased presence and competition of loyalty programs that characterized the early

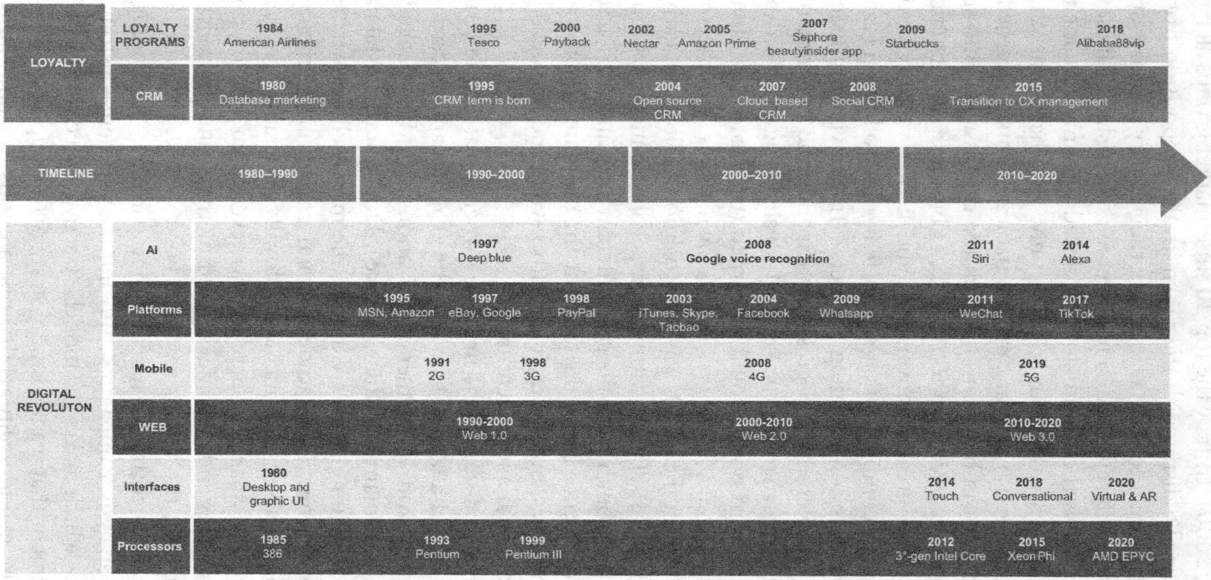

FIGURE 1.3 The information revolution and the evolution of loyalty management.

LOYALTY	LOYALTY PROGRAMS	1984 American Airlines								2007 Sephora beautyinsider app		2009 Starbucks		2018 Alibaba88vip
	CRM	1980 Database marketing	1995 CRM term is born		2002 Open source CRM	2004		2007 Cloud based CRM	2008 Social CRM			2015 Transition to CX management	
TIMELINE		1980–1990	1990–2000			2000–2010					2010–2020			
DIGITAL REVOLUTION	AI		1997 Deep blue			2008 Google voice recognition				2011 Siri	2014 Alexa			
	Platforms		1995 MSN, Amazon	1997 eBay, Google	1998 PayPal	2003 iTunes, Skype, Taobao	2004 Facebook	2009 Whatsapp		2011 WeChat	2017 TikTok			
	Mobile		1991 2G	1998 3G		2008 4G				2019 5G				
	WEB		1990–2000 Web 1.0			2000–2010 Web 2.0				2010–2020 Web 3.0				
	Interfaces	1980 Desktop and graphic UI								2014 Touch	2018 Conversational	2020 Virtual & AR		
	Processors	1985 386	1993 Pentium	1999 Pentium III						2012 3rd gen Intel Core	2015 Xeon Phi	2020 AMD EPYC		

2000s. According to McKinsey, in the year 2000 both in the UK and the US, 50% of major retailers across grocery, mass merchandisers, department stores, chemists, petrol stations and clothing stores operated loyalty programs (Cigliano et al., 2000). In Italy the top 20 supermarket groups all had a loyalty program in place. To distinguish their own loyalty proposition from those of competitors, companies looked to innovate their loyalty program structure.

Over the years, different models had become established. The simplest loyalty program model is the 'stand-alone', a closed system where members earn and spend points with the issuing party only. Another form, the 'affinity' model, is typically used by credit card companies: points are earned wherever the card is used but can be spent only with the card issuer. Soon stand-alone programs became the exception to the rule, as businesses, in an effort to provide customers with greater convenience and higher value rewards, created 'villages' of partner companies that supported point collection (earning partners) and/or redemption (burning partners). In the village model, it is the primary brand/retailer that progressively expands the network of involved parties by adding partners to the original loyalty program. For example, in 2000, Tesco Clubcard points could be earned (or burned) in 7000 stores in the UK, of which only 700 were Tesco's own stores. Another model that gained momentum in the 2000s was the 'coalition' – although early examples of it originate in the 1980s. As with villages, coalition members can get benefits and rewards through a number of different organizations across several industries; the difference lies in the fact that the program is not run by one of the partner companies, but rather, it is jointly owned and managed by all partners, typically through a joint venture.

A consequence and sign of the multiple ownership at play in coalition programs is the choice of a fantasy name for the program and its card, marking it as a different entity from its partner organizations: Air Miles (Canada), Nectar (UK), Payback (Germany), S'Miles (France), Dotz (Brazil), Malina (Russia), Plenti (US) and I-Mint (India) are among the most well-known cases of coalition loyalty programs. Some academics and practitioners employ the term coalition in a broader sense, to include all loyalty programs that have partners (therefore including villages). There are, however, from a business viewpoint, distinctive advantages and challenges posed by the coalition model that make the case for treating the two as separate. For example, in a coalition several loyalty management costs are shared among partners – technology and systems, database analysis, campaign set-up and management, customer care and administration – which makes the model attractive, especially for latecomers to loyalty management that want a loyalty strategy to be up and running quickly. The fact that the major coalitions that operate today around the world originated from the idea of a few innovators that replicated them in different countries favoured the rise of an international loyalty management services industry and makes the story of coalitions one worth telling.

Rise of coalition programs

Air Miles was the first coalition program. The concept was created by Keith Mills, the man who was also behind the Nectar Card, and began operating in the UK in 1988. Consumers who bought products from participating companies were given banknote-like scripts that they could redeem for flights on British Airways. Mills took the idea to the US and Canada in 1991. In the US the idea failed because consumers had to 'clip' barcodes from products of participating manufacturers and mail them to earn miles to redeem as flights from participating airlines – at the very time when retail loyalty programs were substituting 'clipping' with the modern plastic card and when Americans were already strongly engaged with the programs of individual brands (especially airlines) that had enough partners to fulfil the function of multi-brand coalitions. In Canada, by contrast, the coalition recruited large retailers such as Sears, which issued air miles to its loyalty program cardholders, and the scheme flourished. So much so that this retail-driven version was exported to the Netherlands in 1994. In 2003, about 65% of Canadian households and over 53% of Dutch households were collecting Air Miles points.

Once the new ventures were established, Mills and his partners opted to sell their stakes. Air Miles UK was sold to British Airways and the Canadian operation was sold to Alliance Data Systems, a provider of database and CRM solutions. In 2000 Mills began to look again at the UK, where he sought to apply the lessons learned internationally to design a better coalition program and founded Loyalty Management UK. He decided to seek as core partners retailers who were not happy with their own loyalty programs and were keen to enhance their impact by joining forces with other companies. With major companies such as Sainsbury's (that had lost the loyalty program battle with Tesco), BP, Debenhams and Barclaycard among its members, a massive advertising campaign introduced the Nectar scheme to UK consumers in 2002, costing a reported £50 million. Within six months, Nectar had signed up eleven million households, or 50% of the whole UK (Shabi, 2003).

Coalitions, with their national scale and heavy advertising, contributed to accelerating the diffusion of loyalty program membership among consumers, especially in countries where loyalty programs lagged behind, such as Germany, the South American nations and India. The coalition card was everywhere pitched to consumers on the ease of attaining rewards by earning points in one combined account across all sorts of businesses and the simplicity of carrying a single card.

The coalition management venture typically operates by selling to partner companies the right to issue points and buy them back at prices and spreads agreed with each partner (based on each partner's contribution to earning or burning points in large amounts), and by managing promotions and communication to customers on partners' behalf. In addition, they charge partners a fixed fee for administering the program in all its aspects, from planning and developing the strategy, to managing data, points, rewards and IT systems, to providing communication and customer service across various media with individual customers. Exploring the coalition model's pros and cons is outside the scope of this section; suffice it to say that it is vulnerable to conflicts among partners regarding the price of points, conflict due to the overlap of merchandise sold (for example, both Sainsbury's and BP sell gasoline), the different positioning of some partners that might hinder the image of higher profile ones, the ownership of detailed customer purchase histories, the exit of valuable partners that might reduce appeal for consumers, and partners' fear of fostering a brand different from their own. Despite these risks, for over a decade, coalitions have been hugely successful and subject to acquisition and consolidation among the founding ventures, so much so that today we can count on one hand the number of groups running these large schemes worldwide. Some cases of coalitions are presented in Chapter 10.

The industry for 'loyalty management services' is born

The rise of 'loyalty intermediaries' such as the above-mentioned ventures that ran coalition schemes mark the fact that a market for loyalty management services was born. Coalitions were, in essence, cross-industry behavioural databases and applied scientific rigour and state-of-the-art analytical techniques to analyse members' data. They developed segmentation approaches and predictive models to make promotional offers more attractive hence increasing redemption rates for offers and promotions. Coalitions spun off their own consulting divisions to offer their expertise to other companies seeking greater effectiveness and professionalization in their loyalty activities. Their highly trained promotion and loyalty specialists were frequently hired by client companies in need of professionals to establish, run or improve their own loyalty management strategies.

In the mid-2000s, the need for structured, scientific and efficient loyalty management efforts was no longer a niche requirement; it was felt across industries by a growing number of organizations. Additional testimony of this is the fact that during the decade international strategic consulting groups such as KPMG, PWC and A.T. Kearney opened specialized loyalty divisions and offices, a trend that is continuing today. To gain the sustainable advantages of loyalty management strategies, businesses gradually began to embrace the idea that CRM tools were necessary, as the returns of simply having a loyalty program in place had worn off. In turn, the diffusion of loyalty programs stimulated academics and practitioners to develop CRM applications to support the design and management of loyalty programs (Neslin, 2014). Their work sought to address problems such as upselling and cross-selling to members, reducing churn, enhancing loyalty and making the best use of multiple channels, and they provided industry with recommendations based on their research.

Loyalty management was developing an invisible side (CRM) to the visible tools it had been identified with up until then: plastic cards, points, direct mailings, websites, e-newsletters and so on. This is the CRM stage in the history of loyalty management. In the 2000s coalitions had captured large percentages of the population in the countries in which they operated and an increasing number of proprietary customer databases, such as Tesco's, had reached a considerable size. The top 20 retail loyalty programs in Europe, for example, had in excess of a million active cardholders each. Ten of them had over five million. That was more than the hardware and software available in those days could handle (Lugli and Ziliani, 2004).

With retail loyalty program databases recording more and more numbers of customers, FMCG manufacturers, who lacked direct contact with the final customer, developed an interest in partnering with retailers to target consumers with direct offers and targeted promotions. Retailers, on the other hand, were keen to show how effective this type of co-marketing could be because they aimed to increase the amount of marketing contributions from suppliers (to cover the costs of their own loyalty management strategies). In the mid-2000s international manufacturers started introducing specific clauses in supply contracts regarding contributions for targeted marketing activities to loyalty program members by means of 'cooperative CRM' (Lugli and Ziliani, 2004).

For retailers such as Tesco or Carrefour, both of which had already set up platforms for sharing sales data with suppliers, sharing customer analysis looked like a natural next step. Tesco moved forward with dunnhumby, which it had acquired in 2001; other groups set up similar agreements with ad hoc companies as data intermediaries. The favourable trends in hardware and software costs continued throughout the decade and made it affordable even for small and medium-sized companies to start investing in CRM tools and services for the analysis of their own loyalty program customer databases. This too contributed to expanding the market for loyalty, customer databases and CRM, thus attracting more entrants to it.

The digital age: touchpoints, customer journeys and the customer experience

As we review what happened to loyalty management from 2000 to 2020, we should not forget the bigger picture: the explosion of the Web and new mobile devices generated a plethora of available new media that diffused quickly through the first decade of the twenty-first century and in turn concurred to the big data phenomenon. SMS text messaging, websites, email, rich media such as video and animation, instant messaging, blogs, forums and early social networks all showed potential for day-to-day communication with the customer base. The availability of these new channels gave new impetus to customer service and loyalty strategies, including but not limited to loyalty programs, that have communication with the individual at their core.

New digital media allowed entire industries to embrace loyalty management. Think of low-frequency retail sectors: when a customer visits a store only two or three times a year, she is unlikely to make room for a plastic card in her wallet; but she can register online to the store digital loyalty program website, receive emails and mobile promotions. Put simply, CRM and the new digital touchpoints that have emerged in the last two decades have made a retention strategy possible for everyone. As we saw in the first section of this chapter, retention strategies today may be based on loyalty programs, but are not limited to that: they can also take the form of CRM and customer experience management (CEM) approaches (Figure 1.1).

A feature of new media is the fact that it is bidirectional in nature. The customer can employ the same channel of communication she was contacted through to respond directly to the marketing stimulus. And she can initiate that contact at will. Interactivity – the holy grail of relationship strategies – becomes easier to achieve and new digital tools make the interaction measurable. Engagement becomes the buzzword.

It is no wonder that, with the increased focus on engaging customers, interest in gamification as the 'science of engagement' also emerged. According to Paharia (2013, p. 65), gamification 'takes the motivational techniques that video game designers have used for years to motivate players, and use [*sic*] them in nongame contexts'. Such techniques included giving users goals to accomplish, awarding badges, engaging them with competition, encouraging collaboration in teams, giving them status, and enabling them to earn points. Gamification was hailed by some as the new life needed to inject into the loyalty programs that had proliferated but which were no longer able to set the brand aside and change consumers habits. We devote Chapter 6 to discussing engagement and gamification.

In the previous section, we called the period from 1980 to 2000 the age of the loyalty program. Continuing this theme, we call the phase from 2000 to 2020 the age of CRM. Let us recall some of its main features:

1 Loyalty management is no longer synonymous with loyalty program but encompasses an increasing variety of ever more sophisticated tools.
2 Due to the diffusion of CRM, loyalty management begins to mean managing the customer relationship along its lifecycle by means of individual customer data (collected via the loyalty program or otherwise).
3 New types of loyalty programs diffuse, notably coalitions.
4 New digital media are adopted en masse in loyalty management.

5 Promotional intermediaries are born which demonstrate how customer data can be effectively leveraged and which offer loyalty management services and consulting.
6 Loyalty management practices are embraced by new industries that did not have direct access to final consumers or were impaired by a low frequency of visits or long repurchase cycles.
7 Mobile devices profoundly change marketing and because of their intimacy and potential for continuous and ubiquitous interaction are immediately embraced in loyalty management.
8 The industry of loyalty management tools and services is born, comprising CRM vendors, loyalty management platforms and a host of other players. We focus on the structure of the industry in Chapter 8.

From 1980 to the end of the twentieth century, managing loyalty basically meant running a loyalty program. Since 2000, companies have turned to the 'invisible' advantages of loyalty schemes (and related customer databases) – that is, the insight they unlock and its use for targeted marketing activities for retention, upselling, cross-selling and reactivation of selected members of the customer base. In 2020 we entered a new phase in which loyalty management is identified with the design and management of a quality customer experience across the various touchpoints that connect the customer and the brand. The disruption in consumer habits and business activity caused by the pandemic in 2020 and 2021 accelerated marketers' reflection on the importance of a loyal customer base and of touchpoints to encounter them, to continue providing value and a positive experience.

If we look at the evolution of loyalty management as described in this chapter it is possible to notice a continuous attempt by marketers to extend the benefits, privileges and moments in which a customer is recognized as a member. What was the purpose of villages and coalitions, after all? We could say that loyalty management efforts have continuously focused on creating and expanding a 'space of free circulation for the customer' – in which she is identified as an individual customer with unique characteristics derived from data collection at various touchpoints – and provide superior value doing so. The development of CRM tools and the impact of the information revolution only furthered such a trend by spurring on advances in systems for customer identification across touchpoints and in personalization algorithms. Mobile and wearable devices played a major role. In China, services like WeChat truly show how a customer can be placed at the centre of an ecosystem, not to mention Alibaba's vision of a digital loyalty ecosystem, as stated by then CEO Daniel Zhang in 2017: 'We see it as our opportunity to build a unique, global brand alliance, where the loyalty schemes of each brand can be connected to Alibaba's membership system … We want our members to feel like they have a passport to exclusive experiences within the Alibaba ecosystem' (quoted in Chou, 2017, p. 32).

In order to make a customer loyal, companies now consider it necessary that she encounters the brand at the relevant touchpoints along which her shopping journey evolves, be it traditional touchpoints such as the store or newer ones such as apps and digital wallets. If she feels that such an encounter positively contributes to the journey in some way, this translates as a quality customer experience. This might be generated if she feels that her encounter with the brand at the touchpoint is relevant or engaging or personal, is consistent with the stage of the shopping journey or even with the emotional state she is in, or if it adds value in some other way to her journey. Research suggests, as we discuss in Chapter 5, that a positive customer experience leads to loyalty.

In order to orchestrate touchpoint encounters across channels to improve the customer experience, a new framework is emerging: CEM. As stated by the influential work of Homburg et al. (2017), the final goal of CEM is to achieve long-term customer loyalty by designing and continually renewing touchpoint journeys. CEM and loyalty management, therefore, share the same goal: making customers loyal. CEM is, however, still more of a theoretical framework at the moment, whereas loyalty management has proven to be an effective set of tools and approaches that work. These tools and approaches can be the enabler of the CEM framework. A loyalty program, for example, serves the purpose of identifying customers, and CRM serves to provide insights that help create personal and relevant interactions.

In their search to translate the CEM framework into action and put in place a seamless management of touchpoints so that the customer is identified consistently across them and treated accordingly, marketers should look at loyalty management. Since most companies today have some sort of loyalty program or CRM activity already in place, this could be the starting point to move into the next phase that is customer experience management. We elaborate on this in Chapter 5.

The future of loyalty management

What will loyalty management strategies and activities look like in the future? How will the retention approach adapt to competitive arenas where customer demands have changed, technology provides unprecedented opportunities and totally new players have arisen? These are questions that our Observatory receives frequently, and a lot of our work with companies is to facilitate reflection on this. I would like therefore to close this chapter by sharing our approach to gauging future trends in Loyalty Management, and some data that we deem worthy of consideration by managers, regardless of the industry they operate – although, given our academic background, the following framework is particularly suited for retailing.

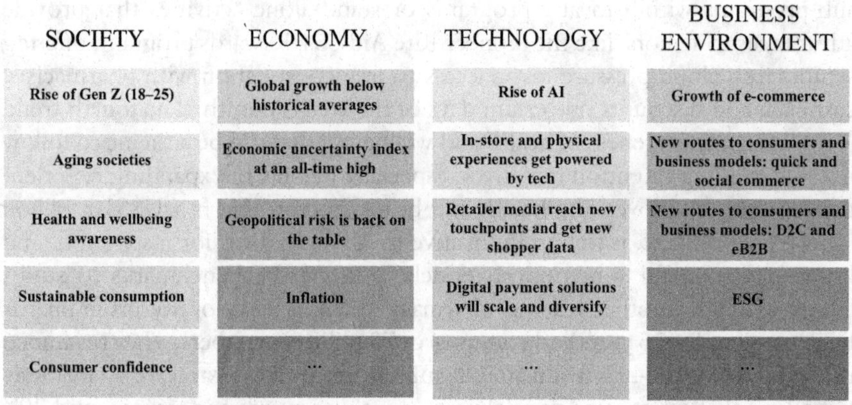

SOCIETY	ECONOMY	TECHNOLOGY	BUSINESS ENVIRONMENT
Rise of Gen Z (18–25)	Global growth below historical averages	Rise of AI	Growth of e-commerce
Aging societies	Economic uncertainty index at an all-time high	In-store and physical experiences get powered by tech	New routes to consumers and business models: quick and social commerce
Health and wellbeing awareness	Geopolitical risk is back on the table	Retailer media reach new touchpoints and get new shopper data	New routes to consumers and business models: D2C and eB2B
Sustainable consumption	Inflation	Digital payment solutions will scale and diversify	ESG
Consumer confidence	…	…	…

FIGURE 1.4   A framework to analyse trends that impact the future of loyalty management.

Source: author's adaptation from Flywheel.

I adapt here the approach of Planet Retail, a retail think tank, recently renamed Flywheel. To understand the outlook for the sector of interest it is useful to look at four groups of trends: society, economy, technology and the business environment (Figure 1.4).

Society comprises demographic and societal trends and it is the group of factors that typically have the most profound impact, especially long-running demographic phenomena. Currently, there are five trends to consider, as far as society is concerned, that we believe require consideration in order to align loyalty management strategies and/or to make sense of signals of other firms' in the market following such trends. The first is the rise of Gen Z, that is the generation aged between 18 and 25 years. Gen Z in 2025 will be 27% of global workforce, they will be the spenders of the future, and they are used to new digital channels and interfaces, and their prominence in society will drive firm's continuous need to refine omnichannel customer experiences. Is your loyalty proposition aligned with Gen Z's expectations? Is it engaging for this generation? We asked Italian companies that employ loyalty programs if their program had been conceived with some consideration for Gen Z and the result is that none was targeting Gen Z. In general, the design of a loyalty program is focused on serving many generations at once, as it assumes that it is enough to have a variety of rewards to cater for all tastes. Specificities in each country's demographic pyramid may explain what has been done so far, but they may represent barriers to taking into consideration other, neglected demographic groups. For example, the second trend is that of aging societies, and here we can consider that in Italy the share of population aged over 65 is 23%, which is incredibly higher than the world's average, that will reach 6% in … 2050! In countries with aging populations loyalty strategists should research the needs and preferences of these target groups, and experiment with special sub-programs within loyalty programs or stand-alone activities that provide advantages to seniors, like the pioneer Rite Aid 65+ Rewards program, offering seniors free blood pressure tests, access to free consultation with pharmacists, cashback and discounts on certain days of the week/month. The fourth trend is the growing awareness of health and wellbeing, that can be a theme to follow in (re)designing retention initiatives, especially in view of expanding experiential rewards. Moreover, the health and beauty sector, that is a US$1.5 billion industry worldwide, is rich in innovative loyalty initiatives for inspiration, and home to successful subscription models, that can be benchmarks to study. Think of CVS, another leading pharmacy chain, whose loyalty program has been running for 25 years and counts over 70 million members. They revamped it in January 2024 introducing a subscription tier, Extracare+ (formerly CarePass) that offers same day delivery, monthly rewards and savings, and 20% off CVS branded products. General merchandise retailers will try their best to enter this lucrative industry, as we see in Amazon's special prices for those who subscribe to repeat shipping of medications and supplements that need to be taken for long periods of time, if not a lifetime. Or hypermarkets and warehouse chains launching health services in subscription, bundling them together with other typical offerings of loyalty programs, to take advantage of the reduction of coverage of public health systems in many European countries. Along with wellness, and related to it, Sustainability is another powerful factor as far as consumer concerns and companies efforts. We devote an entire chapter to analysing how this trend is intertwined with loyalty programs (Chapter 3). Last, but not least, in this area, a factor that should be monitored is the consumer confidence index. It affects current and future spending by consumers, and it also signals to companies the need to strengthen their value propositions and communicate to customers – preferred customers above all – that they have done so. A loyalty initiative is an apt framework to tell customers how being members provides them with a 'shield' against erosion of purchasing power and future uncertainties. This brings us to the second group of trends that need to be monitored – the economy (Figure 1.4). Consumer confidence goes hand in hand with the feeling of economic uncertainty and the return of geopolitical risk on the scene, after decades when it was not as relevant as today. Inflation became top concern for firms and consumers when it spiked in 2022, spurring a variety of initiatives by retailers to strengthen the bond with their loyalty program members: from cheaper subscription options to tying all price reductions to being members, to 'anti-inflation' cheaper alternative product suggestions, powered by AI, for members who shop online. Although inflation has decreased in general in most OECD countries, consumers' worries around this issue tend to linger for much longer, and need to be taken into account. As the readers of this book will probably belong to different countries and continents, it is difficult to pinpoint here other economic trends that have the same relevance for everybody: depending on the region of interest, specific economic factors should be included in the framework. The third area of developments that will greatly influence loyalty strategies, for its transformative potential as far as the customer experience, is technology. We discuss extensively in Chapter 2 how the rise of AI, in its predictive and generative forms, is already changing and empowering loyalty and CX approaches. Retailers' interest in monetizing the access to their customer base is nothing new: however, today, ICTs and AI, consumer acceptance of personalized communication on several touchpoints, and the leading example of some best in class such as Amazon, account for the explosion of the retailer media network phenomenon. This expression designs the business of selling advertising space in a variety of formats by the retailer on their properties (digital and physical) in a coordinated way and being able to target viewers accurately thanks to rich individual data collected from purchase histories and loyalty program interactions. Loyalty programs provide 'zero party data', i.e. data that the member has willingly released for communication and profiling, that become more important today with the pending demise of cookies on the one side and consumers' concerns for privacy on the other. The retail media business is already worth 17% of total digital advertising spending in the US, and twice the amount spent on TV. It is maturing quickly, but it is still unripe and not for everyone, and for this reason we decided not to discuss it in this book. However, the prospect of monetization is serving the purpose of attracting management attention to loyalty programs. Another very powerful technological trend that we observe is the convergence of the loyalty and payment arenas. Digital wallets (which are daily life features for billions of consumers worldwide), 'buy now pay later' and 'pay with points' are examples of the mingling of the two, to provide convenience to customers and richer behavioural profiles to firms for segmentation and provision of value-added services. On this theme, in Chapter 9 we tell the incredible story of Starbuck and the contribution of their wallet to company profitability. Last, but not least, the fourth area of influence for loyalty management is without a doubt the business environment of the firm. Here, everyone reading this book can fill the box with the threats and opportunities specific to their industry, looking at incumbents' strategies and potential entrants, as far as their loyalty efforts and reflections on theirs. As far as retail is concerned, we closely monitor the evolution of e-commerce, not only as a channel to include in the customer journey, but as source of new business models and touchpoints: think of quick commerce, social commerce via livestreaming, direct-to-consumer models ... they all have the potential to attract and retain customers ... to the detriment of whom? We see that more than 20 years after its birth, e-commerce is still producing new disintermediation and reintermediation, with all the competitive consequences in terms of enhanced 'need to retain' customers for incumbents and newcomers. Finally, concerning the business environment, a major impact will be that of environmental, social and governance (ESG) practices. So far, it might have been simply a matter of using the loyalty program to give voice to the company ESG pledges and results. However, as we discuss in Chapter 3, loyalty and ESG might have more in common than we think today: they can stop talking to the consumer, and start engaging the citizen. Maybe, the next phase of loyalty management will be that of citizen experience management.

Note

1 The scoring for this answer is most often based on a scale of 0 to 10. Those who respond with a score of 9 or 10 are called 'promoters', and are considered likely to exhibit value-creating behaviours such as buying more, remaining customers for longer, and making more positive referrals to other potential customers. Those who respond with a score of 0 to 6 are labelled 'detractors' and are believed to be less likely to exhibit such value-creating behaviours. Responses of 7 and 8 are 'passives', and their behaviour falls in the middle. The net promoter score is calculated by subtracting the percentage of customers who are detractors from the percentage of customers who are promoters.

References

Alibaba Group (2023) 'September quarter 2023 results conference call transcript'. Retrievedfromhttps://data.alibabagroup.com/ecms-files/1508695866/34822d0a-3bee-4b88-aaea-ef0f9a519921/EN%20September%202023%20Q%20-%20Alibaba%20Earnings%20Call.pdf (accessed 15 June 2024).

Anderson, E. W. and Mittal, V. (2000) 'Strengthening the satisfaction-profit chain'. *Journal of Service Research*, 3(2), 107–120.

Ascarza, E., Neslin, S. A., Netzer, O., Anderson, Z., Fader, P. S., Gupta, S. and Provost, F. (2018) 'In pursuit of enhanced customer retention management: review, key issues, and future directions'. *Customer Needs and Solutions*, 5(1–2), 65–81.

Baier, M. (1967) 'Zip code: new tool for marketers'. *Harvard Business Review*, 45(1), 136–140.

Beard, Fred K. (2016) 'A history of advertising and sales promotion'. In D. B. Jones and M. Tadajewski, (eds), *The Routledge Companion to Marketing History*, 203–224. Abingdon: Routledge.

Bolton, R. N. (1998) 'A dynamic model of the duration of the customer's relationship with a continuous service provider: the role of satisfaction'. *Marketing Science*, 17(1), 45–65.

Bunting, H. S. (1913) *The Premium System of Forcing Sales: Its Principles, Laws and Uses*. Chicago: Novelty News Press.

Butscher, S. A. (1993) *Customer Loyalty Programmes and Clubs*. Aldershot: Gower.

Chaudhuri, A. and Holbrook, M. B. (2001) 'The chain of effects from brand trust and brand affect to brand performance: the role of brand loyalty'. *Journal of Marketing*, 65(2), 81–93.

Chernev, A. (2017). *The Business Model: How to Develop New Products, Create Market Value and Make the Competition Irrelevant*. Cerebellum Press.

Chou, C. (2017) 'Alibaba's new 88 membership club redefines loyalty'. *Alizila*, 18 August. Retrieved from www.alizila.com/alibabas-new-88-membership-club-redefines-loyalty (accessed 29 January 2019).

Cigliano, J., Georgiadis, M., Pleasance, D. and Whalley, S. (2000) 'The price of loyalty'. *McKinsey Quarterly*, 4, 68–77.

Copeland, M. T. (1923) 'Relation of consumers' buying habits to marketing methods'. *Harvard Business Review*, 1, 282–289.

Day, G. S. (1969) 'A two-dimensional concept of brand loyalty'. *Journal of Advertising Research*, 9(3), 29–35.

Dick, A. S. and Basu, K. (1994) 'Customer loyalty: toward an integrated conceptual framework'. *Journal of the Academy of Marketing Science*, 22(2), 99–113.

Faramarzi, A., & Bhattacharya, A. (2021). 'The economic worth of loyalty programs: an event study analysis'. *Journal of Business Research*, 123, 313–323.

Grönroos, C. (1990) *Service Management and Marketing: Managing the Moments of Truth in Service Competition*. Lexington, MA: Lexington Books.

Grönroos, C. (2006) 'On defining marketing: finding a new roadmap for marketing'. *Marketing Theory*, 6(4), 395–417.

Guenzi, A. (2015) 'Building brand awareness with a bowl of cherries'. *Journal of Historical Research in Marketing*, 7(1), 113–132.

Gummesson, E. (1987) 'The new marketing – developing long-term interactive relationships'. *Long Range Planning*, 20(4), 10–20.

Han, S., Reinartz, W., & Skiera, B. (2021) 'Capturing retailers' brand and customer focus'. *Journal of Retailing*, 97(4), 582–596.

Homburg, C., Jozić, D. and Kuehnl, C. (2017) 'Customer experience management: toward implementing an evolving marketing concept'. *Journal of the Academy of Marketing Science*, 45(3), 377–401.

Jacoby, J. and Chestnut, R.W. (1978) *Brand Loyalty Measurement and Management*. New York: John Wiley and Sons.

Johnson, M. D. and Seines, F. (2004) 'Customer portfolio management: toward a dynamic theory of exchange relationships'. *Journal of Marketing*, 68(2), 1–17.

Keefe, Lisa M. (2004) 'What is the meaning of marketing?' *Marketing News*, 15 September, 17–18.

Keiningham, T. L., Aksoy, L., Cooil, B., Andreassen, T. W. and Williams, L. (2008) 'A holistic examination of Net Promoter'. *Journal of Database Marketing & Customer Strategy Management*, 15(2), 79–90.

Kumar, V. (2015) 'Evolution of marketing as a discipline: what has happened and what to look out for'. *Journal of Marketing*, 79(1), 1–9.

Levitt, T. (1960) 'Marketing myopia'. *Harvard Business Review*, 38(July–August), 24–47.

Liu-Thompkins, Y., Khoshghadam, L., Shoushtari, A. A., & Zal, S. (2022) 'What drives retailer loyalty? A meta-analysis of the role of cognitive, affective, and social factors across five decades'. *Journal of Retailing*, 98(1), 92–110.

Lonto, J. (2000/2013) 'The trading stamp story (or: when trading stamps stuck)'. Retrieved from www.studioz7.com/stamps.html (accessed 12 December 2018).

Lugli, G. and Ziliani, C, (2004) *Micromarketing: Creare valore con le informazioni di cliente*. Turin: UTET.

Mandelli, A. (2018) *Intelligenza artificiale e marketing: Agenti invisibili, esperienza, valore e business*. Milan: EGEA.

Mandelli, A. and Accoto, C. (2014) *Social Mobile Marketing*. Milan: EGEA.

Marshall, A. (1961) *Principles of Economics*. London: Macmillan.

Melnyk, V., Van Osselaer, S. M. and Bijmolt, T. H. (2009) 'Are women more loyal customers than men? Gender differences in loyalty to firms and individual service providers'. *Journal of Marketing*, 73(4), 82–96.

Meredith, G. (1962) *Effective Merchandising with Premiums*. New York: McGraw-Hill.

MFT (2023) 'Expedia Group Q3 2023 earnings call transcript'. Retrieved from www.fool.com/earnings/call-transcripts/2023/11/03/expedia-group-expe-q3-2023-earnings-call-transcrip (accessed 15 June 2024).

Neslin, S. (2014) 'Customer relationship management'. In Winer, R. S. and Neslin, S. A. (eds.), *The History of Marketing Science*, 289–317. New York: World Scientific.

Paharia, R. (2013) *Loyalty 3.0: How to Revolutionize Customer and Employee Engagement with Big Data and Gamification*. New York: McGraw-Hill.

Parisi, D. (2023) Fashion brands are refreshing loyalty programs to increase customer lifetime value, Glossy Retrieved from www.glossy.co/fashion/fashion-brands-are-refreshing-loyalty-programs-to-increase-customer-lifetime-value (accessed 15 June 2024).

Payne, A. and Frow, P. (2005) 'A strategic framework for customer relationship management'. *Journal of Marketing*, 69(4), 167–176.

Petrison, L. A., Blattberg, R. C. and Wang, P. (1993) 'Database marketing: past, present, and future'. *Journal of Direct Marketing*, 7(3), 27–43.

Reichheld, F. (1996) *The Loyalty Effect*. Boston, MA: Harvard Business School Press.

Reichheld, F. and Sasser, Jr., W. E. (1990) 'Zero defections: quality comes to services'. *Harvard Business Review*, September–October. Retrieved from https://hbr.org/1990/09/zero-defections-quality-comes-to-services (accessed 1 March 2019).

Reinartz, W. (2024) 'Firms' focus on brand and customer management: management, development and investors valuations'. Presented at the Marketing Science Institute online seminar, Retrieved from www.msi.org/presentation/presentation-firms-focus-on-brand-and-customer-management-measurement-development-and-financial-consequences (subscription required) (accessed 15 June 2024).

Reynolds, J. (1995) 'Database marketing and customer loyalty: examining the evidence'. *European Retail Digest*, 7 (Summer), 31–38.

Ringold, D. J. and Weitz, B. (2007) 'The American Marketing Association definition of marketing: moving from lagging to leading indicator'. *Journal of Public Policy & Marketing*, 26(2), 251–260.

Shabi, R. (2003) 'The card up their sleeve'. *Guardian*, 19 July. Retrieved from www.theguardian.com/lifeandstyle/2003/jul/19/shopping.features (accessed 12 December 2018).

Shen, L. (2016) 'This is why Starbucks might not be the best stock to buy right now'. *Fortune*, 12 April. Retrieved from http://fortune.com/2016/04/12/sdtarbucks-stock-downgraded (accessed 12 November 2018).

Sheth, J. (2005) 'The benefits and challenges of shifting strategies'. *Customer Management* (MSI conference summary). Cambridge, MA: Marketing Science Institute, 4–5.

Takala, T. and Uusitalo, O. (1996) 'An alternative view of relationship marketing: a framework for ethical analysis'. *European Journal of Marketing*, 30(2), 45–60.

Tapp, A. (2008) *Principles of Direct and Database Marketing*. Harlow: Pearson Education.

Waggoner, F. (1939) *Premium Advertising as a Selling Force*. New York: Harper & Bros.

Webster, Jr., F. E. (1992) 'The changing role of marketing in the corporation'. *Journal of Marketing*, 56(October), 11–17.

Whitten, S. (2016) 'Dunkin' Brands shares jump as loyalty program hits milestone'. *CNBC*, 22 August. Retrieved from www.cnbc.com/2016/08/22/dunkin-brands-shares-rise-tracking-for-best-day-since-july-14.html (accessed 31 January 2019).

Williamson, O. E. (1975) *Market and Hierarchies: Analysis and Antitrust Implications*. New York: Free Press.

Winer, R. and Neslin, A. (2014) *The History of Marketing Science*. Singapore: World Scientific.

Woloson, W. A. (2012) 'Wishful thinking: retail premiums in mid-nineteenth-century America'. *Enterprise and Society*, 13(4), 790–831.

Zaratiegui, J. M. (2004) 'Marshallian industrial districts revisited. Part I'. *Problems and Perspectives in Management*, 49(2), 80–97.

Zeithaml, V. A. (2000) 'Service quality, profitability, and the economic worth of customers: what we know and what we need to learn'. *Journal of the Academy of Marketing Science*, 28(1), 67–85.

Ziliani, C. (1999) *Micromarketing: Le carte fedeltà della distribuzione in Europa*. Milan: EGEA.

Ziliani, C. (2008) *Loyalty Marketing: Creare valore attraverso le relazioni*. Milan: EGEA.

2

THE IMPACT OF BIG DATA AND ARTIFICIAL INTELLIGENCE

Cristina Ziliani

The information revolution

Before the expression 'big data' became popular, scholars and practitioners had been talking about an 'information revolution' for decades. In the late 1980s Peter Drucker, widely regarded as the father of post-war management thinking, identified that the world economy was shifting from being organized around the flow of goods and money to the flow of information. Nicholas Negroponte, architect and founder of the MIT Media Lab, introduced in his book *Being Digital* (1995) the image of the 'atom society' – based on the production of tangible goods – giving way to the 'bit' society – based on the production of information and knowledge and of products and services derived from that information and knowledge.

Relationship marketing scholars predicted in the 1990s that emerging information and communication technologies (ICTs)[1] were going to play a major role in businesses' orientation towards customer loyalty. They were right. Computers, databases and other software applications – from call centre management to analytics – were indeed at the basis of the evolution of direct, database marketing and customer relationship management (CRM). Blattberg, Glazer and Little (1994) clearly saw that developments in ICTs were creating an explosion in the quantity and variety of information available to a growing number of individuals and organizations across the globe. This was going to be a 'marketing information revolution'.[2]

Since their introduction, ICTs have had a close and significant relationship with both marketing and loyalty management. Given the incessant pace of technological progress, amplified – among other things – by the increasing availability of the Internet to half of the world's inhabitants, the embedding of

DOI: 10.4324/9781003400783-2

computing power in everyday objects (the so-called Internet of Things), and the rise of ever more sophisticated software to make sense of the available data, it is worth reflecting on what all this means for marketing, and for loyalty management in particular.

As we articulated in Chapter 1, we see loyalty management as going through four phases in its history. Each is marked by the availability of new technologies and by the progressive expansion they make possible of the ecosystem in which the individual customer is identified and treated accordingly as he or she moves freely across touchpoints. We are now living in the 'loyalty as experience' phase where customer loyalty is pursued and fostered by means of the design (and redesign) of a superior customer experience. Technology, data and the information unlocked by software such as artificial intelligence (AI) algorithms are transforming what human experience is. We 'experience' through a network of touchpoints, many of them new, digital and enriched with sensors whose inputs produce the hyperpersonalization of communication, content and offers in a way that is increasingly relevant to the moment we are at in our journey, regardless of where we or the brand are physically located. This is how far the information revolution has come. Not only it is making ever new tools available to marketers, but it is shaping and redefining the human experience of perception.

This chapter provides some reflections on how this revolution played out in the world of marketing on the evolution of loyalty management and customer experience management (CEM) – and asks what might follow in the future.

Big data marketing and the Stitch Fix case

It has been almost a decade since the phrase 'information revolution' has been substituted by 'big data revolution', an expression that signifies the prominent role of data – and big data – in the transformation of business and society as the product, or by-product, of ICTs. Big data was defined as 'an intentionally subjective definition that refers to datasets whose size is beyond the ability of typical database software tools to capture, store, manage and analyse' (Manyika et al., 2011, p. 1). In incorporating a moving definition of how big a data set needs to be in order to be considered big data, the expression captures how technology is continuously advancing.

Mandelli (2017) describes big data marketing as the evolution of marketing into a new data-based, automated approach whose keywords are: data-driven, customer journey, omnichannel, programmatic, platform economy, automation and hyperpersonalization. She sees this evolution as enabled by the continuous flow of data from the environment and from interactions between customer and brand at various touchpoints, and by newly available intelligence to make sense of and use such data.

Specifically, the big data revolution has impacted marketing on two fronts:

1 *Understanding markets and customers.* Thanks to the improvements in online and offline tracking of individuals and content, it is possible to introduce novel segmentation approaches (think of computer image recognition and image analytics applied to images and videos posted by users) and to understand customer journeys. In turn, journeys that show similarities can be clustered together to define 'personas', which may serve as the basis for …
2 *Managing the customer experience.* This takes the form of not only managing contents and channels/media for communication, but also managing interactions with customers, including personalizing offers, introducing smart and robotic services and designing new intelligent touchpoints, ambients and servicescapes, as will be discussed later in this chapter, and is depicted in Figure 2.1.

The transformation of marketing by big data does not take place at the operational level alone. It has strategic consequences too. Processes become adaptive and interactive, new business models are possible and automation can be applied also to creative aspects of marketing such as content production and product/service design.

Stitch Fix is a telling case in point. Founded in 2011 as a personal styling e-commerce website, it delivers a selection of clothes guaranteed to match each customer's preferences for a monthly subscription fee (Hollis, 2018). In 2023 the company employed 5800 people, including 2000 stylists and 80 data scientists, made $330 million in revenues, had a full assortment of clothes, shoes and accessories for man, woman and child, from which 200,000 shipments are made every week, to 2.8 million active customers (Meisenzahl, 2024; Lake, 2018; Marr, 2018). A new customer starts by filling out a survey describing her fashion and style preferences and provides a rating and feedback on the items she receives.

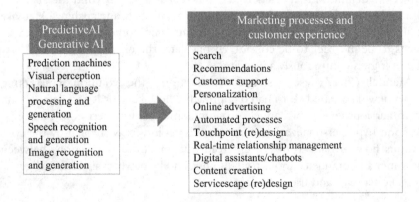

FIGURE 2.1 Impact of AI on marketing and customer experience.

Currently, the company declares that 85% of customers leave feedback on each and every shipment they receive (Ransbotham, 2024). The company's data scientists can then parse through her survey responses and data of how she navigated the Stitch Fix website and other platforms she uses – e.g. social media sites rich in fashion ideas such as Pinterest – to quickly refine suggestions and deliver clothes she is likely to prefer. We are speaking of 4.5 billion text data points (Marr, 2024). They employ image recognition and natural language recognition tools (take, for example, a comment like 'I don't like to show my arms') and feed all that data through recommender engines that select products based on customer preferences, later validated by human stylists who handle the relationship with each specific customer and take the final decision regarding what five pieces of clothing will go in the customer's box that month (Planet Retail, 2018).

Not only this was a new business model for fashion retailing when it appeared, but their use of analytics and AI is bringing creativity in fashion retail to a new level. One of the early forays in the use of AI by Stitch Fix was the creation of new content using deep learning models (that we discuss later in the chapter) on top of their existing personalization engines that selected the items to suggest (Ransbotham, 2024; Bhattarai, 2018). AI tools analysed clothing items that had been top sellers during a specific season and pinpoint best-selling distinctive 'traits' – like, for example, the colour purple, string tops, lace, shoulder-showing sleeves, and so on. Each top-selling item in the season has one or more of such traits but not all of them, and only in some combinations: for example, purple string tops and black lace shoulder-showing blouses sold very well. Why not 'crossbreed' successful items and see what 'offspring' they could generate, carrying some of the 'parent' features with them? Genetic algorithms combined automatically successful features in hundreds of novel ways thus creating fictional items of clothing that did not 'exist' (Gershgorn, 2017). Human stylists eliminate 'ugly' combinations and select a few styles. They then request that partner manufacturers produce a batch of each for trial shipment to customers. In 2018 Stitch Fix successfully marketed 17 AI-designed pieces of clothing under their own label Hybrid Designs, unique to their assortment, thus setting themselves apart from competition and giving marketers a glimpse of a future in which human–machine cooperation would support creative processes. Not surprising, then, that early on they also got excited about large language models (LLMs),[3] using them to support and improve several marketing tasks. Specifically:

a   In order to improve recommendations, it is important to be able to make the most of textual data that is abundant at Stitch Fix, because a lot of the feedback provided by customers is in the form of text. LLM represent text in the form of vectors – known as embeddings: these can be read directly by recommender systems already employed at the company. Therefore, LLM are used to automatically process text data and put it in a form that can be read directly by existing systems to produce higher-quality recommendations.

b   LLM are used for text generation: copy is required to accompany images that are used daily as advertising and served in a personalized way to each customer. The product image is the centrepiece of the ad, and the recommender system takes care of making the selection relevant for each customer, but it needs to be accompanied by captivating text that matches and best describes the image in a way that resonates with the individual. Product descriptions are also needed, given the vast amount of products and the constant changing of the company assortment, to populate the website and other touchpoints where items can be searched or displayed. Generative AI tools at Stitch Fix can produce 10.000 descriptions in 30 minutes, that are then revised by humans in a process that still requires time, but much less compared to having humans creating descriptions anew.

c   More recently, they have focused on the personalized notes that stylists send to each client every time they make a shipment: a new tool powered by OpenAI's GPT-4 enable them to choose from a template and automatically fill out parts of the note such as the content of the shipment, the customer preferences and more, reducing by 20% note-writing time for stylists (Ransbotham, 2024).

d   Another interesting area where they are working is with the vast amount of feedback that customers who have bought from the company dozens of times have provided. The new generative AI tools can create summaries and compress such rich information in more workable bits. Also, over time, it has been possible instead of having separate models (one for women clothes, one for men or one for assisted shopping versus Freestyle, the area of the website where customers get to purchase on their own recommended items without resorting to the human personal stylist) to move to a situation where all the models are in a single centralized place where they leverage all available information about all clients.

e   On the website there is a feature called Complete Your Looks, which helps customers who have previously bought from Stitch Fix pick out items that they have kept, that they own and like, and pair them with other things that might be interesting. This can help customers shop for those themselves right on the site using the feature called Freestyle, or they can save them for their stylists to notice. This is based on a model that has been trained on which items go together in order to help it build outfits in a fully automated way. Such outfit creation model can produce 13 million product combinations daily, that are then used to personalize emails, ads and personalized shopping feeds (Stitch Fix, 2024).

This case illustrates well how far loyalty management has been transformed by technology. The subscription model is a well-known lock-in approach to retention. The business goal of providing customers with superior value and excellent experience hasn't changed. The processes for the extraction and delivery of such value have, and they are increasingly data-based and AI-powered. The emphasis within the marketing information revolution, then, is on the endless possibilities opened up by the analysis and use of data by means of advanced software and algorithms, especially in domains comprised under AI, and, as of today, generative AI, for its creative, innovative potential. Below we reflect on the growing availability of data and its impact on business and marketing, before turning to AI specifically.

The moving frontier of data availability and its impact on business

The word 'data' has been with us since well before computers were invented. It comes from the Latin word *datum*, meaning 'fact', 'description of something that has happened'. To 'datafy' means to describe phenomena in quantitative form so that they can be analysed and easily compared. Datafication refers to observing anything, even things we never thought of as information, such as vibrations of an engine or a person's location, and transforming it into data format; that is, quantifying it (Mayer-Schönberger and Cukier, 2013).

Datafication began well before the digital revolution. Humans have always felt the need to translate phenomena into data in order to analyse it and make sense of reality. Throughout history we have continually added ways of measuring the world: weight, distance, time and so forth. Mayer-Schönberger and Cukier (2013) recall some key milestones:

- In 3000 BC, in Mesopotamia, writing was developed to record and keep track of information about production and business transactions.
- In 200 BC, in Greece, the first version of latitude and longitude was developed to determine where locations were and how long it took to travel from A to B.
- The Romans ran censuses to gather data sets of information in order to levy taxes.
- Arabic numerals, invented in India, travelled to Persia and were later adopted in the West in twelfth century (and entered common use from the fifteenth century).
- In the late fifteenth century, double-entry bookkeeping was invented in Italy by Luca Pacioli, a Franciscan friar, and marked the beginning of the standardized recording of business information.

Clearly datafication is something that is inherent to human nature. Technology is not its cause, but it has been a powerful enabler of the datafication of phenomena not yet quantified. The technologies that support datafication and make digitization and digitalization possible we refer to as ICTs.[4] When talking about ICTs we distinguish three categories. (1) Core technologies are those that enable the storage of data, such as memory disks, and those that process data, such as devices that perform operations and execute instructions: typically, microprocessors. Since data needs to be entered into memory and processors, sensors and readers of various kinds are included here. (2) Access technologies have to do with networks for telecommunication and allow access to data wherever it is located. One example would be routers. (3) Applications are software that enables the actual use of information for specific purposes. Think here of Web browsers or analytics tools.

The development of these technologies began in the early 1950s when the first computer – the mainframe – was invented. They have evolved ever since thanks to the peculiar dynamics of their production processes. These have been popularized as the 'laws' that have governed the development of ICTs to date: Moore's law, Gilder's law, Metcalfe's law and others. The evolution of marketing and loyalty management is intertwined with the availability of data and insights enabled by advances in ICT: for this reason, we briefly recall the laws that govern it and their implications.

In 1965 Gordon Moore, co-founder of Fairchild Semiconductor and Intel, wrote that the number of transistors on a computer chip was doubling every year. The number of transistors expresses the processing power of a microchip. In 1975 he revised that to a two-year doubling period, although looking back at the data it was closer to 18 months (Wilson, 2012). Moore's law means the number of components doubles on each chip and that the device size gets smaller allowing more to be put in the same space. The fact that the power of the computer chip was doubling in a comparatively short time meant that tasks that are hard to perform today will be feasible tomorrow and the cost of equivalent computing power is halving on a similar timescale (Wilson, 2012). Today we speak also of a 'generalized' Moore's law to indicate various trends of exponential improvement in many aspects of ICTs (both computing and communication) such as storage capacity/cost, clock frequency, performance/cost, size/bit, cost/bit, energy/operation, bandwidth/cost and others. These trends impact productivity, efficiency and economic growth (Mack, 2015) and enable the current development of AI, which needs massive computing power.

Gilder's law, proposed by George Gilder, author and prophet of the new technology age (Pinto, 2002), is about communication networks. It states that the bandwidth – that is, the rate of data transfer – of communication systems triples every year. Bandwidth, which is measured in bit per second, grows faster than computing power. While the precise Gilder's prediction may not have held up, the overall trend of increasing network bandwidth has been observed, enabling numerous technological advancements and new applications.

Last but not least, Metcalfe's law, attributed to Robert Metcalfe, originator of the Ethernet and founder of 3Com (Pinto, 2002), asserts that the value of a network is proportional to the square of the number of nodes, that is, the connected users on the system. The number of connected users of the network grows by linear progression and the value of the system – the value of being connected – grows exponentially while the cost per user remains the same. In marketing, this is known as the network effect, which in the simplest terms states that the value of a system is dependent on the number of people using it. Metcalfe's law was advocated to support investment in the Internet, e-commerce and social network booms and draws attention to business models and marketing strategies that promise to connect users and create communities, such as – but not limited to – platforms.

The above trends combined explain the accelerating pace of digitalization, digitization and the big data revolution. Moreover, the frontiers of this revolution are expanding every day, pushed by the embedding of the Internet in objects, by humans carrying the Internet with them wherever they go in their mobile and wearable devices that make the amount of available data for training algorithms expanding every day. In this respect, individuals are contributing to datafication enthusiastically by subjecting themselves to regimes of self-measurement that go far beyond the familiar habits of stepping on a weighing scale every morning … We now count steps, calorie intake, hours of sleep and more, so much so that some scholars have spoken of 'the quantified self' (Lupton, 2016).

Ever more personal aspects of our lives are being quantified: our relationships, our experiences, our moods. Social networks take intangible elements of our daily life and transform them into data. LinkedIn datafies work experiences. X (formerly Twitter) datafies sentiments. As early as 2011 scholars were able to discover the 'pattern of global mood' by analysing the content of a global sample of tweets during each day of the week and by attributing a valence (positive, negative or neutral) to the statements of millions of individuals (Golder and Macy, 2011). Country indexes of emotional states like optimism and anger can be created and fed into stock-trading systems (Mayer-Schönberger and Cukier, 2013). The 'social graph' of individuals on Facebook could be employed for credit scoring. As emotions become data, the opposite is also happening. Alibaba's financial arm Ant Financial calculates individuals' credit scores – named Sesami – based on e-commerce records and payments through the proprietary Alipay wallet, and on the customer's engagement activities such as posting, sharing and commenting online with friends and family. People in China post their Sesami score on dating sites to testify to their reliability and require others to reveal theirs to make sure they are 'real' and accountable (Hvistendahl, 2017).

These examples point towards another feature of the big data revolution. The value of data has been shifting from its primary use (the purpose for which it was collected) to its potential future uses (Mayer-Schönberger and Cukier, 2013). Think of Amazon. It allows other merchants to sell through its websites, thus providing them a service and, at the same time, gains access to information regarding what consumers purchase, which is of significant value to Amazon's own assortment management. In pursuit of such opportunities companies today strive to collect data about customers and partners – often employing loyalty programs and loyalty-building approaches – because they understand the power of analysing, selling and using it for both primary and secondary uses. However, this opens up challenges in how to make customers and partners aware – and how to ask their permission – of the uses the data will be put to if such uses do not yet exist. As AI algorithms become better at recognizing, classifying and recreating human voices and image content, for example, audio and video information stored on platforms by users can be put to totally new uses – and potentially controversial too.[5]

One of the largest contributions to datafication today is from the Internet of Things (IoT). Internet traffic connects more things than it does people. On the one hand, the IoT is often equated with connected home appliances and consumer devices like wearable technologies and cars. However, cyber-physical systems underlie almost all industrial sectors. They involve the acquisition of sensor data from, and the delivery of instructions to, devices that interface with or are part of the real world. Transportation and shipping companies use them for tracking vehicles and packages. Medical systems increasingly rely upon Internet-connected monitoring, diagnostic, and treatment devices. In manufacturing, digital networks are used to manage the handling of materials, optimization of inventories and connection of robotic systems. Local governments are an important IoT constituency in that streetlights, utilities, traffic control systems, and other so-called smart city applications are now part of the Internet ecosystem. In all economic sectors today, cyberspace touches the material world. IoT-collected data are about the actual behaviours of objects and of people's real usage and interaction with objects and services. In consumer markets, as smart home devices (smart thermostats, lighting controls, motion sensors, etc.) become commonplace, brands that can leverage such devices as touchpoints will be able to collect massive amounts of actual usage data that can be put to use with varying degrees of innovation, from control and maintenance to new service design. Moreover, the availability of vast amounts of sensor-collected data is enabling the development of AI algorithms and systems.

How is the big data revolution impacting business and marketing? Traditionally, technological revolutions have been studied for their economic impact in terms of productivity and for the reorganization of industries and supply chains that came as a consequence (Mandelli, 2017). Since Johannes Gutenberg invented the printing press in the mid-fifteenth century, the world has witnessed several waves of technological innovation. Between 1780 and 1840 the application of steam power to production triggered the Industrial Revolution. The steam engine mechanized the great majority of manufacturing processes, beginning with textiles, the most important industrial commodity at the time in Britain, whose price fell by 90% in 50 years while production increased at least 150-fold (Drucker, 2013). In 1829 came the railroad, an innovation that has been defined by many as the truly revolutionary element of the Industrial Revolution since it rapidly changed mental geography. Human beings had become truly mobile. As a new concept of distance was introduced, the horizons of ordinary people expanded for the first time. The next wave of technological revolution can be dated between 1890 and 1950, when both electricity and the automobile were introduced. The information revolution, and AI, are thus the most recent of several waves. Indeed, information revolution's influential analysts McAfee, Rock and Brynjolfsson (2023) stress that business leaders should view AI as a general-purpose technology such as electricity or the steam engine, while considering that its impact on performance and competition will be clear in a few years, not decades.

The information revolution has some peculiar traits. It is happening at a faster pace and it is pervasive: new technologies find application in every industry. Moreover, its cornerstone technology, the computer, has evolved from number cruncher to medium. It has enabled the existence and diffusion of several digital media from email to the Web to social networks – with all the consequences on human communication and society that brings. At the same time, the computer has subsumed several other intelligent technologies. Today maps, calculators, clocks, and an array of other tools that support and expand human intellectual abilities are all accessed via a computer screen. With that computer screen becoming mobile, moreover, all these tools are accessible anytime and anywhere. We may adopt the traditional economic categories to interpret the impact of the big data and AI revolutions, but there is simply much more to it.

Economists have tended to argue that technological innovations are adopted for their positive effects on productivity, because they produce more output with the same input or reduce the cost of one input. ICTs are no exception. However, the input whose cost they reduce is peculiar: information. Changes in the cost of information, especially information connected to the use of markets instead of internal production – a component of so-called *transaction costs* – alter the structure of companies' value chains, markets and indeed entire industries. They enable disintermediation and reintermediation, that is, the reallocation of activities across several players, including new ones, who are connected in networks or ecosystems. This way, new sources of supply that were previously impossible or uneconomical to tap are allowed to enter the product and labour markets. One only needs to think of how Airbnb unlocked the supply of new accommodation options or how Uber brought more underutilized cars to our roads or how Amazon's Web services have provided scalable infrastructure that reduces the need for peak capacity resources. In Chapter 1 we discussed how, thanks to the information revolution, new intermediaries have emerged in the specific domains of marketing services and promotion, contributing to the evolution of loyalty ecosystems and of a market for loyalty management services.

If we consider demand, the big data revolution has unlocked the potential for customers not only to seek out information but to unbundle (or bundle) aspects of products and services that were formerly combined (or separated) by necessity or for profit. It will suffice to cite the practice of watching as many episodes of a TV series as we want. A subscription-based service such as Netflix analyses huge amounts of data on the viewing behaviour of its customer base to create successful TV programs and deliver them in ways that enable new social practices like binge-watching.

At a general level, the literature that explores the impact of the information revolution on business and marketing is immense. Any attempt to summarize it would fall outside the scope of this chapter. However, we may say that most of it has concentrated on the contribution to value creation in terms of efficiency and effectiveness, as was proposed back in 1985 by Porter and Millar. Reflecting on the business impact of the ICT revolution, they stressed that the relevance of the latter is in the unlocking of information, which can create value in the following ways:

- it can improve the strategic decision-making process
- it is a tool for the effective implementation of a given strategy
- it is a source of product and process innovation at company, channel and industry levels
- it enables the building of intangible assets based on information and knowledge.

Years later, McAfee et al. (2012) demonstrated with their research that the more companies characterized themselves as data-driven, the better they performed on objective measures of financial and operational results.

The possibility to give customers what they want in new, more efficient ways translates into new value propositions that deliver what customers did not realize they wanted. Did we know we wanted the Internet in our pockets? Or that we wanted to share music? Many of the new propositions link digital and physical worlds across multiple touchpoints and exploit the availability of data and ubiquitous connectivity. The delivery of these new value propositions requires the rethinking and reimagining of business systems and industry value chains. Those who can access, analyse and exploit relevant information to create new value propositions for products, services or match making have an advantage. The information revolution, for example, allows insurance companies to operate new touchpoints for enhanced customer convenience, such as paying premiums online. However, information on customers' car-related behaviour would allow for the creation of completely new insurance products and services: customers could pay based on the real use of their car, how safe they are as drivers, their car parking and maintenance habits, and so on. The enabling data for such innovation may reside with different players, ranging from car manufacturers to smartphone manufacturers, insurance companies, municipalities and more.

Who can (and will) take advantage of it? Existing players? New information brokers? Industries differ in terms of the potential for value creation from big data and the real possibility of extracting value. Where markets are turbulent, performance is highly variable, transactions are frequent and/or the numbers of potential partners or customers are high, the potential and incentive to mine data to improve understanding and value creation are higher (Brown, Chui and Manyika, 2011). However, capturing such value depends on several factors, starting with competitive pressure from incumbents and new entrants, and encompassing the actual accessibility of data (who owns Alexa's records of interactions with its owner? Who can access them?), the type of decision-making prevalent in the industry, and the adequacy of technological, human and financial resources and skills. Among the latter, the availability of smart software has emerged as a powerful catalyst for the exploitation of big data (Kumar et al., 2016).

Predictive and generative AI in marketing

The advances we have discussed in ICTs have made unprecedented quantities of empirical data available and, at the same time, provided the means to access, store and process them. This has given new impetus to the scientific field of AI, as the burgeoning academic and investor interest in this area in recent years testifies. Worldwide, total corporate investment in AI has increased six-fold since 2016, reaching US$92 billion in 2022, according to Statista (Dencheva, 2023). The number of active AI companies worldwide is around 70,000, one in four being US based (Duarte, 2024).

In 1956 John McCarthy was the first to use the term 'artificial intelligence' in the proposal he co-authored for a workshop at the Dartmouth Summer Research Project. The goal was 'to investigate ways in which machines could be made to simulate aspects of intelligence' (Stone et al., 2016, p. 49). This can still be considered the essential idea that propels research in this area. The Dartmouth workshop created a unified identity for the field and a dedicated research community. The first hundred-year report on AI published by Stanford University offers a working definition: 'AI is a science and a set of computational technologies that are inspired by – but typically operate quite differently from – the ways people use their nervous systems and bodies to sense, learn, reason, and take action' (Stone et al., 2016, p. 4). Nilsson (2010) explains that AI is devoted to making machines intelligent, intelligence being that quality that enables an entity to function appropriately and with foresight in its environment.

Despite the early promise of the 1950s, for decades practical results lagged behind, mainly due to the unavailability of computational power and data. Then, technological progress made it more feasible to build systems that derive solutions from real-world data made available by the Internet and supported by the availability of computing power for storage and processing. As Alibaba's founder Jack Ma put it, 'large scale computing and data are the father and mother of AI' (Ericson and Wang, 2017).

Such advancements have allowed AI to emerge in the past two decades as a profound influence on our daily lives. According to the most recent Stanford University report (Littman et al., 2021), domains where AI breakthrough applications have emerged include medical diagnosis, logistics systems, autonomous driving, language translation, games, and interactive personal assistance. In the analysis they conducted in 2018 of over 400 cases of AI applications, Chui et al. (2018) found that AI was used to support activities where classification, clustering and prevision are useful or necessary to solve problems and take decisions. They saw AI as applied with an incremental orientation, to add value and efficiency to existing processes and products or services. The majority of applications were then for process control, optimization of planning and logistics, customer service and personalization. Only 15% of cases represented solutions that were radically different from what is possible with traditional analytics and software tools (Chui et al., 2018). This was consistent with the beginnings of many technological innovations that later turned into real revolutions. In 2023, Chui (2023) conducted new research along the lines of the previous one and found that the share of organizations that have adopted AI overall has remained steady, at 55%. Less than a third of respondents have adopted AI in more than one business function, suggesting that AI use remains limited in scope. However, the study reveals the explosive growth of generative AI tools (see below). Less than a year after many of these tools debuted, one-third of respondents are using them regularly in at least one business function, and 40% say their organizations will increase investment in AI overall because of advances in generative AI. Speech recognition and generation, natural language processing (understanding and generation), vision, image and video generation, planning, decision-making, and integration of vision and motor control for robotics are among the tasks where AI research has advanced the most, over the past five years (Littman et al., 2021).

Before reflecting on AI's impact on marketing it will be useful to introduce a few more concepts related to AI.

General and narrow AI

An additional driver of progress with AI was the shift in researchers' efforts from building systems that aim at encompassing all aspects of human intelligence – that is, ones that could perform different tasks typical of humans such as image recognition, speech recognition and decision-making, all in the same system – to concentrating on developing systems that focus on a single task, for example a machine that's great at recognizing images but nothing else. In the debate about AI, therefore, two categories of research have coexisted so far: general (or strong) AI and narrow (or weak) AI. General AI research has been surpassed by the fast-advancing results obtained in narrow AI research. However, over the past five years, notable progress has been made in the field of general AI (Littman et al., 2021), specifically as far as: a) the ability for a system to learn in a self-supervised way. A self-supervised model called transformer has become the go-to approach for natural language processing, and has been used in diverse applications, including machine translation and Google web search; b) the ability for a single AI system to learn in a continual way to solve problems from many different domains without requiring extensive retraining for each. One influential approach is to train a deep neural network – that we define below – on a variety of tasks, to make it learn general-purpose, transferable representations, as opposed to representations tailored specifically to any particular task; c) the ability for an AI system to generalize between tasks – that is, to adapt the knowledge and skills it has acquired for one task to new situations.

Machine learning and deep learning

Within AI, machine learning and deep learning are research areas and types of applications which, based on algorithms and powerful data analysis, enable computers to learn and adapt independently. The phrase 'machine learning' was coined in 1959 by Arthur Samuel who defined it as 'the ability to learn without being explicitly programmed' (McClelland, 2017). He invented a computer-checking application that was one of the first programs that could learn from its own mistakes and improve its performance over time. Machine learning is a type of AI research that enables software applications to become more accurate in forecasting outcomes without being specially programmed. Instead of coding specific instructions to perform a particular task, machine learning is a way of 'training' an algorithm so that it can learn how to perform the task autonomously. There are several approaches to training algorithms, which involve several ways of feeding them vast amounts of data with which they adjust themselves and improve. This aspect of AI algorithms is, in our opinion, a notable advance for marketing, and we will elaborate on it further.

Within machine learning, a category of algorithms that can be employed define what is called 'deep learning'. Neural networks are systems based on simulating connected 'neural units', loosely modelling the way that neurons interact in the brain. Neural networks are organized in many layers of interconnected neural units. Each layer specializes in perfecting a specific task and it's this multilayered structure that makes the learning 'deep'. An important implication of deep learning is that the way results are obtained is non-understandable and non-replicable by humans – a sort of 'black box' – hence it is difficult to trace back to eventual biases. This is critical in marketing, when one thinks of the selection of customers for preferential or adverse treatment or the selection of products for recommendation.

Deep learning has powered many of the recent advances in AI: think of ChatGPT, whose public version has reached 100 million users worldwide in two months (Chui et al., 2023) and democratized the discourse and the use of AI in an unprecedented manner thanks to its out-of-the-box accessibility that sets it apart from any previous AI tool and allows anybody who can ask questions to derive value from it. GPT actually stands for 'generative pre-trained transformer'. A transformer is a type of artificial neural network that gets trained on vast quantities of unstructured, unlabelled data in a variety of formats, such as text and audio.[6] ChatGPT is a text generating chatbot, but generative AI can enable capabilities across a broad range of content, including images, video, audio, and computer code. And it can perform several functions such as classifying, editing, summarizing, answering questions, and drafting new content, as we exemplified earlier with the Stitch Fix case and clarify below. Each of these actions has the potential to create value by changing how work gets done across business functions and workflows (Chui et al., 2023). Given the versatility of a foundation model (defined in note 6), companies can use the same one to implement multiple business use cases, differently from the preceding development of deep learning algorithms, that were narrower in scope. For example, a foundation model that has incorporated information about a company's products could potentially be used both to support customer service employees for answering customers' questions and engineers for developing new versions of the products. Such versatility is highly attractive for companies, that could realize benefits faster across a range of use cases. Currently, however, foundation models aren't naturally suited for all applications: for example, large language models have been in the news for answering questions with assertions that are plausible but false, a phenomenon that has been labelled 'hallucination' or 'confabulation'. Neither is generative AI currently suited for directly analysing large amounts of tabular data or solving advanced numerical-optimization problems, which is instead the domain of predictive AI (Chui et al., 2023).

Predictive and generative AI

Predictive and generative AI are two applications of artificial intelligence that both use machine learning to learn from data, but they do it in different ways and have different characteristics and capabilities to solve problems and impact business and marketing productivity. The problems that can be addressed by predictive AI cannot be solved with generative AI and vice versa. Below we define the two AI approaches and give examples of the problems they can solve in marketing (Yao and Koidan, 2024).

Predictive AI is used to predict future events or outcomes based on historical data. Machine learning models designed for prediction identify patterns in historical data and then use those patterns to forecast future occurrences. For example, if we train a predictive machine learning model on customer purchase history data we can then use it to predict which customers will be retained and which other customers will churn in the future. So the output of predictive AI are predictions and forecasts.

Generative AI is a type of AI that can create novel content, such as new text, images, music, and code. It learns from existing data and then generates new data that is similar to the training data. If we train a generative model on a dataset of copy examples (such as product descriptions or advertising jingles) it then generates new product descriptions or new jingles. The output of generative AI is new content.

In the domain of natural language processing (NLP), predictive NLP models can classify text in predefined classes, such as spam or not spam, while generative NLP models can create new text, given a prompt (a social media post or product description). In the field of image processing, predictive models classify images into predefined labels, generative models create new images (Yao and Koidan, 2024). In voice processing, predictive models convert speech to text by predicting how to represent in written the spoken phrases, while generative models create new speech audio from text.

Predictive AI models can achieve very high accuracy, and can automate many tasks; however, they require 'labelled' data, that are expensive and time consuming to obtain, and they need to be retrained periodically to remain accurate.

Generative AI speed up many processes for the creation of content, be it text, code, images or design, and generate innovative ideas; at the same time they can 'hallucinate' as mentioned above, are usually externally created with respect to businesses, with related problems of adaptability to the business specific needs and copyright issues for the used data and the output.

We can say, with Mandelli (2018) that the aspect of human intelligence that has – to date – been best mimicked by AI is the ability to make predictions. Agrawal, Gans and Goldfarb (2018) reason that the rapid interest in and adoption of AI has developed because predictive systems cause a drop in 'prediction costs' and consequently open up opportunities for informed action. In the countless areas of management and marketing (and indeed elsewhere) where the risk of action can be lowered by better prediction, adopting predictive AI offers solutions. Specialists, in turn, have been increasingly translating any sort of decision problem into a prediction problem in order to better address it within the framework of an AI approach and with predictive AI tools. The development of the self-driving car is a case in point. It looked like an unsolvable problem until it was redesigned as the problem of making the predictions a human driver would make in different situations in order to perform the task of driving. The same approach led to success in the above-mentioned field of language translation. As long as translating was considered a task based on putting into a system all the functioning rules of a language, it was too complex to tackle. When looked at as making the agent able to predict what words a human would employ in a context similar to the one at hand, the problem became addressable with machine learning techniques. The same approach greatly improved the accuracy of Google's instant query autocomplete interface, as probably every reader of this book can attest to.

By introducing automation into one of the most critical goals of business and marketing management – optimizing decisions by making better predictions – predictive AI changes the role of human intervention and creates intelligent agents (Kumar et al., 2016). Humans will increasingly have to interact with such agents. In the future there will certainly be an increase in machine–human interactions that will result in totally new experiences and advances in intelligent agent technology (IAT). We are already experiencing this as consumers in the area of customer service robotic assistance, where today we encounter chatbots, communicate with voice assistants and interact with robots in hotels, airports and stores.

Intelligent agents

According to Wooldridge (2002, p. 5), IATs are 'intelligent software or computer systems that are autonomous and possess important properties such as learning, social ability, reactivity, and pro-activeness to perform a set of complex tasks'. Furthermore, Kumar et al. (2016, p. 27) expand the definition in the context of marketing:

> Intelligent agent technologies (IATs) are computational systems that inhabit a complex dynamic environment and continuously perform marketing functions such as (a) dynamic scanning of the environment and market factors including competitors and customers, and firm actions impacting the marketing mix; (b) collaborating and interacting to interpret perceptions, analysing, learning and drawing inferences to solve problems; and (c) implementing customer-focused strategies that create value for the customers and the firm within the boundaries of trustworthiness and policy.
>
> *(Kumar et al., 2016, p. 27)*

As Kumar et al. suggest, AI is powering the development of a variety of IATs that perform marketing activities such as information search (e.g. Web spiders), customer acquisition (e.g. programmatic advertising and retargeting), retention (e.g. recommender systems) and interaction through communication (e.g. personalization and content generation engines), to name but a few.

Figure 2.1 provides a framework to capture how AI applications are impacting marketing. There can be little doubt that AI is one of the catalysts of the

momentous advancement made by the big data revolution that has been with us for over thirty years. We contend that AI will contribute to further transform both the management of the customer experience and the understanding of markets and customers. Figure 2.1 shows how AI has been applied to marketing and how this may lead to improvements in the customer experience. As we discuss in this book, better customer experience drives engagement with products and brands, which in turn positively impacts customer loyalty, and firm performance.

Let's take some of these applications in turn. The nature of predictive AI tools such as prediction machines dramatically improves searching. Successful *search* – the retrieval of sought and unsought but relevant information – is essential for businesses in markets where the available products and services are almost infinite but where consumers' patience is definitely finite. The average online clothing retailer, for example, can have a range easily exceeding 50,000 items: most of them will never be seen by prospects and customers – hence never turned – unless better search options are made available to them (uploading a snapshot of a friend's dress, for example, to search for the same or similar options) and better recommendation algorithms are employed (which can recognize sophisticated attributes of the dress such as the type of garment, its colour, pattern, style and fabric, the brand, the context in which one would wear it – for a party, for the outdoors, etc. – and more).

Search and *recommendation*, in fact, are two sides of the same coin: the coin being the prediction problem. Improving this area would mean giving customers access to a wider yet relevant variety, allowing them to place themselves in a 'niche' instead of settling for the 'average'. From the point of view of the marketer, improved search results and recommendations help sell slow-moving items and thus increase revenues and profits and the ratings of sold goods, since recommended items typically score higher in customers' ratings than non-recommended ones. By streamlining how we search, companies can shorten the customer search-to-shop journey and capitalize on impulse buying. Consumers may experience feelings of discovery, excitement, gratification and empowerment – all of which become embedded in their perceived customer experience. At the same time, the application of generative AI to search will change the customer experience dramatically: Google has been reported to be trialling using its own generative AI to respond to search engine queries with a single best answer – very similar to chatting with AI chatbots like ChatGPT. The experience will be starkly different from looking at a search engine result page with several web pages hyperlinked. Moreover, Google is considering allowing consumers use generative AI-powered search for a fee, in order to cover the growing costs of AI related processing and algorithm training (Shinde, 2024). As new AI tools make the customer experience better, there will be room for extracting value from customers also by charging for their use.

AI–based image and speech recognition will have a significant impact in terms of improving search and recommendation, and consequently the customer experience. For millennials, both young and old, visual search is the technology they are most comfortable with (Wurmser, 2018). Visual search is good for questions that are difficult to verbalize, hence it seems not to cannibalize text search but rather complement it (Wurmser, 2018). More and more businesses offer such functionality on their websites and apps: searching with images is as simple as snapping a photo of a pair of shoes or using a Web app to select a certain image that you found via a Google search. Ultimately, visual search brings online searching closer to the in-store browsing experience.

AI-powered agents help customers to not only find specific items but also the right complements (Butterfield, 2018). Customers upload an image from any source and the software extracts the image's attributes, correlates it with a massive database of products and displays visually similar results as well as relevant recommendations of similar but also complementary products, such as accessories in the case of fashion. The information generated – uploaded photos, results, and customers' consequential actions (click, enlarge, save, discard, purchase, etc.) captured in real time and in context – enrich the user's profile. In November 2018 Zalando launched their Algorithmic Fashion Companion (AFC). Based on a 'training set of over 200,000 outfits created by stylists, the agent suggested those that best matched recent customer purchases, hence offering a curated shopping experience' (Planet Retail, 2018). In 2023 the company introduced its ChatGPT-powered assistant, aimed at making the search and discovery process more natural and intuitive as shoppers can navigate through Zalando's assortment using their own words and expressions. It can suggest items appropriate for a specific event or location and cater to customers looking to combine different activities – like hiking with the beach – and find items suitable for both (Su, 2023).

AI is being applied to the customer experience in the area of voice recognition, too. Voice recognition technology powers voice searches and convert our spoken words into text. AI interprets the text and uses natural language processing and machine learning to produce expected results. Like image recognition, voice and speech recognition build on a natural human trait. Using our voice 'is more natural than using a touchpad or keyboard, takes less brain power, and creates even more opportunity for tech to move further into the background and reduce our reliance on screens' (Cakebread, 2019). The evident advantages of using one's voice to perform tasks, give instructions, search for products and services, place orders and, in general, be heard means that voice-operated services (from search to purchase to post-purchase assistance) will grow exponentially in the future. In 2022, 27% of Google searches were executed through voice. WhatsApp processed 200 million voice messages per day in 2017, that have risen to 7 billion in 2024 (Tiwari, 2017; Economic Times, 2024). The accuracy of voice recognition algorithms has dramatically improved

since IBM's first prototypes in 1995 when the word error rate (WER) – a common metric to gauge the accuracy of voice recognition systems – was 43% (Saon, 2016). It decreased to 15% in 2004, and Google Assistant reached an impressive 4.9% as early as in 2018, close to the average capability of humans, which is a WER[7] of around 4% (van der Velde, 2018).

Since Apple launched Siri in 2011, followed by Amazon's Alexa in 2014 and Google Assistant in 2016, the tech giants have sustained the adoption of voice assistants by popularizing smart devices for the home. In this category smart speaker sales alone rose from 20 million units sold worldwide in 2017 to 200 million units in 2023 (Kinsella, 2018; Statista, 2024). An ever-growing number of smart devices, connected to the Internet and equipped with microphones, cameras, screens, sensors, voice and image recognition and computer vision capabilities will emerge on the market in the future. As more smart objects and devices permeate our daily lives, intelligent voice assistants will become indispensable (Chou, 2018). Moreover, these new smart objects and digital assistants change the 'servicescape' as we know it. Just think of the last time you went to a hotel. It's quite possible that you interacted with a plethora of robotic assistants: your check-in was swift thanks to facial recognition, and a series of smart devices enabled you to manage the temperature and lighting of your room, order entertainment and book other services. Data from such interactions can be used to enrich each customer's profile or derive insights on the needs and wants of the customer base (leading to the better understanding we presented as an outcome in Figure 2.1) and to inform the (re)design of services and of the customer experience.

Digital assistants, thanks to natural language processing, 'understand' voice commands (to ever increasing degrees of accuracy) and are able to produce voice output in natural language that resembles closely what a human would say in response to the command. Advances in this area have been rapid and today natural language processing software can even manage dialects, in countries such as India where this is essential for business, or detect emotions. One area of application of natural language processing for CEM is the development of chatbots – automated *customer support* services powered by AI algorithms – that can process and respond in natural language by text and voice.

Chatbots are becoming increasingly common and represent a new touchpoint in the customer journey. Yao, Zhou and Jia (2018) have analysed hundreds of chatbots employed for the purposes of customer support in a variety of industries. Our own analysis of new services made available to members of major loyalty schemes has found that some companies develop chatbots to provide exclusive services that are intended for retention as well as acquisition of new members to a loyalty initiative and/or to the company. Sephora, the beauty retailer, was an early adopter of chatbots to let customers book in-store appointments with beauty consultants in the nearest store by interacting via text messages on social media. The always-on chatbot now provides beauty product recommendations, tips and product reviews, and how-to videos on product application and skincare. The chatbot has 11% higher conversion rates than other digital touchpoints and Sephora has reported a 50% increase in customer loyalty with the launch of their chatbot (Sprinklr, 2023).

H&M's Kik chatbot provides fashion advice and recommendations to its users. The chatbot uses NLP to understand the user's requests and provide personalized styling tips. Kik is available on the Kik messenger app, with over 15 million monthly active users. It achieved an engagement rate of 86%, with users spending an average of four minutes interacting with the chatbot. Its click-through rate was 8%, which is higher than H&M's email marketing click-through rate of 2% (Sprinklr, 2023).

The game changer of AI in the customer experience raises questions about how customers will engage with touchpoints in the future. Today's customers live in an omnichannel world. Connected devices and the opportunity to interact with them via natural language and image recognition via smart assistants and services are being woven into the fabric of everyday life. The landscape of *touchpoints* will change, and so will the customer's perception of her journey across new and old touchpoints. Brands' access to final consumers will change too. Connected objects and smart devices potentially allow more brands to enter the home and the customer's consideration set. With this come several challenges. Intuitively, voice search will benefit those brands that appear first in search results, while their competitors fall into the shadows (how many pages of search results do we look through?). Thus, businesses unable to compete with the resource-rich and technologically savvy brands risk becoming 'invisible' to customers. Products that have already been present in the customer shopping basket are favoured in terms of their prominence in search results, and sponsored content doesn't necessarily come first. Marketers, therefore, will have to devise strategies to 'win' the intelligent agent, and have their product or brand selected by the smart assistant for suggestion to the customer who is ordering via voice. In other words, new touchpoints will find their unique place in customers' journeys and marketers need to understand and address this in developing appropriate customer experience design strategies.

The new intelligent touchpoints collect data – in any format, structured and unstructured – that can be employed to gain insight and personalize the touchpoint interaction experience by making content and offers available to individual customers according to their tastes and preferences. By employing AI, *personalization* can be taken to new levels. For example, AI tools can help businesses adapt their offer to the context and indeed the specific moment in the customer journey and even to the emotional status of the customer. Not only has facial recognition software been able to map emotions for years; NLP algorithms can detect and decipher emotions, sarcasm and figures of speech (Dhanrajani, 2018). Think of the impact on customer service in a world where chatbots can tell the emotional state of the customer. With prediction capabilities built in, more real-time scoring of customers and prospects will be possible and personalization will be driven less by previously built profiles and more conversationally driven and oriented by contingency factors.

Programmatic *online advertising* is another area where AI has important applications. More accurate predictions will result in improvements in the real-time A/B testing of different advertising solutions, in bidding for inventory and in real-time campaign optimization, thanks to the improved selection of an audience that is more likely to convert. These are just some of the marketing *processes that will become automated* by predictive AI. Let's take another. As is pointed out by Mandelli (2018), *real-time relationship risk management* will become a genuine possibility since algorithms can do a better job of predicting churn from a variety of data (including those on emotions detected in spoken conversations) and can send alerts to marketers or automatically devise retention strategies. The human's role will shift to monitoring processes and choosing among a variety of automatically generated options – as we saw in the case of Stitch Fix and as will be shown to be the case in the advertising and content creation examples below.

Offers, product descriptions and articles related to entire product lines can be automatically composed and personalized by machines. This is one example of how product information can be used to both personalize and automate formerly traditional marketing processes. During Alibaba's 11.11 Shopping Festival, in November 2023, the two e-commerce platforms of the group, Taobao and Tmall, have introduced ten AI-powered features for merchants, and a generative-AI chatbot named Wenwen (which means 'asking' in Mandarin) to answer consumers' queries (Utley, 2023). Since launch in September, the tool has been used by 5 million people, asking on average 8 questions each, daily. It is based on a LLM developed expressly for e-commerce, and users can ask about best deals for them across the thousands that are available and receive personalized recommendations. As for tools for merchants, they assist copywriting, customer service, production of product images and more. Sellers can choose among seven writing styles to create product descriptions that get published 'with one click' on different touchpoints; they can generate product images in seconds, with different positions, backgrounds and situations, to demonstrate product uses and versatility. Real time analysis of sales data prompts sellers with the products to promote. These merchant tools have been used 1.5 billion times during preparation for the Festival and the festival days (Utley, 2023).

Chatbots can take the appearance of an animation – an avatar – to communicate with shoppers in a more engaging way, compared with the dull 'chat box' in the corner of the screen that we are used to. In China, again, many retailers are paving the way. Some 12% of shoppers in the country reported interacting with a virtual customer service agent for complaints or product questions, a 2023 study by consultancy PwC found (Utley, 2024).

AI-powered digital assistants and avatars do not necessarily replace real people; often they complement and enable live employees to serve consumers better. In brand stores on Tmall, for example, human livestreamers and their virtual counterparts cooperate. Human employees are employed for a few hours of the day, to stream demos, share information about new products, and answer consumer queries, and then they pass information to the bots, that take over the rest of the time.

Creative human skills will increasingly be supported – if not substituted – by AI as far as *content (not only advertising) creation*. Today, a significant portion of articles on news sites is written by machines, not by humans. AI tools can turn data into readable texts, indistinguishable from those authored by human beings (Sachin, 2018). Wordsmith, for example, was one of the first content generation agents, used by the Associated Press as early as 2018 to automate most of its financial earnings reports. It produced over 4400 quarterly earnings reports which translate into a 1200% increase compared to manual output (Parbey, 2018). And around the same year we were fascinated by the neuro-storyteller developed by Ryan Kiros at University of Toronto, which combined various AI models to generate stories based on the content of images. One of neuro-storyteller's models was trained on over 14 million passages from romance novels and, when fed with images, generated a short fictional story based on the recognition of its content (Samim, 2015). Today, with ChatGPT-4 and its image creation companion DALL-E widely accessible, we can all do the same in seconds, and are no longer surprised when reading stories like the above.

The filter bubble

The impact of AI undoubtedly goes well beyond marketing. Any discussion about content creation and personalization would not be complete without a reflection on the social consequences of people increasingly living inside their own 'filter bubble' (Pariser, 2011), that is, our own personal unique universe of information that we inhabit online. Ever since 2009 when Google first introduced individualized search results by using each user's past searches to display search results, personalization on the Web – and on digital touchpoints such as social media and apps that have emerged since – has skyrocketed. Pariser (2011) argues that although choosing one medium over another has always implied that we self-select ourselves for certain content (before the age of digital, we still *chose* to read one newspaper rather than another), the personalization bubble online is different. In fact, it is unique to each individual. It is invisible. Many people are not even aware of it. We do not know what gets edited out. With news sites mimicking search engines in (creating and) serving content that has a higher probability of being clicked on, read, forwarded and shared, and with less work performed by humans and more by algorithms, de-bundling and the disappearance of unpopular articles happens in minutes, if not seconds. Friends on social media whose content we do not interact with disappear from our newsfeed. We live inside a narrower image of the world. Because it is built around our behaviour and preferences, our bubble enhances our proclivity to consume content that does not challenge our beliefs. A non-challenging context blunts creativity and openness. This might be good for consumers, particularly if it simplifies choices, but it might not be as good for citizens who, in order to live constructively in peace, need to be aware of differences and learn to accept them (Pariser, 2011). The development and diffusion of ever more powerful AI will exacerbate this and other related risks. Criminals, rogue states, ideological extremists, or simply special interest groups, may make use of deepfake images and video and online bots to manipulate people and the public discourse for economic gain or political advantage (Littman et al., 2021).

A more general and subtle danger is techno-solutionism, or the belief that when given the choice between algorithms and humans, algorithms are always the solution because they are the less biased choice. As AI advances, the temptation to apply AI decision-making to all societal problems will increase. But technology often creates larger problems in the process of solving smaller ones. Amazon, in 2018, found it necessary to discard a proprietary recruiting tool because the historical data it was trained on resulted in a system that was systematically biased against women. Healthcare and criminal justice software has been shown to discriminate against minorities and disadvantaged groups. Automated decision-making may produce skewed results that replicate and amplify existing biases.

The revolution in big data and AI is changing the customer experience as we know it. It is creating value not just by making marketing processes more efficient, but by making them supremely effective since they are now being driven by better prediction, automation and innovation. Value creation is the driver of loyalty. And we are just at the beginning. It is up to each of us to be vigilant so that intelligent tools remain tools that support value creation for everyone.

Notes

1 Although several definitions exist, we follow Khyade and Khyade (2018, p. 2) and understand ICT to broadly mean 'any product that will store, retrieve, manipulate, transmit or receive information electronically in a digital form, e.g. personal computers, digital television, email, robots'.

2 The volume of information worldwide is ever expanding. This is due largely to the fact that the majority of the information that is being produced today is digital; that

is, produced in the binary numeric form that can be manipulated by computers. This transformation from analogue to digital information is enabled by technological advances in digital data creation, processing, storage and transmission. Although the central concept of the modern computer is based on ideas expressed by Alan Turing in 1936, the first prototype wasn't developed until 1964 by Douglas Engelbart and the 1960s marked the evolution of the computer from a specialized machine for scientists to a technology accessible to the general public. Before then information was analogue (paper, books, photographic print) and collecting and analysing it was a huge task. Hilbert (2012) has calculated that in 2000, 75% of the world's stored information was still analogue, while 25% was digital. A radical reversal occurred. By 2007, 7% was analogue and 93% digital, and in 2013 that had accelerated (analogue 2%, digital 98%). Unlike digital, analogue information is no longer growing.

3 Large language models, in the field of artificial intelligence, are algorithms that can recognize and generate text, among other tasks. LLMs are trained on huge sets of data – hence the name 'large' and are built on a type of neural network called a transformer model.

4 Throughout the book we distinguish between digitization and digitalization, two terms often used synonymously. In this we follow Brennen and Kreiss (2014) who, in line with *The Oxford English Dictionary*, define digitization as the 'material process of converting individual analogue streams of information into digital bits' and digitalization as 'the way in which many domains of social life are restructured around digital communication and media infrastructures'.

5 For instance, ChatGPT has been trained on enormous amounts of text, some of which still covered by copyright, and image generating AI systems, like Midjourney, have been sued for copyright infringement.

6 Transformers are a key component of foundation models, that 'power' the generative AI chatbot with which humans interact. Foundation models can be used for a wide range of tasks. For example, a type of foundation model called a large language model can be trained on vast amounts of text that is publicly available on the Internet and covers many different topics.

7 New measures are being created recently, such as NER – that stands for number, edition error and recognition error – to assess the accuracy of a growing array of tools, such as video translation in real time and more (Hughes, 2022).

References

Agrawal, A., Gans, J. and Goldfarb, A. (2018) *Prediction Machines: The Simple Economics of Artificial Intelligence*. Boston, MA: Harvard Business Review Press.

Bhattarai, A. (2018) 'The personal stylists who are training the bots to be personal stylists'. *The Washington Post*, 17 August.

Blattberg, R. C., Glazer, R. and Little, J. D. (1994) *The Marketing Information Revolution*. Boston, MA: Harvard Business School Press.

Brennen, S. and Kreiss, D. (2014) 'Digitalization and digitization'. *Culture Digitally*, 8 September. Retrieved from http://culturedigitally.org/2014/09/digitalization-and-digitization (accessed 24 January 2019).

Brown, B., Chui, M. and Manyika, J. (2011) 'Are you ready for the era of "big data"?'. *McKinsey Quarterly*, 4(1), 24–35.

Butterfield, B. (2018) 'See it, search it, shop it: how AI is powering visual search'. *Adobe Blog*, 12 December. Retrieved from https://theblog.adobe.com/see-it-search-it-shop-it-how-ai-is-powering-visual-search (accessed 17 January 2019).

Cakebread, C. (2019) 'Hey Siri, what are hearables? A new category of wearable emerges'. *eMarketer*, 9 January. Retrieved from www.emarketer.com/content/hey-siri-what-are-hearables (accessed 19 January 2019).

Chou, C. (2018) 'Top tech trends to watch in 2018 from Alibaba scientists'. *Alizila*, 6 February. Retrieved from www.alizila.com/top-tech-trends-to-watch-in-2018 (accessed 19 January 2019).

Chui, M. (2023) 'The state of AI in 2023: generative AI's breakout year'. Retrieved from www.mckinsey.com/capabilities/quantumblack/our-insights/the-state-of-ai-in-2023-generative-ais-breakout-year# (accessed 4 May 2024).

Chui, M., Manyika, J., Miremadi, M., Henke, N., Chung, R., Nel, P. and Malhotra, S. (2018) *Notes from the AI Frontier: Insights from Hundreds of Use Cases.* McKinsey.

Chui, M., Roberts, R., Rodchenko, T., Singla, A., Sukharevsky, A., Yee, L. and Zurkiya, D. (2023), 'What every CEO should know about generative AI'. Retrieved from www.mckinsey.com/capabilities/mckinsey-digital/our-insights/what-every-ceo-should-know-about-generative-ai# (accessed 4 May 2024).

Dencheva, V., (2023) 'AI in marketing revenue worldwide 2020–2028 January 6, 2023'. Retrieved from www.statista.com/statistics/1293758/ai-marketing-revenue-worldwide/#:~:text=In%202021%2C%20the%20market%20for,than%20107.5%20billion%20by%202028 (accessed 6 April 2024).

Dhanrajani, S. (2018) 'Here are the top 10 AI trends to watch out for in 2019'. *YourStory*, 27 December. Retrieved from https://yourstory.com/2018/12/top-10-ai-trends-watch-2019 (accessed 20 January 2019).

Drucker, P. (2013) *Managing in the Next Society.* 2nd edition. London: Routledge.

Duarte, F. (2024) 'How many AI companies are there?' Retrieved from https://explodingtopics.com/blog/number-ai-companies (accessed 22 April 2024).

Economic Times (2024) 'Mark Zuckerberg announces new features for WhatsApp Channels'. Retrieved from https://economictimes.indiatimes.com/tech/technology/mark-zuckerberg-announces-new-features-for-whatsapp-channels/articleshow/106935355.cms?from=mdr (accessed 4 May 2024).

Ericson, J. and Wang, S. (2017) 'At Alibaba, artificial intelligence is changing how people shop online'. *Alizila*, 5 June. Retrieved from www.alizila.com/at-alibaba-artificial-intelligence-is-changing-how-people-shop-online (accessed 5 January 2019).

Gershgorn, D. (2017) 'Stitch Fix is letting algorithms help design new clothes – and they're allegedly flying off the digital racks'. *Quartz*, 16 July. Retrieved from https://qz.com/1028624/stitch-fix-let-an-algorithm-design-a-new-blouse-and-they-flew-off-the-digital-racks (accessed 3 January 2019).

Golder, S. A. and Macy, M. W. (2011) 'Diurnal and seasonal mood vary with work, sleep and daylength across diverse cultures'. *Science*, 333(6051) (30 September), 1871–1881.

Hilbert, M. (2012) 'How much information is there in the "information society"?'. *Significance*, 9(4), 8–12.

Hollis, S. (2018) 'The Stitch Fix story: changing the way millions of people dress with data'. Retrieved from https://jilt.com/upsell/stitch-fix-data (accessed 1 January 2019).

Hughes, J. (2022) 'The future of word error rate (WER)'. Retrieved from www.speechmatics.com/company/articles-and-news/the-future-of-word-error-rate (accessed 7 May 2024).

Hvistendahl, M. (2017) 'Inside China's vast new experiment in social ranking'. *Wired*, 14 December. Retrieved from www.wired.com/story/age-of-social-credit (accessed 3 January 2019).

Khyade, V. B., and Khyade, R. V. (2018) 'Strengthening role of information and communication technology in global society'. *International Academic Journal of Accounting and Financial Management*, 5(2), 42–49.

Kinsella, B. (2018) 'Amazon moves back to top spot for Q3 2018 smart speaker sales – Canalys'. *Voicebot*, 15 November. Retrieved from https://voicebot.ai/2018/11/15/amazon-moves-back-to-top-spot-for-q3-2018-smart-speaker-sales-canalys (accessed 19 January 2019).

Kumar, V., Dixit, A., Javalgi, R. G. and Dass, M. (2016) 'Research framework, strategies, and applications of intelligent agent technologies (IATs) in marketing'. *Journal of the Academy of Marketing Science*, 44(1), 24–45.

Lake, K. (2018) 'Stitch Fix's CEO on selling personal styles to the mass market'. *Harvard Business Review*, (May–June), 35–40.

Littman, M. et al. (2021) 'Gathering strength, gathering storms: the One Hundred Year Study on Artificial Intelligence (AI100) 2021 study panel report.' Stanford University, Stanford, CA, September 2021. Retrieved from http://ai100.stanford. edu/2021-report (accessed 16 September 2021).

Lupton, D. (2016) *The Quantified Self: A Sociology of Self-Tracking*. New York: John Wiley & Sons.

Mack, C. (2015) 'The multiple lives of Moore's law'. *IEEE Spectrum*, 52(4), 31–31.

Mandelli, A. (2017) *Big Data Marketing*. Milan: EGEA.

Mandelli, A. (2018) *Intelligenza artificiale e marketing: Agenti invisibili, esperienza, valore e business*. Milan: EGEA.

Manyika, J., Chui, M., Brown, B., Bughin, J., Dobbs, R., Roxburgh, C. and Byers, A. H. (2011) *Big Data: The Next Frontier for Innovation, Competition, and Productivity*. McKinsey, May. Retrieved from www.mckinsey.com/business-functions/digital-mckinsey/our-insights/big-data-the-next-frontier-for-innovation (accessed 9 January 2019).

Marr, B. (2018) 'Stitch Fix: the amazing use case of using artificial intelligence in fashion retail'. *Forbes Magazine*, 25 May. Retrieved from www.forbes.com/sites/bernardmarr/2018/05/25/stitch-fix-the-amazing-use-case-of-using-artificial-intelligence-in-fashion-retail (accessed 2 January 2019).

Marr, B. (2024) 'How Stitch Fix is using generative AI to help us dress better'. *Forbes Magazine*, 8 March. Retrieved from www.forbes.com/sites/bernardmarr/2024/03/08/how-stitch-fix-is-using-generative-ai-to-help-us-dress-better/?sh=75bcfb3553c2 (accessed 22 April 2024).

Mayer-Schönberger, V. and Cukier, K. (2013) *Big Data: A Revolution That Will Transform How We Live, Work and Think*. London: John Murray.

McAfee, A., Brynjolfsson, E., Davenport, T. H., Patil, D. J., & Barton, D. (2012). 'Big data: the management revolution'. *Harvard Business Review*, 90(10), 60–68.

McAfee, A., Rock, D., & Brynjolfsson, E. (2023) 'How to capitalize on generative AI'. *Harvard Business Review*, 101(6), 42–48.

McClelland, A. (2017) 'The difference between artificial intelligence, machine learning, and deep learning'. *Medium*, 4 December. Retrieved from https://medium.com/iotforall/the-difference-between-artificial-intelligence-machine-learning-and-deep-learning-3aa67bff5991 (accessed 6 January 2019).

Meisenzahl, M. (2024) 'Stitch Fix revenue, customer count decline again in Q2'. Retrieved from www.digitalcommerce360.com/2024/03/05/stitch-fix-revenue-customer-count-decline-again-in-q2/ (accessed 17 April 2024).

Negroponte, N. (1995) *Being Digital*. New York: Alfred A. Knopf.

Nilsson, N. J. (2010) *The Quest for Artificial Intelligence: A History of Ideas and Achievements*. Cambridge: Cambridge University Press.

Parbey, C. (2018) '3 content creation AI that can write a story for you'. 22 November. Retrieved from https://edgy.app/3-content-creation-ai-that-can-write-a-story-for-you (accessed 20 January 2019).

Pariser, E. (2011) *The Filter Bubble: What the Internet is Hiding from You*. London: Penguin.

Pinto, J. (2002) 'The 3 technology laws'. Retrieved from www.jimpinto.com/writings/techlaws.html (accessed 3 January 2019).

Planet Retail (2018) 'Zalando builds machine learning based styling assistant'. 1 November. Available (subscribers only) via: www.planetretail.net/NewsAndInsight/Article/165853 (accessed 19 January 2019).

Porter, M. E. and Millar, V. E. (1985) 'How information gives you competitive advantage.' *Harvard Business Review*, (July). Retrieved from https://hbr.org/1985/07/how-information-gives-you-competitive-advantage (accessed 2 February 2019).

Ransbotham, S. (2024) 'Fashioning the perfect fit with AI: Stitch Fix's Jeff Cooper'. Episode 903 of Me, Myself and AI podcast. Retrieved from https://sloanreview.mit.edu/audio/fashioning-the-perfect-fit-with-ai-stitch-fixs-jeff-cooper (accessed 17 April 2024).

Sachin, S. (2018) 'How does AI work on marketing ads?'. 5 September. Retrieved from www.quora.com/How-does-AI-work-on-marketing-ads (accessed 20 January 2019).

Samim (2015) 'Generating stories about images: recurrent neural network for generating stories about images'. *Medium*, 5 November. Retrieved from https://medium.com/@samim/generating-stories-about-images-d163ba41e4ed (accessed 20 January 2019).

Saon, G (2016) 'Recent advances in conversational speech recognition'. 28 April. Retrieved from https://developer.ibm.com/watson/blog/2016/04/28/recent-advances-in-conversational-speech-recognition-2 (accessed 2 February 2019).

Shinde, J. (2024) 'Google may ask you to pay for AI-powered search soon: is this future of online search?'. Retrieved from www.digit.in/news/general/google-may-charge-money-for-ai-powered-search-soon-future-of-online-search.html (accessed 4 May 2024).

Sprinklr (2023) '15 best chatbot examples from groundbreaking brands'. Retrieved from www.sprinklr.com/blog/chatbot-examples (accessed 7 May 2024).

Statista (2024) 'Sales volume of the smart speakers industry worldwide 2018–2028'. Retrieved from www.statista.com/forecasts/1367982/smart-speaker-market-volume-worldwide (accessed 7 May 2024).

Stitch Fix (2024) 'How we're revolutionizing personal styling with generative AI'. Retrieved from https://newsroom.stitchfix.com/blog/how-were-revolutionizing-personal-styling-with-generative-ai (accessed 22 April 2024).

Stone, P., Brooks, R., Brynjolfsson, E., Calo, R., Etzioni, O., Hager, G., Hirschberg, J., Kalyanakrishnan, S., Kamar, E., Kraus, S., Leyton-Brown, K., Parkes, D., Press, W., Saxenian, A. L., Shah, J., Tambe, M. and Teller, A. (2016) 'Artificial intelligence and life in 2030: One Hundred Year Study on Artificial Intelligence: Report of the 2015–2016 study panel, September 2016'. Retrieved from https://ai100.stanford.edu/2016-report (accessed 7 January 2019).

Su, T. (2023) 'How Zalando uses AI for hyper-personalised customer experiences'. Retrieved from www.drapersonline.com/insight/zalando-on-using-ai-to-create-personalised-experiences-for-consumers (accessed 4 May 2024).

Tiwari, P. (2017) '4 reasons why voice is the future of customer experience'. Retrieved from www.interactions.com/blog/customer-care/4-reasons-voice-future-cx (accessed 19 January 2019).

Utley, E. (2023) 'China's e-commerce industry embraces AI this singles' day'. Retrieved from www.alizila.com/chinas-e-commerce-industry-embraces-ai-this-singles-day (accessed 4 June 2024).

Utley, E. (2024) 'From niche to necessary: the rise of AI-powered virtual avatars in Chinese e-commerce'. Retrieved from www.alizila.com/ai-virtual-avatars-chinese-ecommerce-retail-2024 (accessed 4 June 2024).

Van der Velde, N (2018) 'A complete guide to speech recognition technology'. Retrieved from www.globalme.net/blog/the-present-future-of-speech-recognition (accessed 2 February 2019).

Wilson, J. M. (2012) 'Computing, communication, and cognition: three laws that define the internet society: Moore's, Gilder's, and Metcalfe's'. Retrieved from www.jackmwilson.net/Entrepreneurship/Cases/Moores-Meltcalfes-Gilders-Law.pdf (accessed 3 January 2019).

Wooldridge, M. (2002) *An Introduction to MultiAgent Systems*. Chichester: John Wiley & Sons.

Wurmser, Y. (2018) 'Visual search 2018: new tools from Pinterest, eBay, Google and Amazon increase accuracy, utility'. Retrieved from www.emarketer.com/content/visual-search-2018 (accessed 17 January 2019).

Yao, M., and Koidan, K. (2024) *Applied Artificial Intelligence: A Handbook for Business Leaders*. 2nd edition. Middletown, DE: TOPBOTS.

Yao, M., Zhou, A. and Jia, M. (2018) *Applied Artificial Intelligence: A Handbook for Business Leaders*. Middletown, DE: TOPBOTS.

3
LOYALTY AND SUSTAINABILITY

Cristina Ziliani

Sustainability: everyone's priority?

In 2023 US travel and hospitality companies were polled about how they were currently integrating sustainability into their loyalty programs (iSeatz, 2023). They declared they were offering customers bonuses or incentives for booking sustainable options (45%), contributed a portion of revenue to sustainability causes or organizations (37%), offered sustainability-related redemption options (32%) or had a statement reflecting their committment to sustainability (30%). Only 15% declared they had not integrated sustainability at all into their loyalty program.

These results echoed what we had been observing in Italy, where, in 2022, 47% of businesses revealed that they would introduce offers and rewards related to 'values', including sustainability, and 30% intended to completely reorganize their loyalty program around sustainability (Osservatorio Fedeltà, 2022). That year we dedicated a webinar to discussing the crossing of loyalty and sustainability, and it attracted over 280 marketing/loyalty managers. We also carried out a first round of collection of international cases of loyalty programs that incorporated elements of sustainability that retrieved 58 cases. In 2023 our yearly survey of Italian businesses confirmed that 29% intended to completely reorganize their loyalty program around environmental and social sustainability.

On an international scale, the Antavo (2023) global customer loyalty report asked companies what (socially and environmentally) sustainable actions were currently rewarded by their loyalty programs or planned to be offered in the near future, and 70% mentioned charitable contributions (48% planned, 22% currently), 66% indicated adoption of sustainable behaviour (51% planned, 15% currently), 64% purchase of ethical products (51% versus 13%).

DOI: 10.4324/9781003400783-3

In sum, managerial attention to the intersection between sustainability and loyalty is high, while the ways in which this is translated into practice vary widely. However, underpinning the variety of efforts – from adding sustainable options to rewarding members for supporting charities or behaving sustainably – is the implicit assumption that customers care about sustainability, and see value in companies' adjusting their proposals accordingly. Or is it so? Why 28% of the sustainability-friendly loyalty programs that we registered in 2022 seem to have disappeared only two years later, in 2024?

The stream of reports and data showing that consumers say they care about sustainability and, more generally, about companies' environmental, societal and governance (ESG) efforts, is endless. Especially younger generations are called to the fore, when change towards sustainability in management and marketing practices is advocated. Recent surveys, including those conducted by IBM with NRF and the Baker Retailing Center at the University of Pennsylvania, for example, found between half to two-thirds of US consumers said they will pay more for sustainable products (Case, 2023). However, there are more shades to the picture. According to GfK Consumer Life data, over half (53%) of US consumers think more sustainable products cost too much. And research by Usrey et al. (2020) showed that consumers consider products explicitly claiming green attributes as less effective than conventional alternatives, in certain categories. A joint study by McKinsey and Nielsen (2023) looked beyond the self-reported intentions of US consumers and examined their actual spending behavior and established that sales growth of products making ESG claims outpaces products not featuring them: however, the study does not demonstrate a causal relationship that indicates whether consumers bought these brands *because* of the ESG-related claims or for other reasons. For instance, the study does not control for factors such as marketing investments, distribution, and promotional activity.

When asked about the importance that a brand support 'good causes' to make them loyal, 86% of Italian consumers say it is important: in the same survey, however, when asked to rank loyalty program rewards from most to least preferred, support to environmental causes comes at the 14th place for Gen X and even lower (15th) for Gen Z; donations to environmental (social) charities and organizations follow at the 16th and 20th places (out of a total of 22 types of rewards). In the mentioned iSeatz (2023) survey, we find similarly contradictory results: 55% of consumers say they would choose one loyalty program over another if it prioritized sustainability; however, the same consumers put the availability of more sustainable options at the bottom of the list of 'what would make you use your loyalty program more often or spend more'! We will get back later in the chapter to this 'attitude-behaviour gap', i.e. the good intentions not followed by actions.

In this chapter we discuss how companies are addressing ESG goals with their loyalty strategies: we do this by revising 58 cases that we collected based on secondary sources in spring 2022 and 31 additional cases that we detected in 2024, for a total of 89 cases and 20 industries. We will then present what consumer psychology, neuroscience and social science research has found to be working (and not working) in prosocial loyalty programs. Finally, we reflect on the peculiarity of sustainable behavours – as opposed to conventional purchase and engagement behaviours, that are the typical target of loyalty activities – to support the design of effective sustainable loyalty programs, rewards, mechanisms and related communication.

What loyalty and sustainability have in common

Our 2023 survey (see Chapter 8) asked companies to articulate what was the relationship between their strategy for sustainability and their loyalty program, and here are the results: only in 13% of cases the loyalty program is seen as an integral part of the company's ESG strategy; 52% of businesses strive to make loyalty program members aware of the company's ESG efforts, but the loyalty program is focused on other matters; finally, for 35% of businesses the loyalty program and the company's ESG strategy proceed along two separate and independent routes.

It is understandable that a total redesign of one's loyalty program around sustainability and sustainable behaviour would not be desirable for every company: at the same time, as much as the majority of businesses today undertake some steps towards ESG goals, keeping those sealed away from one's loyalty strategy may lead to missed opportunities. In fact, we argue that loyalty and sustainability have more in common than one would think.

In Chapter 1 we examined how customer loyalty has grown in relevance in the hierarchy of company goals over the past forty years, as the competitive environment in many sectors has increasingly favoured retention over acquisition. As a result, loyalty management, i.e. the compound of practices aimed at fostering customer loyalty, has evolved, from the establishment of loyalty programs that reward desired customer behaviours, to the use of customer data to develop individual customer relationships to maximize CLTV, as far as the design/redesign of touchpoints and entire journeys to provide a positive experience for preferred customers.

As this customer-focussed shift in strategic thinking was taking place, another one was under development: the evolution of a 'social and environmental conscience' of the firm, as Figure 3.1 illustrates. It was around the turn of the twentieth century that the discourse around corporate social responsibility (CSR) emerged, defined as the focus of the business on ethical conduct and social impact. According to Mohr et al. (2001), CSR refers to 'a company's commitment to minimizing or eliminating any harmful effects and maximizing its long-run beneficial impact on society' (p. 47). The environment took center stage in this 'responsibility' framework with the beginning of the

FIGURE 3.1 The evolution of loyalty management and the sustainability orientation of the firm.

twenty-first century: as awareness of the antropic causes of climate change grew, the word 'sustainability' was employed more and more to define the idea that it is possible to live and to produce in a way that satisfies human needs and also preserves a healthy physical environment. More recently, the abbreviation ESG (environmental, societal and governance) was coined to denote specific criteria that can be employed to assess how businesses are performing in their endeavour to be accountable for their conduct not only in environmental terms but also social ones. Therefore, the term sustainability is now employed commonly to generally refer to both social and environmental aspects – and so will it be in this chapter, unless otherwise specified.

As ESG metrics started to be adopted by financial bodies to evaluate the desirability of investing in a business, the discourse about sustainability has rapidly taken up an urgency and inescapability for top management that it did not have before.

Here is the first point in common between loyalty and sustainability: they are corporate goals that have grown constantly in relevance over the years to occupy public discourse and attain strategic importance – they are now so called 'C-suite concerns'. They share a forward-looking nature: investiment and committment, patience and sacrifices are requested now, in view of greater good in the future.

Secondly, these two goals are connected in the process of value creation: on the one hand, the loyalty of customers, employees and investors grants financial sustainability to the business hence making resources available that can be invested in environmental and social sustainability efforts. From this viewpoint, therefore, loyalty as a profit generator is necessary to provide the finances for the business' sustainability goals. On the other hand, as long as such efforts to make the business socially and environmentally sustainable are perceived as of value by customers, employees and investors, this contributes to strengthening their loyalty to the business. As Kumar (2019) points out, consumers are making decisions not just on product selection or price, but also on what a brand stands for. Numerous studies have shown that CSR activities might be an effective way for companies to strengthen brand image (Ganesan et al., 2009), attract and retain customers (Sen et al., 2009), enhance employee commitment and job satisfaction (Vlachos et al., 2013) and improve financial performance (Luo and Bhattacharya, 2009), just like loyalty strategies. This relationship could therefore play out as a self reinforcing circle.

Thirdly, both strategies encompass customers, employees and investors. Fourth, they have their own specific metrics: it has taken forty years to see retention rate, CLTV and other customer-related success measures be used to describe corporate performance (Reinartz, 2023), but now they are widely adopted in the majority of industries and growing faster than brand-related success measures. We can hypothesize that ESG metrics will spread fast. For all the above, marketers need to explore ways to grow ESG and loyalty together and support their virtuous circle. Will the paths of loyalty and sustainability eventually meet? The analysis of how loyalty management strategies are dealing with company's sustainability efforts, that we conduct in the next session, gives us hope: some businesses have developed initiatives that aim to accompany customers in a lifelong journey of learning and getting better at doing good to the planet and to others. Their activities are not only for members of the brand's loyalty program or customers of the company, but open to everyone. The attention is as much on rewarding as it is on education. Some even reward for reducing consumption and spending…in a word, they seem to speak to individuals not as much as consumers, but as citizens – responsible dwellers of a resource-strained planet. Perhaps the meeting point of ESG and loyalty management is taking a step beyond customer experience management (Figure 3.1), and thinking and acting in terms of citizen experience management.

How loyalty programs have embraced sustainability so far

Kumar notes that the implementation of pro-social loyalty programs that embed the business's social and environmental responsibility in loyalty program design by focusing on societal or environmental causes is an emerging trend (Kumar, 2019). Flacandji et al. stress that:

> since CSR is strategically important to companies, potentially positioning them accordingly by highlighting their social and/or environmental values (Einwiller et al., 2019), developing a green loyalty program can be a promising way to heighten engagement as well as to attract and retain customers (Sen et al., 2009).

(Flacandji et al., 2023, p. 465)

A 'green' loyalty program is a form of pro-social loyalty program that specifically rewards consumers for green behaviours, according to Liu and Mattila (2016). In practice, this can take many forms, as loyalty program propositions vary from offering the possibility to donate one's points to an environmental protection institution, on the one hand, to the launch of an app for members to educate them regarding sustainability, on the other.

In order to explore the variety of propositions, as far as pro-social loyalty programs (with a particular attention, albeit not exclusive) to green loyalty programs, in 2022 we started a dedicated reasearch effort. Desk research conducted on a variety of secondary sources retrieved 58 cases of loyalty programs or loyalty initiatives that contained some elements of environmental concern across 12 industries and 10 countries, from Air Canada to Zooplus. In March–April 2024 each and every case of the 2022 sample was revisited, and 31 additional cases added, in an attempt to appreciate the evolution of green loyalty programs over time and capture a more comprehensive picture of the phenomenon. It must be noted that out of the original 58 cases, 17 appeared to be no longer in operation in 2024 (28%), as it was not possible to retrieve any news or information more recent than those collected during the first round of research. Therefore, the analysis of sustainable loyalty programs we conduct in this section is based on 72 cases (57% operating also in 2022 and 43% added in 2024) that appear to be in activity as this book goes to press (Table 3.1 gives the full breakdown of active and inactive programs).

The most represented industries in the sample are clothing (25%), beauty (21%), retail chains (such as supermarkets, petfood, furniture, petrol – 16%) and transport (8%), and in total 20 sectors are represented. As far as the country of operation of the loyalty programs, Europe and Middle East comes first (56%), followed by North America (32%) and Asia-Pacific (12%). As for structure, 30% of programs/activities have tiers and points, while 35% have points only, the remainder have none (35%).

63% of the sustainability initiatives we analysed were part of a formal loyalty program and were accessible only to loyalty program members; 37% of activities, on the other hand, were part of the brand's general value proposition, stood separate from the eventual loyalty program, and are accessible regardless of loyalty program membership. For example, in the beauty industry, brands such as Noble Panacea, Ilia and Farmacy Beauty offer recycling programs that send envelopes and labels for returning empty product pots or used shoes and garments free of charge to anyone who request them. Others like MAC and Kiehl's welcome product returns in store. Fashion brands typically offer vouchers in return for taking/sending in used clothes, not exclusively the brands' own, but sometimes belonging to other brands too. US brand Eileen Fisher offers a US$5 voucher for returning Eileen Fisher used items to the

TABLE 3.1 Reviewed programs in the 2022 and 2024 research efforts

2022 sample, still active in 2024	Added in 2024	2022 sample, apparently inactive in 2024
Air Canada	Acqua e Sapone	Alibaba
BeerHawk	AirFrance	Amazon smile
Best Western	American Express	Brewdog
Binee	Brakes Bros	Cogo
Boots	ChinaChemGroup	Epic impact
Coop Danmark	Coca-Cola	FourState
Co-op (UK)	COS	GeneralMills
Costa Coffee	Crai	GoodVibes
Credo Beauty	Eileen Fisher	Jet Blue
Cuyana	Enel	Leroy Merlin
Decathlon	FAB Bank	Maakola
EB Game	Face the Future	MakeupEraser
Etihad	Farmacy Beauty	McDonald's
Fiat	GHA Hotels	REM beauty
Girlfriend collective	Grill'd	SAM's club
H&M	Hera	Vans
IHG hotels	Ilia	Veja
Ikea	Iren	
JohnLewis	Mac	
Jules	Meow Meow Tweet	
Kiabi	Noble Panacea	
Kiehl's	Petronas	
Kroger	Puma	
L'Occitane	Qatar Airways	
Lufthansa	Raiffeisen bank Romania	
Lush	Starewood Hotels (1 Hotels)	
Madewell	The Warehouse Group	
Mango	Timberland	
Marks & Spencer	TOMS	
Nature et Decouverte	Universal Standards	
Plae	Urban outfitters	
PointsforGood		
Qantas		
REI		
SephoraUS		
Tentree		
The Body Shop		
The Gap		
The North Face		
YvesRocher		
Zooplus		

store or online and resells them in a dedicated section of their website. Shoe brand PLAE provides parents the opportunity to turn in their kids' used PLAE shoes and buy new or used ones – no membership required. In the utilities sector, Italian company Hera has launched a program to educate consumers on how to reduce their environmental impact, especially their energy consumption, that is free to join for anyone. Hera customers, however, besides learning, can earn reductions on their bills based on specific energy saving behaviours.

We therefore see two approaches as for the entanglement of the sustainability activity with the loyalty program:

1 A stand-alone program, especially for recycling used products, with no connection to the company loyalty program, that might even not exist.
2 A proper loyalty program where earning or/and burning options are connected to sustainability, for example donating one's points to a good cause and/or earning points for sustainable behaviours.

We will get back to the variety of forms this second option can take.

First, we look at the 'good causes' embraced by the activities and loyalty programs analysed. Environmental goals dominate in 70% of cases, social causes are the concern of 22%, while 8% of programs span both areas of sustainability. In turn, environmental programs can be oriented to compensating customers' environmental impact, for example by planting trees, or to reducing such impact, for example by choosing new generation aviation fuels that are less polluting, or recycling plastic. Often programs offer both compensation and reduction options.

Social sustainability programs offer support to a variety of charities (90% of cases), while the remaining 10% aimed for inclusion goals. Providing disadvantaged citizens, especially children, with education, access to better nutrition, sport activities, healthcare, mental health services are among the supported causes. In the case of companies with local presence, such as hotel chains or retail stores, some loyalty programs associate a local charitable organization to the local branch, to enhance impact on the local community, while in other cases a single or few organizations is/are chosen at national level as the recipient of donations. Members of the Petronas Mesra Rewards loyalty program, for instance, can donate their points to two causes: a company providing solar energy home systems for families living without electricity or to the national technical university in Malaysia. Members of the Co-op in the UK are strongly encouraged at multiple occasions during the year to choose their local community charity for donations: when they make such choice (easily on the app or website, from a geolocalized list showing first organizations nearest to the member), they are entered in a sweepstake to win £500 for themselves and £5000 for the chosen charity.

In 2022, the analysis led to classifying loyalty programs in three groups, based on increasing committment of the company to the cause of sustainability. We replicated such classification in 2024 on the entire sample of 72 cases. Given the managerial perspective that we take on loyalty management throughout this book, we deemed interesting a classification aimed to elicit if and how the company contributed to the sustainability effort touted by the loyalty program, as outlined below. However, there are other possible ways to categorize prosocial loyalty programs for example, an interesting distinction is the one among programs where (i) it is the member to be rewarded, (ii) it is a third party that benefits (so called altruistic loyalty programs – for example, when members buy Zooplus own label Zoolove petfood products, the company donates 10% of the product price to an animal welfare charity that changes every month), or (iii) both the individual and a third party are rewarded. However, we are not going into this detail in the remainder of the section.

Resuming the above-mentioned classification based on the company's committment to sustainability, as displayed in Figure 3.2, the 'starting point' for a loyalty program to embrace sustainability is when it allows members to donate their points/discounts/vouchers or own money to a related endeavour, be it a/many charity/ies of their choice, or designated by the company. In this first case, that we label 'entry level sustainability' it is the member who is doing all the effort (in other words she is earning the loyalty program currency by spending with the company), while the company is not directly committing resources, if not marginally, by choosing the charity/ies and communicating the option/s to members. The expenditure burden is on the customer. An example of this case is the loyalty program of Vietnam Airlines, that has designed an emotional campaign to subsidize surgery for disadvantaged children in Vietnam: it is the airline' loyalty program members, by donating their miles (which they have acquired by spending on flights and other products) that contribute to the cause. The campaign is devised to encourage, in the end, members to acquire more miles, and spend miles on the cause. The airline, apparently – as mentioned above we base our analysis on published sources,

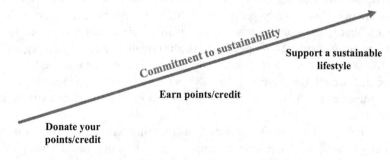

FIGURE 3.2 Loyalty strategy commitment to sustainability.

and might therefore lack relevant information on what companies are possibly doing behind the scenes – is not contributing. The same can be said of Flyingblue, the loyalty program of Airfrance and KLM, that has selected a range of well known international charitable organizations such as Unicef, the Red Cross, Médicins sans Frontières and WWF, to receive customers' donations of miles, that the organizations will use as such for their own travel needs, therefore increasing usage of the mentioned airlines' services. In most other programs belonging to this 'entry level' tier, such as American Express, the mentioned charities receive the donations but in the form of money.

In Australia, quick service restaurant chain Grill'd has a straightforward loyalty program to encourage repeat visits in which, when 8 visits are reached, members get a free burger or have the option to donate a meal to a local charitable organization. Beauty company Yves Rocher similarly offer members who reach 150 points to redeem them for a 10 Euro voucher or to have a tree planted.

A contrasting approach is adopted by Co-op supermarkets in the UK: members can donate 1% of their grocery spending with the supermarket to a cause of their choice, and Co-op doubles the amount by donating directly another 1%: the deeper committment of the business, compared to the 'entry level' case, is evident. Kroger in the US and the Warehouse Group in New Zealand follow a similar approach with customers choosing the charity that will benefit and the company matching or doubling their donations. Farmacy Beauty allows donation to Feeding America of up to 600 points (equivalent to US$30) and matches the donation with the same amount. Air Canada's Aeroplan loyalty program matches the amount of miles a member decides to devote to offsetting their flight emissions, plus an additional 20%, by transferring the total amount to the offsetting partner Offsetters. These cases exemplify the 'second level' in the classification of loyalty programs' committment to sustainability displayed in Figure 3.2: instead of 'donating your points' this is called 'earn points/discounts' to signify that the company is spending money directly on each member, by accruing her some form of reward, or directly disboursing funds proportionately to the individual's efforts towards sustainable goals. An interesting case is that of British foodservice wholesaler Brakes, that launched their loyalty program in 2023. Everytime customers redeem their cashback, the company has a tree planted via a certified reforestation program. In the first year of operation, 10,000 small businesses have signed up and 23,000 trees have been planted. So, on the second step of the ladder, in Figure 3.2, we see the company directly spending resources to accrue benefits to the member or the chosen third party based on the member's sustainable behaviours.

Sustainable behaviours are defined in literature as 'actions that result in decreases in adverse environmental impacts as well as decreased utilization of natural resources across the lifecycle of the product, behavior, or service'

(White et al., 2019, p. 24). In the 72 cases sample, these actions are rewarded with points in 40% of cases, with discounts or vouchers (20%), with both (8%), whereas 31% of programs encourage sustainable behaviours or provide opportunities for them but do not reward them.

In practice, what behaviours are encouraged/rewarded with points or discounts/vouchers by pro-social loyalty programs? We aknowledge the presence of 32 distinct behaviours, that can be grouped in three areas.

The first area is called 'spending' because the company rewards a specific purchase choice made by the customer, typically the one with the least environmental impact, among possible ones, or the customer is called to disbourse money, as in the case of compensating her flight emissions. Specifically (in brackets the name of the company):

- Choose a recycled paper cup, not a plastic one (Costa Coffee).
- Buy organic products (versus non-organic products) (Carrefour France).
- Buy fairtrade and sustainable products from the assortment (L'Occitane).
- Buy one kilo (or 5 items) of used Kiabi garments in the 'New Life' corner of the store (Kiabi).
- Buy eco-designed products (Decathlon).
- Choose store pick up, instead of home delivery or other ways to make the online order more sustainable, such as grouping items (Facethefuture).
- Book an eco-friendly lodge (Qantas).
- Buy energy and water saving products such as thermostats, bulbs, water filters (Iren).
- Offset the CO_2 emissions of your flight, or car, or home by employing your miles or adding a surcharge to your bill (Etihad, Qantas).
- Use the product (drive the electric Fiat 500 car) (Fiat).

The second area of behaviours that are rewarded is called 'circularity' in that they are concerned with recycle, return, reuse, reduce and trade in. Specifically:

- Recycle plastic bottles (Coca Cola Indonesia) or cosmetics' packaging (Credo Beauty, Boots, John Lewis, M.A.C., Kiehls, Lush) by taking them back to the store.
- Return empty beer kegs (PerfectDraft).
- Refill cosmetics bottles (the Body Shop).
- Recycle garments by taking them back to the store (Mango, COS, Puma, John Lewis, The North Face) or sending them back to the online retailer (Cuyana, Eileen Fisher, Madewell).
- Rent selected clothing items instead of purchasing them (H&M).
- Take used school uniforms to the store (Marks & Spencer) that will be sold by Oxfam to fund community projects.
- Have your shoes repaired instore (Veja).

- Buy (and sell) a preused garment from the Renewal section of the brand website (Urban Outfitters).
- Trade or buy preowned videogames and related products (EBGames).
- Take your old IKEA forniture back to the store for resale (IKEA).
- Recycle your old consumer electronics products by taking them to the dedicated kiosk (Binee).
- Trade in or buy used sport gear instore or on the Re/supply dedicated website (REI).
- Rent sporting goods instead of purchasing them (Decathlon).
- Bring your reusable bag for shopping (North Face).
- Ask the hotel you want to skip housekeeping (IHG hotels, BestWestern).
- Travel with less luggage (Etihad).

In the ChinaChem Group Hearts program, members earn points for their shopping in the group's malls but also when they engage in Quests, that are opportunities for doing good in Hong Kong. These activities include spending time with the elderly, with children, with the less fortunate, collecting rubbish from parks and public spaces, connecting with nature, visiting art and culture places. The points can be redeemed for vouchers and discounts on products and experiences, from restaurants to outdoors activities, parties on one's birthday and more.

Fashion brand Cuyana gives cash or credit in the loyalty program to customers who send preowned Cuyana bags and clothes back for recycling, reselling or donating. The benefitting organization is the HEART Foundation for women starting a new life after abuse: on their premises a 'store' is populated with preowned Cuyana products that the women can 'shop' for free.

In the Kroger recycling program, customers collect plastic and send it out to partner organization Terracycle for recycling, hence receiving points that can only been spent for donations to a charity of choice or to Kroger's Zero Hunger | Zero Waste foundation. Schools and organizations can participate too by setting up an account and receive multiple points.

IKEA Family members can join the Sell Back program to resell their IKEA forniture back to the company. After an evalution based on photos, the customer takes the piece back to the store where it is displayed in a special corner for preowned items and receives a voucher for up to 30% of the product original price, to spend on a subsequent visit.

Timberland customers can join the Community loyalty program that, besides providing points for purchases and engagement activities, offer opportunities for participating in events such as refurbishing clothes and accessories, making seed bombs, doing volunteer work in local communities, taking part in educational events on environmental and social sustainability.

Etihad has introduced the Conscious Choices program alongside the regular frequent flyer one; customers who undertake a variety of behaviours – from travelling with less luggage to offsetting the emissions of their flight – earn badges. Once the first badge is earned, the customer starts accumulating miles with her sustainable behaviours that concur to her status in the regular loyalty program. Qantas has introduced the Green Tier, alongside its tiered frequent flyer program. Members of the latter who complete five activities to be chosen among emission offsetting, sustainable travel, energy saving, choosing ecofriendly products, or donating to charities and community, can access the Green Tier for a year, and maintain membership every year by completing another round of ecofriendly activities. Benefits are recognition (green frequent flyer card and green app), points and opportunity to have Qantas offset 3 tonnes of CO_2, while there are no spillover effects onto the customer status in the regular program.

The third area of behaviours that are rewarded is called 'knowledge/ information sharing' and comprise activities to increase customers' knowledge about sustainability, in general or related to their own behavior, testing such knowledge also via gamification, share it with others via social media posting or through the loyalty program itself. Here they are:

- Create your energy profile by activating a free energy consumption monitor service with the utility company (Enel).
- Read educational content on energy reduction tips and answer the subsequent quiz or share two different pieces of such content on social media (Iren).
- Take the quiz on sustainable behaviours knowledge (Iren).
- Take the 'ecological footprint' test to assess how sustainable is your behaviour (L'Occitane, Raiffeisen Bank).
- Use the 'my footprint' feature of the retailer app to see the carbon footprint of all grocery categories purchased by the customer in the past few months (Coop Danmark).
- Post pictures of yourself involved in ecofriendly activites (Girfriend Collective).
- Post pictures of yourself using specific hashtags (Make Up Eraser).

During our analysis of the digital touchpoints of the brands, such as their websites, app and social network pages, we were able to notice that the sustainability loyalty program/effort was salient in the majority of cases (80%): it was prominent, or at least easy to locate on the homepage and in the navigation bar. We noticed that some companies had a dedicated app for the sustainable loyalty program (29%), while the majority devoted an area of their multipurpose app to it (71%). Here are two cases of programs with a dedicated app.

Coop Danmark, the leading supermarket chain in Denmark, launched their carbon footprint app in 2020 to allows shoppers to track their carbon footprint when shopping. By signing up for the free app and using their membership card at checkout, shoppers can see, on the app, the carbon footprint of each individual item and category purchased. The app will also make suggestions (such as using potatoes instead of rice as the carbon footprint of potatoes is 4 times less than that of rice). The app also allows shoppers to compare their footprint with the average customers, and track progress over time in the adoption of more ecofriendly product choices. Coop Danmark has also made the workings of the app available to other retailers free of charge.

#genHerazioni is the program developed in 2023 by Italian utilities company Hera, open to customers and to anyone who wants to learn and engage in more sustainable living. It is free to join and participants earn two types of currencies – Ecocoins and Actionpoints – for a range of activities: reading or watching content on sustainable behaviours, testing one's knowledge on sustainability by playing games, instant wins and quizzes. Hera customers can win points by participating in sweepstakes only if they reduce their energy consumption: every month they can check online or in app the difference between the current month consumption versus the previous one and can access the draw only if there is a positive balance. The program stimulates aspiration to proficiency in sustainability thanks to a tier structure.

These latter cases, in our view, take a further step in the engagement of the company with sustainability: the educational purpose is evident, even more than the rewarding part. These apps present themselves as companions for leading a more sustainable life, learning and doing better over time. The fact that their functionalities are open to non-members too enhances their prosocial aim. It is interesting to note that in 2022 we were able to record the existence of more programs belonging to this third case (Figure 3.2) that we labelled 'Sustain a lifestyle', such as Alibaba's green program, but they seem no longer active in 2024. Alibaba Group announced in 2022 a carbon-tracking mini program that monitors shopper behavior across the Alibaba ecosystem, rewarding consumers for making eco-friendly choices. Consumers can collect points through 70 'low-carbon behaviors' such as taking public transport, purchasing energy-efficient appliances and selling unused items on Alibaba's second-hand digital marketplace. Points can be used to claim digital badges and shopping discounts on Alibaba's various e-commerce platforms. However, no news of the program has been published after the 2022 announcement.

To support consumers in their efforts to live more sustainable lives, new startups appear everyday. Some of them seem to have been short lived, while others have gone past their initial steps and seem to have gained a place in the loyalty arena. An example of the former is Epic Impact, that aimed to become a platform for companies selling sustainable products and services, and for companies willing to offer sustainable options as rewards for their loyalty program members. The 'one stop shop' fot ethical, sustainable living would make it easier for consumers to make sustainable choices and reward them when making purchases on the platform, thus attracting more businesses and users. Unfortunately it seems to have become inactive since 2022. On the contrary, an example of the latter, now entering their sixth year of operation is Points for Good, an Indian platform that enables members of loyalty and employee programs to redeem their points to make a donation towards a cause they care for like helping a child against malnutrition, educating girls in rural areas, providing clean drinking water, empowering women, protecting the environment, and helping increase the resources available for the charities registered on the platform, to continue their good work. Points for Good declares to have raised over 75 million points, supporting 16 charities, and over 107 projects, empowering over 150 million members from 20 bank partners and over 1000 corporate partners to donate their loyalty and employee reward points.

Overall, our analysis has shown the development of loyalty programs and activities that aim to retain customers by appealing to their interest for environmental causes across many industries. Approaches vary: the simple enabling of donations from the part of the customer is the most common, also for its easy implementation. It is easy to add it to an existing loyalty initiative, and also to expand it by adding more causes or rotating them, to keep the offer interesting and fresh. The variety of active behaviours that loyalty programs have pinpointed as suitable for being rewarded seems to have plateaued: we have listed above over 30 different activities customers can engage with to do good and get rewards in the form of points/discounts or both currently offered by loyalty programs around the world, and such list has changed little between 2022 and 2024. As for the more ambitious endeavours that provide tools for self education, monitoring and support for ethical living in the long term, that we registered in 2022, some seem to have stalled or be closed, while we look forward to witness whether others become established in consumers' routines over time. This brings us to the need to understand how individuals respond to loyalty offers when they entail sustainable behaviours. In the following section we look at what academic research has found so far on this regard.

How customers respond to prosocial loyalty programs

Despite the growing popularity of prosocial loyalty programs, academic research is still scarce, and little is known as far as how customers respond to them. Here we share results from the few published experiments conducted to ascertain whether members (and non-members) see value in prosocial loyalty programs, compared to ordinary ones, and what are the outcomes of membership.

The starting point, when discussing prosocial loyalty programs, as we noted earlier, is whether they increase perceived value, compared to conventional ones. Flacandji et al. (2023) note:

the economic benefits related to rewards that customers may derive from their green behavior may be similar to those of a conventional program. However, the economic costs of green loyalty programs include the effort that customers need to exert when undertaking certain green purchase or non-purchase behaviors: e.g. looking for information about which green products are eligible, planning new green non-purchase behaviors and so on. These economic costs might lead customers to perceive green loyalty program designs as less valuable in economic terms than a conventional loyalty program.

(Flacandji et al., 2023, p. 474)

As far as psychological costs, adopting sustainable behaviours may be challenging, as this might entail changing one's habits, making abstract evaluations of future impact of one's actions, and so on (see next section). Finally, with regard to green altruistic loyalty programs, i.e. programs not rewarding consumers but benefitting an environmental action organization, when monetary rewards are offered to environmental charities and not to members, there might be potential negative consequences on perceived economic value. Flacandji et al. (2023) designed an experiment, involving over 1000 consumers, to test the perceived value – composed of psychological and economic value – of conventional loyalty programs, green loyalty programs rewarding green purchase behaviour, green loyalty programs rewarding green non purchase behaviour and finally altruistic green loyalty programs, benefitting a third party.

The experiment found that all three green loyalty programs score higher than the conventional loyalty program as far as psychological value. This can be explained by the fact that self esteem is enhanced by the green behaviours, and/or by feeling more special and recognized for personal values. As far as economic value, the design of the green loyalty program plays a role in determining its perception, compared to a conventional loyalty program. Here, when the loyalty program rewards 'green' spending, it looks the same as a conventional program to consumers – the 'transactional nature seems to dominate on the green aspect of the transactions' – while customers see more favourably the green non transactional loyalty program than the others. Finally, green altruistic loyalty programs are confirmed, as in previous research, to be not effective drivers of intention to join (Eason et al., 2015) or to enhance participation in an loyalty program (Hwang and Choi, 2020).

In a nutshell, the study showed green loyalty programs rewarding green non-purchase behavior deliver the highest economic and psychological value compared to other green loyalty programs. As a result, this type of loyalty program appears to be the best choice in terms of optimizing perceived value. If we turn to our sample of cases discussed in the previous section, it is therefore worrying to see a trend towards the adoption of altruistic programs, rather than programs where it is members that get rewarded for their green behaviour: such loyalty programs may cost less for the company, but they might fail to involve current customers and prospects.

Another interesting academic study regarding green loyalty programs has to do with their mitigating effects on by-standers perception of the preferential treatment being reserved to members of a loyalty program or club. Given that customer prioritization practices (think of priority boarding for airline loyalty program members) are ubiquitous, it is in the interest of companies to mitigate negative perception of those customers that are excluded. When bystanders observe other customers' (members') preferential treatment, they are likely to feel irritated or envious and, consequently, react negatively to the service provider or perceive reduced satisfaction. Rewarding guests for their own eco-friendly behaviors offers an easy justification for customer prioritization. The psychological mechanism explaining the positive impact of a green loyalty program on bystanders' satisfaction with their own consumption experience is the perception of the firm's 'prosociality'. Moreover, the findings of this study indicate that preferential treatment associated with a 'go green' loyalty reward program is as effective as traditional programs in enabling members to signal their status.

Bazaraa et al. (2022) address the topic of the use of incentives to encourage voluntary green program participation. They also point out that no research so far has examined how the different levels of the different types of incentives moderate the individual response to green loyalty programs, considering not only participants, but also non-participants. They conduct three experiments to examine how manipulating the type (self-benefiting incentives and other-benefiting – altruistic – incentives) and level (low, high) of incentive can affect the relationship between participation in voluntary green programs and satisfaction. They also introduce the role of 'warm glow' in mediating such a relationship: 'Warm glow is the positive feeling people experience due to the moral satisfaction induced by contributing to the common good of the environment' (Andreoni, 1990). It explains why people decide to engage in pro social behaviours, aside from pure altruism. People experience a personal, direct utility when contributing to public good, which is of value in itself, apart from any increase in the public good. The research showed that participating in voluntary green programs increased warm glow, which helped to improve service satisfaction compared to not participating in these programs. Different types and levels of incentives can influence the causal relationship between green program participation, warm glow, the customer experience and service satisfaction. Results show that most people are willing to participate in green programs when available, convenient, and easy to use. However, if managers consider only the satisfaction of people who choose to participate in green loyalty programs, then using high self-benefiting incentives or low or high other benefiting incentives is good. However, if managers consider the satisfaction of all groups of customers (participants and non-participants of green programs), which might be desirable, then using high self-benefiting incentives is the best option, as this is the only incentive scheme resulting in the highest satisfaction levels among both groups. As this might require quite a budget, then the second-best option to impact satisfaction of both groups of customers is using no incentives at all.

The psychological factors that facilitate adoption of sustainable behaviours and how to leverage them: the SHIFT framework

Historically, marketing attention to sustainable behaviours has translated into the quest for the 'green consumer', by segmenting the market in search of this specific, hopefully sizable and profitable, segment. More recently, interest has shifted to identifying the predictors of sustainable consumption, and of sustainable consumption change. Several authors have contributed to this endeavour (e.g. Steg and Vlek, 2009; Peattie, 2010; Gifford and Nilsson, 2014). In this section we choose to present the work of White et al. (2019) because their SHIFT framework is the broadest, offering practitioners, as well as scholars, all the major factors that literature has found to influence the adoption of sustainable behaviour.

SHIFT is an acronym, standing for: Social influence, Habit formation, Individual self, Feelings and cognition, and Tangibility as the drivers of sustainable behaviour, that the authors derived from a comprehensive analysis of over 300 related academic papers. As mentioned earlier in this chapter, the 'attitude-behaviour gap' as far as sustainability, i.e. the good intentions not followed by actions, is the major challenge for marketers, and also one of the reasons why loyalty programs can help to encourage sustainability, in that they are traditionally intended to determine behaviour by sapient use of incentives.

However, one should not acritically extend what is known about the effect of incentives, rewards and loyalty program design to sustainable behaviours, in that the latter differ greatly from conventional purchase and engagement behaviours that loyalty programs typically address.

Sustainable behaviours are choices where individuals are required to postpone a self-indulgent behaviour in order to obtain a positive result later on, a result that is abstract in nature and benefits not only the individual who is making the sacrifice, but also others.

When designing actions to drive adoption and/or upholding of sustainable behaviours, therefore, it is necessary to consider the following critical points of such behaviours:

- They present a trade-off between 'me' and 'the others', in that individuals typically act in view of self interest, but here they need to sacrifice it, to obtain a positive result that happen to benefit others too.

- The long-term horizon, because often the results are not immediately seen but require time to accumulate or be sizable, such as obtaining a forest by planting a tree at a time.
- The need for collective action to have an impact, that may lead individuals to doubt their own self efficacy (what difference am I making?).
- The need to substitute what is basically a habit with a new, conscious behaviour, and habits are hard to change because they save mental energy, whereas conscious behaviour requires leaving 'autopilot' and taking charge of a deliberate course of action.
- The abstraction, because concepts like CO_2, emissions, environmental impact, are difficult to visualize. Below we draw from White et al. (2019) to explore the above characteristics of sustainable behaviour and propose how to best address them to make sustainable behaviour more likely to be pursued and sustained.

The 'me–others' trade off

Often when it comes to sustainable behaviours, consumers perceive them as burdensome to the individual, as they require effort, costs and sometimes the acceptance of lower quality or aesthetics (e.g. 'ugly' organic fruit). At the same time, these sustainable behaviours have positive environmental and/or social consequences that go 'beyond the self'. A sort of internal conflict therefore arises in the consumer: purchases usually serve to satisfy oneself, one's needs and desires, while sustainable behaviours put what is 'outside oneself' first, such as the environment, others, future generations.

It therefore becomes useful to create 'framing', that is, to induce clients to think in terms of a broader self, to put them in a mental condition in which they think of themselves as less individualistic and more connected to others. Some practical examples:

- Make individuals feel like 'agents' of change. This will give a feeling of empowerment and a real possibility of having an effect on change.
- Leverage 'moral identity'. Subjects with a high 'moral identity' want to behave virtuously towards a wider sphere of subjects than other individuals. Talking to customers, making them feel like individuals with a high moral sense, can be an effective lever, for example by making them think about how they are helping future generations.

Individuals want to have a positive idea of themselves, and what they buy and consume also serve this purpose. Learning that our actions have negative consequences (on sustainability or otherwise) induces defensive behaviors that hinder messages and changes. Individuals seek information that confirms their self-concept. So the way is to create a positive association between the idea of oneself and sustainable behavior.

Individuals want to perceive themselves as consistent. If someone or ourselves points out to us that we have behaved sustainably at a certain time, we will more likely do so in the future. Here then is the importance of personal commitment gestures, such as 'signing a pact with nature'. Again for consistency, if we are sustainable in one area of our action, we will be more likely to be sustainable in others (the 'positive spillover' phenomenon), which has implications for retention. Pointing out to people that their behaviors ARE sustainable leads them to persevere. 'In these five years you have had these results and effects on the environment ...' This example goes in the direction of making people feel like agents of change and effective, as mentioned above and below.

Self-efficacy. Individuals engage in a behavior if they have the perception that it will have an impact ('there's no point in me doing it'). It is necessary to find ways to demonstrate to the customer that she has an impact (for example with before and after images etc.).

In particular, positive associations with sustainable behaviour should be aimed for. There is not much research in this sense: perhaps the best-known example is the positive association 'sustainable food-health'. It is conceivable that sustainability has positive associations with health, outdoor life, nature, local and fresh foods. Therefore, connecting the company's offer and communication to strong trends such as outdoor living, 'vibrant living', staying healthy should be effective.

It could be useful to leverage the positive emotions of moral elevation and awe that we feel when we witness exemplary behavior on the part of our peers. These are emotions that 'take us outside of ourselves', expanding the self and making us more inclined to altruistic behaviors. Furthermore, since certain natural landscapes, such as high mountain peaks, can inspire similar emotions, we could work on the association of these themes.

A final idea concerns making CS more socially desirable for the individual by connecting them to an aspirational role model, for example a sports celebrity.

The long-term horizon

A second criticality of sustainable behaviours concerns the fact that a long-term horizon is necessary for them to bring results. So, inevitably, when the individual engages in sustainable behaviours, some of the consequences will arrive not immediately but in the future, in some cases even beyond the life horizon of the individual himself. This trait also makes sustainable behaviours different from traditional consumption behavior. The literature demonstrates that benefits in the future are less desirable than immediate ones, and less effective in spurring action. Thinking that the repercussions are so far from today can reduce the sense of self-efficacy mentioned before, which every individual spontaneously seeks, i.e. the feeling of having an impact on the outside world. And feelings of frustration may arise that lead to inaction. Finally, there is another mechanism at play: self-control or self-regulation. Just think of the example of going on a diet and then giving in to temptation: it is difficult to hold back from ice cream today in view of a benefit that will only come much later – fitting into your favorite dress. In the case of sustainable behaviour, not only is a sacrifice made now for a future benefit, but this benefit is 'broader than us' or falls on others, as illustrated at the previous point.

Since research shows that those who are under-resourced (e.g. tired, exhausted, etc.) are unable to self-control and easily give in to impulse and compensatory behaviors, it may be useful to address people in a way that makes them feel less tired, more relaxed, perhaps with images, sounds or something else. The association with the mountains or other relaxing land-scapes in this sense can go in the right direction.

Positioning the benefits of sustainable behaviour as close to the 'self' can be effective in overcoming self-control difficulties. For example, think about com-municating the vegan eating style as good for health, rather than good for the environment. The different relevance of the message for the individual emerges immediately.

Another way to overcome the perception of sacrifice (this applies to this point as well as the previous one) is to use the positive emotional effect that doing something good for others has on individuals (the abovementioned 'warm glow', or 'warm light of good'), making it perceived as the positive consequence that comes direcly from the sustainable behaviour.

Finally, since some approaches have short-term effects (e.g. the use of incen-tives) while others appeal to longer perspectives (leveraging consistency, self-concept, customer values), a CRM strategy has the advantage of being able to orchestrate a mix of tools and messages that act on short-term behavior with others that work to make them last over time.

The need for collective action

A third peculiarity of sustainable behaviour is that, for the result to arrive, other individuals must also engage in the same behavior. Therefore the theme of social influence in this field is very relevant: by social influence we mean the effect whereby observing (or knowing) others engaging in the same actions leads the individual to a greater perception of collective effectiveness. To stim-ulate sustainable behaviour, the use of communications and messages that emphasize collective actions and collective efficacy could be very useful. For example:

• Using messages that communicate the result achieved and/or the result that will/could be achieved at different levels of numbers of customers engaged – showing the 'landslide' effect – could be effective; a 'competi-tion' to recruit 1000, 2000 or 10,000 friends, resulting in the saving of 10, 20 or 100 forests that are not cut down, could be the theme of a member get member action, but also of a digital game, a quiz or something else.

- The emotion that is often leveraged in this area is the pride of belonging to a group. You could also use the feeling of hope: 'Our customers give concrete hope to the environment: here's what we did together ...'
- Collective action is also linked to the theme of tangibility, that we discuss below. In communication it is appropriate to use metaphors that give a tangible image of the collective impact. This applies both if communication is used to give 'framing' to the consumer and to transfer information to her in the most effective way (example: together this year we recycled an amount of rubbish the size of the Empire State Building).
- When informing and describing the benefits or advantages of sustainable behaviour, using measures on a collective rather than individual scale may be more effective. For example, 'A thousand inhabitants of London who use our energy means ...' etc.

The need to substitute a habit with deliberate behaviour

Many behaviors – even non-sustainable ones – become automatic. The consumer puts them into action without thinking about it anymore. Habits are difficult to change, since replacing them with more conscious behavior requires mental energy (which the habit instead saves).

Give feedback. Providing the consumer with specific information on how she is doing (or a certain activity is going) can be effective, especially if it refers to past behavior, or the behaviors of others.

The abstraction

Sustainable behaviours are often considered abstract, difficult, with an uncertain outcome. Likewise, their consequences sound abstract, even if immediate and local: think of consequences such as energy efficiency or air quality. Unlike other consumer behaviors, therefore, the consequences of sustainable behaviours are less clear and more uncertain.

In uncertain situations, individuals tend to refer to others, to their behaviors and expectations: the so-called 'social norm' is used and 'social influence' becomes relevant. This is noteworthy because, if a sustainable behaviour is not familiar, what others do tend to prevail, and the individual does not feel like deviating. Social norms, or what is socially appropriate to do in a given context, are powerful influencers. For example, composting, recycling, conserving energy, choosing food from sustainable sources, choosing eco-friendly means of transport, staying in green hotels and installing solar panels have become, to varying degrees, social norms. But not in all geographical areas or population groups. Social identity concerns our perception of belonging to groups. If the individual perceives her belonging, if she 'sees herself as a member of the group', she will be more likely to behave like the group.

Making the customer feel part of a group that has sustainable behaviors increases effectiveness. Since individuals wish to see the groups to which they belong positively and see them excel, especially in public contexts, underlining the superior and shared identity of the group and talking about the results achieved are two approaches that increase the effectiveness of messages because they make them more acceptable.

Social desirability refers to whether individuals engage in behaviors to make a positive impression on others. Therefore, certain products or behaviors must be made socially acceptable and in particular we must act against possible negative perceptions (e.g.: driving an electric car is not 'manly'). Here testimonials can play a role. Engaging publicly (visibly) in the group is more likely to lead to the behavior (whether the customer wears the program pin is a variable that predicts future behavior).

Abstractness can bring with it a risk of demotivation – the so-called 'green fatigue' phenomenon: the individual feels demotivated and therefore reduces the drive to conserve sustainable behaviour and can return to previous and unsustainable habitual choices. Some strategies to avoid demotivation, are:

- Make people think about the benefits for themselves and their loved ones.
- Communicating the local and nearby impacts for the city, the neighborhood, the region can work. Leverage people's attachment to a specific place and use current experiences, such as a heat wave.
- Concrete communication. Communicate the immediate impact and the clear steps to take immediately to make a difference (with images and narratives). How, not just why.
- Encourage the desire for intangibility. Shifting attention to the sharing economy, to experiences, to digital products to suggest that needs can be satisfied in a different way and without material goods.
- To activate positive emotions, visual communication is very useful: images and videos arouse much more emotional reactions than texts and words.
- Use the sharing by our loved ones, peers, and group members, of images and thoughts connected to positive emotions related to sustainability. For example, sharing a photo of ourselves while we go to work by bike, perhaps in the context of a contest to show our sustainable way of life: this is how the so-called 'emotional contagion' is exploited.
- Give information. Lack of exposure or confusing information hinders sustainable behaviour. Therefore, providing information on desirable or undesirable behaviors and their consequences is useful. It emerges from research that it is above all important to provide basic information on why a certain behavior or product is sustainable, and information that is not too detailed. Furthermore, giving information alone is not useful, but must be combined with other tactics, in particular those that leverage emotions.

In sum, green loyalty programs offer greater psychological value than a conventional loyalty program as they reinforce the customers' self-esteem. They can increase overall positive evaluation of the self: the positive impact customers have on the environment can lead them to perceive greater self-worth (Venhoeven et al., 2016). However, given the peculiar traits of sustainable behaviours as opposed to traditional engagement or spending behaviours, marketers should consider the SHIFT framework when designing green loyalty programs. Moreover, given the 'attitude-behaviour gap' that occurs quite often with green behaviours, research should go beyond survey and scenario experiments, and move to the field. Looking at what real life loyalty programs are doing, and hopefully sharing results in the managerial community can help achieving success in pairing sustainability with loyalty. We hope this chapter can contribute to this aim.

Acknowledgements

We are deeply grateful to Silvia Chessa and Clelia Galvano, junior researchers with the Observatory in 2024, who performed the data collection and analysis on the sample. We alone are responsible for mistakes and omissions.

References

Andreoni, J. (1990) 'Impure altruism and donations to public goods: a theory of warm-glow giving'. *The Economic Journal*, 100(401), 464–477.

Antavo (2023) 'Global customer loyalty report – loyalty pays back'. Retrieved from https://antavo.com/reports/global-customer-loyalty-report-2023 (accessed 11 January 2024).

Bazaraa, D. A., Mahrous, A. A. and Elsharnouby, M. H. (2022) 'How manipulating incentives and participation in green programs affect satisfaction: the mediating role of warm glow.' *Journal of Cleaner Production*, 362, 132306.

Case (2023) 'Consumers care about sustainability – but will they pay more?'. Retrieved from https://nrf.com/blog/consumers-care-about-sustainability-will-they-pay-more (accessed 26 March 2024).

Eason, C. C., Bing, M. N. and Smothers, J. (2015) 'Reward me, charity, or both? The impact of fees and benefits in loyalty programs'. *Journal of Retailing and Consumer Services*, 25, 71–80.

Einwiller, S., Lis, B., Ruppel, C. and Sen, S. (2019) 'When CSR-based identification backfires: testing the effects of CSR-related negative publicity'. *Journal of Business Research*, 104, 1–13.

Flacandji, M., Passebois Ducros, J. and Ieva, M. (2023) 'Redesigning loyalty marketing for a better world: the impact of green loyalty programs on perceived value'. *Journal of Service Theory and Practice*, 33(4), 465–487.

Ganesan, S., George, M., Jap, S., Palmatier, R. W. and Weitz, B. (2009) 'Supply chain management and retailer performance: emerging trends, issues, and implications for research and practice'. *Journal of Retailing*, 85(1), 84–94.

Gifford, R. and Nilsson, A. (2014) 'Personal and social factors that influence pro-environmental concern and behaviour: a review'. *International Journal of Psychology*, 49(3), 141–157.

Hwang, J. and Choi, L. (2020) 'Having fun while receiving rewards? Exploration of gamification in loyalty programs for consumer loyalty'. *Journal of Business Research*, 106, 365–376.

iSeatz (2023) 'Booking, personalization, sustainability, and payments: the tipping point for travel loyalty in 2023'. Retrieved from www.iseatz.com/blog/tipping-point-travel-loyalty-2023 (accessed 26 March 2024).

Kumar, V. (2019) 'Global implications of cause-related loyalty marketing'. *International Marketing Review*, 37(4), 747–772.

Liu, S. Q. and Mattila, A. S. (2016) 'The influence of a "green" loyalty program on service encounter satisfaction'. *Journal of Services Marketing*, 30(6), 576–585.

Luo, X. and Bhattacharya, C. B. (2009) 'The debate over doing good: corporate social performance, strategic marketing levers, and firm-idiosyncratic risk'. *Journal of Marketing*, 73(6), 198–213.

McKinsey and Nielsen (2023) 'Consumers care about sustainability – and back it up with their wallets'. Retrieved from www.mckinsey.com/industries/consumer-packaged-goods/our-insights/consumers-care-about-sustainability-and-back-it-up-with-their-wallets# (accessed 26 March 2024).

Mohr, L. A., Webb, D. J. and Harris, K. E. (2001) 'Do consumers expect companies to be socially responsible? The impact of corporate social responsibility on buying behavior'. *Journal of Consumer Affairs*, 35(1), 45–72.

Osservatorio Fedeltà (2022) 'I nuovi confini della Loyalty' [in Italian]. Retrieved from www.osservatoriofedelta.unipr.it/pubblicazione/14487/white-paper/i-nuovi-confini-della-loyalty/

Peattie, K. (2010) 'Green consumption: behavior and norms'. *Annual Review of Environment and Resources*, 35, 195–228.

Reinartz, W. (2023) 'Firms' focus on Brand and customer management: management, development and investors valuations'. Presented at the Marketing Science Institute online seminar. Retrieved from www.msi.org/presentation/presentation-firms-focus-on-brand-and-customer-management-measurement-development-and-financial-consequences [subscription required] (accessed 15 June 2024).

Sen, S., Du, S. and Bhattacharya, C. (2009) 'Building relationships through corporate social responsibility', in D. J. Macinnis, C. W. Park and J. R. Priester (eds), *Handbook of Brand Relationships*. New York: Routledge.

Steg, L. and Vlek, C. (2009) 'Encouraging pro-environmental behaviour: an integrative review and research agenda'. *Journal of Environmental Psychology*, 29(3), 309–317.

Usrey, B., Palihawadana, D., Saridakis, C. and Theotokis, A. (2020) 'How downplaying product greenness affects performance evaluations: examining the effects of implicit and explicit green signals in advertising'. *Journal of Advertising*, 49(2), 125–140.

Venhoeven, L.A., Willem Bolderdijk, J. and Steg, L. (2016) 'Why acting environmentally-friendly feels good: exploring the role of self-image'. *Frontiers in Psychology*, 7, 1–8.

Vlachos, P. A., Panagopoulos, N. G. and Rapp, A. A. (2013) 'Feeling good by doing good: employee CSR-induced attributions, job satisfaction, and the role of charismatic leadership'. *Journal of Business Ethics*, 118, 577–588.

White, K., Habib, R. and Hardisty, D. J. (2019) 'How to SHIFT consumer behaviors to be more sustainable: A literature review and guiding framework'. *Journal of Marketing*, 83(3), 22–49.

4

WHAT WE KNOW ABOUT LOYALTY PROGRAMS

Marco Ieva

What is a loyalty program?

Loyalty programs started to be adopted in the early 1980s and have gained influence across multiple industries since (Berry, 2013). The majority belong to the retail industry (Colloquy, 2017), and in the Unites States, companies invest an astonishing $2 billion in them (Taylor et al., 2015). On average, almost one third of the marketing budget (28%) is devoted to customer loyalty and CRM (Antavo, 2024). They have been widely studied in academia and are regarded by marketers as a key marketing tool and customer experience touchpoint. Unsurprisingly, there has been no shortage of attempts to define loyalty programs. The American Marketing Association (AMA) defined what it called 'frequent shopper programmes' as 'continuity incentive programmes offered by a retailer to reward customers and encourage repeat business'.[1] Several scholars have identified further features. Bijmolt, Dorotic and Verhoef (2011) pointed out that loyalty programs flourish across multiple industries both in business-to-business (B2B) and business-to-consumer (B2C) settings.

Kumar and Reinartz (2018) identified them as marketing processes that reward customers for certain behaviours they undertake with brands, for instance repeat purchases, engagement with the brand assets, and so on. loyalty programs provide consumers with benefits that include tangible rewards and statuses. They provide companies with identifiable advantages such as increasing the likelihood of retaining members and gaining insight on purchases at an individual level. loyalty programs generate switching costs, since members lose value if they decide to switch to another company (Leenheer et al., 2007), and switching costs play a role in reducing customer switching

DOI: 10.4324/9781003400783-4

behaviour (Pick and Eisend, 2014). Companies can leverage customer insight to deploy personalized and targeted marketing activities, such as customized offers (see Breugelmans et al., 2015; Liu, 2007). A recent review of more than one hundred studies published from 1990 to 2020 has found robust evidence that loyalty programs enhance customer loyalty (Belli et al., 2022).

Loyalty programs include distinct typologies of marketing programs that differ in many ways. Several terms have been employed to refer to them. Indeed, we could make a long list, where reward programs, frequency reward programs, loyalty cards or schemes, points cards, advantage cards, frequent flyer programs and frequent shopper programs would feature among others (see Bijmolt, Dorotic and Verhoef, 2011). However, in all cases the underlying concept of an loyalty program is that customers enrolled in one are encouraged to maintain or increase their spending with a given company in exchange for some asset – points, coupons, stars, air miles, etc. – that can be converted into products and services. Kumar and Reinartz (2018) identified four distinct goals, all or some of which loyalty programs are designed to accomplish:

- building attitudinal and behavioural loyalty
- generating efficiency profits
- generating effectiveness profits
- achieving value alignment.

Let's take these in turn. Attitudinal loyalty involves a positive customer perception and attitude towards a particular product or service or company, while behavioural loyalty refers to the actions that customers undertake with respect to a product or service. Both are key forms of loyalty and usually correlate – although one does not necessarily imply the other. Efficiency profits are profits resulting from a change in customer purchase behaviour brought about by membership of an loyalty program. Effectiveness profits are medium-term or long-term profits generated by improvements a company makes to a product offering, communication or promotion on the basis of information gathered though the loyalty program. Finally, value alignment refers to the possibility of aligning marketing efforts and related investment with the value of customers targeted by the loyalty program.

According to Kim et al. (2021) the loyalty programs can have different effects in many stages of the relationship between companies and customers, namely in the customer acquisition, onboarding, expansion, and retention stages. First, loyalty programs have a key role in the acquisition stage by increasing the expected value of products and services and initiate the relationship with customers. Low or no joining fee, convenient enrolment, immediate rewards at subscription and clear rules for redeeming rewards can be of help in this phase. After joining the program and starting to buy from the company, customers enter the onboarding stage. In this stage, developing feeling of gratitude is important for a loyalty program as well as managing the first impression customers have of the program. In this stage the company should pay attention to reward value, visibility and exclusivity to ensure that new members can progress in the program, keeping their motivation and engagement high. After a while, members enter the expansion stage, meaning that they have been enrolled in the program for a while and they are familiar with it. In this phase, the program should rely more on soft and indirect rewards (rewards that are more experiential and less related to the core business of the company). Soft and indirect rewards can increase the customer's perception of status and status demotion should be carefully evaluated to avoid negative consequences. Finally, the loyalty program can be effective also for customers in the retention stage: they have been members for a long time and need to be maintained and engaged. In this respect, the loyalty program can be employed to create and develop customer habits in interacting with the company, thus reducing the risk of customer churn. loyalty programs can have a positive effect in the retention stage by keeping customers motivated to stay with the company by means of status-exclusive rewards.

To summarize, loyalty programs should be flexible enough to accommodate different strategies and goals depending on the stage of the relationship the customer is in loyalty programs can also play a different role depending on the customer journeys' stage and on the industry of reference (Steinhoff and Zondag, 2021): loyalty programs can provide personalized suggestions that can ease the information search stage, increase purchase value when making the purchase decision, and offer reassurance in the post purchase stage for loyalty program members.

Clearly, success in achieving these goals depends on how an loyalty program can influence customer behaviour. Blattberg, Kim and Neslin (2008) identified three key elements of loyalty programs that aim to do this: the points-pressure mechanism, rewarded behaviour and personalized marketing. The points-pressure mechanism influences customers to accelerate their purchases as they draw nearer to gaining a certain reward. The receipt of a program reward can increase the strength of the relationship between the customer and the company. Personalized marketing involves the delivery of offers and communications tailored to an individual and aimed at triggering an attitudinal and behavioural response, something we will return to later in this chapter.

Scholars have identified four key components of loyalty programs: membership requirements, program structure, point and reward structure, and program communication (see Liu and Yang, 2009; Bijmolt, Dorotic and Verhoef, 2011; Breugelmans et al., 2015). Next section discusses these components in more detail and reviews the recent literature on each before moving on to address a specific type: the coalition loyalty program.

Membership requirements

Membership requirements refer to the rules that define how customers are to be enrolled in loyalty programs. We can identify two specific aspects: (1) voluntary versus automatic enrolment; (2) open versus closed enrolment. loyalty programs commonly offer voluntary enrolment, meaning customers are asked if they want to join. This leads to self-selection: customers that are enrolled in the loyalty program have chosen to be members and thus probably differ in some meaningful way from customers that have decided not to join. On the one hand, customers who have a positive attitude towards the company might be more inclined to be members of an loyalty program. On the other hand, customers who are sensitive to promotional activities might also be keen to join.

There are many variables to take into account when understanding why customers join an loyalty program, as supported by empirical research. For example, Demoulin and Zidda (2009) and Gómez, Arranz and Cillán (2012) identified several drivers positively or negatively related to the likelihood of completing a voluntary subscription to an loyalty program in a supermarket retail setting: shopping enjoyment, individual desire for privacy, perceived scheme disadvantages, perceived scheme advantages, perceived complexity, distance from the store, and attitudinal and behavioural loyalty. They found that customers who regard shopping as a hedonistic activity, are more reluctant to share their personal information with a company, or who are sceptical about the advantages of an loyalty program (for example, if it has an overly complicated points accrual mechanism or structure) are less likely to subscribe. By contrast, the perceived benefits stemming from subscribing can positively influence the decision to join. Attitudinal and behavioural loyalty is also a factor: the higher the positive attitude towards the retailer, or the amount of time spent with the retailer, the higher the likelihood a customer will join its loyalty program. Customers who live close to the store are also more likely to become loyalty program members, probably a consequence of the convenience of having a store nearby.

Whatever the motivations to join, voluntary enrolment is certainly the most employed enrolment mechanism. In this respect, one of the most frequently used key performance indicators (KPIs) for loyalty programs is the percentage of transactions and turnover that is accounted for by loyalty program members out of the total number of transactions and amount spent in the store made by all customers. These figures tend to vary depending on the industry. For instance, in Italy, consumer surveys run by the Loyalty Observatory (see Chapter 8) showed that the turnover related to loyalty program members in grocery retailing might reach percentages higher than 80% of the total turnover, while in consumer electronics, in the pharmacy sector or in apparel this figure is usually much lower, reaching 50–60% at maximum.

Automatic enrolment, which is less commonly deployed, means that customers join an loyalty program upon their first purchase of a given product and service. From that moment the company can automatically track future transactions made by the customer. Unfortunately, there is not much research on the difference in terms of effectiveness of automatic versus voluntary enrolment. The main benefit of automatic enrolment is that it allows companies to track the purchase behaviour of all the customers purchasing at least one product. Hence, no selection bias arises when evaluating the effects of an loyalty program using this enrolment type. However, automatic enrolment can have several downsides. For example, customers may perceive the enrolment mechanism itself as a limitation of their freedom of choice and might then be sceptical of the related advantages of the program. Moreover, since the customer is to be identified at first purchase, this implies requesting personal information and creating a new customer profile, tasks that can be time-consuming. This process may irritate the occasional customer, and may prevent some from completing the purchase altogether. Finally, the General Data Protection Regulation (GDPR) on data privacy valid in Europe call for further legal evaluations of the feasibility of automatic enrolment.

The second aspect of enrolment mechanism is the decision to make an loyalty program open to everybody or restricted to customers with certain requirements. The latter are commonly known as closed or 'selective' loyalty programs. Esmark, Noble and Bell (2016) studied the extent to which an open versus closed loyalty program could be more effective in fostering consumer attitudes towards the company such as gratitude, in-group identification and loyalty. Their main findings were as follows. First, open loyalty programs seemed to be more effective in the grocery industry while closed loyalty programs were more effective in those businesses where the hedonic component plays a stronger role, such as travel services, restaurants and coffee shops. Second, both open and closed loyalty programs contributed to enhancing customer loyalty but in a different manner depending on the stage of the customer relationship, in their study identified as beginning and growth, maturity, decline.

At the beginning and growth stage, there was no difference in the effectiveness of open versus closed loyalty programs. At the maturity stage, both types of loyalty programs were effective in fostering loyalty. Specifically, open loyalty programs positively influenced customer in-group identification (the consumer belief of being consistent with the image of the average program member). In-group identification, in turn, had a positive effect on loyalty intentions. By contrast, closed loyalty programs influenced gratitude, which arises when a customer feels that the company has adopted a behaviour that leads to advantages for the customer (see Raggio et al., 2013). Gratitude also impacted loyalty intentions. Finally, when the relationship was in the declining stage, closed loyalty programs were more effective at developing in-group identification in customers, thus leading to higher customer loyalty. Therefore, the closed loyalty program was shown to be useful in retaining customers more likely to abandon the company and restoring the quality of the relationship with them.

Customers can join a closed loyalty program by invitation or by paying a membership fee. The membership fee is a lump sum paid upon enrolment or a periodical subscription fee that is charged, for instance, every month or year. One of the most famous closed loyalty programs is Amazon Prime, which requires customers to pay a membership fee in order to enrol and enjoy its benefits (e.g. no delivery costs, access to entertainment services, etc.). Given that loyalty programs can entail huge investment in terms of money and effort, companies can use the membership fee to help cover their costs and thereby offer more valuable and meaningful benefits to customers. However, a membership fee can discourage some consumers from joining if they perceive the advantages as failing to justify the membership fee or if they are put off by being tied in to an annual paid subscription.

Ashley, Gillespie and Noble (2016) studied the effect of membership fees on consumer perceptions of loyalty programs. Their study found that fee-based loyalty programs were likely to attract consumers who felt committed to the company and were willing to spend with it. They also found that fee-based programs can increase the revenues of the loyalty program: in addition to the fee received, such loyalty programs are able to elicit a more favourable perception of the program and, in turn, increase the average customer spend after enrolment. Their findings offer an important lesson in how to increase the likelihood that customers will join a fee-based loyalty program. The answer is related to the interaction between the membership fee and the accrual system. If the membership fee is low, it is better to offer a simple accrual system, one that can be easily understood and keeps the customer focused on the benefits of the program rather than on price. Where the membership fee is high, increasing the perceived complexity of the accrual system contributes to increasing membership intentions because it triggers a more comprehensive evaluation of the costs and benefits of the program rather than an evaluation of the fee alone. In addition, Iyengar, Park and Yu (2022) have focused on the effectiveness of subscription programs, when the membership fee is paid on a yearly basis. They have found a positive impact of the subscription on purchase behaviour, especially in the first two months of the subscription. Moreover, according to their study, the subscription increases the purchase frequency and the amount spent on new purchased products compared to the pre-subscription period, with a positive total impact on profits.

Program structure

Breugelmans et al. (2015) identified two main program structures: frequency reward and customer tier. Frequency reward programs assign points based on how much or how frequently a customer spends and rewards are achieved depending on certain point thresholds. Customer tier programs have a hierarchical structure:

customers are classified into tiers according to their purchase behaviour in a previous period (for example, gold, silver and bronze customers) and the classification is typically reviewed every year (see Bijmolt et al., 2018). While frequency reward programs are employed in settings where purchase occasions tend to be more frequent (for example, in supermarket retailing), customer tier programs are generally employed in service sectors such as aviation, banking, car rental, and hospitality. This reveals that the type of structure is also clearly linked with the type of business.

Gopalakrishnan et al. (2021) tested the effectiveness of a non-tiered loyalty program that was rewarding customers by means of a coupon offered every 100 dollars spent, in the hairdresser sector. They analysed the impact of the loyalty program on several KPIs, such as average ticket, average inter-purchase time, propensity to churn and Customer Lifetime Value. While the program did not have any impact on the average ticket, a positive and significant effect of the loyalty program in reducing average inter-purchase time (3 days lower on average) and churn probability was assessed.

Comparing the two program structures, non-tiered versus tiered loyalty programs, Kopalle et al. (2012) found that customer tier was more effective than frequency reward in driving loyalty because it continually provides benefits once the customer belongs to a high tier, whereas the frequency reward component displays a short-term impact only. This is due in part to the effect of points pressure, which pushes the consumer to reach a certain threshold to gain a reward, and in part to the effect of receiving the reward itself, which triggers subsequent short-term purchase behaviour. Tier structures have also been found to drive gratitude towards the company (see Steinhoff and Palmatier, 2016), specifically when advancement within the program hierarchy is earned (see Eggert, Steinhoff and Garnefeld, 2015). It should be noted, however, that these results varied slightly according to the industry of reference and gender of program members: apparently men were more likely to be engaged in a customer tier program if their status was made visible to others.

Chaabane and Pez (2017) added yet more insight on this topic. They found that the effectiveness of frequency reward versus customer tier depended on the congruence between the program and the brand concept. They classified brand concepts as symbolic and functional. Symbolic brands satisfy the needs of self-expression and self-enhancement and are related to the expression of a status – Ferrari is a good example of a symbolic brand. Functional brands, by contrast, are brands that solve practical issues and provide more tangible benefits – Chevrolet could be included in this typology. The authors found that symbolic brands perceived a hierarchical loyalty program structure as more congruent with their brand concept and this congruency was reported to lead to increased loyalty to the surveyed companies. However, frequency reward and customer tier were found to be equally congruent with a functional brand concept. These studies thus provide evidence for the superiority of a multi-tier loyalty program in driving loyalty, at least in certain circumstances.

It is, however, worth mentioning what has been referred to in many studies as the dark side of customer tier loyalty programs. The first issue relates to the situation when customers receive endowed – rather than achieved – elevated customer status. If the status is not perceived as a customer personal achievement, consumer scepticism arises. This scepticism might hamper the effectiveness of the status upgrade in driving customer loyalty (see Eggert, Steinhoff and Garnefeld, 2015). Marketers are therefore advised to frame the higher status offered to consumers as a reward for the customer behaviour, leaving to the customer the final decision of whether to change or keep their current status. In this regard, Yu et al. (2022) show the role of feedback strategies in influencing loyalty program members in tiered loyalty programs: the customization of progress feedback in the loyalty program can be effective in persuading members to keep their tier level. Feedback strategies can be 'looking-back', namely stressing how much progress the loyalty program member has already done, or 'looking-forward', highlighting the remaining progress the loyalty program member has to do to retain the level. Their study found that low-tier members are more likely to retain their level when exposed to a looking-back strategy, while for high-tier customers the opposite occurs: looking-forward strategies are more effective in retaining their tier.

Moreover, consumer tier demotion – when a customer, due to spending below threshold/previous period, is shifted to a lower tier – represents a second key issue. Quite simply, individuals are more sensitive to tier demotions than they are to tier promotions. Tier demotions may thus have a higher negative effect on trust, commitment and loyalty than do the positive effects of tier promotions (see Van Berlo, Bloemer and Blazevic, 2014). Banik (2023) found that status demotion negatively affects customers' satisfaction, word-of-mouth, and share-of-wallet. In addition, customers attributing the cause of their status demotion to the firm's policy changes display lower level of satisfaction, word-of-mouth and share-of-wallet.

According to Ramaseshan and Ouschan (2017), this is more evident for high-status consumers than it is for low-status consumers. To take a hypothetical example, Gold customers that are shifted to a lower tier (Silver) are more likely to display negative reactions in terms of purchase behaviour than Silver customers that are shifted to the lower tier (Bronze).

The third issue is more strategical: marketers planning to introduce a customer tier program should understand that the termination of that program might seriously harm the relationship with those customers accustomed to accessing benefits related to the highest program tiers (Bijmolt et al., 2018).

Point and reward structure

The main issues, as outlined by Breugelmans et al. (2015), concerning the point and reward structure of an loyalty program revolve around the design of the points accrual system and type of rewards offered in both frequency reward and customer tier programs. Companies managing loyalty programs can take advantage of what are known as the points pressure effect and rewarded behaviour effect (see Taylor and Neslin, 2005; Bijmolt et al., 2018). The points pressure effect occurs when a customer is approaching a certain threshold that triggers a reward and accelerates her purchases in order to gain it more quickly. To elicit this effect, companies must avoid two common mistakes, outlined by Bijmolt et al. (2018) and Drèze and Nunes (2011): (1) setting thresholds that are too easy to reach and consequently demotivate customers; and (2) setting thresholds that are too high and thus discourage occasional customers from engaging with the program. The rewarded behaviour effect occurs when a customer receives the reward and experiences feelings of joy and happiness that reinforce engagement with the loyalty program and might lead to a positive change in purchase behaviour (Colliander, Söderlund, and Szugalski, 2016). Even though this effect appears to be a significant driver of a long-term relationship with customers (according to Taylor and Neslin, 2005), there are some caveats that should not be overlooked: the duration of this effect is short term, from two to seven weeks, and tends to be different depending on the characteristics of the customer and their previous engagement with the loyalty program (see Taylor and Neslin, 2005; Kopalle et al., 2009).

Timing is critical here. Two issues need to be taken into account: the difference between achieving an immediate versus a delayed reward, and the points expiration policy (that is, the amount of time that members have at their disposal to accrue points in order to achieve a reward). Regarding the former, Roehm and Roehm (2011) found that consumers favoured delayed rewards if those rewards fit with their personal values. Regarding the latter, unredeemed points can become an issue for some companies, which tend to cope with it by introducing points expiration policies. Consumer personal characteristics might help explain the likelihood that a program member will redeem points or would rather accumulate them. Hwang et al. (2016) found that young consumers were more likely to redeem points compared with older consumers. Moreover, according to their study, high-income consumers were more likely than low-income consumers to redeem points. These results indeed suggest that companies should be willing to differentiate their marketing actions related to points redemption depending on the personal (in this case, socioeconomic and demographic) characteristics of members. As a matter of fact, Li et al. (2024) focus on the link between customer relationship characteristics in loyalty programs and point redemption behaviour in services. Data show that customers with higher purchase depth (extent of customers' usage of the services of a service provider) and redemption recency (expressed as number of days since last redemption) are more likely to redeem points. However, customers with higher purchase breadth (purchases made in distinct categories of services), purchase recency (expressed as number of days elapsed since the last purchase), redemption depth (the extent of customers' usage of loyalty points of the firm) and redemption breadth (the diversity of services redeemed with points from the firm) display a lower probability to redeem. Finally, they found that, with reference to redeemers only, customers with higher purchase breadth and purchase recency will redeem a higher number of points.

Breugelmans and Liu-Thompkins (2017) found that establishing a points expiration deadline elicited a positive effect on purchase behaviour. However, in their study, this positive impact was identified only for those consumers that displayed a higher degree of flexibility in their purchases. Consumers that tended to buy fewer products with the company offering the loyalty program and shopped across multiple stores were more flexible in managing their purchases and adapting their behaviour with respect to the points expiration policy. In contrast, those who already spent a significant amount of money with the company were less likely to adapt their purchase behaviour to comply with the expiration policy. Hence, they perceived the expiration policy as a restriction on their flexibility, which for them made the program less appealing.

As far as rewards are concerned, there are usually two categories: hard and soft rewards. Arbore and Estes (2013) offered definitions for these terms. Hard rewards are tangible benefits, including, for instance, discounts, free products and monetary incentives. Soft rewards are intangible benefits, mostly psychological, relational or emotional, that include preferential treatment, status visibility, priority check-in and special events. Previous research has found that consumers tend to prefer tangible rewards (see Keh and Lee, 2006). Soft rewards have been found to drive attitudinal loyalty, namely commitment (see Bridson, Evans and Hickman, 2008), whereas tangible rewards contribute to developing higher behavioural loyalty (see Meyer-Waarden, 2015). Belli et al. (2022) analysed the role of different types of rewards on loyalty program effectiveness, measured in terms of customer loyalty, across findings from more than one hundred academic studies. They have found that loyalty programs that provide hard rewards in the form of discounts (e.g. discounts on product prices available to loyalty program members only) have weaker impacts on customer loyalty than loyalty programs that do not provide discounts: loyalty programs offering discounts tend to generate more loyalty to the program rather than loyalty to the company offering the loyalty program. loyalty programs offering hard rewards in the form of savings (coupons that can be redeemed after reaching a certain points threshold) display stronger effects on customer loyalty than loyalty programs that do not offer a savings feature. Finally, they found that loyalty programs offering exclusive soft rewards for their members (i.e. exclusive access to special events or product lines) have higher impact on customer loyalty than loyalty programs that do not offer exclusive rewards.

Usually, what we observe in practice is that both hard and soft rewards are strictly linked to the core business of the company. For instance, airline industry loyalty programs might offer fast check-in or supermarket retailers might offer coupons on the next purchase in their stores. Meyer-Waarden (2015) found that rewards aligned with the image of the company were more effective in driving loyalty intentions.

Program communication

The fourth component, communication, plays a vital role in the management of an loyalty program. First, at a strategic level the loyalty program should be fully integrated in the marketing strategy of a company with all the other touchpoints that the company can directly or indirectly manage or monitor. Second, the effectiveness of an loyalty program might be related to how companies frame their communication of the points-earning mechanism or decide how consumers are going to be informed about their points-balance status (for instance, if automatically or not).

Bonezzi, Brendl and De Angelis (2011) found that when consumers were motivated to reach a given points threshold and were at the beginning of their goal pursuit, they took as a reference their initial state, namely the amount of points already collected. Consumers approaching the end goal, by contrast, took as a reference their desired end state, namely the amount of points they needed to reach. However, individuals in the middle – that is, neither close to the start nor to the end of the goal pursuit process – were demotivated to pursue the final goal. These findings point to the importance of framing messages in an effective way to avoid members remaining stuck in the middle of the goal pursuit process, as we have seen also previously, when referring to tiers and feedback strategies.

According to the study of Ku et al. (2018), messages that highlight the amount of money that should be spent to achieve a reward or the loss stemming from consumer inaction were more likely to erode intention to redeem the reward. However, this effect occurred only for those individuals that were 'stuck in the middle'. More research is needed in this area to assess how companies can design communications to maximize consumer engagement with their programs.

The importance of communications has been also highlighted by Bies, Bronnenberg and Gijsbrechts (2021), that have measured the impact of push messages on consumer spending and redemption behaviour. Specifically, they found that push messages have a strong impact on redemption and a moderate effect on consumer spending. More importantly, the timing of those messages plays a role: early messages have higher impact on spending and lower on redemption, while the opposite occurs for messages sent close to the expiry date of the loyalty program. High spending customers (before the program launch) seem to react more favourably to push messages compared to low spending customers. Finally, it should be recalled that loyalty programs open great opportunities for marketers to personalize email marketing communications. As shown by Zhang and Liu-Thompkins (2024), companies can identify different customer segments based on their loyalty program tier level and goal distance. Their findings suggest that companies should employ personalized communications in loyalty programs with affective versus cognitive message appeals, depending on the type of customer segment, to achieve higher effectiveness.

What is clear from our discussion in this section is that the four key components of loyalty programs – membership requirements, program structure, point and reward structure, and program communications – are not mere trivial aspects but key considerations that any company must take into account when designing a program. As the body of evidence suggests, deciding whether an loyalty program should be open or selective, include a membership fee or not, adopt a frequency reward or customer tier structure, harness the points pressure or rewarded behaviour effects, and so on, are all matters that must be considered carefully alongside a myriad of different customer variables and being mindful of the long-term costs and challenges that might arise from having to make alterations or wholescale changes to the program design. It is imperative too, regardless of how an loyalty program is designed, that its benefits and features are communicated to customers clearly and that program communication is both integrated into the overarching company marketing strategy and designed to maximize individual customer engagement.

Coalition loyalty programs

Before we move on to assess how loyalty programs achieve the four goals identified by Kumar and Reinartz (2018), it is worthwhile saying something about the coalition model given its distinct characteristics, economic relevance and diffusion. Payback, Nectar and Dotz are leading examples of this type of program today, but the concept dates back to the late 1980s (as we discussed in Chapter 1). Coalition loyalty programs are unique in that they seek to bring together a group of different partners, usually active in different sectors, such as the retail and service sectors (see Moore and Sekhon, 2005). They allow members to earn points when shopping at any of the different partners of the program and usually involve partners that cooperate to create a unified coalition program and a third non-participating party that manages its operations. As some scholars have noted, there are benefits to both companies and customers in joining a coalition loyalty program (see De Noni, Orsi and Zanderighi, 2014).

For companies:

- It allows them to cross-sell and cooperate to achieve mutual gain by expanding the customer base for customer relationship marketing activities (Dorotic, Bijmolt and Verhoef, 2012).
- Because the costs of introducing and running an loyalty program are shared among partners, the financial burden placed on individual companies is limited (Capizzi and Ferguson, 2005). This is particularly appealing to local and smaller companies.
- Costs are also saved because the company managing the program has the skills and infrastructure necessary to maximize the usage of the information collected through it and effectively manage the different loyalty marketing activities (Nath, 2005).
- Since a coalition loyalty program enables customers to earn and burn points for purchases across a wide range of product categories, they may be more appealing to some consumers and lead to higher enrolment rates than traditional loyalty programs.

Customers enjoy benefits too:

- They can earn points faster without increasing their spending with a company. Customers don't need to spend more on a single product category to earn more points but can simply switch the same spending on a given category to a different company that is a partner in the program.
- They can enjoy a wider variety of rewards, which are usually aligned with the business of the companies joining the coalition.

There are, however, significant risks in adopting a coalition loyalty program. First, the program might lose focus and meaning if too many and diverse partners are included (Kumar and Reinartz, 2018). Second, each partner will bring to the program a customer base that differs in size, turnover and, more importantly, points-earning patterns. Therefore, it is not a simple task for the company managing the coalition to plan marketing activities and achieve cooperation among partners. On the one hand, the major partners in a coalition loyalty program might invest more in the program and demand more attention from the company managing it. On the other hand, the minor partners might be unwilling to cooperate if they feel that the program is not delivering substantial results for their business. While there are coalition programs that were able to achieve success in Germany and United Kingdom, there is also evidence of unsuccessful coalition loyalty programs, for example the closure of both Nectar in Italy in 2016 and of the American Express coalition program, Plenti, in the United States in 2018. Schumann, Wünderlich and Evanschitzky (2013) further explored the 'dark side' of coalition loyalty programs by studying the spill-over effect of a service failure for a company that is active in a coalition loyalty program. Their study found that service failure caused by one partner in a coalition loyalty program does not simply impact the other partners. The negative consequences are, in fact, extended to the coalition program as a whole. If catastrophic, it is hard to see how the program can recover. Belli et al. (2022) have found, based on multiple studies, that coalition loyalty programs are as effective as single-firm loyalty programs in stimulating customer loyalty. Therefore, the company decision to join a coalition should take into consideration aspects more related to cost and control related factors, such as allowing for sharing costs versus sharing customer data with partners.

In Chapter 10 two case studies of coalitions are presented: Dotz, from Brazil, and yuu Rewards, from Singapore.

How successful are loyalty programs?

We've discussed the key features of loyalty programs. But how do loyalty programs perform in reality? Several studies have attempted to measure this. This section reviews the existing evidence of the performance of loyalty programs in achieving the four goals outlined in the first section. It looks at the influence of loyalty programs on customer loyalty attitudes and behaviours, and thus how they generate efficiency profits from the resulting changes in customer purchase behaviour, before moving on to discuss how they contribute to medium-term and long-term profits and function to pursue value alignment.

Before delving into the literature, it is important to keep in mind, in the case of programs that adopt voluntary enrolment (the vast majority), that customers self-select: they *choose* to enrol in loyalty programs. It is important to account for this self-selection bias in order to estimate the actual effect loyalty programs have. Otherwise, there is the tangible risk that we overestimate the impact loyalty programs have. Usually, consumers who are more prone towards a given company tend to join its loyalty program. Evidently this is one, but not the only, reason why their behaviour is different from consumers who do not join the program. Leenheer et al. (2007) highlighted this issue by demonstrating that a methodology that ignores self-selection bias estimates that loyalty programs lead to a 30% increase in share of wallet. When taking into account self-selection bias that percentage drops dramatically to 4%. One cannot overemphasize the importance of employing sound and proper statistical methods that take bias into account when measuring program performance.

Influence on attitudinal loyalty

There is a plethora of studies that have focused on the influence of loyalty programs on both attitudinal and behavioural loyalty. But these have tended to analyse the short-term effects of loyalty programs in driving customer attitudes and intentions.

Attitudinal loyalty – often expressed as commitment, satisfaction or positive perceptions, and generally measured by means of consumer surveys – has been regarded by many as a key performance metric and antecedent to behavioural loyalty (see Furinto, Pawitra and Balqiah, 2009; Dorotic, Bijmolt and Verhoef, 2012). It is important because it prevents program members from switching to other companies that might offer programs with better perceived benefits' (see Hansen, Deitz and Morgan, 2010) and supports a company in retaining customers and driving long-term purchase behaviour effects. Some scholars have argued that loyalty programs might be more effective in building attitudinal loyalty for those customers who are already prone to develop a relationship with the company (see Dholakia, 2006; Daams, Gelderman and Schijns, 2008). Others have observed that enhancing how consumers perceive an loyalty program and its rewards might lead to increased attitudinal loyalty to the company (see Demoulin and Zidda, 2008; Furinto, Pawitra and Balqiah, 2009).

Other studies have focused on how loyalty programs can actually drive attitudinal loyalty. Stathopoulou and Balabanis (2016) found that members' positive perception of program benefits led to increased trust and satisfaction, while Kang, Brashear-Alejandro and Groza (2015) discovered that values and benefits were significant antecedents to both company and program loyalty. Consumer perception of the values and benefits of enrolling in a loyalty program is the key driver of loyalty to that program. In turn, loyalty to the program may lead to loyalty to the company through a specific mechanism: the consumer-company identification, in which consumers are attracted by the company brand and begin to identify themselves with it. The loyalty program itself may help to develop, or even initiate, the bond between company and consumer and this has been shown to contribute to increasing attitudinal loyalty to the company.

Along the same lines, Brashear-Alejandro, Kang and Groza (2016) found that delivering non-monetary incentives to loyalty program members can be a valuable means of driving feelings of identification. In addition, Söderlund (2019) found that evoking customers' membership status drives higher feeling of belonging, leading in turn to higher customer satisfaction, for loyalty program members compared to loyalty program non-members. Ma, Li and Zhang (2018) studied the effects of loyalty programs in service sectors and found both positive and negative consequences for attitudinal loyalty. On the one hand, tangible rewards, preferential treatment and perceived status exerted a positive effect on customer relationship quality. However, perceived status can also backfire. Ma, Li and Zhang (2018) found that for gold program members who had developed a high perception of their status, the joint offering of preferential treatment and tangible rewards led them to develop entitlement behaviours. They started to expect preferential treatment and extra efforts from the company, and such expectations negatively affected satisfaction, profitability, and ultimately, the relationship with the company. Vilches-Montero et al. (2018) found that consumer perceptions of the innovativeness and competitive advantages offered by an loyalty program can drive attachment to it and, in turn, increase store loyalty. This relationship was, again, found to vary depending on gender. For men, the perceived competitive advantages of the program were significantly related to store loyalty; for women, the perceived innovativeness of the loyalty program was a significant antecedent to store loyalty.

Finally, Gorlier and Michel (2020) found that loyalty program rewards also positively affect members' self-expansion. Self-expansion is the degree to which one person experiences a relationship with another subject or entity as a driver of increased knowledge, skills, abilities, positive life changes, and new experiences. Specifically, their study showed that special rewards, meaning rewards that are perceived as novel and arousing, allow consumers to expand their self-worth, thus leading to an increase in attitudinal outcomes, such as brand identification, intention to recommend, and overall evaluation.

Influence on behavioural loyalty

If an attitudinally loyal customer is someone who perceives a brand, product or program in a positive way and feels, internally, committed and satisfied with it, a behaviourally loyal customer is someone who takes specific positive actions in respect of that brand, product or program (e.g. maintaining his purchases or recommending the company/brand to others). The same customer can be one without being the other, and although attitudinal loyalty can be an antecedent to other forms of loyalty (as is argued by many of the aforementioned scholars), it is not necessarily so. So, to move beyond studies that look at how loyalty programs affect customer perceptions and attitudes, we now turn to those that focus on how they perform in changing purchase behaviour and influencing customer behavioural loyalty. There is evidence to suggest that loyalty programs may do this over time, if not in the short term. Dorotic, Bijmolt and Verhoef (2012) offered an extensive review of how loyalty programs influence customer behaviour and Belli et al. (2022) have expanded and updated this review. Specifically, by reviewing effects from more than one hundred studies, Belli et al. (2022) found that loyalty programs have a stronger impact on behavioural loyalty than on attitudinal loyalty. And this result reinforces the importance of measuring success of loyalty programs on multiple outcomes such as affective and behavioural loyalty.

Several early studies were conducted measuring the impact of loyalty programs on purchase behaviour in aggregate terms (e.g. Cigliano et al., 2000) and found that loyalty programs, in the first year of introduction, increased average sales by a percentage ranging from 1 to 3% in grocery retailing and 5% to 8% in department stores. It is clear that these percentages were also related to the key characteristics of the industry and company in question. For instance, research has found that, when the degree of competitiveness in the market is high and when the number of loyalty programs in the market increases, the aggregate effect of each program is significantly reduced (see Kopalle and Neslin, 2003; Liu and Yang, 2009). Moreover, other studies have shown that while big brands seem to achieve benefits from introducing an loyalty program because they can count on a big share of customers, small firms launching the loyalty program as a late competitive response seem to encounter a higher risk of failure (see Meyer-Waarden and Benavent, 2006). A more recent study (Bombaij and Dekimpe, 2020) has assessed the impact of loyalty programs on sales across a large sample of 358 grocery retailers from a broad cross-section of 27 western and eastern European countries. Their study found a positive effect of simpler loyalty program variants, namely those offering direct and immediate rewards, on retailer sales productivity (measured as total sales divided by sales area expressed in square meters). However, their study also highlights the role of contingency factors that could weaken or strengthen this effect: country characteristics, type of accrual mechanism, type of rewards, belonging to coalition loyalty program, etc. This reveals how complex it is to identify the combination of factors leading to maximize the success of a loyalty program.

When reviewing the effects of loyalty programs on purchase behaviour at the individual customer level, purchase frequency, share of wallet and purchase volume are generally regarded as the relevant KPIs. As we have stated before, loyalty program members displayed higher spending than non-members in many previous studies (e.g. Meyer-Waarden, 2008). However, when accounting for self-selection, there is evidence to suggest that the positive effects of loyalty programs on purchase behaviour may be limited to short-term loyalty marketing activities only, such as instant reward programs. The mentioned study from Gopalakrishnan et al. (2021) estimated the effectiveness of a standard loyalty program: the authors did not find an impact on the average amount spent, but they found a positive and significant impact on frequency and likelihood to remain with the company.

Instant reward programs are short-term programs that reward consumers upon the act of purchase with small prizes per fixed spending (see Minnema, Bijmolt and Non, 2017). Generally speaking, these rewards are part of a collectable set and encourage customers to come back to the point of sale in order to obtain new rewards that are part of the collection (e.g. coffee cups, knives, small toys). Some companies also offer rewards to customers if they purchase specific products or brands.

Early studies in this respect showed that instant rewards programs increased average spending levels by 6% during the promotional period (see Taylor and Neslin, 2005). Minnema, Bijmolt and Non (2017) estimated the substantial effects of instant reward programs in a grocery retailing setting and found that these initiatives had a positive impact on the frequency of visits to the store but do not affect the number of products bought. This impact was much stronger for customers taking an active part in the reward collection. Moreover, delivering a free gift associated with the purchase of a given product was reported to increase the probability that the involved consumers would choose that brand and was particularly effective when coupled with a price discount. A study from Bombaij, Gelper and Dekimpe (2022) analysed almost 100 instant reward programs and found that they are effective in increasing sales with a sales lift on average equal to 4%.

The evidence on the long-term effects of loyalty programs, and indeed the effectiveness of long-term loyalty programs, is mixed: while some studies report positive effects on purchase behaviour, others display no such effects. Specifically, across grocery retailing, airline services and insurance there is evidence for an increase in purchase frequency and volume and share of wallet driven by loyalty programs (see Verhoef, 2003; Leenheer et al., 2007). The highest effects are reported just after the introduction of the loyalty program. With respect to Customer Lifetime Value (CLV), Gopalakrishnan et al. (2021) found that the loyalty program significantly increases CLV computed on a five-years horizon, obtaining a 29.5% lift.

Many studies have reported a 'ceiling effect' in the impact of loyalty programs depending on the customer segment of reference (e.g. Bolton, Kannan and Bramlett, 2000; Lal and Bell, 2003). Heavy buyers tend to have less room to increase their spending as a consequence of the loyalty program because they are already top spenders. Therefore, the effects of the loyalty program might be more visible and significant for customer segments that are low or medium spenders.

Melnyk and Bijmolt (2015) investigated the effects of introducing and terminating a loyalty program on the likelihood that customers will stay with the company and increase their spending with it. Their study spanned different industries: food, telecommunications, petrol, financial services, utilities and retail. The results show that loyalty programs that provided members-only services and special events had a positive effect on loyalty intentions when the program was first introduced. When the program was terminated, there was no significant decrease in terms of loyalty intentions, which means that the impact of members-only services and special events was still lasting. Moreover, the authors found that at the introduction stage, program structure and point and reward structure were key influences on the behaviour of members. The negative effects of terminating a loyalty program are largely dependent on the competitive environment and how long a customer has been a member of the program.

Despite this evidence in favour of the effectiveness of loyalty programs, other studies conclude that loyalty programs do not substantially change consumer behaviour (see e.g. Bellizzi and Bristol, 2004; Meyer-Waarden and

Benavent, 2006). The mixed picture reveals the key role played by contextual factors such as customer segments, settings, industries and program design in the study of loyalty program performance. It is, then, very challenging to provide a definitive answer on the impact of loyalty programs. However, from this updated review of previous studies, several key insights do emerge:

- loyalty programs are related to change in customer attitudes and behaviours, but this change is driven by a complex set of different factors that very often are not under the control of the company.
- The chosen program structure and reward and points-earning mechanism are key drivers of the impact of loyalty programs.
- Marketers should carefully measure the short-term results of loyalty programs by considering different KPIs and different customer segments to capture the potential heterogeneity of effects.

There is no simple and unique answer to the question of how effective loyalty programs are in influencing attitudinal and behavioural loyalty. This is largely due to the complexity of assessing their performance in terms of variables that are empirically challenging. We believe, rather, that the greater value of loyalty programs lies in their effect on profits and their capacity to provide value alignment opportunities.

Influence on profits and value alignment

Kumar and Reinartz (2018) define effectiveness profits as those profits that companies can achieve by relying on a better knowledge of their customer base through the information obtained through loyalty programs. Utilizing loyalty program-generated data, companies can customize their offer and tailor communications to customers segments and individuals. Moreover, they can take informed decisions regarding other aspects, such as assortment, merchandising and promotional strategy, by relying on customer data at an individual level. Hence companies can use loyalty programs at a strategic level to learn about customer preferences and use this actionable data in a way that could result in a win-win situation for both the customer and the company.

Kumar and Reinartz (2018) understand value alignment as the capability to serve each customer by investing monetary and non-monetary efforts that are in line with the value that each customer brings to the company. By following this path, the company ensures that the profits received are aligned with the costs needed to serve any given customer. The risk of value alignment is that each customer might be treated differently. Thus, value alignment is advisable and feasible only when there is high heterogeneity in customer spending and if the characteristics of a given business allow it to implement this kind of differentiation: i.e. customers or customer segments can be distinguished by employing direct and personal means of communication. It is plain, then, that both effectiveness profits and value alignment have several requirements that need to be met if they are to work. It is not easy for any company to achieve these goals and develop a significant competitive advantage.

Studying the effects of loyalty programs on effectiveness profits and value alignment is a challenging task and this explains why there is a lack of academic literature on this topic. To this aim, studies should adopt a long-term approach and track how companies, internally, take advantage of the customer information gathered through the development of an loyalty program. However, the success story of the Tesco Clubcard program in the 2000s could be considered a good example on how loyalty programs can contribute to generating effectiveness profits and achieving value alignment by leveraging individual customer information. In this respect, Humby, Hunt and Phillips (2003) have explained how Tesco achieved outstanding results by relying on customer data to take informed decisions on many different marketing aspects and deliver customized offers to customers.

The evolution of loyalty programs in the last decade

Among practitioners across different countries and industries there is a growing concern regarding the need to re-design loyalty programs. The growth of digital channels and AI have changed the customer journey and provided new ways to interact with customers in different contexts. In such an environment, consumers may develop a dimmer view of the benefits of loyalty programs that rely on 'traditional' reward catalogues and plain discounts, which may be in danger of becoming outdated. Breugelmans et al. (2015) identified three new key trends in loyalty marketing associated with the digital transformation:

- The growth of coalition loyalty programs and the need to develop partnerships among players in different industries.
- The growth of the mobile channel, which can change the whole experience customers have with an loyalty program.
- The rise of intermediaries that can aggregate information on loyalty program membership and compare the terms and conditions of scores of loyalty programs with the click of a button, thus allowing consumers to choose programs that offer the most value.

Chen, Mandler and Meyer-Waarden (2021) have updated the above trends by identifying key paths for future developments:

- The move from plastic loyalty cards to digital loyalty cards would allow to connect the loyalty programs with many other devices and sources of information; this would translate into the development of a loyalty program application ecosystem, with the integration of many connected objects, such as wearables, smart home appliances, personal assistants (e.g. chatbots, voicebots), and other sensors. This would allow companies to access new types of data to be correlated with member' behaviours: heart rate, blood pressure, dietary information (e.g. allergies), sleep quality and sports performance.

- Developments in artificial intelligence allow companies to employ advanced analytical capabilities with the aim of extracting insights from the large amounts of data collected every day; this would increase the accuracy and the timeliness of predictions implemented on customer purchase and non-purchase behaviour.

Moreover, in the last five years companies have re-designed their loyalty programs to stimulate and reward pro-social actions within the points accrual mechanism as highlighted in Flacandji et al. (2023). We discuss such study in detail in Chapter 3. This trend is ongoing even though it is challenging to assess the actual effectiveness of pro-social loyalty programs in economic terms.

Companies across the world are forging other pathways to loyalty program innovation too. loyalty programs are increasingly rewarding non-transactional customer behaviour. Some loyalty programs are expanding their points-earning mechanisms to include the option of collecting points by reading pro-social or branded content or by undertaking engagement actions, such as answering to surveys, logging in on apps or websites, playing simple games or answering quizzes, or sharing their personal data with the company.

Using monetary incentives to rewards customers for taking specific non-purchase actions is also a key factor in the rise of the referral reward program. Referral reward programs (also called 'member get member' programs) are now established in many industries. They acquire customers by providing incentives to existing customers to recommend the company to new customers (Jin and Huang, 2014). Orsingher and Wirtz (2018) studied the key drivers of referral reward program effectiveness and found that the face value of the incentive was a key positive driver of the recommenders' perceived attractiveness of the incentive. The perceived attractiveness of the incentive led, in turn, to higher intention to recommend the company. However, if the face value of the incentive was too high, recommenders were worried about being negatively perceived by their peers and this was shown to hamper the likelihood they would recommend the company to others.

Loyalty programs as a customer experience touchpoint

While most of the literature on loyalty marketing has focused on the specific features and effects of loyalty programs, there is a growing stream of studies related to customer experience management and touchpoints that have considered loyalty programs as an example of the latter (see e.g. Wind and Hays, 2016). As defined by Duncan and Moriarty (2006), touchpoints are all verbal and non-verbal incidents in which an individual perceives and con- sciously relates to a given firm or brand. We discuss the new literature on touchpoints in greater depth in Chapter 5, but it is relevant to the present discussion to briefly review the findings from those studies that have analysed the role of the loyalty program as a touchpoint among others in a given com- pany's repertoire (e.g. its website, store and mobile app).

According to Verhoef et al. (2009), loyalty programs have the potential, just like any other touchpoint, to shape the customer experience and thus contribute towards achieving customer satisfaction and loyalty. The question that inevitably arises is to what extent loyalty programs are more or less impor- tant than other touchpoints in driving experience and loyalty. Mohd-Ramly and Omar (2017) studied the role of store attributes, including loyalty pro- grams, as antecedents to the customer experience in the retail sector. They hypothesized that customer satisfaction may lead to an improved customer experience. The results from their study show that loyalty programs were the second most important driver of the customer experience after store atmos- phere. Though more research is needed to confirm a positive and substantial relationship between loyalty programs and customer experience, Mohd-Ramly and Omar's study is a good indication that an association between the two exists.

In a similar vein, Ieva and Ziliani (2018a, 2018b) and Ziliani and Ieva (2018) focused on the relationship occurring between touchpoint frequency and positivity and loyalty intentions. They measured, by means of a survey, three dimensions of touchpoint interaction: reach, frequency and positivity. Each of these terms requires brief explanation. Touchpoint reach, defined by Romaniuk, Beal and Uncles (2013), is the indication of whether a customer has been exposed or not to a given touchpoint over time. Touchpoint fre- quency is the frequency of exposure to a given touchpoint over a specific period of time (see Baxendale, Macdonald and Wilson, 2015). Touchpoint positivity is the customer's affective response when encountering a given touchpoint in a period of time (again, Baxendale, Macdonald and Wilson, 2015).

These three variables were measured with reference to any touchpoint (store, website, mobile app, loyalty program, etc.) relevant to the setting of reference. Through this method it was possible to identify the relative role played by loyalty programs – as far as the frequency and positivity of exposure are concerned – in their relationship with loyalty intentions. By means of a segmentation study, Ieva and Ziliani (2018a) found that, in a grocery retail setting, the customer segments displaying higher exposure to all the different touchpoints, including loyalty programs, were positively related to higher loyalty intentions, namely a willingness to disclose private information to the company, a relationship commitment and positive word of mouth. In a study that followed soon after, Ieva and Ziliani (2018b) investigated the relationship between touchpoint reach, frequency and positivity and loyalty intentions considering around 20 different touchpoints in the mobile communication services industry. Loyalty intentions were measured including different perspectives: the extent to which a customer intended to say positive things about the provider, to recommend it to others, to consider it as their first choice for mobile services, and to increase their use of its services in the future. Their results showed that being exposed to loyalty programs was positively related to higher loyalty intentions, but that there was no evidence of a relationship between positive affective response to loyalty programs and loyalty intentions.

In another study, Ziliani and Ieva (2018) focused on how touchpoint frequency and positivity were related to relationship commitment and positive word of mouth towards a grocery retailer. The results were completely different from the 2018b study. This time affective response to loyalty programs had a positive and significant relationship with both relationship commitment and positive word of mouth towards the retailer, while frequency of exposure to loyalty programs had no significant relationship with the two outcomes. This, thus, suggests that the role of loyalty programs in terms of frequency and positivity on loyalty intentions is very specific and may change depending on the setting, in this case mobile communication services versus grocery retailing. The key message for us here, however, is that loyalty programs played a role in influencing loyalty intentions even when their role was considered in the context of a broader, more comprehensive study of all available touchpoints. Of course, it should be highlighted that these three studies did not control for the selection bias occurring with loyalty programs: customers exposed to the loyalty program may have had different characteristics (such as a more positive attitude towards the retailer) than those not exposed to it.

What next for research on loyalty programs?

The aim of this chapter has been to review the existing literature on loyalty programs to provide an updated overview of what we currently know about what they are, how they work and what they can achieve. It would be remiss to end this chapter without offering some reflections on potential areas for future research.

First, the design of the point and reward structure is a challenging task that requires many key decisions. Management and marketers, short on time or lacking the resources, often base these decisions on gut instinct or personal preferences rather than sound rational analysis and that is an understandable reality. However, there are several questions for researchers and practitioners alike to consider. The first challenge is how to define the ratio between the amount spent and number of points issued to members, what we have described in this chapter as the points-earning mechanism. Should points be granted for a specific amount spent or for purchasing certain products in certain categories? What is the optimal points-earning mechanism that maximizes engagement and effectiveness in terms of future spending without hurting profits? The second relates to customer tier programs. What is the best number of tiers? Can more tiers encourage higher spending? What are the optimal thresholds that should be employed to shape each tier? With a higher number of tiers there is also higher risk that consumers experience demotion more frequently, with the related negative consequences.

Second, the impact of digital technology is changing how consumers interact with loyalty programs. Many programs can be accessed through smartphone apps where customers can gain points, check in real time their current point status and request their rewards. They can also glean which purchase or non-purchase actions are required to meet a certain threshold. It would be interesting to understand how digital technology can impact the way customers engage with loyalty programs. Is mobile capable of boosting engagement with the loyalty program? Can the mobile channel increase the control customers want to have on their points and program goals?

Third, members of Generation Z (the post-millennials loosely defined as those born between the mid- to late 1990s and 2010) are gaining purchasing power and are emerging as a new and valuable customer segment for companies (see Chapter 1). Previous studies have shown that age plays a significant role in explaining consumer preference for loyalty programs (see Ieva and Ziliani, 2017). However, another study comparing how loyalty is formed among generations (Baby Boomers, Generation X and Generation Y) did not find any generational differences (Whalen Bowen, and Baloglu, 2023). Questions will inevitably arise about the appeal of loyalty programs to this new generation. Will loyalty programs be able to catch the attention of Generation Z? How will the meaning of loyalty differ for this generation? Will the traditional reward catalogue disappear with the rise of digital collections and mobile apps? Should companies adapt their engagement strategies to meet the characteristics of Generation Z? The same questions will arise soon for the upcoming generation, Generation Alpha.

Fourth, in the current omnichannel scenario there is a greater need to identify consumers across channels and especially at every interaction with any touchpoint. loyalty programs could be very important in tracking consumers any time they encounter the brand and they could be integrated with new connected devices and touchpoints, linking traditional data with new types of data such as biometric data, data related to the surrounding environment, etc. If consumers are going to identify themselves by means of the loyalty card, personal code, mobile application or username and password, companies can recognize them, address their complaints and register their preferences and purchase intentions in a seamless way, provided they can reconcile the information across multiple (old and new) touchpoints. loyalty programs, then, could become central to the (re-)design of a true omnichannel strategy that enables a company to deliver a seamless customer experience. Indeed, loyalty programs might just be the starting point to involve the customer, track their purchase and non-purchase activity, and communicate with them in a personalized way.

There is work to be done then. loyalty programs currently absorb a huge amount of efforts and resources, but they are key marketing tools that gain valuable and actionable customer insight and help drive, in certain circumstances, customer attitudes and behaviours. The world of the consumer is rapidly changing, and given the growth of digital technology and the changes in needs and expectations, companies must now keep pace by monitoring and revising their loyalty programs in a way that responds to new challenges and is consistent with all the other touchpoints that contribute to the customer experience.

Note

1 Until recently the AMA published this definition in its online dictionary at www.ama.org, but the dictionary now no longer appears on the website. It is, however, a widely known definition and believed to be the first attempt to categorize loyalty programmes.

References

Antavo (2024) 'Global customer loyalty report'. Retrieved from https://antavo.com/reports/global-customer-loyalty-report-2024 (accessed 4 July 2024).

Arbore, A and Estes, Z. (2013) 'Loyalty program structure and consumers' perceptions of status: feeling special in a grocery store?'. *Journal of Retailing and Consumer Services*, 20(5), 439–444.

Ashley, C., Gillespie, E. A. and Noble, S. M. (2016) 'The effect of loyalty program fees on program perceptions and engagement'. *Journal of Business Research*, 69(2), 964–973.

Banik, S. (2023) 'Exploring the effects of status demotion in hierarchical loyalty programs'. *Journal of Strategic Marketing*, 31(5), 1087–1106.

Baxendale, S., Macdonald, E. K. and Wilson, H. N. (2015) 'The impact of different touchpoints on brand consideration'. *Journal of Retailing*, 91(2), 235–253.

Belli, A., O'Rourke, A. M., Carrillat, F. A., Pupovac, L., Melnyk, V. and Napolova, E. (2022) '40 years of loyalty programs: how effective are they? Generalizations from a meta-analysis.' *Journal of the Academy of Marketing Science*, 50(1), 147–173.

Bellizzi, J. A. and Bristol, T. (2004) 'An assessment of supermarket loyalty cards in one major US market'. *Journal of Consumer Marketing*, 21(2), 144–154.

Berry, J. (2013) 'Bulking up: the 2013 Colloquy loyalty census'. 25 June. Retrieved from www.totalcustomer.org/2013/06/25/whitepaper-download-2013-colloquy-loyalty-census (accessed 24 February 2019).

Bies, S. M., Bronnenberg, B. J. and Gijsbrechts, E. (2021) 'How push messaging impacts consumer spending and reward redemption in store-loyalty programs'. *International Journal of Research in Marketing*, 38(4), 877–899.

Bijmolt, T. H. Dorotic, M. and Verhoef, P. C. (2011) 'Loyalty programs: generalizations on their adoption, effectiveness and design'. *Foundations and Trends in Marketing*, 5(4), 197–258.

Bijmolt, T. H. Krafft, M., Sese, F. J. and Viswanathan, V. (2018) 'Multi-tier loyalty programs to stimulate customer engagement'. In R. W. Palmatier, V. Kumar and C. M. Harmeling (eds), *Customer Engagement Marketing*, 119–139. Cham: Palgrave Macmillan.

Blattberg, R. C., Kim, B. D. and Neslin, S. A. (2008) 'Why database marketing?' In R. C. Blattberg, B. D. Kim and S. A. Neslin (eds), *Database Marketing*, 13–46. New York: Springer.

Bolton, R. N., Kannan, P. K. and Bramlett, M. D. (2000) 'Implications of loyalty program membership and service experiences for customer retention and value'. *Journal of the Academy of Marketing Science*, 28(1), 95–108.

Bombaij, N. J. and Dekimpe, M. G. (2020) 'When do loyalty programs work? The moderating role of design, retailer-strategy, and country characteristics'. *International Journal of Research in Marketing*, 37(1), 175–195.

Bombaij, N. J., Gelper, S. and Dekimpe, M. G. (2022) 'Designing successful temporary loyalty programs: an exploratory study on retailer and country differences'. *International Journal of Research in Marketing*, 39(4), 1275–1295.

Bonezzi, A., Brendl, C. M. and De Angelis, M. (2011) 'Stuck in the middle: the psychophysics of goal pursuit'. *Psychological Science*, 22(5), 607–612.

Brashear-Alejandro, T., Kang, J. and Groza, M. D. (2016) 'Leveraging loyalty programs to build customer–company identification'. *Journal of Business Research*, 69(3), 1190–1198.

Breugelmans, E., Bijmolt, T. H., Zhang, J., Basso, L. J., Dorotic, M., Kopalle, P., Minnema, A., Mijnlieff, W. J. and Wünderlich, N. V. (2015) 'Advancing research on loyalty programs: a future research agenda'. *Marketing Letters*, 26(2), 127–139.

Breugelmans, E. and Liu-Thompkins, Y. (2017) 'The effect of loyalty program expiration policy on consumer behavior'. *Marketing Letters*, 28(4), 537–550.

Bridson, K., Evans, J. and Hickman, M. (2008) 'Assessing the relationship between loyalty program attributes, store satisfaction and store loyalty'. *Journal of Retailing and Consumer Services*, 15(5), 364–374.

Capizzi, M. T. and Ferguson, R. (2005) 'Loyalty trends for the twenty-first century'. *Journal of Consumer Marketing*, 22(2), 72–80.

Chaabane, A. M. and Pez, V. (2017) '"Make me feel special": are hierarchical loyalty programs a panacea for all brands? The role of brand concept'. *Journal of Retailing and Consumer Services*, 38, 108–117.

Chen, Y., Mandler, T. and Meyer-Waarden, L. (2021) 'Three decades of research on loyalty programs: a literature review and future research agenda'. *Journal of Business Research*, 124, 179–197.

Cigliano, J., Georgiadis, M., Pleasance, D. and Whalley, S. (2000) 'The price of loyalty'. *McKinsey Quarterly*, 4, 68–77.

Colliander, J., Söderlund, M. and Szugalski, S. (2016) 'Multi-level loyalty program rewards and their effects on top-tier customers and second-tier customers'. *Journal of Consumer Marketing*, 33(3), 162–171.

Colloquy (2017) 'Loyalty census 2017'. Retrieved from www.the-cma.org/Contents/Item/Display/327325 (accessed 26 February 2019).

Daams, P., Gelderman, K. and Schijns, J. (2008) 'The impact of loyalty programmes in a B-to-B context: results of an experimental design'. *Journal of Targeting, Measurement and Analysis for Marketing*, 16(4), 274–284.

De Noni, I., Orsi, L. and Zanderighi, L. (2014) 'Coalition loyalty-programme adoption and urban commercial-network effectiveness evaluation'. *International Journal of Retail & Distribution Management*, 42(9), 818–838.

Demoulin, N. T. and Zidda, P. (2008) 'On the impact of loyalty cards on store loyalty: does the customers' satisfaction with the reward scheme matter?'. *Journal of Retailing and Consumer Services*, 15(5), 386–398.

Demoulin, N. T. and Zidda, P. (2009) 'Drivers of customers' adoption and adoption timing of a new loyalty card in the grocery retail market'. *Journal of Retailing*, 85(3), 391–405.

Dholakia, U. M. (2006) 'How customer self-determination influences relational marketing outcomes: evidence from longitudinal field studies'. *Journal of Marketing Research*, 43(1), 109–120.

Dorotic, M., Bijmolt, T. H. and Verhoef, P. C. (2012) 'Loyalty programmes: current knowledge and research directions.' *International Journal of Management Reviews*, 14(3), 217–237.

Drèze, X. and Nunes, J. C. (2011) 'Recurring goals and learning: the impact of successful reward attainment on purchase behavior'. *Journal of Marketing Research*, 48(2), 268–281.

Duncan, T. and Moriarty, S. (2006) 'How integrated marketing communication's "touchpoints" can operationalize the service-dominant logic'. In R. F. Lusch and S. L. Vargo (eds), *The Service-Dominant Logic of Marketing: Dialog, Debate, and Directions*, 236–249. Abingdon: Routledge.

Eggert, A., Steinhoff, L. and Garnefeld, I. (2015) 'Managing the bright and dark sides of status endowment in hierarchical loyalty programs'. *Journal of Service Research*, 18(2), 210–228.

Esmark, C. L., Noble, S. M. and Bell, J. E. (2016) 'Open versus selective customer loyalty programmes'. *European Journal of Marketing*, 50(5/6), 770–795.

Flacandji, M., Passebois Ducros, J., and Ieva, M. (2023) 'Redesigning loyalty marketing for a better world: the impact of green loyalty programs on perceived value'. *Journal of Service Theory and Practice*, 33(4), 465–487.

Furinto, A., Pawitra, T. and Balqiah, T. E. (2009) 'Designing competitive loyalty programs: how types of program affect customer equity'. *Journal of Targeting, Measurement and Analysis for Marketing*, 17(4), 307–319.

Gómez, B. G., Arranz, A. M. G. and Cillán, J. G. (2012) 'Drivers of customer likelihood to join grocery retail loyalty programs: an analysis of reward programs and loyalty cards'. *Journal of Retailing and Consumer Services*, 19(5), 492–500.

Gopalakrishnan, A., Jiang, Z., Nevskaya, Y. and Thomadsen, R. (2021). 'Can non-tiered customer loyalty programs be profitable?'. *Marketing Science*, 40(3), 508–526.

Gorlier, T. and Michel, G. (2020) 'How special rewards in loyalty programs enrich consumer–brand relationships: The role of self-expansion'. *Psychology & Marketing*, 37(4), 588–603.

Hansen, J. D., Deitz, G. D. and Morgan, R. M. (2010) 'Taxonomy of service-based loyalty program members'. *Journal of Services Marketing*, 24(4), 271–282.

Humby, C., Hunt, T, and Phillips, T. (2003) *Scoring Points: How Tesco is Winning Customer Loyalty*. London: Kogan Press.

Hwang, J. H., Chung, J., Kim, J. W., Lee, D. and Yoo, W. S. (2016) 'Antecedents to loyalty point redemption: implications for customer equity management'. *Journal of Business Research*, 69(9), 3731–3739.

Ieva, M. and Ziliani, C. (2017) The interplay between customer experience and customer loyalty: which touchpoints matter. Paper presented at *20th Excellence in Services International Conference*, University of Verona, Verona, Italy, 7–8 September.

Ieva, M. and Ziliani, C. (2018a) 'Mapping touchpoint exposure in retailing: implications for developing an omnichannel customer experience'. *International Journal of Retail & Distribution Management*, 46(3), 304–322.

Ieva, M. and Ziliani, C. (2018b) 'The role of customer experience touchpoints in driving loyalty intentions in services'. *The TQM Journal*, 30(5), 444–457.

Iyengar, R., Park, Y. H. and Yu, Q. (2022) 'The impact of subscription programs on customer purchases'. *Journal of Marketing Research*, 59(6), 1101–1119.

Jin, L. and Huang, Y. (2014) 'When giving money does not work: the differential effects of monetary versus in-kind rewards in referral reward programs'. *International Journal of Research in Marketing*, 31(1), 107–116.

Kang, J., Brashear-Alejandro, T.and Groza, M. D. (2015) 'Customer–company identification and the effectiveness of loyalty programs'. *Journal of Business Research*, 68(2), 464–471.

Keh, H. T. and Lee, Y. H. (2006) 'Do reward programs build loyalty for services? The moderating effect of satisfaction on type and timing of rewards'. *Journal of Retailing*, 82(2), 127–136.

Kim, J. J., Steinhoff, L. and Palmatier, R. W. (2021) 'An emerging theory of loyalty program dynamics'. *Journal of the Academy of Marketing Science*, 49(1), 71–95.

Kopalle, P. K. and Neslin, S. A. (2003) 'The economic viability of frequency reward programs in a strategic competitive environment'. *Review of Marketing Science*, 1(1), 1–39.

Kopalle, P., Neslin, S. and Sun, B. (2009) 'A dynamic structural model of the impact of loyalty programs on customer behavior'. In S. Samu, R. Vaidyanathan and D. Chakravarti (eds), *AP – Asia-Pacific Advances in Consumer Research*, vol. 8, 265–266. Duluth, MN: Association for Consumer Research.

Kopalle, P. K., Sun, Y., Neslin, S. A., Sun, B. and Swaminathan, V. (2012) 'The joint sales impact of frequency reward and customer tier components of loyalty programs'. *Marketing Science*, 31(2), 216–235.

Ku, H. H., Yang, P. H. and Chang, C. L. (2018) 'Reminding customers to be loyal: does message framing matter?' *European Journal of Marketing*, 52(3/4), 783–810.

Kumar, V. and Reinartz, W. (2018) 'Loyalty programs: design and effectiveness'. In V. Kumar and W. Reinartz (eds), *Customer Relationship Management*, 179–205. Heidelberg: Springer.

Lal, R. and Bell, D. E. (2003) 'The impact of frequent shopper programs in grocery retailing'. *Quantitative Marketing and Economics*, 1(2), 179–202.

Leenheer, J., Van Heerde, H. J., Bijmolt, T. H. and Smidts, A. (2007) 'Do loyalty programs really enhance behavioral loyalty? An empirical analysis accounting for self-selecting members'. *International Journal of Research in Marketing*, 24(1), 31–47.

Li, C., Swaminathan, S. and Kim, J. (2024) 'Point redemption in loyalty programs: the role of customer relationship characteristics and their implications for service providers'. *Journal of Service Research*, online ahead of print.

Liu, Y. (2007) 'The long-term impact of loyalty programs on consumer purchase behavior and loyalty'. *Journal of Marketing*, 71(4), 19–35.

Liu, Y. and Yang, R. (2009) 'Competing loyalty programs: impact of market saturation, market share, and category expandability'. *Journal of Marketing*, 73(1), 93–108.

Ma, B., Li, X. and Zhang, L. (2018) 'The effects of loyalty programs in services: a double-edged sword?' *Journal of Services Marketing*, 32(3), 300–310.

Melnyk, V. and Bijmolt, T. (2015) 'The effects of introducing and terminating loyalty programs'. *European Journal of Marketing*, 49(3/4), 398–419.

Meyer-Waarden, L. (2008) 'The influence of loyalty programme membership on customer purchase behaviour'. *European Journal of Marketing*, 42(1/2), 87–114.

Meyer-Waarden, L. (2015) 'Effects of loyalty program rewards on store loyalty'. *Journal of Retailing and Consumer Services*, 24, 22–32.

Meyer-Waarden, L. and Benavent, C. (2006) 'The impact of loyalty programmes on repeat purchase behaviour'. *Journal of Marketing Management*, 22(1–2), 61–88.

Minnema, A., Bijmolt, T. H. and Non, M. C. (2017) 'The impact of instant reward programs and bonus premiums on consumer purchase behavior'. *International Journal of Research in Marketing*, 34(1), 194–211.

Mohd-Ramly, S. and Omar, N. A. (2017) 'Exploring the influence of store attributes on customer experience and customer engagement'. *International Journal of Retail & Distribution Management*, 45(11), 1138–1158.

Moore, G. and Sekhon, H. (2005) 'Multi-brand loyalty cards: a good idea'. *Journal of Marketing Management*, 21(5–6), 625–640.

Nath, S. (2005) 'Choosing the right loyalty programme'. *European Retail Digest*, 48(3), 53–56.

Orsingher, C. and Wirtz, J. (2018) 'Psychological drivers of referral reward program effectiveness'. *Journal of Services Marketing*, 32(3), 256–268.

Pick, D. and Eisend, M. (2014) 'Buyers' perceived switching costs and switching: a meta-analytic assessment of their antecedents'. *Journal of the Academy of Marketing Science*, 42(2), 186–204.

Raggio, R. D., Walz, A. M., Godbole, M. B. and Folse, J. A. G. (2013) 'Gratitude in relationship marketing: theoretical development and directions for future research'. *European Journal of Marketing*, 48(1/2), 2–24.

Ramaseshan, B. and Ouschan, R. (2017) 'Investigating status demotion in hierarchical loyalty programs'. *Journal of Services Marketing*, 31(6), 650–661.

Roehm, M. L. and Roehm, H. A. (2011) 'The influence of redemption time frame on responses to incentives'. *Journal of the Academy of Marketing Science*, 39(3), 363–375.

Romaniuk, J., Beal, V. and Uncles, M. (2013) 'Achieving reach in a multi-media environment: how a marketer's first step provides the direction for the second'. *Journal of Advertising Research*, 53(2), 221–230.

Schumann, J. H., Wünderlich, N. V. and Evanschitzky, H. (2014) 'Spillover effects of service failures in coalition loyalty programs: the buffering effect of special treatment benefits'. *Journal of Retailing*, 90(1), 111–118.

Söderlund, M. (2019) 'Can the label "member" in a loyalty program context boost customer satisfaction?'. *The International Review of Retail, Distribution and Consumer Research*, 29(3), 340–357.

Stathopoulou, A. and Balabanis, G. (2016) 'The effects of loyalty programs on customer satisfaction, trust, and loyalty toward high-and low-end fashion retailers'. *Journal of Business Research*, 69(12), 5801–5808.

Steinhoff, L. and Palmatier, R. W. (2016) 'Understanding loyalty program effectiveness: managing target and bystander effects'. *Journal of the Academy of Marketing Science*, 44(1), 88–107.

Steinhoff, L., and Zondag, M. M. (2021) 'Loyalty programs as travel companions: complementary service features across customer journey stages'. *Journal of Business Research*, 129, 70–82.

Taylor, G. A. and Neslin, S. A. (2005) 'The current and future sales impact of a retail frequency reward program'. *Journal of Retailing*, 81(4), 293–305.

Taylor, M., Buvat, J., Nambiar, R., Singh, R. R. and Radhakrishnan, A. (2015) 'Fixing the cracks: reinventing loyalty programs for the digital age'. Retrieved from www.capgemini.com/resources/fixing-the-cracks-reinventing-loyalty-programs-for-the-digital-age (accessed 26 February 2019).

Van Berlo, G., Bloemer, J. and Blazevic, V. (2014) 'Customer demotion in hierarchical loyalty programmes'. *The Service Industries Journal*, 34(11), 922–937.

Verhoef, P. C. (2003) 'Understanding the effect of customer relationship management efforts on customer retention and customer share development'. *Journal of Marketing*, 67(4), 30–45.

Verhoef, P. C., Lemon, K. N., Parasuraman, A., Roggeveen, A., Tsiros, M. and Schlesinger, L. A. (2009) 'Customer experience creation: determinants, dynamics and management strategies'. *Journal of Retailing*, 85(1), 31–41.

Vilches-Montero, S., Pandit, A., Bravo-Olavarria, R. and Chao, C. W. F. (2018) 'What loyal women (and men) want: the role of gender and loyalty program characteristics in driving store loyalty'. *Journal of Retailing and Consumer Services*, 44, 64–70.

Whalen, E. A., Bowen, J. T. and Baloglu, S. (2023) 'Comparison of generational loyalty models and loyalty programs for Millennial, Generation X, and Baby Boomer hotel customers'. *Journal of Hospitality and Tourism Insights*, 7(4), 2328–2346.

Wind, Y. J. and Hays, C. F. (2016) 'Research implications of the "beyond advertising" paradigm: a model and roadmap for creating value through all media and non-media touchpoints'. *Journal of Advertising Research*, 56(2), 142–158.

Yu, I., Liu, C., Yang, M. X. and Zeng, K. J. (2022) 'Looking-forward or looking-back: feedback strategies in tier-based hotel loyalty programs'. *International Journal of Hospitality Management*, 102, 103164.

Zhang, J. and Liu-Thompkins, Y. (2024) 'Personalized email marketing in loyalty programs: the role of multidimensional construal levels'. *Journal of the Academy of Marketing Science*, 52(1), 196–216.

Ziliani, C. and Ieva, M. (2018) 'The role of touchpoints in driving loyalty: implications for omnichannel retailing'. *Micro & Macro Marketing*, 27(3), 375–396.

5

MANAGING CUSTOMER EXPERIENCE TO FOSTER LOYALTY

Marco Ieva and Giada Salvietti

Customer experience as a multidimensional concept

In one of the most important and seminal articles on customer experience, Pine and Gilmore (1998) pointed out that consumers were seeking not just products and services but also experiences. To understand to what extent an experience differs from a service, it is worth recalling the brilliant example provided by these two authors in their article. They referred to an American TV series: *Taxi*. In this sitcom, Iggy, a cab driver, aims to be the best taxi driver in the world. As part of this goal, he transforms the standard taxi ride into a true experience by serving sandwiches and drinks, conducting tours of the city, and singing Frank Sinatra songs. Iggy wants to engage his customers and create a memorable experience that is distinct from the service itself. The taxi service is just the setting for the whole experience. Pine and Gilmore's article on the 'experience economy' was to kickstart a proliferation of studies focusing on customer experience. An emerging concept in the late 1990s, customer experience now plays a key role for practitioners and academics. The proliferation of channels has dramatically increased the number of opportunities for interactions between consumers and companies within the customer journey (Hall and Towers, 2017). This is putting increasing pressure on companies to design and manage the customer experience in a seamless way across multiple channels.

Before we talk about customer experience in a book about loyalty management, it is important to clarify what we mean by it. We deem it necessary to focus on the definition and explanation of this concept by highlighting the different stages of its theoretical development.

Attempts to define it were made by Holbrook and Hirschman (1982), Pine and Gilmore (1998) and Schmitt (1999). These authors focused on the role

DOI: 10.4324/9781003400783-5

of emotions and feelings that consumers experience in the whole shopping process and thus adopted an experiential view of consumer behaviour. They pointed out that companies are called to sell personal and memorable experiences rather than simply products and services. Developing entertaining experiences, then, is now seen as a task not confined to the entertainment industry but one to be embraced by companies in different industries. In the contributions to this area that followed (e.g. Addis and Holbrook, 2001; LaSalle and Britton, 2003), the whole consumption process starts to be considered as an experience: the involvement in the experience is recognized to occur at different levels (emotional, cognitive, etc.) and takes place at every interaction between the company and the consumer. Just selling memorable experiences then is not enough. Companies are called to take a further step. They should design and manage the customer experience at every interaction between the company and the customers to match their expectations.

Lipkin (2016) offers a comprehensive classification of the literature in this area by identifying two streams of studies: one regards the customer experience as a subjective experience, the other stresses the contextual and event-specific element of it. In the first stream, customer experience is seen as a subjective experience that occurs due to external stimuli that are capable of influencing how customers perceive a given experience. In this respect, these studies do not see the customer as a passive receiver of external stimuli but take into account the two-way interactions that occur between customers and companies. Within the contextual approach, customer experience is seen as created and co-created through multiple touchpoints. Along this line, Carù and Cova (2007) argue that customers live a continuum of consumption experiences. These experiences can be constructed by the consumer themselves, developed by the company, or co-created by the company and the consumer.

In more recent years, academics have increased their efforts to define customer experience by issuing several definitions that could help to clarify the concept. The most important and widely accepted definitions of customer experience available both in business and academia are:

- 'Customer experience is the internal and subjective response customers have to any direct or indirect contact with a company' (Meyer and Schwager, 2007, p. 2).
- 'Customer experience is comprised of the cognitive, emotional, physical, sensorial, spiritual, and social elements that mark the customer's direct or indirect interaction with (an)other market actor(s)' (De Keyser et al., 2015, p. 23).
- 'Overall, we thus conclude that customer experience is a multidimensional construct focusing on a customer's cognitive, emotional, behavioral, sensorial, and social responses to a firm's offerings during the customer's entire purchase journey' (Lemon and Verhoef, 2016, p. 71).

- 'Customer experience is the evolvement of a person's sensorial, affective, cognitive, relational, and behavioural responses to a firm or brand by living through a journey of touchpoints along pre-purchase, purchase, and post-purchase situations' (Homburg et al., 2017, p. 8).

These definitions highlight several key characteristics of the customer experience:

- It is a complex and multidimensional construct that involves multiple components that are cognitive, emotional, behavioural, sensorial and social.
- It is strictly personal in that it might engage each customer differently as far as each level is concerned (e.g. rational, emotional, sensorial, physical).
- Even though it has a strong personal nature, it occurs in social environments; customer experience is therefore shared within institutional and social structures that make its nature as interpersonal.
- It has a temporal dimension based on contact with a whole set of touchpoints that allow customers to encounter a given company; for this reason, it should be seen as a continuum in time, given that relationships with customers are increasingly based on multiple interactions (Klaus et al., 2013).
- It is a dynamic process that cannot be restricted to just the purchase or the service delivery stage; on the contrary, it encompasses the whole customer journey across all the different situations before, during and after the purchase.

The multidimensionality of the customer experience is a key conclusion coming from all the presented definitions (Bonfanti, 2018). Customer experience has indeed a multidimensional structure composed of elementary components (Gentile et al., 2007). Moreover, the customer experience can be intended as a general and broad concept. However, it could also specifically refer to particular aspects of a company offering, such as a brand (e.g. Brakus et al., 2009) or the service offer, or even the store or website (Verhoef et al., 2009; Bustamante and Rubio, 2017). This reveals the need for both practitioners and academics to define and shape the customer experience by taking into account the diverse contextual factors that may contribute to it. As such, it is worth briefly describing the four key constructs of customer experience:

- brand experience
- service experience
- retail customer experience
- online customer experience.

Brand experience

The definition of brand experience starts from the consideration that consumers encounter various specific brand-related stimuli, namely brand-identifying colours, brand shapes, slogans, mascots, and brand characters. These elements are strongly related the brand identity (e.g. logo), its packaging, and marketing communications (e.g. advertisements) and can be associated with all the environments and situations where the brand is marketed or sold (e.g. stores, events). Thus, Brakus et al. (2009, p. 53) conceptualize brand experience as: 'subjective, internal consumer responses (sensations, feelings, and cognitions) and behavioural responses evoked by brand-related stimuli that are part of a brand's design and identity, packaging, communications, and environments.' They posit that brand experience consists of four separate, though related, dimensions: sensory, affective, intellectual and behavioural. Brand experiences may vary in intensity, in valence and in time: they can be strong or weak, positive or negative, long or very short.

Service experience

Service experience is a key construct in the service domain to understanding value creation and concerns the consumption of experiences rather than goods (Jain et al., 2017). According to Jaakkola et al. (2015), service experience involves dynamic, experiential and relational activities and interactions. It is important to distinguish between customer experience and service experience, since they are often used to refer to the same concept. As highlighted by Bustamante and Rubio (2017), customer experience and service experience should not be used interchangeably; while service experience is limited to the subject who is actually experiencing the service, customer experience includes all the direct and indirect interactions occurring between the customer and the entity that is providing the experience.

Retail customer experience

In the retailing context, customer experiences specifically stem from the interaction with the different elements of the retail mix (i.e. price experience, promotion experience). This in-store experience arises from both elements that are under (e.g. merchandising) and outside (e.g. influence from peers) the control of the retailer. The in-store/retail customer experience specifically takes into account the cognitive, emotional, social and physical responses to a service that results from the customer shopping visit to the physical retail store (Bustamante and Rubio, 2017).

Online customer experience

Finally, customer experience may be referred to the online context. This distinction stems from the consideration that those involved in online experiences are not only shoppers but visitors and actual users of a technological system (Cho and Park, 2001). For this reason, academics have developed a specific construct, namely the online customer experience or online shopping experience. Klaus et al. (2013, p. 445) define the online customer experience as the 'customers' mental perception of interactions with a company's value proposition online. These mental perceptions in turn drive a set of outcomes, namely benefits, emotions, judgments (including perceived value) and intentions.' Rose et al. (2012) specifically develop a concept of online customer experience as a psychological state in the form of a subjective response to the digital assets of the retailer. Specifically, the customer undertakes a cognitive and affective processing of information stemming from the website. Trevinal and Stenger (2014, p. 324) define the online shopping experience as 'a holistic and subjective process resulting from interactions between consumers, shopping practices (including tools and routines) and the online environment (e.g. shopping websites, online consumer reviews, and social media)'. They highlight the complexity of this type of customer experience, given that online shoppers interact in both online and offline contexts (in a specific place, time, with or without a companion's presence …). As it will be further discussed such complexity has later led to new constructs of customer experiences that take into account customers' seamless journeys across online and offline environments.

Dimensions of customer experience

In the studies on the different types of customer experience, there are similarities and differences in how they identify its dimensions. Presented below is a summary of the six dimensions of customer experience that have been identified by the main studies on the topic: cognitive, emotional, social, sensorial, physical and lifestyle. These dimensions are also referred to as strategic experiential modules (Schmitt, 1999). Customer experience is conceptualized as the 'sum' of cognitions, feelings, sensations, and social and physical responses triggered by an experience provider.

Cognitive dimension

The cognitive dimension of the customer experience (some authors refer to this dimension as intellectual) has to do with all the cognitive efforts occurring during the experience. For instance, while a customer is in the store, he or she might be involved in thinking about the displayed assortment or about how a given product could be used to achieve a given outcome. Cognition is defined as the ability to process information acquired from what individuals perceive and learn and from their subjective characteristics (Bustamante and Rubio, 2017). Scholars claim that cognition is the first state of the customer experience occurring before the affective response, because cognition primarily processes acquired knowledge (Vinhas Da Silva and Faridah Syed Alwi, 2006). The cognitive dimension of the customer experience has to do with all the mental responses to the brand or store stimuli that involve customers (Schmitt, 1999). To clarify, mental responses are basically thoughts, ideas, or memories, among others (Bustamante and Rubio, 2017). The creativity or the problem-solving skills of the customer could be stimulated by the offering of a given brand and retailer, leading to an increase in their attention to, for example, the product quality and the displayed information. Positive thoughts and memories could be elicited when in contact with a given product, brand or store. In turn, these cognitive responses are supposed to lead to strong, enduring attitudes towards the object if the stimulus has sufficiently persuasive content (Wright, 1973).

Emotional dimension

The affective or emotional component relates to the generation of emotions and moods within the affective system. The affective system can be defined as a 'valenced feeling state', that includes emotions and moods as key elements (Richins, 1997). There is a difference between emotions and moods: the former is related to stimuli that elicit them and are usually stronger, while moods tend not to be linked with a specific stimulus and are lower in intensity (Erevelles, 1998). With reference to the customer experience, the affective dimension largely involves emotions rather than moods given that the experience is created by responses to stimuli, specifically touchpoints (Bustamante and Rubio, 2017). Emotions are mental states arising as a consequence of cognitive evaluations of events or thoughts and are usually associated with physical reactions, such as facial expressions or body movements (Cacioppo and Gardner, 1999). We can refer to emotions such as interest, joy, surprise, sadness, anger and disgust. Emotions are very powerful drivers of behaviour, and they have the potential to influence how individuals process information.

Why are they so important to the customer experience? Marketing stimuli have the potential to drive consumers to feel emotions that shape affective experiences (Bustamante and Rubio, 2017). Positive affective experiences can then have a positive impact on multiple customer behaviours that are key for companies, such as positive word of mouth, intention to re-patronize a store and willingness to pay more. Emotions can also be negative and can negatively influence the development of positive experiences and the related customer behaviours. This is why when considering the affective dimension of customer experience both positive and negative emotions should be taken into account (Fornerino et al., 2006).

Social dimension

The social (or relational) dimension of the customer experience is gaining increasing relevance due to the growth of social media and the proliferation of touchpoints that allow consumers to interact not only with the company but also with each other. The social component has to do with the extent of human interaction that takes place in online and offline environments and to the social identity of an individual and his or her linkage to a specific group of people (Brun et al., 2017; Bustamante and Rubio, 2017). In this respect, it is believed that the social context – which involves the whole set of interactions and relationships among people – of the experience is relevant to influence how consumers live this experience. Two key elements shape the social dimension of the customer experience: consumer-to-consumer and employee-to-consumer interactions. Companies are willing to leverage the social aspects of the experience by encouraging consumers to consume products together, to feel a part of a community that shares not only the products but the values and ideals that are related to those products. Moreover, previous research has shown that peer observation is a very influential touchpoint in retailing (Baxendale et al., 2015). Hence, the social context is not only capable of providing an 'augmented' experience but also of directly influencing how the experience takes place. In the offline environment, the retail store is a natural drive of human interactions: shoppers meet sales assistants and other shoppers and social relationships are built (Hu and Jasper, 2006). As far as the online environment is concerned, social media, messenger applications such as WhatsApp and Telegram and online customer support such as live chats are key drivers of online human interactions.

Sensorial dimension

The sensorial component of the customer experience is related to how external stimuli affect the senses of consumers (Gentile et al., 2007). Hence, it has to do with the perception of experience through the senses: sight, hearing, touch, taste and smell (Brun et al., 2017). Different means could be employed to enhance the sensorial dimension of the customer experience. The usage of a particular smell, the control of light and music in the store, the design and the images employed in the development of a website could all elicit a sensory response in consumers. This could have an impact on how consumers perceive their experience with the brand or in the store.

Physical dimension

The physical (or pragmatic/behavioural) component was identified by Bustamante and Rubio (2017) when studying the in-store customer experience as a physiological response to environmental stimuli in the store. This response is intended as a state of comfort or lack of comfort that is elicited by the environment. This is a dimension that is specific to the in-store customer experience and that could be assimilated, to a certain extent, to the pragmatic/behavioural dimension that has been identified when conceptualizing customer experience in general terms (Bustamante and Rubio, 2017). As a matter of fact, the pragmatic/behavioural component has to do with all the physical acts that characterize a given experience. Gentile et al. (2007) highlight that this specific dimension should not be considered as usability, because it is does not simply refer to the usage of a product after the purchase. This component embraces all the actions undertaken at the different stages of the customer journey. As Brun et al. (2017) point out, there is no consensus among scholars on the measurement of this dimension. According to Brun et al. there are two main issues that hamper it. First, this dimension is very hard to capture in some industries such as banking where customers do not engage in particular behaviours. Second, the measures employed to identify the behavioural dimension might not only be related to the experience itself. For instance, reviewing many times the bank account has been employed is one indicator to measure the behavioural dimension of the customer experience in banking. However, this type of behaviour is also strongly correlated with consumer perceived risk.

Lifestyle dimension

The lifestyle dimension has been identified by Gentile et al. (2007) and further developed by Trevinal and Stenger (2014). These authors conceptualize it as the summary of values and beliefs that become manifest by behaving in a certain consistent manner, hence by consistently adopting a lifestyle. Trevinal and Stenger found in their qualitative study that this component is largely evident across three key elements: shopping orientation (that could be hedonistic/utilitarian), the daily routines that are associated with online shopping, and individual values, such as privacy concerns and political issues, that are related to shopping choices. This component has not been studied and quantitatively measured in further studies. We could argue that scholars might find it challenging to capture the specific characteristics of this dimension, given that expressing a lifestyle is something that might include, for instance, sensorial, physical and cognitive aspects of the customer experience.

Understanding each dimension and how they differ offers the possibility of measuring the customer experience and making it actionable for marketers.

The development of a proper measure of customer experience is the concern of the next section.

Measuring customer experience

Measuring customer experience has been regarded both as a pressing marketing issue (Verhoef et al., 2009) and a very challenging task in marketing research for academics and practitioners (Lemon and Verhoef, 2016; Flacandji and Krey, 2020). Despite the challenge, measuring something is the first step towards managing it. Companies that are able to measure and identify strengths and weaknesses of the customer experience that they deliver can change how they design and implement it. Palmer (2010) already predicted that measuring customer experience would be a key but at complex issue for academics.

Lemon and Verhoef (2016) provide a rich description of the key challenges and metrics that have been adopted in marketing in the last 20 years by researchers and managers to try to tackle this challenge. By updating their valuable work with the most recent developments in customer experience measurement, we could summarize the different available measures of customer experience in four segments:

- customer feedback metrics
- service experience quality
- measures based on strategic experiential modules
- shopping experience memory scale

By employing these metrics, managers can measure customer experience at different levels. First, customer experience could be measured with reference to the most recent experience of the customer or as a summary of multiple experiences that occur in a given period of time. Second, customer experience could be measured with reference to a specific touchpoint (e.g. the experience with the customer service), with an environment (e.g. the in-store customer experience) or with the set of touchpoints encountered in different environments. Depending on the needs of the company, measures can be customized and results interpreted accordingly.

All four groups of metrics have something in common: they are based on surveys of customers and not on behavioural data or other sources. This, of course, carries both advantages and limitations. The survey allows companies to extract more detailed information on the customer experience and to discover the drivers of a given behaviour. However, running a survey involves taking many decisions that can significantly influence the final results: the sampling, the wording of questions, the channel employed to administer the survey, the means undertaken to address the non-response and response biases.

Not to even mention the risk that the engaged respondents fill in the survey without paying attention to the questions just to achieve the reward related to survey completion. And this is in line with recent criticism that has arisen around the usage of panels of respondents such as Amazon MTurk (Ford, 2017). Hence, despite the following discussion on which metric is more appropriate to represent and summarize the customer experience, the methodological rigour adopted to administer any survey is critical to a successful measurement. A good expression summarizing this point is a wisdom known among many researchers: doing research is more a matter of bias management. Thus paying attention to reducing biases in research should be the first concern when running a survey. Now the reader is sufficiently worried about the potential influence of researchers on results, let us review in detail the different categories of metrics!

Customer feedback metrics

Customer feedback metrics are measures that aim to capture how customers perceive a part of the whole experience with the company or a brief summary of the whole experience (Lemon and Verhoef, 2016). Just to make it clear, the two most popular metrics in this category are customer satisfaction and net promoter score, which we discussed in Chapter 1. One relevant difference between them is that, according to Zeithaml et al. (2006), net promoter score is more suitable to measuring future behaviour, whereas satisfaction is oriented towards measuring past behaviour as far as the relationship with the company is concerned. We could, rather, see these metrics as a proxy for customer experience measures rather than true ones.

The reader might justifiably ask, then, why customer satisfaction and net promoter scores are employed at all. The answer lies in the fact that these two metrics are quite simple; both are generated from answers given by respondents and analysed by companies. Moreover, even if we are to consider them proxies for true measurement, there is evidence of a significant, if small (according to some reported cases), correlation between these two metrics and firm revenue growth and other financial metrics (see e.g. Reichheld, 2003; Keiningham et al., 2007; Van Doorn et al., 2013). Hence, we could assume that an increase in customer satisfaction or in the net promoter score might be somehow related to an increase, for instance, in revenues. Intuitively, this has a certain appeal to marketers who are maybe obliged to rely on such simple metrics rather than look for more complex and insightful alternatives.

Service experience quality

The second group of metrics refers to the service experience quality metrics that have been developed in recent years, starting with the work of Parasuraman et al.

(1988) and Zeithaml et al. (1996) and progressing to the measures developed by Klaus and Maklan (2012) and Klaus et al. (2013). In this respect, it is important to stress, as highlighted by Bustamante and Rubio (2017), that this group of measures has been developed by researchers in the domain of services marketing that tend to consider customer experience and service experience as interchangeable concepts. Moreover, all these measures are multi-item scales.

The service quality measure (SERVQUAL) developed by Parasuraman and his colleagues is a reliable and multidimensional measure that has been employed as a proxy for customer experience. Its importance and relevance can be understood just by looking at the citation metrics of the article that launched this measure in 1988. According to Google Scholar, more than 30,000 academic and non-academic works have cited it in 30 years. The SERVQUAL was developed to measure perceived quality, which is the overall consumer evaluation of an entity in terms of excellence or superiority (Parasuraman et al., 1988).

It is a multidimensional scale, given that it measures perceived quality across five different dimensions: reliability, assurance, tangibles, empathy and responsiveness. SERVQUAL is employed to provide an evaluation of the perceived quality of a service both at the level of each of these five service dimensions and at the overall level, across them all. The five dimensions can be explained as follows:

- Tangibles: the perceived quality of physical facilities, equipment and appearance of personnel.
- Reliability: the extent to which the company is capable of performing the service in a precise and reliable manner.
- Responsiveness: the extent to which the company is available and willing to support customers and provide help promptly.
- Assurance: the ability of the company, through their staff, to show knowledge and friendliness and to develop trust in its customers.
- Empathy: the extent to which the company is able to devote personal and careful attention to each customer to express caring with respect to his or her needs.

It is evident that this measure is not capable of capturing the full meaning of the customer experience nor measuring each of the customer experience dimensions. However, this is indeed a good starting point towards the assessment of the quality of the service experienced by customers.

As a matter of fact, starting from the concept of service quality, Klaus and Maklan (2012) have adopted a measurement of customer experience that is based on how customers perceive or subjectively judge the components of the service experience, namely service experience quality. In this respect, service experience quality is considered as an updated formulation of the traditional service quality concept. In their conceptualization, Klaus and Maklan (2012) argue that specific and concrete service attributes are the drivers of perceptual attributes. These perceptual attributes, which are consumer evaluations of the service, are the elements that define the four customer experience quality dimensions: product experience, outcome focus, moments of truth and peace of mind. The dimensions can be described as follows:

- Product experience could be considered the extent to which the customer perceives that they have multiple options to choose from and that they can compare offers. In this respect, the authors are referring to the customer's feeling of choosing what they prefer at any stage of the shopping process. Moreover, this dimension also involves the feeling of being under the ongoing care of the company that makes the whole shopping experience very easy and smooth.
- Outcome focus has to do with the orientation that customers have to stick with the same company in order to get the desired results rather than look for offerings from competitors or question the quality of the offering of the current provider.
- Moments of truth refer to the extent to which the customer perceives that the company was flexible and caring enough to meet their needs and to manage service failures or critical requests in the proper manner. This dimension also includes the perceived risk felt by customers during these interactions, namely the perceived risk that is related to a service failure or to a pain point.
- Finally, peace of mind involves the evaluation of all the interactions between the customer and the service provider, taking into consideration all the stages of the customer journey. This dimension is more related to the emotional aspects of the experience with the service provider and the creation of a relational bond between customer and company.

Klaus and Maklan incorporate these four dimensions in the final scale, which they call the customer experience quality (EXQ) scale and which they adopt as a general measure of customer experience in further works (e.g. Klaus and Maklan, 2013). The EXQ scale is based on the customer point of view, captures the value of a company offer when it is experienced by the customer, encompasses the stages before and after the service delivery and considers behavioural and intentional measures (Klaus et al., 2013). Despite these strengths, Klaus et al. (2013) do point to the limitation of EXQ, which is its limited empirical validation, and develop the scale further in the banking context. This last work results in quite a change to the EXQ scale. Four dimensions become three: brand experience (not to be confused with that developed by Brakus et al., 2009), service (provider) experience and post-purchase experience. These three new dimensions can be described thus:

- Brand experience involves how the customer perceives the brand and all the elements that are employed to take a decision in the pre-purchase stage of the customer journey.
- Service (provider) experience is associated with the customer–company interaction; specifically, in the case of the banking industry, it has to do with the bank branch, the staff and the specifics of the banking service that is provided. This dimension is related to accessibility, how the service delivery works, evaluation of the personal interactions undertaken and the setting of service delivery.
- Post-purchase/consumption experience is related to the part of the experience that follows service delivery, such as the development of the relationship with the company, the attachment to the company and service recovery situations.

This review of the development and further validation of the EXQ scale in its different versions leads us to formulate several considerations:

- In terms of actionability, the EXQ could indeed be appealing to practitioners and even easy to interpret for customers, given that each dimension is related to concrete situations in the experience with the service provider.
- The EXQ might have some issues in terms of generalizability, given that it seems more appropriate to measure the experience in services rather than the customer experience in other contexts. Nevertheless, a follow-up study by Kuppelweiser and Klaus (2021) demonstrated the validity of the EXQ scale in both B2B and B2C contexts, thus improving the operationalization of customer experience management in different contexts.
- The four dimensions identified by the scale seem not to be in line with the generally employed conceptualization of the customer experience as a multidimensional construct that involves cognitive, affective, sensorial, social and behavioural dimensions; this is, of course, due to the different theoretical background on which the scale relies.

Despite its limitations (outlined by Lemon and Verhoef, 2016), the EXQ has been recently employed as a measure of the customer experience, namely by Roy (2018), thus proving to still be an actionable option for both scholars and practitioners. In the fourth paragraph we will describe in details the implications of the results from Roy's study.

Measures based on strategic experiential modules

The third group of customer experience metrics has been developed in alignment with the conceptual framework of Schmitt (1999) that identifies strategic experiential modules. In this respect, customer experience is seen as the mixture of cognitions, feelings, sensorial, social and physical responses driven by the provider of the experience (Bustamante and Rubio, 2017). Therefore, these measures seem more in line with the conceptual framework of customer experience that has attracted the most attention and support among scholars. This typology of scales seeks to capture the result of a continuum of multiple experiences that occur throughout a series of interactions between the consumer and the stimuli that are somewhat related to the company. Hence, the respondent is supposed to recall what he or she has stored in their long-term memory.

In this area, we can find different types of measures of customer experience that are related to the setting where the experience takes place or that attempt to measure the experience with a specific entity, for instance a brand or store. In this respect, we can identify several strategic experiential modules scales:

- Brand experience scale, as developed by Brakus et al. (2009).
- In-store/retail customer experience scale, as developed by Bustamante and Rubio (2017) (while some previous scales exist, they could be considered the first to attempt it in this domain).
- General customer experience scales applied to specific contexts such as retailing, retail banking or travelling; Brun et al. (2017) and Srivastava and Kaul (2016) provide some examples of scales developed from the work of Schmitt (1999), Gentile et al. (2007) and Brakus et al. (2009).

According to Brakus et al. (2009), the brand experience scale aims to measure four experience dimensions – sense, feel, think and act. In their conceptualization, brand-related stimuli such as colour, shape, design, slogans and brand characters have the potential to impact one or multiple experience dimensions at the same time. The twelve items of the scale, in the view of the authors, measure the extent, namely the intensity, to which the respondent has lived an experience with a brand along the sensory, affective, intellectual or behavioural dimensions. Is the experience emotionally intense? Does it trigger the customer to think? Does it drive their senses? How far does the experience with the brand invite the customer to act or to complete certain actions due to brand-related stimuli? Moreover, it is worth highlighting that this scale is not aimed at capturing the outcomes of just one cross-sectional incident with the brand but measures the experience stemming from a series of multiple interactions between the customer and all the different brand-related stimuli.

This scale, then, could be useful to managers and practitioners willing to assess the extent a brand is able to involve its customers and to understand the impact that the experience with a given brand might have on other consumer attitudes, such as brand personality, satisfaction and loyalty.

The in-store/retail customer experience scale developed by Bustamante and Rubio (2017) aims to capture the specific experience lived by the customer in the physical store. The authors of the scale conceptualize the in-store customer experience as a subjective internal response to all the elements that are part of the physical environment of the store. Among these responses, interaction with other customers or with store associates is also included as an important part of the experience. One key characteristic of this scale is that it considers all the physical and sensorial responses to the store stimuli as part of one unique dimension. Hence, the physical dimension of the experience is not disentangled from the sensorial one. While previous scales in this area (e.g. Bagdare and Jain, 2013) take into account only the affective dimensions of the retail experience or adapt the brand experience scale to the store environment (e.g. Srivastava and Kaul, 2016), this measure is based on a full theoretical development of the in-store customer experience that has been empirically tested by the authors. The scale goes beyond the hedonic side of the experience and measures the cognitive, affective, physical and social dimensions. This measure is then different from other scales in this area and aims to capture the mental responses to the in-store stimuli, the emotions aroused by the environment, the extent of social interaction occurring between the customer and store associates or other customers and, finally, the physiological responses to the interaction with different retail stimuli. As a result, the in-store customer experience includes 15 items in total. It represents an important tool for retailers to evaluate how good they are at delivering a successful in-store customer experience and to understand the extent to which a positive experience can be translated into loyalty or purchase behaviour.

The generic customer experience scale of Brun et al. (2017) is designed based on the theoretical works of Schmitt and Gentile et al. and developed based on Brakus's brand experience scale. Specifically, this scale aims to capture the whole experience of a customer with a given company, regardless of the environment or channel where the experience takes place. The scale includes both the positive and negative affective dimensions and distinguishes between the sensorial and the behavioural dimensions. It includes 21 items measuring the cognitive, positive affective, negative affective, sensorial, social and behavioural dimensions. While its general scope might be considered an advantage, a related disadvantage is its low flexibility in measuring customer experiences that occur in specific contexts. For this reason, researchers who aim to measure the experience customers have with a brand or store are advised to employ instead the scales formulated by Brakus et al. (2009) and Bustamante and Rubio (2017) respectively.

Shopping experience memory scale

Last but not least, academic research has seen the recent development of the shopping experience memory scale, which aims to capture the memory of the shopping experience, specifically the extent to which the customer is able to recall the experience, the extent to which a given experience is memorable.

The authors of this scale (Flacandji and Krey, 2020) agree with the view of Kahneman (2011) that customers are willing to repeat an experience lived in the past exclusively because of the memory that is associated with that past experience. Flacandji and Krey have developed a scale that is based on theory and empirical evidence to capture customers' memories that are related to the consumption experience. This scale has been specifically developed for the retail context and involves 14 items measuring four different main dimensions: attraction, structure, affect, social.

Attraction captures the capability of the retail environment and the products to attract the customer; hence to what extent the customer perceives the experience as appealing. Structure measures the key elements of the memory of the experience, such as its vividness, accessibility and coherence; it assesses how far the customer is able to recall the details and temporal sequence of the experience. Affect refers to all the emotions felt when recalling the experience; for example, has the experience elicited positive feelings and a general feeling of comfort? The social dimension captures whether the recalled experience has a social meaning; recalling the experience might lead the consumer to perceive himself as an important part of a group or to have something valuable to share with others. Given that this an emerging scale, it would be interesting to see to what extent this scale can explain customer loyalty or loyalty attitudes in general compared to the strategic experiential modules scales.

To summarize, some further considerations are needed to put all these scales into context. Academics and practitioners are currently working to improve the measurement of customer experience, such a complex construct. We have reviewed different approaches that stem from different theoretical perspectives and goals. While the service experience quality and the strategic experiential modules scales have been increasingly adopted by academics in retailing and consumer services, customer feedback metrics are still widely employed by practitioners in industry. However, given the importance of the concept of 'memorable experiences', the shopping memory scale might be employed in the future to understand if the memory of the experience is actually the key drive to measure. Despite this attention to measuring customer experience, two issues remain unaddressed. How can companies manage the customer experience, and what is its effect on customer attitudes and behaviours? We will tackle these two topics in the following paragraphs.

Customer experience management and touchpoints

To develop and manage the customer experience, practitioners have in recent years started to adopt a new managerial framework that has taken the name of customer experience management (Homburg et al., 2017). Since the 2000s, the recognition of customer experience has led to companies seeing its management as an increasingly important activity. Puccinelli et al. (2009) and Grewal et al. (2009) have fostered the relevance for companies to design and manage the customer experience, while Palmer (2010) has argued the need for a concrete meaning of customer experience management beyond the hype initially associated with the term. A clear and well-defined framework of customer experience management was, until very recently, still missing. As a matter of fact, while the concept of customer experience was taking a well-defined shape, customer experience management was still an emerging managerial practice rather than a well-structured strategic approach.

Homburg et al. (2017) have addressed this gap. Their influential work has helped define the key characteristics of customer experience management. The customer experience management framework is a firm-wide management approach to designing customer experience. The final goal of customer experience management is achieving long-term customer loyalty by designing and continually renewing touchpoint journeys (Homburg et al., 2017). Organizations that are able to properly manage the customer experience are more likely to obtain gains such as higher employee satisfaction, customer satisfaction and, more importantly, higher revenues (Rawson et al., 2013; McColl-Kennedy et al., 2019).

At this point the reader might ask what the difference is between customer relationship management (CRM) and customer experience management (CEM), given that both approaches share the final goal of achieving long-term customer loyalty. It's a valid question. CRM is regarded as a data-driven process that implies planning, implementing and monitoring the set of relationships occurring with customers (Payne and Frow, 2005). CRM is involved with collecting data on the customer to react to his purchasing behaviour patterns with marketing actions. The focus of the second approach, then, is more oriented towards the analysis of the customer to implement specific actions that are aimed at specific goals.

Dimensions of customer experience management

CEM is conceptualized by Homburg et al. (2017) as a managerial framework that is oriented towards the customer experience by adopting an active and not reactive approach. Specifically, CEM involves three main dimensions: cultural mindset, strategic direction and capabilities. All three dimensions refer to the cultural orientation towards customer experience, the strategy to shape it and the firm's capabilities to adapt and renew the designed experiences. Let us, drawing on Homburg et al., clarify each one in turn.

Cultural mindset

Cultural mindset involves three main elements that a company should recognize in its DNA: achieving an ongoing commitment throughout the organization towards the creation of experiences at each touchpoint; understanding that touchpoint journeys across pre-purchase, purchase and post-purchase stages are key factors that should be considered in daily decision-making; cooperating with company partners with a goal to aligning the different touchpoints that the customer encounters in the same shopping situation. In this regard, the company needs to take into account the customer experience and the related touchpoints in every decision that is going to affect the customer. Thus a key element in CEM is the focus on touchpoints. As a matter of fact, strategic direction and firm capabilities are specifically concerned with managing touchpoints.

Strategic direction

Strategic direction refers to all the strategies that aim to maximize the coordination among touchpoints in order to provide a seamless experience that is flexible depending on the situation but that develops throughout all the different touchpoints. To this aim four elements are key:

- Achieving a thematic cohesion of touchpoints in line with the brand image developed by the company and its related elements (thematic cohesion of touchpoints).
- Ensuring the consistency of all touchpoints in delivering experiences that are thematically linked to the brand (consistency of touchpoints).
- Improving the link between situations where the customer is exposed to certain touchpoints and the features of each touchpoint that is present in that situation (context sensitivity of touchpoints).
- Integrating all touchpoints across online and offline channels to deliver an omnichannel customer experience that prevent customers from perceiving barriers and differences across channels (connectivity of touchpoints).

Capabilities

Finally, a firm's capabilities refer to the extent to which it is able to perform a series of ongoing activities to manage touchpoints. Specifically:

- Planning customer journeys around its touchpoints and assigning requirements across company functions on how to address the different moments and places of these journeys (touchpoint journey design).
- Assigning priorities in terms of monetary, human and time resources to a given set of touchpoints in a flexible manner based on data collected through the different touchpoints (touchpoint prioritization).
- Coordinating the set of touchpoints by reflecting on what the touchpoint journey orientation within the company is (touchpoint journey monitoring).
- Developing and checking key performance indicators for each touchpoint with the goal of renewing existing touchpoint journeys or developing new ones (touchpoint adaptation).

Establishing the cultural mindset, strategic direction and capabilities towards customer experience enables a company to regard the customer experience as the core concept of the company strategy with the final goal of fostering long-lasting customer loyalty.

Role of touchpoints

In reviewing Homburg et al.'s conceptualization of CEM, we can quickly see that the set of touchpoints available to a company is the very playground in which customer experience is designed. More, we might follow Jain et al. (2017) and say that touchpoints are in fact the determinants of the customer experience. It is thus also worth reviewing the main studies that have dealt with the role of touchpoints in delivering a successful customer experience.

Touchpoints can be defined as the verbal and non-verbal incidents that any person perceives and relates to a firm or a brand (Duncan and Moriarty, 2006). Hence, they should be regarded as an episode of direct or indirect encounter with a firm (Lemon and Verhoef, 2016). From this definition we can understand that the concept of touchpoint is much broader than other related concepts that have been employed in the past, such as media or channel. Already we are faced with a definitional challenge: what should be considered a touchpoint and what not? This is one of the most difficult decisions to make when adopting a touchpoint perspective. To find a solution, we should look to the evidence from previous studies in this domain.

Previous studies on the topic, such as Baxendale et al. (2015), do not mention specific criteria based on which touchpoints should be selected, aggregated or disentangled. Some studies, to cope with the overwhelming variety of touchpoints, have decided to disregard those that reach only a low number of customers (e.g. Romaniuk et al., 2013). Others employ specific lists of touchpoints that are worth considering depending on the type of setting or interest (e.g. Zahay et al., 2004; Romaniuk et al., 2013; Li and Kannan, 2014; Baxendale et al., 2015; Wind and Hays, 2016; Hallikainen et al., 2019; Ieva and Ziliani, 2018a; Ieva and Ziliani, 2018b; McColl-Kennedy et al., 2019; Wagner et al., 2020). For instance, in retail settings the touchpoints that have been identified include traditional media, in-store, telephone, salesforce, catalogues, loyalty programs, mobile apps, email, word of mouth, and so forth. Therefore, touchpoints are not restricted to a specific domain but can be physical, digital or even personal interactions, such as a friend or a shop assistant who recommends a particular brand (Voorhees et al., 2017).

Classifying touchpoints

To handle the explosion in the last few decades of touchpoints, scholars have attempted to provide classifications to help group them into different categories. For example, Lemon and Verhoef (2016) have classified touchpoints based on who is responsible for managing any given one: brand-owned, partner-owned, customer-owned and social/external. Touchpoints are defined as brand-owned if the company itself is managing them: for example, a loyalty program or a product. Partner-owned touchpoints are managed by the company and a partner, such as another company (e.g. coalition loyalty programs) or a service provider (e.g. a digital agency that is in charge of the social media communications of the company). Customer-owned touchpoints are those that cannot be influenced by the company since they are under the full disposal of the customer. Examples include a customer deciding her preferred method of payment among those available or a customer producing user-generated content about a given brand. Finally, the social/external touchpoints are those occurring in social contexts: peer observation, as shown by Baxendale et al. (2015), is a very influential touchpoint. A typical situation is when we are seated in a restaurant and we see what the person sat at the next table is eating. Or we spot a nice car while we are driving home from work.

Lemon and Verhoef's classification is indeed very clear, and it is important to have an organizing framework to understand and utilize touchpoints. However, as the authors recognize, this classification has to cope with the variety and dynamics of business situations, where the difference between brand-owned touchpoints and partner-owned touchpoints or between customer-owned and social touchpoints might be not so well-defined. In the first case, the best example might be a loyalty program: every decision on the touchpoint is taken by the company, but the program might rely on the IT platform of a technology provider (the partner) and a system error might influence the performance of that touchpoint and the related customer experience, and thus harm the company. Hence, in this case, what is conceptually a brand-owned touchpoint could, in fact, be considered partner-owned. In the second case, a review on TripAdvisor by a customer about his positive experience in a hotel is, at first at least, a customer-owned touchpoint – it cannot be influenced by the hotel owner. However, when the review is shared and seen by other customers it becomes a social touchpoint too – it could influence the choice of other customers.

Another classification proposed by Manser Payne et al. (2017) differentiates between personal versus non-personal touchpoints: to what extent is there a human component in a given interaction with a customer? This classification is worth highlighting because it could be increasingly important in the future given that companies are likely to increase the adoption of digital assistants and chatbots. In this respect, it would be interesting to understand whether personal touchpoints are more or equally effective than non-personal touchpoints. Answering this question will lead to a shift in the investment that companies devote to technology versus human staff. Sometimes, in the same customer journey, a customer will interact first with a chatbot, which then links the customer to a person in charge of customer service who might be better equipped to fix the issue.

Other studies have distinguished between firm-initiated and customer-initiated touchpoints (e.g. Anderl et al., 2016). Here the point is to distinguish among touchpoints depending on who is starting the interaction: has the company contacted the customer? Or has the customer visited its webpage or written to it? Classifying touchpoints is indeed a tricky business but it is important for marketers to clarify the key characteristics and categories of the touchpoints they manage daily. Moreover, specific classifications and labels have been proposed with reference to digital touchpoints. Straker et al. (2015) have classified digital touchpoints in four different categories: functional touchpoints, social touchpoints, corporate touchpoints and community touchpoints. Email and websites are examples of functional touchpoints and their purpose is to provide diversion, functionality and interaction. Social touchpoints include social media, where the key feature is the extent of interaction that they allow. Corporate touchpoints aim to achieve customer feedback: FAQs, customer feedback forms, and the like. Finally, community touchpoints have in common a strong cohesion among users: blogs are, for instance, included in this category.

Assessing touchpoints

Studies have been undertaken to assess the role of touchpoints, specifically in the business-to-consumer (B2C) setting. The key considered variables in this domain are the reach, frequency and positivity of exposure to touchpoints.

Reach

Reach has to do with the fact that a given customer has been exposed or not exposed to a given touchpoint. Why is achieving reach important? The capability of addressing the right customer segment with the right touchpoint is key for media placement (Romaniuk et al., 2013). In this regard, studies on touchpoint reach have found that the extent to which brand users versus brand non-users are able to recall touchpoint exposure significantly differs. Specifically:

- Brand users are more likely to recall having been exposed to the advertising of the brand (Vaughan et al., 2016).
- TV advertising, gift packs, in-store displays/promotions and outdoor advertisements reach average brand users (Romaniuk et al., 2013).
- Social media and word of mouth have been found to reach heavy brand users (Romaniuk et al., 2013).

Frequency

As far as the frequency of exposure to touchpoints is concerned, studies have focused on its relationship with loyalty intentions and its impact on brand attitudes. Ieva and Ziliani (2018a) have segmented consumers based on frequency of exposure to touchpoints in a retail setting. They found that consumers can be largely segmented based on the intensity of the exposure to all the touchpoints rather than based on the exposure to a given set of specific touchpoints. Moreover, the exposure is significantly and positively related to loyalty intentions: more loyal customers tend to encounter more frequently their main retailer through all the different touchpoints. Ieva and Ziliani (2018b) also studied the relationship between frequency of exposure and loyalty intentions in a mobile services setting. They found that the higher the willingness to recommend the company and to stay as a long-term customer, the higher the likelihood of recalling exposure to certain touchpoints, such as the store, the website, email, mobile app, word of mouth and loyalty programs.

Frequency of exposure also impacts brand attitudes (Campbell and Keller, 2003) and brand consideration changes (Baxendale et al., 2015). Specifically, Baxendale et al. (2015) have conducted a study on brand touchpoints in four consumer categories: electrical goods, technological products, mobile handsets and soft drinks. Their study found that frequency of exposure to brand advertising, peer observation, in-store communications and retailer advertising has a positive effect on brand consideration: higher frequency of touchpoint exposure (expressed by a natural log decay) increases the likelihood that consumers will consider that brand in their consideration set.

Positivity

It should be clarified that positivity is the valence of the affective response to a touchpoint (Baxendale et al., 2015). Previous studies have found that positivity drives spending and repeat purchase intentions (Arnold and Reynolds, 2009) and that it is positively correlated with satisfaction (Westbrook and Oliver, 1991) and commitment (Ahluwalia et al., 2000). Why is positivity so important? How a customer lives the experience with a given touchpoint in affective terms is actually embodied in how they evaluate that touchpoint and this evaluation is believed to influence brand-related cognitions that will occur in the future (Baumeister et al., 2007). Affective responses have been recently found to impact loyalty intentions (Ou and Verhoef, 2017; Ieva and Ziliani, 2018b). Baxendale et al. (2015) have also discovered positive effects on brand consideration of all touchpoints they considered (traditional earned, such as editorial and news coverage, brand advertising, word of mouth, peer observation, in-store communications and retailer advertising). Specifically, Ieva and Ziliani (2018b), in the mobile services setting, have found that touchpoint positivity stemming from the interactions with customer service, mobile messaging, provider website, TV and cinema advertising, the physical store, mobile apps, word of mouth and provider store associates is positively related to customer loyalty.

Prioritizing touchpoints

As we can see, the findings on touchpoint reach, frequency and positivity in the B2C setting support the view that touchpoints differ in their relationship with consumer attitudes, such as loyalty intentions. Thus companies should prioritize touchpoints depending on their effects on consumer attitudes. Digital touchpoints and touchpoints in business-to-business (B2B) settings have also attracted specific attention. As far as the role of digital touchpoints is concerned, Hallikainen et al. (2019) have identified a broad range of segments in terms of their preferences for digital touchpoints. For instance, their segmentation has found anti-digital consumers (people who do not like digital touchpoints) but also digital enthusiasts (consumers that are keen on using new touchpoints and channels as soon as they are available to the public). Wagner et al. (2020) have shed light on the role of touchpoints in the online environment in influencing how channels are evaluated. Specifically, they found that the type of digital touchpoint through which consumers interact and its level of development affect how the online channel is perceived.

The omnichannel customer experience across touchpoints

In a retailing environment where physical, digital and mobile channels are provided, touchpoints enable customers to freely roam across channels in their search and purchase journeys. From the perspective of customer experience, this implies the emergence of new and more complex forms of experience, whose shape depends on the contextual elements of each channel visited by customers. The omnichannel customer experience, specifically, addresses seamless experiences across all of the retailers' channels and encompasses all of the customer journey stages (Rahman et al., 2022). Various studies have addressed this emerging construct – mostly by focusing on specific aspects: channel integration perception (Shen et al., 2018), touchpoint management (Homburg et al., 2017); technology quality (Calvo et al., 2023), and so on. Recently, literature has identified the most complete form of omnichannel customer experience, the so-called 'phygital customer experience (PH-CX)', a holistic vision that encompasses customer journeys from physical to digital settings and vice versa (Klaus, 2021; Batat, 2022). Phygital is defined as 'a combination of both physical elements and digital devices, platforms, technologies, extended realities, online platforms and so forth' (Batat, 2022, p. 3) aimed towards offering unique and immersive experiences. The concept of 'phygital' stresses the need to offer suitable customer experiences integrated into customers' tangible and intangible needs, whose value for customers is consistent across settings. Conceptualizations of omnichannel customer experience attempt to identify dimensions synthesizing a wide variety of touchpoints, services, or other enablers connecting channels for customers, each with different characteristics. One of the most notable attempts, by Rahman et al. (2022) proposes that customers use omnichannel attributes in each of the cues they encounter in their journey in order to evaluate the experience as a whole. As such, it is possible to use these omnichannel dimensions to measure the overall corresponding experience, as well as a checklist of elements providing an excellent omnichannel customer experience. The nine dimensions so identified are:

- Value: it reflects the customers' judgment on whether the omnichannel retailer's product and pricing is appropriate.
- Personalization: it involves the extent to which the omnichannel retailer is able to offer tailored services, products and transactional environments to satisfy its customers' individual needs.
- Customer service: it measures the support services provided across all channels at all stages of the customer journey.
- Consistency: it evaluates product assortment and pricing consistency across channels.
- Delivery: it evaluates the extent to which delivery and pick-up services are provided in any channel.
- Product returns: involves customers' experiences with the retailer's handling of product returns and replacements.
- Social communications: it reflects the reputation mechanisms across channels through which customers infer the omnichannel retailer's quality.
- Information safety: concerns the safety measures aimed at protecting customers personal or financial data across channels.
- Loyalty programs: this final dimension elevates the loyalty program – its points-accrual dynamics and the rewards it offers – to the role of a major enabler that can both provide omnichannel perception and significantly affect the customer experience in multiple channels.

Customer experience and customer loyalty

This last section aims to provide empirical evidence in favour of one of the main assumptions of this chapter: a better customer experience can increase customer loyalty. This is also the reason why we are addressing the topic of customer experience in this book. We see it as the latest stage in the 'evolution' of loyalty management. There is indeed wide consensus that customer experience is a driver of customer loyalty (Jain et al., 2017). The intuitive idea behind this relationship is that having a positive customer experience contributes to further develop the relationship between the customer and the company, thus leading to higher customer loyalty in the long run. This consideration is assumed to be valid in different B2B and B2C contexts, in different industries and for different types of customers. Below we are going to briefly review the main results from the most recent studies that have studied the relationship between customer experience measures with customer loyalty measures. First, we present their findings on the relationship between EXQ and customer loyalty. Second, we show the results from previous research on the relationship between the customer experience scale and strategic experiential modules and customer loyalty. By comparing these two streams of studies we can draw relevant and robust conclusions on the role of customer experience in driving long-term customer loyalty.

EXQ and customer loyalty

Klaus and Maklan (2013) and Klaus et al. (2013) have studied the relationship between customer experience measured by means of the EXQ scale and a series of constructs that are employed as measures of customer loyalty or as proxies for it: customer satisfaction, loyalty intentions and word of mouth. The contexts of reference where these relationships have been studied are as follows: mortgages, fuel and service stations, retail banking and luxury goods. Both studies consistently show that the customer experience is significantly and positively related to customer satisfaction, loyalty intentions and word of mouth.

Roy (2018) takes a step further by measuring how the effect of customer experience on loyalty intentions (and satisfaction and word of mouth) changes when considering the following: a hedonic (e.g. restaurant) versus utilitarian (e.g. banking) service and first-time versus regular customers. Roy takes a longitudinal perspective, thus observing changes occurring over time. Results show that the positive impact of customer experience on customer loyalty is significant in both utilitarian and hedonic settings. However, it is stronger in the case of the hedonic setting than the utilitarian one. This means that customer experience seems to matter more for settings where the affective component has a predominant role and less in settings that are more concerned with rationality. A second result of the study regards the estimation of customer experience effects for a first-time customer. Specifically, results show that for a first-time customer, their experience has a positive effect on customer satisfaction but no effect on customer loyalty and word of mouth. This means that customer satisfaction is the most immediate outcome of customer experience, while loyalty and word of mouth can be influenced only with a continuum of multiple experiences.

In fact, findings from the same study show that the impact of customer experience on customer loyalty, satisfaction and word of mouth increases with time. Specifically, if the first-time customer is then converted into a regular customer, the impact of customer experience on customer loyalty is stronger. According to Roy, these results are in line with the theoretical argument of consumer attitude formation over time. In the first experience, the customer is only capable of developing satisfaction as an immediate attitude if the experience is positive.

However, with the occurrence of multiple subsequent experiences, the learning process undertaken by the customer leads to the development of attitudinal and behaviour loyalty. These findings have key implications for managers in terms of the attention that should be paid to first-time customers versus regular customers.

Finally, the aforementioned study by Rahman et al. (2022) on omnichannel customer experiences tested and measured their effectiveness on five outcomes: customer satisfaction, word-of-mouth, share-of-wallet, trust towards the retailer and, naturally, customer loyalty. Not only the study provides evidence of omnichannel customer experiences driving loyalty, but also suggests that certain dimensions of the experience have a stronger impact on the various outcomes. The authors apply an importance performance mapping analysis, aimed at identifying which dimensions – among nine identified from academic literature – contribute the most to customer loyalty. Results show that, besides the offer of a loyalty program encompassing the retailer's multiple channels, the dimensions of customer service, value, and social communication are the most critical for customer loyalty (Rahman et al., 2022). Practitioners are therefore advised to consider the customer experiences they are currently offering in terms of which elements are most contributing to driving loyalty and proceed to measure them accordingly by means of robust measures.

Strategic experiential modules and customer loyalty

The stream of studies adopting measurement scales based on strategic experiential modules (e.g. cognitive, affective) has tested the role of customer experience or its related constructs, such as brand experience and in-store customer experience, on customer loyalty and customer satisfaction. Within this stream of studies, research has also tried to capture, where possible, not only the overall effect of customer experience, but also the effect of each dimension of customer experience on customer loyalty.

Impact of customer experience on customer loyalty

Brun et al. (2017) have studied the impact of each customer experience dimension on customer loyalty and how the type of channel investigated, whether online or offline, moderates this effect. Their study was conducted in the banking and travel industries. Results show that, on average, the cognitive and social dimensions have a positive impact on customer loyalty, whereas the negative affective and behavioural dimensions have a negative effect. No overall impact was found to stem from the sensorial or positive affective dimensions. Moreover, these results tend to vary slightly depending on the channel considered (e.g. the bank brand or travel agency versus online home or travel agency banking), whether online or offline, and on the considered industry, whether banking or travel. For instance, the social dimension has a stronger effect on loyalty in the offline environment than online for both banking and travel, while the cognitive dimension has a stronger effect online for banking and offline for travel. Srivastava and Kaul (2016) have estimated the effect of customer experience on share of wallet, attitudinal and behavioural loyalty. Their study finds that customer experience has a positive and significant effect on attitudinal and behavioural loyalty but no effect on share of wallet.

Impact of brand experience on customer loyalty

Brakus et al. (2009) have studied six different categories of product brands, such as computers, cars, drinking water, sneakers, clothes and newspapers. They found that brand experience has a positive and significant effect on customer satisfaction and, through customer satisfaction, on loyalty. The rationale behind this result is strictly linked with the true nature of an experience: given that a brand involves the senses and elicits good feelings, customers (who are, after all, humans and seek stimuli that produce gratification) might want to receive such stimuli again. This result is then in line with the results on the effect of the general customer experience construct on loyalty.

Impact of in-store experience on customer loyalty

Bustamante and Rubio (2017) have estimated the effect of the in-store customer experience on satisfaction with the retail store and customer loyalty – specifically store loyalty – in a retail fashion context. Their study shows that the customer experience lived in the store has a positive effect on satisfaction and store loyalty and that a positive in-store customer experience is a key driver of the customer relationship with the retailer.

References

Addis, M. and Holbrook, M. B. (2001) 'On the conceptual link between mass customisation and experiential consumption: an explosion of subjectivity'. *Journal of Consumer Behaviour: An International Research Review*, 1(1), 50–66.

Ahluwalia, R., Burnkrant, R. E. and Unnava, H. R. (2000) 'Consumer response to negative publicity: the moderating role of commitment'. *Journal of Marketing Research*, 37(2), 203–214.

Anderl, E., Schumann, J. H. and Kunz, W. (2016) 'Helping firms reduce complexity in multichannel online data: a new taxonomy-based approach for customer journeys'. *Journal of Retailing*, 92(2), 185–203.

Arnold, M. J. and Reynolds, K. E. (2009) 'Affect and retail shopping behavior: understanding the role of mood regulation and regulatory focus'. *Journal of Retailing*, 85(3), 308–320.

Bagdare, S. and Jain, R. (2013) 'Measuring retail customer experience'. *International Journal of Retail & Distribution Management*, 41(10), 790–804.

Batat, W. (2022) 'What does phygital really mean? A conceptual introduction to the phygital customer experience (PH-CX) framework'. *Journal of Strategic Marketing*, 1–24.

Baumeister, R. F. and Vohs, K. D. (2007) 'Self-regulation, ego depletion, and motivation'. *Social and Personality Psychology Compass*, 1(1), 115–128.

Baxendale, S., Macdonald, E. K. and Wilson, H. N. (2015) 'The impact of different touchpoints on brand consideration'. *Journal of Retailing*, 91(2), 235–253.

Bonfanti, A. (2018) *Customer shopping experience: Le sfide del retail tra spazio fisico e digitale*. Turin: Giappichelli.

Brakus, J. J., Schmitt, B. H. and Zarantonello, L. (2009) 'Brand experience: what is it? How is it measured? Does it affect loyalty?' *Journal of Marketing*, 73(3), 52–68.

Brun, I., Rajaobelina, L., Ricard, L. and Berthiaume, B. (2017) 'Impact of customer experience on loyalty: a multichannel examination'. *The Service Industries Journal*, 37(5–6), 317–340.

Bustamante, J. C. and Rubio, N. (2017) 'Measuring customer experience in physical retail environments'. *Journal of Service Management*, 28(5), 884–913.

Cacioppo, J. T., Gardner, W. L. and Berntson, G. G. (1999) 'The affect system has parallel and integrative processing components: form follows function'. *Journal of Personality and Social Psychology*, 76(5), 839–855.

Calvo, A. V., Franco, A. D. and Frasquet, M. (2023) 'The role of artificial intelligence in improving the omnichannel customer experience'. *International Journal of Retail & Distribution Management*, 51(9/10), 1174–1194.

Campbell, M. C. and Keller, K. L. (2003) 'Brand familiarity and advertising repetition effects'. *Journal of Consumer Research*, 30(2), 292–304.

Carù, A. and Cova, B. (2015) 'Co-creating the collective service experience'. *Journal of Service Management*, 26(2), 276–294.

Cho, N. and Park, S. (2001) 'Development of electronic commerce user-consumer satisfaction index (ECUSI) for Internet shopping'. *Industrial Management & Data Systems*, 101(8), 400–406.

De Keyser, A., Lemon, K. N., Klaus, P. and Keiningham, T. L. (2015) *A Framework for Understanding and Managing the Customer Experience*. Marketing Science Institute working paper no. 15-121. Cambridge, MA: Marketing Science Institute.

Duncan, T. and Moriarty, S. (2006) 'How integrated marketing communication's "touchpoints" can operationalize the service-dominant logic'. In R. F. Lusch and S. L. Vargo (eds), *The Service-Dominant Logic of Marketing: Dialog, Debate, and Directions*, 236–249. Abingdon: Routledge.

Erevelles, S. (1998) 'The role of affect in marketing'. *Journal of Business Research*, 42(3), 199–215.

Flacandji, M. and Krey, N. (2020) 'Remembering shopping experiences: the shopping experience memory scale'. *Journal of Business Research*, 107, 279–289.

Ford, J. B. (2017) 'Amazon's Mechanical Turk: a comment'. *Journal of Advertising*, 46(1), 156–158.

Fornerino, M., Helme-Guizon, A. and Gotteland, D. (2006) 'Mesurer l'immersion dans une expérience de consommation: premiers développements'. Paper presented at *Actes du XXIIème Colloque international de l'Association Française du Marketing*, Nantes, 11–12 May.

Gentile, C., Spiller, N. and Noci, G. (2007) 'How to sustain the customer experience: an overview of experience components that co-create value with the customer'. *European Management Journal*, 25(5), 395–410.

Grewal, D., Levy, M. and Kumar, V. (2009) 'Customer experience management in retailing: an organizing framework'. *Journal of Retailing*, 85(1), 1–14.

Hall, A. and Towers, N. (2017) 'Understanding how millennial shoppers decide what to buy: digitally connected unseen journeys'. *International Journal of Retail & Distribution Management*, 45(5), 498–517.

Hallikainen, H., Alamäki, A. and Laukkanen, T. (2019) 'Individual preferences of digital touchpoints: a latent class analysis'. *Journal of Retailing and Consumer Services*, 50, 386–393.

Holbrook, M. B. and Hirschman, E. C. (1982) 'The experiential aspects of consumption: consumer fantasies, feelings, and fun'. *Journal of Consumer Research*, 9(2), 132–140.

Homburg, C., Jozić, D. and Kuehnl, C. (2017) 'Customer experience management: toward implementing an evolving marketing concept'. *Journal of the Academy of Marketing Science*, 45(3), 377–401.

Hu, H. and Jasper, C. R. (2006) 'Social cues in the store environment and their impact on store image'. *International Journal of Retail & Distribution Management*, 34(1), 25–48.

Ieva, M. and Ziliani, C. (2018a) 'Mapping touchpoint exposure in retailing: implications for developing an omnichannel customer experience'. *International Journal of Retail & Distribution Management*, 46(3), 304–322.

Ieva, M. and Ziliani, C. (2018b) 'The role of customer experience touchpoints in driving loyalty intentions in services'. *TQM Journal*, 30(5), 444–457.

Jaakkola, E., Helkkula, A. and Aarikka-Stenroos, L. (2015) 'Service experience co-creation: conceptualization, implications, and future research directions'. *Journal of Service Management*, 26(2), 182–205.

Jain, R., Aagja, J. and Bagdare, S. (2017) 'Customer experience: a review and research agenda'. *Journal of Service Theory and Practice*, 27(3), 642–662.

Kahneman, D. (2011) *Thinking, Fast and Slow*. New York: Farrar Straus Giroux.

Keiningham, T. L., Cooil, B., Aksoy, L., Andreassen, T. W. and Weiner, J. (2007) 'The value of different customer satisfaction and loyalty metrics in predicting customer retention, recommendation, and share-of-wallet'. *Managing Service Quality: An International Journal*, 17(4), 361–384.

Klaus, P. (2021) 'Viewpoint: phygital – the emperor's new clothes?'. *Journal of Strategic Marketing*. doi:10.1080/0965254X.2021.1976252

Klaus, P. and Maklan, S. (2012) 'EXQ: a multiple-item scale for assessing service experience'. *Journal of Service Management*, 23(1), 5–33.

Klaus, P. and Maklan, S. (2013) 'Towards a better measure of customer experience'. *International Journal of Market Research*, 55(2), 227–246.

Klaus, P., Gorgoglione, M., Buonamassa, D., Panniello, U. and Nguyen, B. (2013) 'Are you providing the "right" customer experience? The case of Banca Popolare di Bari'. *International Journal of Bank Marketing*, 31(7), 506–528.

Kuppelwieser, V. G. and Klaus, P. (2021) 'Measuring customer experience quality: the EXQ scale revisited'. *Journal of Business Research*, 126, 624–633.

LaSalle, D. and Britton, T. A. (2003) *Priceless: Turning Ordinary Products into Extraordinary Experiences*. Boston, MA: Harvard Business School Press.

Lemon, K. N. and Verhoef, P. C. (2016) 'Understanding customer experience throughout the customer journey'. *Journal of Marketing*, 80(6), 69–96.

Li, H. and Kannan, P. K. (2014) 'Attributing conversions in a multichannel online marketing environment: an empirical model and a field experiment'. *Journal of Marketing Research*, 51(1), 40–56.

Lipkin, M. (2016) 'Customer experience formation in today's service landscape'. *Journal of Service Management*, 27(5), 678–703.

Manser Payne, E., Peltier, J. W. and Barger, V. A. (2017) 'Omni-channel marketing, integrated marketing communications and consumer engagement: a research agenda'. *Journal of Research in Interactive Marketing*, 11(2), 185–197.

McColl-Kennedy, J. R., Zaki, M., Lemon, K. N., Urmetzer, F. and Neely, A. (2019) 'Gaining customer experience insights that matter'. *Journal of Service Research*, 22(1), 8–26.

Meyer, C. and Schwager, A. (2007) 'Customer experience'. *Harvard Business Review*, 85(2), 116–126.

Ou, Y. C. and Verhoef, P. C. (2017) 'The impact of positive and negative emotions on loyalty intentions and their interactions with customer equity drivers'. *Journal of Business Research*, 80, 106–115.

Palmer, A. (2010) 'Customer experience management: a critical review of an emerging idea'. *Journal of Services Marketing*, 24(3), 196–208.

Parasuraman, A., Zeithaml, V. A. and Berry, L. L. (1988) 'Servqual: a multiple-item scale for measuring consumer perceptions of service quality'. *Journal of Retailing*, 64(1), 12–40.

Payne, A. and Frow, P. (2005) 'A strategic framework for customer relationship management'. *Journal of Marketing*, 69(4), 167–176.

Pine, B. J. and Gilmore, J. H. (1998) 'Welcome to the experience economy'. *Harvard Business Review*, 76, 97–105.

Puccinelli, N. M., Goodstein, R. C., Grewal, D., Price, R., Raghubir, P. and Stewart, D. (2009) 'Customer experience management in retailing: understanding the buying process'. *Journal of Retailing*, 85(1), 15–30.

Rahman, S. M., Carlson, J., Gudergan, S. P., Wetzels, M. and Grewal, D. (2022) 'Perceived omnichannel customer experience (OCX): Concept, measurement, and impact'. *Journal of Retailing*, 98(4), 611–632.

Rawson, A., Duncan, E. and Jones, C. (2013) 'The truth about customer experience'. *Harvard Business Review*, 91(9), 90–98.

Reichheld, F. F. (2003) 'The one number you need to grow'. *Harvard Business Review*, 81(12), 46–55.

Richins, M. L. (1997) 'Measuring emotions in the consumption experience'. *Journal of Consumer Research*, 24(2), 127–146.

Romaniuk, J., Beal, V. and Uncles, M. (2013) 'Achieving reach in a multi-media environment: how a marketer's first step provides the direction for the second'. *Journal of Advertising Research*, 53(2), 221–230.

Rose, S., Clark, M., Samouel, P. and Hair, N. (2012) 'Online customer experience in e-retailing: an empirical model of antecedents and outcomes'. *Journal of Retailing*, 88(2), 308–322.

Roy, S. (2018) 'Effects of customer experience across service types, customer types and time'. *Journal of Services Marketing*, 32(4), 400–413.

Schmitt, B. (1999) 'Experiential marketing'. *Journal of Marketing Management*, 15(1–3), 53–67.

Shen, X. L., Li, Y. J., Sun, Y. and Wang, N. (2018) 'Channel integration quality, perceived fluency and omnichannel service usage: the moderating roles of internal and external usage experience'. *Decision Support Systems*, 109, 61–73.

Srivastava, M. and Kaul, D. (2016) 'Exploring the link between customer experience–loyalty–consumer spend'. *Journal of Retailing and Consumer Services*, 31, 277–286.

Straker, K., Wrigley, C. and Rosemann, M. (2015) 'Typologies and touchpoints: designing multi-channel digital strategies'. *Journal of Research in Interactive Marketing*, 9(2), 110–128.

Trevinal, A. M. and Stenger, T. (2014) 'Toward a conceptualization of the online shopping experience'. *Journal of Retailing and Consumer Services*, 21(3), 314–326.

Van Doorn, J., Leeflang, P. S. and Tijs, M. (2013) 'Satisfaction as a predictor of future performance: a replication'. *International Journal of Research in Marketing*, 30(3), 314–318.

Vaughan, K., Beal, V. and Romaniuk, J. (2016) 'Can brand users really remember advertising more than nonusers? Testing an empirical generalization across six advertising awareness measures'. *Journal of Advertising Research*, 56(3), 311–320.

Verhoef, P. C., Lemon, K. N., Parasuraman, A., Roggeveen, A., Tsiros, M. and Schlesinger, L. A. (2009) 'Customer experience creation: determinants, dynamics and management strategies'. *Journal of Retailing*, 85(1), 31–41.

Vinhas Da Silva, R. and Faridah Syed Alwi, S. (2006) 'Cognitive, affective attributes and conative, behavioural responses in retail corporate branding'. *Journal of Product & Brand Management*, 15(5), 293–305.

Voorhees, C. M., Fombelle, P. W., Gregoire, Y., Bone, S., Gustafsson, A., Sousa, R. and Walkowiak, T. (2017) 'Service encounters, experiences and the customer journey: defining the field and a call to expand our lens'. *Journal of Business Research*, 79, 269–280.

Wagner, G., Schramm-Klein, H. and Steinmann, S. (2020) 'Online retailing across e-channels and e-channel touchpoints: Empirical studies of consumer behavior in the multichannel e-commerce environment'. *Journal of Business Research*, 107, 256–270.

Westbrook, R. A. and Oliver, R. L. (1991) 'The dimensionality of consumption emotion patterns and consumer satisfaction'. *Journal of Consumer Research*, 18(1), 84–91.

Wind, Y. J. and Hays, C. F. (2016) 'Research implications of the "beyond advertising" paradigm: a model and roadmap for creating value through all media and non-media touchpoints'. *Journal of Advertising Research*, 56(2), 142–158.

Wright, P. L. (1973) 'The cognitive processes mediating acceptance of advertising'. *Journal of Marketing Research*, 10(1), 53–62.

Zahay, D., Peltier, J., Schultz, D. E. and Griffin, A. (2004) 'The role of transactional versus relational data in IMC programs: Bringing customer data together'. *Journal of Advertising Research*, 44(1), 3–18.

Zeithaml, V. A., Berry, L. L. and Parasuraman, A. (1996) 'The behavioral consequences of service quality'. *Journal of Marketing*, 60(2), 31–46.

Zeithaml, V. A., Bolton, R. N., Deighton, J., Keiningham, T. L., Lemon, K. N. and Petersen, J. A. (2006) 'Forward-looking focus: can firms have adaptive foresight?' *Journal of Service Research*, 9(2), 168–183.

6

FOSTERING LOYALTY THROUGH ENGAGEMENT AND GAMIFICATION

Giada Salvietti

From customer engagement to customer loyalty

Customer engagement has been described as a psychological state affecting customers' relationships with companies and brands that greatly exceed mere involvement (Brodie et al., 2011). As a consequence, it entails many advantages that caught the attention of practitioners and academics alike. In fact, studies addressing its positive effects on consumers – that in turn improve corporate performance and profitability (Brodie et al., 2011) – are manifold. Engaged customers have more significant, proactive and interactive relationships with brands than their non-engaged counterparts, under multiple perspectives that go beyond purchase. Behaviours exhibited by engaged customers extend beyond individual transactions and may include pre- or post-purchase experiences (Van Doorn et al., 2010). They are more prone towards spreading positive word-of-mouth as well as providing recommendations and referrals deemed credible by peers (de Oliveira Santini et al., 2020). Also, engaged customers actively participate with companies in the co-creation of experience and values (Brakus et al., 2009), and may even contribute to new product and service development (Hoyer et al., 2010). Finally, engaged customers usually display a stronger preference for premium price and lower price sensitivity than non-engaged ones, thus proving more profitable for companies (Ramkumar et al., 2013).

This variety of outcomes can be traced back to customer engagement being a multidimensional concept, affecting the cognitive, the emotional and/or the behavioural sphere. According to Patterson et al. (2006), customer engagement interactions are characterized by three components embodying each

DOI: 10.4324/9781003400783-6

dimension: (a) absorption, which is the level of customer concentration on the company/brand and corresponds to the cognitive dimension; (b) dedication, or the customers' sense of belonging to the company/brand, which reflects the emotional dimension; and (c) vigour, the customers' level of energy and mental resilience exerted during the interaction, which represents the behavioural dimension.

It is important to note that customer engagement – and each of its three dimensions – may be of variable intensity, due to its nature as a psychological state tied to a relationship. As such, on the one hand, customers may evolve from 'non-engaged' to 'highly engaged' and vice versa following an interaction with the brand. On the other hand, engagement may be temporarily inactive and entering a dormancy period, with the possibility to be later reactivated (Brodie et al., 2011). An important implication is that carefully crafted marketing strategies and initiatives can change customer engagement intensity, thus influencing customers' preferences and behaviours following their response to the interactive stimuli provided (Bolton, 2011).

Alongside other relational concepts, customer engagement stands out for its long-term consequences, that include self-brand connection, emotional brand attachment and customer loyalty (Brodie et al., 2011). The nexus between customer engagement and loyalty, as its outcome, has been widely explored, encompassing both behavioural and attitudinal loyalty. For example, it has been shown that engagement with non-purchase activities captures customers' attention, making them more receptive to information received about companies and products, which in turn results in increased patronage intention (Vivek et al., 2012).

The study by Hollebeek (2011) delves into the connections between customer engagement and loyalty by proposing a segmentation criterion based on low and high levels of both constructs. As reported in Table 6.1, four segments are identified:

- Low engaged customers are divided into 'exits' and 'apathists'. Exits are likely to switch to a different brand or category, due to their lower loyalty levels, whereas 'apathists' still display comparatively high levels of loyalty. These customers did not develop a significant relationship with the brand but are still loyal due to their inertia: choosing another alternative would require excessive effort.
- High engaged customers include 'activists' and 'variety seeker'. Activists are the most engaged, loyal and therefore desirable customers. Finally, variety-seekers are highly engaged but they tend to defect from the organization to explore novelties in the same product category

Such segmentation constitutes a guideline for companies on how to manage customer engagement while focusing on the most promising targets. As for

TABLE 6.1 Customer segmentation according to engagement and loyalty

	Customer engagement low	*Customer engagement high*
Customer loyalty high	Apathists	Activists
Customer loyalty low	Exits	Variety seekers

Source: adapted from Hollebeek (2011)

what concerns low-engaged customers, focusing on apathists might increase their attitudinal disposition towards the brand through awareness, thus encouraging their migration towards the activists' segment. As for high-engaged customers, companies must take into account that even activists might be exposed to fatigue during their relationship, needing engagement to be revamped. Companies should therefore maintain them to the optimal engagement level. Variety seekers, for their part, would benefit from re-engagement actions oriented at winning them back, at least temporarily.

Managing customer engagement

Due to its complexity, managing customer engagement requires a systematic process, that starts with the identification of the ways such engagement is manifested in customers' attitudes, emotions and behaviours and ends with the design of targeted actions (Van Doorn et al., 2010). Not only companies should develop capabilities and resources dedicated to customer engagement management, but they should also clearly identify, beforehand, the critical aspects affecting customer-brand interactions.

As what concerns this first aspect, companies must define the places and contexts where customer engagement is manifested. This involves identifying which channels – and within them, which initiatives – are driving engagement (i.e. online vs. offline venues; one-to-may vs. one-to-one interactions, etc.). This first evaluation is functional and preliminary to the assessment of customer engagement and of its outcomes, in the short and in the long term.

Such assessment may then require the use of an established scale to examine customer engagement and determine the strengths and weaknesses of specific engagement strategies.

Among customer engagement scales developed in literature over the years, it is worth mentioning Vivek et al. (2014) scale, as it offers an assessment based on the relational interplay between customers and the company or brand. In this light, the scale measures two dimensions that are concerned with the customer's individual relationship with the company/brand, and a third dimension that incorporates the network of social connections surrounding such relationship (Vivek et al., 2014; p. 407):

1 Conscious attention: defined as 'the degree of interest the person has or wishes to have in interacting with the focus of their engagement', it provides a proxy of the intensity of the customer's involvement.
2 Enthused participation: 'the zealous reactions and feelings of a person related to using or interacting with the focus of their engagement', which captures the customer's emotional commitment to the relationship.
3 Social connection: is described as 'the enhancement of the interaction based on the inclusion of others with the focus of engagement, indicating mutual or reciprocal action in presence of others'.

By addressing these three dimensions, the scale proposed is representative of the interactive and reciprocal relationship between engaged customers and the company or brand, as well as its meaningfulness and connectedness.

As anticipated, other scales have been later developed, specific to customer engagement in relation to sectors, domains or touchpoint (Chan et al., 2014; Romero, 2017). In certain contexts, the relationship between customers and companies relies heavily on the presence of human agents acting as the embodiment of the brand and its values: this is the case of many B2B and B2C services. Moreover, across different contexts, the need for social connections – i.e. to include other peers in the relationship – is variable to the point it may even be irrelevant or extremely relevant (Vivek et al., 2014). Finally, some touchpoints might be so effective that customers may be engaged with the touchpoint itself rather than with the company providing said touchpoint, and in a different way. This is the case of customer engagement with the loyalty program, that will be further explored later. Besides the aforementioned differences, from a strategic point of view, companies operating across multiple touchpoints or channels may find extremely useful to understand whether initiatives carried out in one channel to foster customer engagement provide positive spillover effects on other channels (e.g. if creating engagement on social media also drives in-store visits and purchases, etc.) (Bolton, 2011).

Moving forward with the analysis, as what concerns the design of targeted actions to improve customer engagement, companies are called to intervene on its antecedents. In this sense, extant studies from literature may provide guidance to identify key aspects. Customer engagement has been found to be driven by customer satisfaction, by positive emotions and trust (de Oliveira Santini et al., 2020). A major concern for companies, is, therefore, to identify whether some aspects of the experience provided can be improved or mended. Customer feedback – especially concerning complaints – represents powerful insight to be addressed in a redesign effort that will lead to future engagement. Studies on service failure and recovery clearly show that companies' actions can turn negative customer engagement into a positive one, thus creating value other than resolving a threat (Voorhees et al., 2009). Once they revise the experience provided to customers, companies may then nurture Customer

Engagement processes by defining new actions and initiatives able to stimulate customers' participation and involvement. The scale and nature of such actions are proportional to the company's provision of channels and touchpoints. Some companies, for example, may need to create dedicated locations to foster their customers' engagement, such as establishing customer communities or creating dedicated websites or platforms (Demangeot and Broderick, 2016). Other social incentives involve creating competitive contexts or activities where customers obtain status levels recognizable by their peers (Wirtz et al., 2013). One of the most widespread engagement techniques relies on granting customers rewards and incentives for carrying out a certain activity, such as writing reviews (Ryu and Feick, 2007).

Context in customer engagement

Customer engagement is heavily affected by the context in which the interaction between the brand or company and the customer takes place (Hollebeek, 2011). Changes in the context can affect the level of customer engagement with the brand over time, as the number of available engagement interactions may sensibly vary, as well as their costs (sustained by both companies and customers alike). The advent of the digital transformation has revolutionized customer engagement management, by providing many more accessible environments for interactions to occur. Similarly, different contexts may imply differences in customer preferences and perceived costs and efforts as well as in the company's assets and expertise (Fernandes and Esteves, 2016). As such, differences in the engagement initiatives adopted by firms are once again attributable to contextual factors, both internal and external. Among touchpoints creating engagement, we decided to dedicate a paragraph to loyalty programs, as major contributors to loyalty fostered through customer engagement; also, we will explore new technologies enabling enrichment of traditional touchpoints.

Customer engagement and loyalty programs

Loyalty programs are traditionally considered as one of the most powerful tools to foster loyalty through engagement. Being members of a loyalty program usually allows customers to benefit from a privileged relationship with the company, as well as a differentiated experience compared to that offered to non-members (Gupta et al., 2018). Moreover, multi-tier loyalty programs provide varying levels of tangible rewards and intangible benefits, thus integrating a variety of engaging stimuli (Bijmolt et al., 2018). Members are in fact exposed to unique benefits and experiences (Breugelmans et al., 2015).

The latest studies about engagement and loyalty programs led to the isolation of the loyalty program engagement concept, which was introduced to distinguish between customer engagement specific to the loyalty program offered and overall customer engagement oriented towards the brand itself. loyalty program engagement has been therefore conceptualized as a measure comprising several behaviours specific to the loyalty program context, that reflect customers' responses to the program's stimuli (Bruneau et al., 2018). The six behaviours identified – which also constitute the scale measuring loyalty program engagement – include but are not limited to actions traditionally indicating participation in a loyalty program, such as redeeming rewards (Steinhoff and Palmatier, 2016), and the hierarchical order in which they are provided displays an increase in the effort and proactivity exerted by consumers. Loyalty program engagement, therefore, involves:

- proactive use of the loyalty card
- point-redemption activities
- changes in one's purchase behaviours to take advantage of the loyalty program's offers, reserved to members
- information sharing concerning the loyalty program
- careful consideration of the information received about the loyalty program
- proactive search of such information.

The integration within a single framework of a variety of engagement behaviours is also consistent with the existence of multiple degrees of engagement, that come with a different intensity. For example, card users-only or redeemers-only might be doing so out of habit, thus reflecting a low level of engagement. This also suggests that traditional, individual measures, might not be sufficient to signal customer engagement.

Despite allowing a separate evaluation of customer engagement specific to this instrument, loyalty program engagement is not isolated per se. Research has in fact demonstrated that loyalty program engagement improves overall customer engagement and customer loyalty (Meyer-Waarden et al., 2023), acting as a driver. This happens because it establishes customers' presence in the relationship with the brand, which was built through the loyalty program (Bruneau et al., 2018). The study by Meyer-Waarden et al. (2023) also identifies elements of the loyalty programs driving loyalty program engagement: the researchers found that the perceived value of rewards offered by the program may heavily impact on engagement. Such value is defined in terms of financial value, personalization and preferential treatment experienced by customers, that may vary in accordance with customers' individual preferences and characteristics (Ashley et al., 2016). Finally, loyalty program engagement is subject to contextual variance, as differences are found in diverse retailing sectors as what concerns relations with its antecedents and outcomes (Meyer-Waarden et al., 2023).

Customer engagement and new tools and technologies

Among emerging directions for customer engagement development, new technologies represent huge opportunities companies should start exploring, in search of synergies with the online and offline touchpoints they already implemented (Lim et al., 2022).

Artificial intelligence (AI) is a first venue for future improvement of customer engagement, both in the collection and processing of customer data. AI-enabled tools (such as enhanced mobile apps, voice and image recognition, self-service technology) can improve customer engagement by delivering timely messages and recommendations, across multiple platforms, personalized in line with customer preferences. Moreover, AI can allow integration of multiple campaign, it can help tracking and recording customer insights and it can support their analysis through machine learning of big data, leading to more precise customer segmentation (Kumar et al., 2019).

Virtual and augmented reality follow as tools to foster customer engagement (Hollebeek et al., 2020). The use of virtual reality (VR) holds the potential to create personalized, immersive and engaging customer experiences; in this sense, it provides a virtual environment that companies may dedicate to customer engagement. Augmented reality (AR) overlays digital elements to the physical environment customers are visiting, that can be activated through mobile phones' cameras. AR allows marketers to design sensory, enjoyable and playful experiences in a real-world setting, enabling engagement with more freedom for customers – who, unlike with VR, do not need a headset to participate in the experience.

On the one hand, the implementation of these tools allows companies to create engagement within each single customer visit to the physical or digital environment, which is particularly crucial to initiate relationships with new customers or in contexts where interactions are particularly swift, such as e-commerce websites (Demangeot and Broderick, 2016). On the other hand, they also support and enhance new ways through which engagement is created. Storytelling is a first technique that has been greatly enhanced by the introduction of VR and AR technologies, as they help providing customers with significant experiences, of compelling and emotional content, to be shared later in the form of personal stories (Lim et al., 2024). Moreover, AI tools can be used to help companies track customer-generated content and promote the co-creation of future storytelling across platforms (Lim et al., 2022). Similarly, gamification can benefit from these technologies in enhancing the experiences designed and making them more attractive, thus increasing the number of motivated customers adhering to gamified programs (Koivisto and Hamari, 2019).

Although relatively new in research and practice, the concept of gamification holds a huge potential for fostering customer engagement and customer loyalty, which companies have just started to explore and implement. The following paragraphs will be therefore dedicated to framing gamification and its outcomes and identify the mechanisms through which it influences customers' engagement and loyalty intentions.

What is gamification?

Gamification has been defined as the use of game-design elements in non-gaming contexts (Deterding et al., 2011), or the 'process of enhancing a service with affordances for gameful experiences in order to support user's overall value creation' (Huotari and Hamari, 2012, p. 25). Formally, gamification first appeared, as a term and as a concept, in 2010. During that year's Dice Conference held in Los Angeles, Jesse Schell, CEO of Schell Games and professor at CMU in Pittsburgh, made a speech in which he described a near future in which gaming would extend to everyday life, in a convergence with real life. Since then, gamification has become increasingly pervasive in a wide range of areas, from education (Landers and Landers, 2014), to human resource management (Kim, 2018), to marketing and retailing (Poncin et al., 2017; Souiden et al., 2018), as a means to motivate users and promoting certain actions, behaviours or emotional responses.

It is worth stressing the difference between 'gaming' and 'gamification', since the latter only adapts a few elements of gaming to diverse contexts. In gaming, the entertainment of the user-player is the ultimate goal of the entire experience, even in contexts in which the subtext intends to convey values; in gamification, such entertainment is the mere means by which to make the experience more interesting and enjoyable for users-customers. That is because gamification is oriented at promoting an activity, a service, a product, a brand, while eliciting emotions and behaviours. Moreover, the term 'gamification' itself recalls 'game' rather than 'play', hinting that entertainment is structured and subject to precise rules, as opposed to the purposeless spontaneity of play (Deterding et al., 2011).

The elements used to gamify activities and experiences can be manifold and include – but are not limited to – self-representation with avatars; 3D environments; narrative; feedback; reputations, ranks and levels; competition subject to explicit rules; teams; parallel communication systems; time pressure (Reeves and Read, 2009). In order for gamified experiences to be effective, these elements must be integrated into a carefully designed experience by adopting a reasoned process. A first insight from literature is that game design elements are pertaining to different levels of abstraction, thus indicating a hierarchy in their implementation. Five levels of abstraction have been identified: Table 6.2 presents the elements from the most concrete to the most abstract.

So far, various gamification conceptual models have been proposed in academia and practice, to provide guidance when designing gamified experiences.

TABLE 6.2 Game design elements and levels of abstraction

Element	Definition
Interface design patterns = Badges, levels or leaderboards	Interaction design components that explicitly qualify the interface
Game mechanics = Time-based or resource-based constraints; turns	The complex of structure and rules that constitute the mechanics of the game, recurring throughout the gameplay
Design principles = Long-lasting gameplay, clear objectives, variety of playing styles	Guidelines for approaching a design problem or solution
Conceptual models of game design units = MDA (mechanics-dynamics-aesthetics), challenge, trivia, alternate realities	Different models of design, concerning either the game's components or its overall experience
Game design methods = Playtesting*, value-based game design	Practices and processes specific to game design

Source: adapted from Deterding et al. (2011) and Deterding (2015).

* Playtesting refers to processes through which selected players have access to a game's early version (or some of its sections) in order to test for bugs and design flaws before the game is released to the market. By now, playtests have become an established part of games' quality control process.

The first models were originated from game design frameworks, among them, the dominant one is the so-called 'MDA', which stands for 'mechanics, dynamics and aesthetics' (Hunicke et al., 2004). The MDA approach formalizes the three game design elements of rules, system and fun, into mechanics, dynamics and aesthetics, respectively, that constitute the gaming experience for users. The mechanics element consists of all algorithms constituting the game structure, such as the game rules and the existence of points, levels, leaderboards, missions, etc. Dynamics define how the mechanics are executed in the game, based on the single player's and, eventually, other players' inputs; as such, they may determine the game's overall complexity and influence players' understanding of the rules. Finally, aesthetics are the desirable emotional responses evoked in the player when interacting with the dynamics and mechanics. The model also displays the designers' and players' perspectives as opposite: designers have full control over mechanics, partial control over dynamics and could only anticipate players' emotional responses; by contrast, players are immediately exposed to the Aesthetics, and only over time they come to understand dynamics first and mechanics later (see Figure 6.1).

The main insight emerging from the MDA framework is that designers always have to consider the users' perspective so as to provide an experience-based and therefore interesting design.

Subsequent gamification frameworks drew from the MDA but adapted its elements: for example, in Werbach et al.'s (2012) framework, aesthetics are

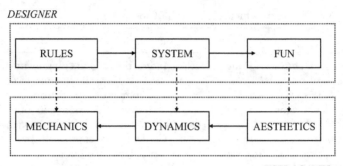

FIGURE 6.1 MDA game design framework.

Source: adapted from Hunicke et al. (2004).

replaced by components, since gamification is concerned only with the user experience. Moreover, Werbach et al. reorder the three elements according to their level of abstraction: dynamics are conceptual and serve the purpose of establishing the gamified experience's structure; mechanics include all processes encouraging users' involvement and driving their actions; and components include all concrete tools allowing the gamified system to be put into practice.

Where the aforementioned frameworks, based on structural elements, contribute specifically to the design of gamified experiences, other, more extensive, models, also formalize the stages dedicated to gamification processes' planning and management. For example, a first attempt called the 6D framework included the definition of the business objective and the target behaviours that the gamified experience should elicit. Another well-known model is the Octalysis framework (Chou, 2015), which identifies eight core drives gamification should elicit through motivators so as to provoke behaviours.

In their review of gamification frameworks in academic literature, Mora et al. (2017) identified more than 35 frameworks, many of which have been developed for specific contexts (17 in the business domain, 6 in education and learning, etc.). Across these many diverse frameworks, however, we were able to identify some common principles that should be integrated into the gamified experiences in order to elicit users' responses.

- **Principles leading to a behavioural response**: clear and relevant objectives; immediate feedback; positive reinforcement post-actions; guided sequential paths; simplified user experiences.
- **Principles eliciting emotional responses by fuelling a positive self-perception**: individual goals; adaptive content; multiple choices available and user's self-determination.
- **Principles allowing social interactions**: competition; social comparison; social norms.

Gamification as a customer engagement approach

As anticipated, gamification has been adopted in multiple contexts and has proven useful to elicit behavioural and attitudinal responses on a variety of targets, including customers, employees, students, etc. In all of these areas, several studies have investigated and acknowledged the effects, mostly positive, of gamification.

Gamification has been found to improve learning processes by stimulating creative and critical thinking, and by allowing clearer understanding through edutainment (Sailer and Homner, 2020). As what concerns emotions, gamification has the potential to drive the senses of enjoyment, flow, satisfaction, autonomy, accomplishment and mastery, that are traditionally induced by games and gameplay elements (Alsawaier, 2018). Moreover, gamification can be considered as a 'motivational information system' (Koivisto and Hamari, 2019). In the context of games, the experiences provided make the product itself intrinsically motivating, thus sustaining the user's future engagement and repeated usage. Gamification takes this approach a step further, as similar motivational effects are transferred towards the activity or behaviour the user is expected to perform. Finally, gamification has potential impacts on behaviours such as teamwork and performance improvement, or participation and engagement. In this sense, Harwood and Garry (2015), propose the view of gamification as a customer engagement approach to design effective experiences. According to this study, gamification fosters engagement-related behaviours through emotional responses and motivational states. Moreover, gamified experiences creating Engagement also contribute to customer engagement's own outcomes, such as improvement of brand-customer relationships through trust and commitment and customer loyalty.

There are many psychological and sociological theories supporting gamification's various effects. Regarding motivation, a commonly used theoretical framework is the self-determination theory (SDT) (Ryan and Deci, 2000; Ryan et al., 2006). According to the SDT – and to its derived theories – individuals find motivation towards performing a certain behaviour in intrinsic reasons (i.e. related to the current activity itself) or in extrinsic reasons (e.g. related to incentives and benefits, interpersonal relations, etc.). Games, as well as gamified activities, respond specifically to the internal motivational needs of autonomy, competence and relatedness. Playing is an autonomous activity, as users adhere voluntarily. Competence is achieved through the gameplay, where users are facing and overcoming challenges designed to be accessible (Deterding, 2015). Relatedness, which refers to acceptance and recognition, is achieved through the social environments created within or around the gamified activity (Koivisto and Hamari, 2019). Further studies also addressed the influence of gamification on reinforcing individuals' extrinsic motivation, through the expectancy value theory (EVT). All gamified activities, in fact, include rewards of different nature, which users will obtain by performing the desired behaviour (Vassileva, 2012). Among these mechanisms, the most common are:

- *Points and rewards*: a certain amount of points are awarded to the user for task completion (e.g. in-game challenges, referrals, reviews, purchase, etc). Points have an extrinsic value for customers in accordance with the rewards they could obtain by cumulating them, and an intrinsic value related to their role as immediate positive reinforcement. Structures may be less or more complex, such as those involving *achievements*, bonuses that users can get by completing specific goals and usually include additional points or items. Rewards themselves may vary from in-game prizes to discounts, coupons and personalized offers to be used in the real world.
- *Badges*: symbols, coats of arms and trophies that certify the fulfilment of a specific objective. They stimulate continued action through motivation mechanisms related to both competence and affiliation: on the one hand, users achieve badges because of the skills they perfected or the effort they put through; on the other hand, badges are recognized among other players and therefore serve as status symbols.
- *Levels and status*: levels gained through in-game experience document users' progress and are used to classify and segment them based on their performances. Users can always access their own level and requirements to advance; moreover, interfaces such as rankings and leaderboards track and display users' progresses to the whole community, which promotes competition and, sometimes, cooperation.
- *Missions, challenges and goals*: missions foster competition, curiosity and, in turn, continuity in participation. Challenges and 'striving for results' motivate and attract users, to the point that sometimes certain areas or functionalities are subordinate to the completion of certain missions. By completing missions and challenges, users are therefore rewarded both intrinsically and extrinsically. In order for the experience not to be frustrating, goals must be clearly communicated and well-defined; also, missions' difficulty can be adjusted based on the increase of the user's skills.

Besides these mechanisms, gamified experiences and environments must also be able to elicit emotions, which happens under certain circumstances. According to the flow theory (Csikszentmihalyi, 1990, 2014), users are able to experience a state of total involvement whenever individuals are faced with tasks that reflect their abilities and that they perceive as within their reach, whenever they are so immersed to lose their self-consciousness and time perception, and whenever their control over the interactions is maximized. Games and gamified experiences, therefore, may achieve such an emotional response by means of well-defined goals, rules, challenges and feedbacks (Zichermann and Cunningham, 2011). These emotions, in turn, fuel customer engagement with the gamified activity first – thus ensuring continued interaction – and the desired behaviour later.

Discussing a concrete application of these principles can be useful to understand how gamified elements of an experience create engagement within customers. The study by Hamari (2017) consists of a gamification intervention on a marketplace with the purpose of increasing both customer engagement and customers' transactions (i.e. the desired behavioural outcome). The setting of the experiment was a marketplace dedicated to peer-to-peer trading services: customers from a narrow local community – specifically, a major university in Finland – could buy and sell goods and services, as well as conclude non-monetary transactions such as borrowing and carpooling. The experiment lasted about two years and involved the monitoring of customers' actions before and after the implementation of the gamified experience. A total of 2989 users were involved, divided into two homogeneous groups: 1410 were in the control group (i.e. their behaviour was tracked during the year before the gamification intervention) and 1579 were exposed to the experiment (i.e. they registered on the marketplace after the implementation of the gamified mechanisms and were followed over the next year). The gamification intervention consisted of the introduction of badges and missions. The badges were design in line with those available on the gaming platforms Steam and Xbox Live: all badges had a different name, visual and description, thus providing clear goals and feedback to the user related to the actions undertaken. For example, badges were awarded for general use activity (logging in or browsing), carrying out transactions, interacting with questions or comments about listed goods and services; also, other additional badges were designed for specialty actions, such as a Christmas-themed badge for donations during the month of December. An additional level of challenge was introduced through a statuses-based system: all badges in fact could be obtained in three levels (Bronze, Silver and Gold). Bronze badges were obtained after performing the required activity twice, Silver required six actions, and Gold required fifteen actions, thus pushing the customer to be very active on the marketplace. Such a system, therefore, implemented both principles leading to a behavioural response and principles eliciting a positive self-perception.

A final mechanism was introduced to encourage social interactions, as unlocked badges in the user's profile became visible to every other user.

Metrics used to measure and compare behaviours before and after the gamification intervention included: the number of trade proposals published on the marketplace, the number of comments posted, the number of pages viewed individually by each user, and the number of transactions completed. Results were analysed by controlling for the network effect (i.e. the number of active users on the platform at time of registration, which can contribute to increasing Engagement), and the users' length-of-relationship with the marketplace.

After one year from the introduction of the badge system, three of these metrics displayed a significant increase:

- Page views per user increased from 45 to 83.
- The number of comments posted was five times higher than before (from one comment every 10 users to one comment every 2 users).
- Similarly, the average number of transactions increased from one transaction every 10 users to one transaction every 2 users.

Following the introduction of the gamified mechanism, therefore, users were most likely to use the service and actively interact with the marketplace, with a significant growth of their engagement interactions and behaviours.

Gamification in loyalty management

Gamification and loyalty are closely related by nature: many gamification mechanisms, in fact, share substantial logics with loyalty initiatives, first and foremost with loyalty programs. The points-reward mechanisms are typical of loyalty programs, and so are statuses, which are a core feature of tier-based schemes. As such, gamifying loyalty initiatives and programs may benefit from structural synergies between the elements of gamification and the characteristics of loyalty tools.

Studies concerning gamification and loyalty programs demonstrated its role in increasing customer loyalty, intention to enrol in the loyalty program and active participation to the loyalty program. This emerges clearly from the study conducted by Hwang and Choi (2020), who tested the effectiveness of a gamified loyalty program against a 'traditional' one. The study involved around 200 participants in an online experiment conducted through a mobile app. The control version of the loyalty program had a traditional point-accrual structure based on each dollar spent by customers, whereas the gamified version introduced a lottery-based (bingo) mechanism, in line with the Starbucks Bingo Challenge. Every 200 points collected, customers enrolled in both loyalty programs could redeem them for a $5 reward, either a coupon they could use on their next purchase or a donation to a local charity. Users were randomly assigned to one or the other loyalty programs and were asked to fill out a satisfaction questionnaire, stating their intention to participate by downloading the program app. Results from the study showed that satisfaction with the loyalty program increased on average by 13% for the gamified program, and so did the intention to actively participate in the loyalty program. Gamification, however, did not change the preferences for 'individualistic' or 'altruistic' rewards. These results are in line with established research on loyalty programs, that demonstrate that attractive loyalty programs stimulate loyalty towards the loyalty program itself and enhance customer satisfaction (Yi and Jeon, 2003). It can therefore be inferred that gamified loyalty programs are perceived as more attractive by members, appearing to their eyes as new, innovative and interesting (Hofacker et al., 2016).

Beyond loyalty programs, gamification has been found to positively foster other loyalty-related behaviours and attitudes. Evidence from research has shown that gamification does improve retention in highly competitive environments (see Zhang et al., 2023, on the mobile payment market), and patronage intention (Hamari, 2017).

Although gamification is most of the time discussed or applied in the online context – applied through digital touchpoints – it can be effectively extended to offline environments as well (so-called 'analogue gamification'), and it can give rise to hybrid forms. Gamification can therefore be adapted to loyalty initiatives that are increasingly becoming omnichannel. This is the case of an interesting study developed in a sports retailing context was conducted by Högberg et al. (2019). The field experiment involved around 400 customers recruited in-store and was conducted in the store itself. All customers received a smartphone and were asked to seek out six different locations (i.e. areas of the store, dedicated to different sports), where they would perform a task. In the 'control' version of the activity, the smartphone would not provide any gamified element besides the informational hints identifying the locations. On the contrary, the smartphone in the gamified version was equipped with a series of functionalities incorporating game mechanics. At each location, participants would receive sports-related quizzes: they had a 30 seconds-time limit to answer each question, they would receive individual feedback (visual: green or red lights and textual: correct or incorrect answers) and also information about other participants' responses, cues and functions to help them answer questions, and a progress bar. At the end of the activity, all participants would receive a 20% discount coupon, to be used the same day. Participants in the control group of the experiment would receive the discount coupon only for participating in the activity, whereas participants in the gamified activity would receive the discount coupon only after successfully completing 4 out of 6 quizzes. At the end of the activity, customers were asked to disclose about their enjoyment and engagement with the activity, the satisfaction with the reward received, and their attitude towards the retailer. Results showed that gamification is also effective in creating in-store hedonic value through enhanced customer experiences, and that it causally affects positive affect towards the retailer – thus fostering attitudinal loyalty. The study by Högberg et al. (2019) also provides insights over effectiveness of different gamification mechanisms on specific goals. In this study, the quiz-based mechanism was not effective neither on reward satisfaction nor on steering customers towards a specific purchase in-store (although it did work on creating engagement and attitudinal loyalty, which is consistent with other studies on digital engagement – see Kunkel et al., 2021).

The context- and goal-related effectiveness of gamification mechanisms is, in fact, an aspect that is being currently investigated by academic research and that constitutes one of the major future directions for both researchers and practitioners. From a managerial point-of-view, it becomes in fact crucial to understand which mechanisms better serve the business' purposes. Other future research directions concern the use of gamification for companies to promote green and socially sustainable behaviours. As anticipated in Chapter 3, in recent years, many companies have started integrating sustainability within their loyalty initiatives and programs, (re)designing experiences, programs and communities where information is shared and conscious behaviours are promoted. Gamification might therefore encourage customers' engagement in these activities and create balance between for-profit and non-for-profit companies' objectives (Liu et al., 2024).

References

Alsawaier, R. S. (2018) 'The effect of gamification on motivation and engagement'. *The International Journal of Information and Learning Technology*, 35(1), 56–79.

Ashley, C., Gillespie, E. A. and Noble, S. M. (2016) 'The effect of loyalty program fees on program perceptions and engagement'. *Journal of Business Research*, 69(2), 964–973.

Bijmolt, T. H., Krafft, M., Sese, F. J. and Viswanathan, V. (2018) 'Multi-tier loyalty programs to stimulate customer engagement'. *Customer Engagement Marketing*, 119–139.

Bolton, R. N. (2011) 'Comment: Customer engagement: Opportunities and challenges for organizations'. *Journal of Service Research*, 14(3), 272–274.

Brakus, J. J., Schmitt, B. H. and Zarantonello, L. (2009) 'Brand experience: what is it? How is it measured? Does it affect loyalty?'. *Journal of Marketing*, 73(3), 52–68.

Breugelmans, E., et al. (2015) 'Advancing research on loyalty programs: a future research agenda'. *Marketing Letters*, 26, 127–139.

Brodie, R. J., Hollebeek, L. D., Jurić, B. and Ilić, A. (2011) 'Customer engagement: conceptual domain, fundamental propositions, and implications for research'. *Journal of Service Research*, 14(3), 252–271.

Bruneau, V., Swaen, V. and Zidda, P. (2018) 'Are loyalty program members really engaged? Measuring customer engagement with loyalty programs'. *Journal of Business Research*, 91, 144–158.

Chan, T. K., Zheng, X., Cheung, C. M., Lee, M. K. and Lee, Z. W. (2014) 'Antecedents and consequences of customer engagement in online brand communities'. *Journal of Marketing Analytics*, 2, 81–97.

Chou, Y.-K. (2015) *Actionable Gamification: Beyond Points, Badges, and Leaderboards*. Fremont, CA: Octalysis Media.

Csikszentmihalyi, M. (1990) *Flow: The Psychology of Optimal Experience*. New York: Harper Perennial.

Csikszentmihalyi, M. (2014) 'Play and intrinsic rewards'. In M. Csikszentmihalyi, *Flow and the Foundations of Positive Psychology*, 135–153. New York: Springer.

de Oliveira Santini, F., Ladeira, W. J., Pinto, D. C., Herter, M. M., Sampaio, C. H. and Babin, B. J. (2020) 'Customer engagement in social media: a framework and meta-analysis'. *Journal of the Academy of Marketing Science*, 48, 1211–1228.

Demangeot, C. and Broderick, A. J. (2016) 'Engaging customers during a website visit: a model of website customer engagement'. *International Journal of Retail & Distribution Management*, 44(8), 814–839.

Deterding, S. (2015) 'The lens of intrinsic skill atoms: a method for gameful design'. *Human-Computer Interaction*, 30(3–4), 294–335.

Deterding, S., Dixon, D., Khaled, R. and Nacke, L. (2011) 'From game design elements to gamefulness: defining' gamification'. Paper presented at the *15th International Academic MindTrek Conference: Envisioning Future Media Environments*, Tampere, Finland, 28–30 September.

Fernandes, T. and Esteves, F. (2016) 'Customer engagement and loyalty: a comparative study between service contexts'. *Services Marketing Quarterly*, 37(2), 125–139.

Gupta, S., Gupta, T. and Shainesh, G. (2018) 'Navigating from programme loyalty to company loyalty'. *IIMB Management Review*, 30(3), 196–206.

Hamari, J. (2017) 'Do badges increase user activity? A field experiment on the effects of gamification'. *Computers in Human Behavior*, 71, 469–478.

Harwood, T. and Garry, T. (2015) 'An investigation into gamification as a customer engagement experience environment'. *Journal of Services Marketing*, 29(6/7), 533–546.

Hofacker, C. F., De Ruyter, K., Lurie, N. H., Manchanda, P. and Donaldson, J. (2016) 'Gamification and mobile marketing effectiveness'. *Journal of Interactive Marketing*, 34(1), 25–36.

Högberg, J., Ramberg, M. O., Gustafsson, A. and Wästlund, E. (2019) 'Creating brand engagement through in-store gamified customer experiences'. *Journal of Retailing and Consumer Services*, 50, 122–130.

Hollebeek, L. D. (2011) 'Demystifying customer brand engagement: exploring the loyalty nexus'. *Journal of Marketing Management*, 27(7–8), 785–807.

Hollebeek, L. D., Clark, M. K., Andreassen, T. W., Sigurdsson, V. and Smith, D. (2020) 'Virtual reality through the customer journey: framework and propositions'. *Journal of Retailing and Consumer Services*, 55, 102056.

Hoyer, W. D., Chandy, R., Dorotic, M., Krafft, M. and Singh, S. S. (2010) 'Consumer cocreation in new product development'. *Journal of Service Research*, 13(3), 283–296.

Hunicke, R., LeBlanc, M. and Zubek, R. (2004) 'MDA: a formal approach to game design and game research'. Paper presented at the *AAAI Workshop on Challenges in Game AI*, San Jose, California, 25–26 July.

Huotari, K., and Hamari, J. (2012) 'Defining gamification: a service marketing perspective'. Paper presented at the *16th International Academic MindTrek Conference*, Tampere, Finland, 3–5 October. https://doi.org/10.1145/2393132.239313

Hwang, J. and Choi, L. (2020) 'Having fun while receiving rewards?: Exploration of gamification in loyalty programs for consumer loyalty'. *Journal of Business Research*, 106, 365–376.

Kim, T. W. (2018) 'Gamification of labor and the charge of exploitation'. *Journal of Business Ethics*, 152(1), 27–39.

Koivisto, J. and Hamari, J. (2019) 'The rise of motivational information systems: a review of gamification research'. *International Journal of Information Management*, 45, 191–210.

Kumar, V., Rajan, B., Gupta, S. and Pozza, I. D. (2019) 'Customer engagement in service'. *Journal of the Academy of Marketing Science*, 47, 138–160.

Kunkel, T., Lock, D. and Doyle, J. P. (2021) 'Gamification via mobile applications: a longitudinal examination of its impact on attitudinal loyalty and behavior toward a core service'. *Psychology & Marketing*, 38(6), 948–964.

Landers, R. N. & Landers, A. K. (2014) 'An empirical test of the theory of gamified learning: the effect of leaderboards on time-on-task and academic performance'. *Simulation & Gaming*, 45(6), 769–785.

Lim, W.M., Rasul, T., Kumar, S. and Ala, M. (2022) 'Past, present and future of customer engagement'. *Journal of Business Research*, 140, 439–458.

Lim, W. M., Jasim, K. M. and Das, M. (2024) 'Augmented and virtual reality in hotels: impact on tourist satisfaction and intention to stay and return'. *International Journal of Hospitality Management*, 116, 103631.

Liu, X., Zhou, Z., Yuen, K. F. and Wang, X. (2024) 'Green and gamified! An investigation of consumer participation in green last-mile from a gamification affordance perspective'. *Journal of Retailing and Consumer Services*, 79, 103808.

Meyer-Waarden, L., Bruwer, J. and Galan, J. P. (2023) 'Loyalty programs, loyalty engagement and customer engagement with the company brand: consumer-centric behavioral psychology insights from three industries'. *Journal of Retailing and Consumer Services*, 71, 103212.

Mora, A., Riera, D., González, C. and Arnedo-Moreno, J. (2017) 'Gamification: a systematic review of design frameworks'. *Journal of Computing in Higher Education*, 29, 516–548.

Patterson, P., Yu, T. and De Ruyter, K. (2006) 'Understanding customer engagement in services'. *Proceedings of ANZMAC 2006 Conference, Brisbane*, 4(6), 1–8.

Poncin, I., Garnier, M., Mimoun, M. S. B. and Leclercq, T. (2017) 'Smart technologies and shopping experience: are gamification interfaces effective? The case of the Smartstore'. *Technological Forecasting and Social Change*, 124, 320–331.

Ramkumar, R., Kumar, A., Janakiraman, R. and Bezawada, R. (2013) 'The effect of customers' social media participation on customer visit frequency and profitability'. *Information Systems Research*, 24(1), 108–127.

Reeves, B. and Read, J. L. (2009) *Total Engagement: How Games and Virtual Worlds Are Changing the Way People Work and Businesses Compete*. Cambridge, MA: Harvard Business Press.

Romero, J. (2017) 'Customer engagement behaviors in hospitality: customer-based antecedents'. *Journal of Hospitality Marketing & Management*, 26(6), 565–584.

Ryan, R. M. and Deci, E. L. (2000) 'Intrinsic and extrinsic motivations: classic definitions and new directions'. *Contemporary Educational Psychology*, 25(1), 54–67.

Ryan, R. M., Rigby, C. S. and Przybylski, A. (2006) 'The motivational pull of video games: a self-determination theory approach'. *Motivation and Emotion*, 30, 344–360.

Ryu, G. and Feick, L. (2007) 'A penny for your thoughts: referral reward programs and referral likelihood'. *Journal of Marketing*, 71(1), 84–94.

Sailer, M. and Homner, L. (2020) 'The gamification of learning: a meta-analysis'. *Educational Psychology Review*, 32(1), 77–112.

Souiden, N., Ladhari, R. & Chiadmi, N. E., (2018) 'New trends in retailing and services'. *Journal of Retailing and Consumer Services*, 52, 286–288.

Steinhoff, L. and Palmatier, R. W. (2016) 'Understanding loyalty program effectiveness: managing target and bystander effects'. *Journal of the Academy of Marketing Science*, 44, 88–107.

Van Doorn, J., Lemon, K. N., Mittal, V., Nass, S., Pick, D., Pirner, P. and Verhoef, P. C. (2010) 'Customer engagement behavior: theoretical foundations and research directions'. *Journal of Service Research*, 13(3), 253–266.

Vassileva, J. (2012) 'Motivating participation in social computing applications: a user modeling perspective'. *User Modeling and User-Adapted Interaction*, 22, 177–201.

Vivek, S. D., Beatty, S. E. and Morgan, R. M. (2012) 'Customer engagement: exploring customer relationships beyond purchase'. *Journal of Marketing Theory and Practice*, 20(2), 122–146.

Vivek, S. D., Beatty, S. E., Dalela, V. and Morgan, R. M. (2014) 'A generalized multidimensional scale for measuring customer engagement'. *Journal of Marketing Theory and Practice*, 22(4), 401–420.

Voorhees, C. M., Baker, J., Bourdeau, B. L., Brocato, E. D. and Cronin Jr, J. J. (2009) 'It depends: moderating the relationships among perceived waiting time, anger, and regret'. *Journal of Service Research*, 12(2), 138–155.

Werbach, K., Hunter, D. and Dixon, W. (2012) *For the Win: How Game Thinking Can Revolutionize Your Business (Vol. 1)*. Philadelphia, PA: Wharton digital press.

Wirtz, J., Den Ambtman, A., Bloemer, J., Horváth, C., Ramaseshan, B., Van De Klundert, J. & Kandampully, J. (2013) 'Managing brands and customer engagement in online brand communities'. *Journal of Service Management*, 24(3), 223–244.

Yi, Y. and Jeon, H. (2003) 'Effects of loyalty programs on value perception, program loyalty, and brand loyalty'. *Journal of the Academy of Marketing Science*, 31(3), 229–240.

Zhang, L., Shao, Z., Benitez, J. and Zhang, R. (2023) 'How to improve user engagement and retention in mobile payment: a gamification affordance perspective'. *Decision Support Systems*, *168*, 113941.

Zichermann, G. and Cunningham, C. (2011) *Gamification by Design: Implementing Game Mechanics in Web and Mobile Apps*. Sebastopol, CA: O'Reilly Media.

7

USING CUSTOMER INSIGHT IN RETAIL MANAGEMENT

Michela Giacomini and Miriam Panìco

Customer insight

Behind every sales dollar there is a customer

Everybody needs to buy food on a regular basis and when they do so they leave with retailers millions of data points through their transactions. More information still is available when one uses a loyalty card because the retailer can easily track the history, habits and needs of every customer. The availability and processability of such a wealth of data is the reason why customer insight has found such fertile ground within the retail industry, and why customer analytics has increased and evolved massively in the last three decades, enjoying the proliferation of data sources (online, offline and third-party) and increasingly sophisticated models with which to utilize them. Here we retrace the steps of the customer insight evolution by presenting the types of analysis that retailers usually employ.

Customer insight in the retail industry starts with the basic view of business performance as being a combination of stores and products and then adds various dimensions of customer behaviour, such as frequency, recency, spend, acquisition and retention, each being behavioural aspects of the customer experience (as discussed in Chapter 5). A simple example is the decomposition analysis of key performance indicators (KPIs) whereby analysts try to decompose the effects of sales performance (see Figure 7.1) and demonstrate that every shift in sales is due to a change in customer behaviour.

In the past, these data referred to in-store behaviour only. Today, of course, a multichannel or purely online retailer wants to better understand its customers and the differences between online, offline and cross-shopping customer

DOI: 10.4324/9781003400783-7

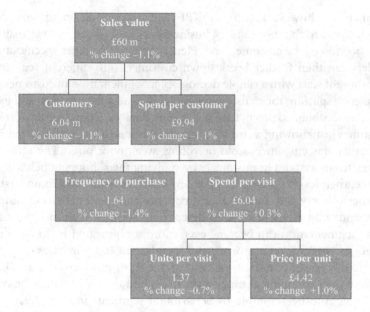

FIGURE 7.1 Decomposition analysis.

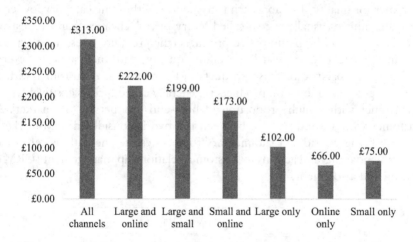

FIGURE 7.2 Spend per customer by customer group.

behaviour. Customers shopping cross-channel are actually more valuable to retailers, as is illustrated in Figure 7.2, which presents the spend per customer by customer group of an anonymized European retailer. It has therefore become fundamental to increase sales for bricks-and-mortar and multichannel retailers to understand the characteristics and needs of this group in order to move more customers online.

Sometimes, however, customer KPIs and decomposition analysis are not enough to get to the root cause of business performance, as changes may affect only a portion of the customer base. Hence the need for more specific analysis. Retailers can then further break down customers into different segments. A retailer might start with a simple demographic segmentation of customers – for example, by splitting their customer base by age and affluence. Age and income data can be obtained from national census data or from customer surveys. Sometimes just knowing a customer's postal address can give a good indication or whether this customer is old or young, wealthy or poor. The retailer can then try to understand its customers by studying their shopping behaviour, for instance, their level of loyalty or price sensitivity. A simple way to understand a customer's loyalty is to look at their frequency and spent per week: customers who spend and visit more are considered more engaged than those that don't.

The segmentation can become even more sophisticated by looking at the 'categories coverage': a customer who spends a lot but purchases only in two or three categories (e.g. pasta, frozen meals, fresh produce) is very likely to complete their shopping at other retail stores and therefore cannot be considered loyal. Another example of behavioural segmentation, as already mentioned, is price sensitivity. By looking at the type of products purchased over time, this segmentation aims to understand if customers are looking for price or rather for quality. The approach is to identify within one category low-end priced products (usually the so-called 'entry prices', cheaper than the rest of the category) and high-end priced products (the premium ones, most expensive in the category and usually of higher quality) and understand for every customer the balance of these products in their baskets. A customer with a high proportion of low-end products is generally called 'price-sensitive', while a customer with a high proportion of high-end products is 'up-market'. A customer with a good balance between the two is considered 'mid-market'. Despite being considered rudimentary today, these segmentations can drive recommendations and actions for customer relationship management (CRM), pricing and assortment.

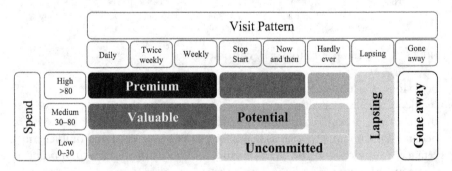

FIGURE 7.3   Customer shopping habits – a proxy for loyalty.

For example, retailers use these to:

- drive the frequency and spend of non-loyal customers through personalized offers
- reward and retain the most valuable customers
- retain and attract more customers by improving the pricing perception through better prices or more adequate assortment (particularly if a store has few loyal customers and a high proportion of price-sensitive customers).

And the list of examples could go on.

For retailers who aspire to know their customers better, customer insight enables the bespoke clustering of customers using a mix of demographic and shopping data, often informed by detailed attitudinal research on customer motivations. Each further division of the customer base helps uncover more detail on how a retailer is performing for different segments of the market-place. This further step in segmentation might be a lifestyle segmentation to identify macro-groups of customers with similar behaviours, needs and motivations, or something more specific like a health segmentation to identify micro-groups of customers with similar dietary habits (i.e. organic, vegan, sporty, etc.). Figure 7.4 presents an example of lifestyle segmentation and demonstrates how the split into groups is correlated with customers' price sensitivity.

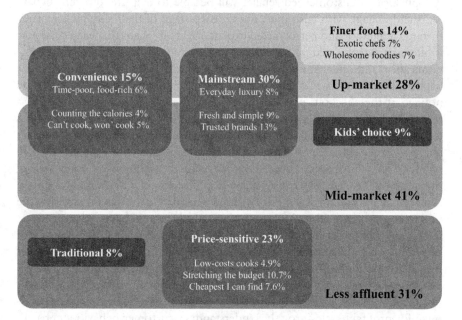

FIGURE 7.4   Example of lifestyle segmentation.

From clusters to personalization

To help retailers grow, all this understanding and analysis needs to trigger two important questions: 'why is this happening?' and 'what should I do about it?' And in today's multichannel world, responding is even more complex because customers are continuously exposed to multiple stimuli and therefore there is ever more and variegated data. Retailers' understanding must be quick, in real time and at the customer level. Answering these questions involves delving into the customer shopping journey (that we see as composed of the phases we call discover → shop → buy → reflect) and understanding the journey of every customer.

Looking at the customer journey, the questions a retailer wants an answer to become even more numerous.

1 To begin with, how do customers think about a retailer? What does its brand stand for? On what occasions would a customer shop at a particular store? How does the customer look for information about products?
2 How does the customer shop? Online or in-store? When? Where? Why?
3 What do they purchase? How do they pay? Are they collecting points or using a coupon?
4 And then, what are their thoughts after the purchase? Are they sharing the experience with friends or online? Will they shop here again?

A sophisticated customer-led retailer will be able to map the different behaviours and engage with customers during each stage of their shopping journey through a relevant and personalized experience. This means that each customer is offered a personalized path to higher levels of engagement via relevant communication and offers at each step. Even more relevant when the engagement happens in real time while shopping online. For example, a customer might be notified at the checkout phase if the product that she usually buys in a given time cycle has been missed or forgotten. The algorithm identifies that it is time to be repurchased. We will see a clear example of customer engagement later on in this chapter (Step 2: Strategic price and promo analysis). Equally, if there seems to be a problem at the 'shop' stage of the shopping journey (either online or offline), customer insight can help diagnose the barriers. This can be achieved by using statistical models that help to analyse the dynamics within the purchasing process such as looking at the way customers choose what products to pick up, but factoring in other influencing elements such as the importance of promotions, the exposure to communication and so forth. Once a retailer has built and validated robust models of how customers calculate the attractiveness of their brand and how they decide to buy different products in different circumstances, it is a relatively short step to prescribing smart changes to optimize for profitable sales growth. Understanding customer behaviour through the shopping journey will allow retailers and brands to respond to customers' needs in a more relevant way and, as a result, improve perception, which is anyway a long-term investment.

From past understanding to future forecasting

No retailer would put their strategies entirely in the hands of automated decision-making tools. However, scenario-forecasting category management tools and self-learning targeting algorithms show the extent to which the close integration of customer insight and retail management has become a modern reality. Scenario-forecasting tools allow managers to build 'what if' scenarios; for example, what's the effect of changing the prices of certain products? What happens to the sales of other products in the same category? Is there any cannibalization effect? And what happens to a certain customer group or to total performance? These kinds of forecasting and optimization models allow the retailer to take conscious and targeted decisions for pricing, promotions, assortment and space. Self-learning targeting algorithms are even more sophisticated, providing an automated diagnosis of the performance and the reasons behind it. There is no longer an analyst running hundreds of deep dives to identify the reason for poor performance; the machine automatically diagnoses the effect of multiple factors and detects and isolates the relevant ones.

From customer insight to capability/level management

We generally say that a company is customer-focused when customer insights are not just responding to quick ad hoc questions in order to understand and fix specific issues (a tactical approach) but when insights are regularly built to drive business decisions and strategic plans, to manage marketing and commercial levers in a customer-oriented way. Unfortunately, some retailers buy insights reporting or tools just to use the data, without having a clear understanding of where they are today, what they need, what they want to get out of the data or if they have the right resources or the right company culture. This behaviour can lead to ineffectual decisions. That's why we always recommend that our partners start from an assessment of capability, to *assess a retailer's existing sophistication in planning and execution* in any business area – from data, through loyalty and CRM, to pricing, promotions, assortment and so on. Such an approach explores the current tensions and practices in a detailed manner in order to identify *opportunities to progress along the capability ladder* at the right pace, taking into account business and customer needs and organizational readiness. This assessment generally gives an indication of where the retailer is for all business areas on:

- Strategic planning: the extent to which the actual planning aligns and supports the strategic objectives of the business.
- Process and governance: the presence and extent of established and embedded processes and adherence to them.
- People and integration: the specific roles, functions and structures within the organization, and centres of power.
- Customer understanding and data: the integration of data and customer insight into decision-making.
- Tools and reporting: the existence and use of supporting tools on delivering improved insight, planning and execution.
- Supplier collaboration: ways of working with suppliers.

Understanding at what level the retailer sits for each of these levers is the most important starting point to understanding how to grow and make the most of insights and data.

Figure 7.5 demonstrates the significance of the promotional lever. A retailer which doesn't use customer data but is driven only by the previous year's actions or trading experience is at the lowest level. The first data that are usually collected are competitive indexes as well as competitor information such as promotions they are running and how. This data can be used to set some promotional rules or identify competitive promotional prices (e.g. prices should never be 5% higher than that of the main competitors). Only 20% of retailers use customer data to build better promotions or understand which

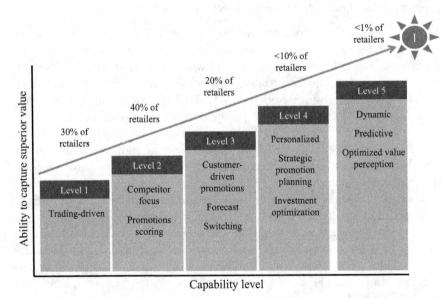

FIGURE 7.5 A retailer's capability levels.

products attract more customers and how customers behave when exposed to certain promotions (building 'what if' scenarios). The number of retailers that adopt even more sophisticated customer analysis is very limited and below 1%. Before using new customer data or building new tools, a retailer needs to know where it is in this journey and where it wants to go.

As we said before, we recommend that our partners start from an assessment of their capabilities to understand the *existing sophistication of planning and execution* in any business area. Retailers could be at different stages in any area. Some retailers, for instance, are pretty advanced in using data for their loyalty and CRM programs but still only take trading-driven decisions on pricing, promotions and assortment. It's important to run an assessment that allows retailers to focus on the levers that are most relevant to driving the loyalty of their target customers – and this is generally best understood through customer research.

Category management

Category management is a very important business approach: finding out what the customer wants will help retailers provide a better offer and shopping experience in every category. With the right category management in place, the customer receives the right assortment offering with optimal prices at the right placement in stores. We have demonstrated that successful category management should be customer-oriented, which means driven by customer insight rather than by old habits or intuition, in order to have a clear understanding of what customers want. However, it should also consider the financials and strategic decisions already taken by the company and be operationally manageable. This evolution in category management is what we call category leadership. The typical questions that a retailer should ask are listed in Figure 7.6 and most can be answered using data insights.

Improvements in category management represent a huge source of benefit to retailers: by applying an evolved, customer-centric category management approach, retailers' sales in the category can increase by more than 3%.

Category roles

One of the first questions to ask is always: how can I prioritize the categories most likely to drive customers to my stores? Retail is a highly competitive environment; unsurprisingly, we would all like to be the best at everything – but we can't afford to be. We have to make choices. Making tough choices is at the heart of successful category management. Some categories and some marketing levers are more important in driving sustainable growth than others. The challenge is knowing how to identify those categories, so you can make choices about where to invest.

CUSTOMER	FINANCIAL	STRATEGIC	OPERATIONAL
How can I focus on what is really important to customers in each category?	Which categories should I be investing in more – and less?	How can I make the customer's experience in categories reflect the strategic choices we make as a business?	How do I ensure my teams focus on activities that will really grow my categories, rather than trying to do everything everywhere?
How can I prioritize the categories most likely to drive customers to my stores?	How do I prioritize categories that are good for my bottom line?	How can I ensure all the resources at my disposal are aligned to my strategic priorities?	What targets should I set for each of my marketing levers?
How can I merchandise my categories more effectively for customers?	How can I get greater return on investment on all my category activities?		How can I get the best support from my suppliers and ensure we are aligned?

FIGURE 7.6   Key questions for successful category management.

Strategic choices can be taken when building category roles to identify groups of categories that may have the same strategic function for the retailer. Category roles will be useful for answering data-driven questions like: 'which categories are most important – both to the business and to my customers – and why?' Answering this question enables the definition of roles for each category.

In Figure 7.7 the 'importance to customer' is a composite score, built using customers KPIs like sales and frequency of purchase within the category. But it can also be enhanced using market research information, asking customers how much they value and how they shop in any specific category. The 'importance to retailer' is also a composite score and is based on performance versus the previous year and versus the market, where performance is generally calculated comparing this year's sales and margin versus those of the previous year. The matrix in Figure 7.7 will help the retailer to understand where the company needs to develop, win, control or protect. Business actions will be formalized according to the category roles, such as investing in the right levers (such as pricing, promotions and assortment) for the different categories or recovering some margin from those defined as 'control' in the category roles map. Now, this may sound like an obvious approach to managing categories, but it never fails to surprise us just how many retailers are still operating in silos with different categories being managed in isolation and out of sync with the overall objectives of the business. As the retail climate gets more and more challenging, the effective use of resources within category management will be essential for retailers to do well.

Every retailer has four resources they can spend on their categories:

Importance to customer

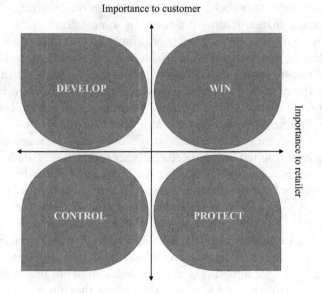

FIGURE 7.7   Category roles map.

- Money – how much should we invest in pricing, promotions or communications activity to drive the category?
- Time – how much should we allocate to managing and reviewing categories?
- People – who should we dedicate to managing which categories and what are the priorities?
- Space – how much should be allocated to different categories in-store?

Every category is in competition for these resources. How they are optimally allocated should depend on the category's priority and this should be intrinsically linked to the overall strategy for the business. More analysis will be required to understand what the right action is for every category: for instance, is it pricing, promotions or assortment? Examples of the analysis required to take business decisions will be illustrated in the paragraphs that follow.

Customer-oriented assortment

Assortment is an important business lever to consider when reviewing a category. It responds to the question above about resources in space: how much should be allocated to different categories in-store? Here is an example of how tough category choices were implemented to drive strategic change within one large European retailer through a rationalization of ranges. To make the shopping experience easier for customers, this retailer wanted to simplify assortment and reduce range across all food categories in-store, removing duplication while retaining market-leading products. In some categories, the range was reduced by up to 30%. By focusing on customer metrics rather than just commercial metrics, this retailer was able to identify and protect the products most important to customers (not necessarily the best-selling lines but those key to driving customer traffic and creating cross-selling opportunities, with low cannibalization of other products). With a 2% average uplift in sales, 1.4% volume growth and improved availability, the results were extremely positive for both retailer and customers. The smaller range and increased space in-store for remaining lines resulted in improved customer satisfaction. Paradoxically, the reduction in choice actually made it easier for customers to find what they were looking for, adding speed, ease and convenience to the overall shopping experience. A tough choice to make but ultimately the right one.

At the base of the described example there are analyses such as customer decision trees built using the substitutability index, that we explain below. A customer decision tree is a data-driven hierarchical clustering approach which provides a model for how shoppers make decisions about which products to purchase in a category and identifies the criteria they use to evaluate those products. Substitutability is an index which indicates how customers substitute products in their basket and is derived from looking at all customers' historical baskets. Let's take an example based on mayonnaise and assume that a retailer sells two brands (A and B) of 500-gram bottles. If product A is out of stock and customers who usually buy that product move to product B, then it means that the two products are substitutable. If product A is on promotion, and customers who usually buy that product move to product B, again it means that they are substitutable. If instead, customers don't switch it means that the products represent different needs and are not substitutable. In this case, basket analysis is more important than other research because, as we have seen from experience, what customers say is sometimes very different from what customers do.

In Figure 7.8 you can see a simple example of a customer decision tree for the oral care category. The tree shows how customers shop within the oral care category: a toothbrush and toothpaste are two separate needs, and a customer will never substitute a toothbrush with toothpaste! At a deeper level we understand that when a customer looks for a sensitive toothpaste, he or she will look for a specific brand. If a customer loves Brand 1, any product within that brand will be fine with them, while Brand 3 lovers will look for either paste or gel. Brand 3 gel is, therefore, a specific need, and the retailer should guarantee assortment coverage of Brand 3 gel in all its stores, including small ones. It's very interesting to notice that every retailer, or even every format within one retailer, could have different customer decision trees because their shoppers, and therefore their needs, will be different.

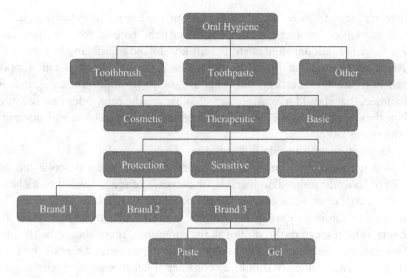

FIGURE 7.8 Example of a customer decision tree.

Customer-oriented assortment means identifying the best products to cover all customer needs and new needs may lead to unexpected new assortment opportunities that aren't being addressed. The best products are usually associated with business KPIs, such as sales combined with customers KPIs, frequency of purchase and spend per customer. When running a category review, a retailer should try to keep in its assortment the most important products for customers and remove the less important ones, but cover all the needs available – in all its stores' clusters, even the smallest local ones. It is important to note, however, that using customer data alone provides an internal view only, certainly more insightful than it has ever been before but still missing the gap analysis that market data can provide. For a proper range to be defined, retailers can gain a great deal from analysing competitors' data and sales. In e-commerce, there is less of a space issue, but it's still important to propose the products that are more appealing to customers to guarantee a complete coverage of needs and a positive shopping experience. It's also fair to say that even for e-commerce, no warehouse in the world could store all the products available on the market.

Space optimization

Another important business lever that responds to the space question is the layout of stores and the space allocated to every single category. Of course, this is more relevant to physical stores. Retailers must deliver a positive shopping experience that drives high performance. But sometimes managing multiple formats, store size and, as a consequence, layouts can be very challenging.

There are many tools on the market which provide space optimization, as well as planogram or layout recommendations. At the base of these sophisticated tools there is again data and customer insight, linked to information about the physical dimensions of products and space in stores. Analysis will support retailers to answer questions like what are the most important categories for customers that should have more space? What are the categories that sell more when they get more space? What's the right order of products and categories in the stores' aisles?

Space optimization analysis is based on elasticity models: all historical sales, coupled with information about the space available, must be collected and analysed to understand if an increase or decrease of space has led to a change in sales. More elastic categories will have more space than less elastic ones. The analysis and algorithms are quite complex because there are always space constraints to be respected: the sum of all the categories' space should be the same of the space available in-store. On top of this, the shape and size of the products within each category should be considered because some categories (like water in Italy, for instance) may come in big six-bottle packs and require a minimum space that is quite large, compared to other categories like spices that, again in Italy, take very little space. The analysis will provide the recommended space per category.

Category adjacencies, which means categories that should have an adjacent position in the layout for an eased customer shopping experience, can be identified using simple analyses such as the basket analysis mentioned earlier to identify products that are usually purchased together by customers. An example in the Italian market could be pasta with tomato sauce or oil; this indicates

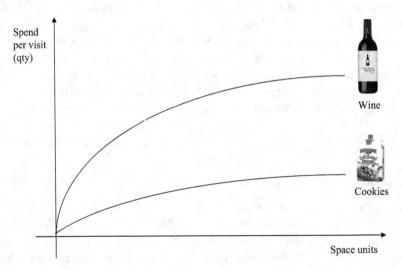

FIGURE 7.9 Elasticity curves examples.

that the three categories should be possibly in close proximity or sequence within the store.

Value for customers

Another critical resource investment point is money: how much should we invest in the category to drive customers' value perception? Every customer perceives a certain value for the products or services they want to buy, which is the gain that the customer will receive versus the price they can pay. Retailers generally want to understand what the average value perception of their customers is to be able to improve their offer and, as a consequence, increase loyalty and attract new customers. There are several analyses that can be run and many tools that can be purchased to understand and optimize the value for customers, from simple descriptive analyses to very sophisticated optimization and simulation tools. However, there is not a standard and fixed process: a retailer should adopt the solutions which better respond to its maturity level and its objectives, as already discussed. Here we give a simple example of a retailer's journey towards understanding what drives its customers' perception of value.

Step 1: Value driver research

A retailer who wants to analyse the value for customers should start by finding out what customers think about the existing offer. Understanding if a customer thinks the retailer is cheap or expensive is usually quite simple but identifying the drivers for value perception is from it. Certainly, regular prices and promotions play a big role, but these are far from the only factors. We all know, for instance, that communication is very important. A clear flyer with rounded and highlighted discounts or signage on the shop floor announcing promotional offers can condition customer perception and behaviour. Assortment is important as well: retailers proposing several 'entry prices' or fantasy brands can be perceived as cheap, while those offering only premium products can be perceived as expensive. Perception is then conditioned significantly by the actual offers of competitors in the area. Overall, we say that there are seven levers driving price perception.

A retailer who wants to prioritize actions for its business plan should start by understanding which levers are diving the price perception of its customers.

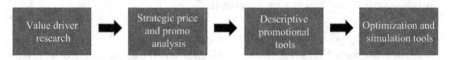

FIGURE 7.10   Retailer journey to improve customers' value perception.

FIGURE 7.11 Drivers of price perception.

Step 2: Strategic price and promo analysis

Pricing and promotion are usually the most important levers to determine value perception. Understanding how customers react to the changes in prices and promotions is fundamental to building the right value proposition, which can lead to better perception and therefore higher customer purchases. As pricing and promotion are part of the same 'ecosystem' just presented, we believe that they should be analysed and understood together in order to build integrated plans. Here is a list of questions that should be answered when building an integrated pricing and promotion plan:

- What are the important products for customers?
- How many price-sensitive customers shop in the stores and what products are important to them?
- How do customers react to price changes?

To answer these questions, retailers need to deploy some of the customer insights we discussed earlier in the chapter.

1 The first step is building measures of price sensitivity, which means identifying customers that prefer purchasing cheaper items, like entry prices, fantasy brands or private labels. Price-sensitive customers are generally more perceptive and reactive.

2 The second step is building composite rankings to identify the most important products for customers, based on simple KPIs like customer penetration (percentage of customers buying the product), customer penetration
for price-sensitive customers (or for other target customers groups such as
loyals), sales or quantity of products, and so forth. We might call the composite ranking 'importance to customers'.
3 The final step is building measures of price elasticity. Price elasticity
expresses how much sales can change as a consequence of price variation.
Accurate price elasticity estimates are usually built using a long history
(usually at least two years, to account for seasonal variation) and looking
at all the possible price variations, including price and promotional
changes. As we have already explained, we believe it's very important to
keep the two levers together to understand customer reactions to all possible changes.

This type of analysis can result in a very simple matrix that can lead to important strategic decisions (Figure 7.12).

In the Hi-Lo corner, we find products with high price elasticity but low
importance to customers. The strategy for these products is to regularly run
strong promotions and partially recover margins by increasing the regular
price. For products in the Hybrid corner, both prices and promotions are very
important and therefore these products should have a very competitive regular

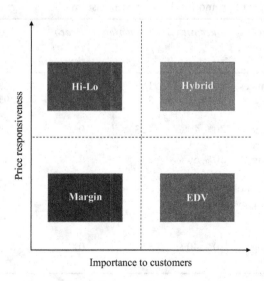

FIGURE 7.12 Matrix for taking strategic decisions based on price and promo
analysis.

price and be promoted regularly with competitive promotional prices. Products in the EDV (everyday value) corner are instead good candidates for an everyday-low-price regime with very good prices but a lack of promotions; promotions are not elastic and therefore do not generate more sales. Finally, products in the Margin area are ideal candidates to recover margins in both levers. This type of matrix is normally used to provide strategic category guidelines to buyers and category managers.

Step 3: Descriptive promotional tools

Category managers also need to understand the performance of previous offers and this usually happens through simple promotional reports that contain descriptive sales and customers KPIs, like the report presented in Tables 7.1 and 7.2. This report includes some exemplary KPIs; however, a retailer could tailor the report adding other KPIs or building different views, like summary tables, trend charts or multidimensional interactive views.

These kinds of reports are usually refreshed after every promotional campaign in order to provide real-time information to buyers and category managers. Whatever the view or the visualization tool is, it's important to understand how customers react to promotions to identify good promotions or drop bad ones. In Tables 7.1 and 7.2, for instance, we can see that important customer KPIs include:

TABLE 7.1 Example of promotional report with customer KPIs (part one)

Product	Category	Discount (%)	Promotional price	Reach (basket penetration)	Loyal customers reach	New customers attracted
AAA	Soya sauces	30%–40%	185	0.3%	32%	48%
BBB	Refinery sugar	0%–10%	36	0.6%	29%	67%
CCC	Weighted candies	30%–40%	423	0.2%	37%	5%
DDD	Drinking water	50%–60%	34	0.9%	24%	13%
EEE	Low-alcohol beverages	0%–10%	51	0.4%	23%	7%
FFF	Mineral water	30%–40%	25	0.3%	33%	7%
GGG	Drinking water	30%–40%	51	0%	31%	3%

TABLE 7.2 Example of promotional report with customer KPIs (part two)

Product	Category	Promotional sales	Cannibalized sales within the category	Incremental sales	Recommendation
AAA	Soya sauces	605,510	-17,171	568,438	Strongly recommended
BBB	Refinery sugar	543,580	-12,851	156,108	Acceptable
CCC	Weighted candies	611,385	-71,634	518,697	Avoid
DDD	Drinking water	296,867	-44,773	180,757	Strongly recommended
EEE	Low-alcohol beverages	617,310	-222,717	331,922	Avoid
FFF	Mineral water	260,392	-102,635	142,435	Avoid
GGG	Drinking water	300,674	-88,480	130,212	Recommended

- Reach: what proportion of all customers shopping purchase the product?
- New customers attracted: of all customers who buy into the offer, how many are new to the category? Or for the store?
- Incremental sales for the category: the difference between observed sales and expected sales (forecasted as if the product was not in promotion) can be considered incremental sales. And these are generally sales coming from existing customers buying more products or new customers attracted by the promotion.
- Cannibalization indicates how customers are switching between products. That is, if Coca-Cola is on promotion, what happens to the sales of other cola products? Again, this is built by forecasting sales for all the products in the category when Coca-Cola is not on promotion and comparing the result to what happens to Pepsi or other cola products when Coca-Cola is on promotion.

This kind of analysis is very useful and allows retailers to cut the tails of bad promotions and improve the overall performance of the promotional periods through improved sales and margin.

Step 4: Optimization and simulation tools

Retailers who have very good historical data, dedicated and skilled resources and a considerable budget can think about purchasing an optimization tool.

Advanced tools embed very sophisticated science in forecasting and optimization, which can support simulation scenarios. Where it is feasible, we recommend buying such a tool since building algorithms from scratch would take even numerous expert analysts considerable time (definitely more than a year!). This kind of tool eliminates guesswork from pricing by introducing a superior rule-based pricing engine that can determine the appropriate pricing based on a range of targets. Pricing rules can be automatically managed across thousands of products and categories. Pricing usually includes:

- Minimum and maximum gross margin rules.
- Brand rules to ensure budget brand products are priced lower than premium brand products.
- Product size rules to maintain the price per unit of measurement (e.g. price per litre) within product families (e.g. different sizes of Coke Zero).
- Product importance rules to allow different rules to be applied to the most and least important products to the retailer's customers.
- Competitor product rules to help maintain a retailer's price position against individual competitor products.

Optimization functionalities enable retailers to reach specific objectives in respect of the defined rules, such as:

1 Maximize the performance of each category in line with the role assigned to it by the retailer (i.e. maximize profit in a profit-driver category).
2 Meet the budgetary needs of each category (i.e. quarterly and half-year budgets on revenue, margin and profit).
3 Maximize the performance of a category with a focus on target customers.

Finally, these tools provide extensive simulation capabilities so that category managers and analysts can create and compare many different scenarios: what happens if we run a specific promotion in a certain period? What happens if we drop the regular prices by 5% in the everyday-low-price line? What happens if we change some promotional mechanics? And so on. Simulations use forecasting science to provide the estimated scenario. The best underlying customer demand models incorporate both promotion and non-promotion data to provide the retail industry with the best possible forecasting accuracy. Throughout our experience, we have been able to reach very high levels of accuracy. Figure 7.13 provides an example of forecasting accuracy for some categories' revenues.

This signals a great revolution for retailers. They can finally take very informed, customer-oriented and effective decisions.

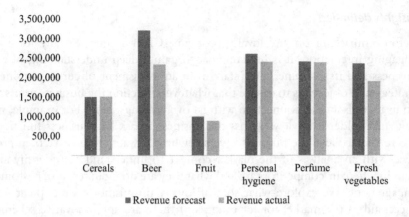

FIGURE 7.13 Example of forecasting accuracy by category.

From insight to activation

In this section we discuss an important strategic marketing lever to connect, influence and establish a durable relationship with customers, in which insights play a fundamental role: 'customer engagement'. Any single interaction with a customer can be defined as a form of customer engagement. Therefore, by 'customer engagement strategy' we mean any form of customer loyalty program, lifecycle marketing, CRM or digital experience program. We explain how the knowledge gained from customer-driven insights can help the business to understand customer behaviours, needs, motivations, preferences and interactions that can be used to make better decisions and to personalize the customer experience. Some of the most common client concerns and questions we help to solve relate to whether or not to have a loyalty program or whether to change it or embed digital experiences. We believe marketers must think beyond the scope of their questions and demonstrate loyalty to their customers with propositions that put their needs first in every interaction with the company. Successful companies in this space are rewarded by customers not only with purchases but with their attention, positive word of mouth and long-term preferences for the brand.

Delivering stand-out customer engagement propositions requires a deep knowledge of customer wants and needs, an understanding of business goals and objectives and an approach proven to work. Our approach to helping businesses with customer engagement strategies is called the 'insight to activation process'. It is a roadmap composed of three macro steps:

1 insights definition
2 engagement strategy development
3 activation plan.

Insights definition

Before embarking on any loyalty program, CRM strategy or any form of engaging interaction, it is fundamental to gain a deep understanding of the business and its customers. We start from an assessment of current business strategy and objectives to ensure that whatever direction the business wants to go in there is a clear connection with its overarching vision. For example, we run stakeholder interviews across the business to ask key business functions where they believe the business is versus where it wants to go. We then proceed with an analysis of the market context to understand and identify any gaps in where its competitors are and what they are doing in terms of customer engagement. We explore what sort of loyalty propositions are popular and successful in the market, or for example if there are any innovative schemes that are covering emerging customer needs, and where the business we are helping sits in this respect.

Once we have gained this contextual knowledge, it is then possible to run an analytical study of customers' behaviour, their needs and their unique characteristics that will complete the overall picture. We believe that a combination of different analyses and different levels of detail can help to support customer engagement at scale. We frequently see companies invest large amounts of money in expensive market research that does not lead to actionable insights because it does not also take into account actual customer behaviour. Therefore, through a combination of insight layers we can work to understand:

- What customers need and value, in order to understand where to focus investment across the shopping stages/mindsets: discover → shop → buy → reflect.
- The customer DNA (see below), to create a customer language and identify unique characteristics.
- The customers' current value, their potential one, and winnable potential. One example is measuring how customers spend and visit but also in how many categories they shop. This means identifying and understanding the loyal customers and predicting those that have high potential to become loyal, reduce their loyalty or who are at a high risk of defection.

Let us look at the first two points in more depth since they are significative inputs in understanding customers and giving shape to customer engagement strategies. The first point, understanding customer needs, is a crucial step in shaping a customer engagement strategy. At dunnhumby we approach this with an in-depth and action-oriented package of insights-generating activities that incorporate qualitative research, customer needs mapping, and behavioural analysis to describe how to better engage customers to increase their frequency, spend, engagement and preference for the brand. We investigate what customers are looking for in a great shopping experience and describe how well every competitor within the market is doing to meet these expectations. By fusing the attitudes collected with traditional marketing research with real customer behaviour (by analysing loyalty card and transactional data), we are able to put the customer at the heart of the strategy definition, define where to play and identify areas to build propositions. This work allows our partners to build a customer engagement contact plan which delivers actions that respond to the identified needs of customers and therefore reduce any risks that might come from ignoring those needs. For example, starting from the fundamental human and emotional needs of customers, such as the desire to be in control and be recognized, we ask if those needs are being fulfilled in the specific retail context and how this differs by individual. Once those needs have been established, we measure how well the retailer is currently satisfying those needs. Moreover, we look at how those needs evolve along the four mindsets/stages of the shopping journey (discover → shop → buy → reflect). While the shopping journey may look linear, customers can jump between mindsets during their shopping journey. With this insight, we can create actionable output in the form of needs-based propositions for priority customer groups and demonstrate how these can support the retailer's initiatives. Similarly, understanding customer DNA is another important phase of research we conduct to better understand customers, their motivations and what attracts them to the brand. Figures 7.14 presents a case study of a French retailer that illustrates how this is done at dunnhumby.

Only by connecting and combining the different layers of insights can we gather the right set of inputs to help businesses to understand where the opportunities are, which groups of customers to invest in and which propositions to develop to best meet the needs of these priority customers while delivering against business objectives.

Engagement strategy development

With the insight work completed, it is then possible to move on to the development of an engagement strategy. The insight inputs drive the creation of a final assessment that defines the existing and potential future customer experience. They enable our consultants to validate business requirements by cross-checking business objectives with customer objectives to ensure that both are met and confirming that what the business wants to do responds to the needs of the customer. It is then possible to elaborate some viable options for customer engagement propositions (e.g. programs to avoid customers from lapsing) which we then workshop with the business. This drives the definition of the characteristics of the customer engagement propositions and, through a customer lens, establishes the customer's reasons to believe in the program

Customer at the Heart

Case Study

Working with a French retailer to engage and reward customers

CHALLENGE

The retailer was delivering customer propositions mainly driven by business objectives rather than customer preferences, e.g. categories or products purposes, leading to:

- reduced frequency and average spend per customer
- decrease in customer engagement.

OBJECTIVES

- Understand the individual behaviour of each customer, their unique characteristics and preferences.
- Gain deeper insights to be translated into a customer-driven and multichannel engagement plan, which is unique, highly personalized and relevant.

ACTION ONE – Over 200 variables were grouped into four dimensions of 'customer DNA'.

ACTION TWO – 37 customers were identified and divided into three types.

ACTION THREE – 12 priority personas were selected, representing 28% of clients and 55% of sales.

FINAL STEP

These were then translated into a customer-driven engagement plan.

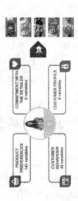

FIGURE 7.14   Case study 1: Customer at the heart.

and the designed customer experience. How the program is structured will determine what it will cost and expected returns.

The development of an engagement strategy proceeds with diagnosis, definition and design:

1 Diagnosis work, which looks at:

 a The current 'as is' program and touchpoints to be validated against customer and business needs through the results of the insight work.

 b The current competencies (capabilities), evaluated across technology, operations, people, processes, governance and channels to determine if they meet the future orientation. We want to answer questions such as: what technical infrastructure, data and software integration is available?

 c A review of industry benchmarks, case studies and any other relevant research to input in the proposition development; that is, we perform an analysis of competitors to benchmark the business propositions versus the key competitors.

2 Definition work, which looks at:

 a The vision and the proposition to deliver against customer needs and business objectives. This work outlines the future customer experience vision, showing what a customer would experience compared to the present day. For example, we live the experience to see what it feels like for a customer against given customer experience pillars, which means ensuring that what we are developing makes the experience for the customer accessible, relevant, trustable and easy. These are the four key elements that come out again and again over the last 30 years of dunnhumby's customer research and studies on engagement strategies.

 b The development of a 'to be' strategy: the communication approach and any commercialization strategy aimed at involving external partners or suppliers to participate in the program. We look at the level of personalization, the required data, content, technology, and so on. We develop a strategy and capability roadmap showing the data, science, propositions, technology, resources and organization structure phased over time to realize the vision and opportunities.

 c The creation of a business case to quantify the financial opportunities in terms of customer potential, campaign uplifts, reach and return on investment (ROI) for a combination of activities.

3 Design work, which looks at:

 a The design of the potential future customer experience with a contact strategy, touchpoints, and mechanics across the journey. This means planning the 'who gets what' proposition, the message, the offer, the treatment and the where (channels) and when (timing) across a range of always-on, planned, tactical and triggered communications.

Figure 7.15 presents an example of the work completed for a Canadian retailer where the steps described above were applied.

Execution plan

With the insight and engagement strategy stages complete, this third and final phase of the 'insight to activation' process involves execution, evaluation and optimization, which in turn, activates the feedback loop again to better adjust and evolve any proposition or activity to the customer.

Execution

This is a very sensitive phase, in that often even a brilliant program or proposition could fail if not supported and communicated properly across the business and to customers. We strongly believe in and support the development of a plan for launching the program with customers and employees, ensuring the processes are in place to deliver a seamless experience. Again, customer insight plays a fundamental role in this planning stage before the program or proposition goes live in the market – in the development of the right content to use when briefing communication agencies on understanding what customers should think, feel and do; in briefing the company headquarters, stores and employees through trainings; in communicating the program to suppliers, pre-launching to staff and possibly trialling it with selected groups of customers.

Evaluation

Insights continue to feed into the process through the measurement of the impact of the customer engagement activities. This enables improvements and makes the investment accountable to the business. This is when the business needs to identify the key questions it needs answers to, such as:

1 How much incremental revenue was generated from the campaign?
2 What was the ROI of CRM or digital campaigns?
3 Which customers are most engaged in the CRM and digital channels?
4 What channels, customer segments or tactics are driving the greatest margin and sales uplift?

This process involves the definition of customer and business KPIs to evaluate and the creation of reports reflecting that. Figure 7.16 gives an example of our approach to measurement.

Customer Loyalty Design

Case Study

Working with Metro to design a new loyalty programme for the Quebec region

CHALLENGE

The grocery retailer was seeking to become more customer-centric and as such, wanted to develop a mechanism for identifying, rewarding and communicating with customers.

ACTIONS

An internal and competitor assessment of the loyalty programme design was undertaken covering:

- business case
- program definition and design
- customer research (concepts, mechanics, branding)
- guidance on the IT provider decision and solution
- identification of the pilot market and test
- development of the launch plan
- achieving organizational buy-in
- creating an ongoing member communications plan
- reporting and KPI measurement.

No.1
Retail loyalty program in Canada, 2014

2.4m
members

Metro piloted and rolled out the loyalty programme.

FIGURE 7.15 Case study 2: Customer loyalty design.

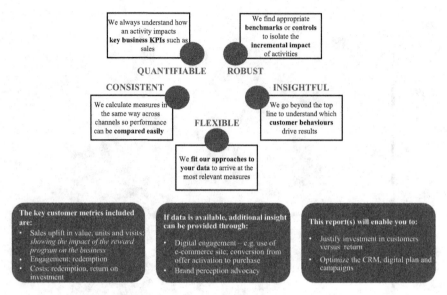

FIGURE 7.16   Measuring customer and business KPIs.

As Figure 7.16 shows, our approach to evaluation is developed across five key elements:

- Quantifiable: any customer engagement activity is defined with a set of measurable metrics (KPIs). Therefore, after the execution of the activity, we evaluate the impact for any agreed KPI; for example, the number of sales generated, level of customer participation, and so on.

- Robust: often customer engagement activities run on top of mass commercial plans, during seasonal periods or otherwise can be influenced by several external factors. To evaluate impact by isolating those aspects we find appropriate benchmarks and statistical control groups that allow us to measure the isolated effect of the activity. For example, in an email campaign to a selected group of customers, we remove a small group of control customers (with the exact same profile as those contacted), who will not receive any communication. In this way, we can then measure if there is a sales uplift by comparing the behaviour of the two groups in the campaign and non-campaign (or pre-campaign) period.

- Consistent: this means that measures are calculated in the same way across all the channels that are used as part of the program so that a comparison of results can be carried out.

- Insightful: the evaluation is not only focused on sales results, which is the end goal; we also look at the components that have driven that result; in particular, the different customer behaviours that have driven it, linking it up with the plan of actions that was activated.

- Flexible: the approach must be flexible and adapt to the business's available data to find the best evaluation solutions (e.g. there might be customer data points that are fundamental to gain a clear view of customer behaviour but that are not available to the business, such as the single customer view which allows one to identify the same customer across the different touchpoints).

Optimization

The evaluation is also very important to optimize future activities. Optimization is possible only after the following steps:

- Quantification of the ROI of the program to drive incremental investment.
- Repetition of the activities that drive the greatest ROI.
- Focus on the most valuable shoppers within the program.
- Understand how different channels and messages affect the program engagement.
- ROI and long-term shopper value.
- Test and learn hypotheses through experimental design and evaluation. For example, it is important to test what the right number is of consecutive communications to the different groups of customers since a loyal customer would have a different approach compared with a less loyal customer, where the frequency of purchase is definitely lower. Another example could be testing a different subject in an email campaign to see which is more effective at driving email-open rates.

Change management

All retailers have a lot of customer and transaction data. Deciding to analyse the data is a big step change but not enough for a company to become data-driven and customer-oriented. We have seen many examples of retailers analysing the data but not taking actions from the insights gained; or again, retailers building impressive plans but not implementing the decisions taken; or lastly, companies who have tried to implement data-driven plans but don't know anything about the level of compliance in-store or about the results achieved. To become data-driven and customer-oriented, every company needs a change management program which includes the following five steps:

1 use data to better understand customers' needs
2 create and embed a common customer language
3 align people, processes and systems
4 engage 'the army of your people'
5 show tangible change in-store and online.

It is worth noting that most companies do only the first step. Indeed, the first step encompasses everything we have described in this chapter: analyse and understand customer data. In the rest of this chapter, we will describe the steps that follow it.

Create and embed a common customer language

Bringing customer-first to life requires a common language about customers, starting with understanding shopping habits and terms such as price sensitivity, store segments, lifestyles, customer communications, customer promises, and so forth. The challenge is to speak the language to as many people in your organization as often as possible. A good place to start is with a customer-focused purpose and vision. The purpose establishes what a retailer stands for, what its identity is, why and for whom it exists. A retailer should express this both to customers and to employees. The vision should be based on an authoritative knowledge of customers and the market. Who the most loyal customers are, their behaviours and preferences; how the company competes to attract and retain them. This should guide decision-making at all levels. One important element of a common customer language is the notion of 'customer promises' – a concept which aims to focus an organization on delivering a consistent customer experience every day from every part of the business. By unifying what really matters to customers into a simple set of commitments, customer promises are measures of how effectively a brand delivers on its brand promises.

Practically speaking, customer promises help to:

- Identify opportunities to become closer to the customer and to create a customer-first mindset within your business.
- Provide a structure for a customer strategy to ensure that all functions and roles can consistently prioritize and take action in ways that are most valuable to customers.
- Anchor the common customer language in a way that is easy to understand across business functions.
- Unite all employees (at all levels) to practise customer-first initiatives.

Customer promises should be:

1 Priorities that are important to customers, in the voice and language of the customer.
2 Data-led, based on structured research from the customer up (rather than top-down from management).
3 Benchmarked to allow the measurement of progress over time.

Through the customer promises, customers themselves tell businesses where they should start, and what good looks like when they deliver it.

For example, Tesco uses the following promises to make its 'Every little helps' slogan explicit to customers:

- the aisles are clear
- I can get what I want
- the prices are good
- I don't queue
- the staff are great.

Align people, processes and systems

Bringing customer-first to life and inspiring people to do their best for customers will require changes to supporting structures and processes within a company. Of all the steps, this one presents the greatest challenge: to align the business systems around the customer and the data. Customer-first organizations display a single-minded focus on loyal customers – growing this segment and increasing their lifetime value. They set up systems to retain and grow customer loyalty over time. They track, measure and report on customer initiatives such as customer promises or customer-focused KPIs. They implement a process that aligns the customer with strategic plans and reviews, using the customer's perspective as a filter through which to evaluate future plans. Measuring results is a very important step in order to monitor if data-based processes are happening and if they are having an impact on customers. Only through the analysis, understanding and usage of the results can the process last and improve over time.

Becoming customer-first means investing resources in:

1 capabilities to analyse customer behaviour, segment customers and create personalized communications
2 measurement of projects results
3 capabilities that enable organizational change
4 training programs for employees
5 performance measures aligned with customer-first initiatives
6 recognition and rewards for employees who put the strategy into action.

This long-term view transcends the traditional retail instinct to make decisions based on current market trends without considering the lasting impact that these choices – such as matching competitor prices or other 'me too' tactics – may have on customer relationships. The reality is that the best relationships are nurtured. This requires time and investment. By focusing on long-term relationships with loyal customers, retailers can build a path to growth with them at the centre.

TABLE 7.3 Example of change in employees' KPIs

Before	After
Executive compensation is tied exclusively to sales and margin.	Customer KPIs contribute 33% to compensation bonuses.
Merchandising team target is % margin.	Target driving $ margin and/or profit.
Assortment rationalized to drive % margin by category.	Optimized to drive visits and sales of entire store.
Pricing strategy focuses on competitiveness.	Focus on price perception.

Engage 'the army of your people'

All the stakeholders in the company need to be informed, aligned, engaged and inspired. We have seen examples of companies in which the CEO was pushing for the change but middle management was not aligned and had different KPIs. The result? Change didn't happen. At the same time, if middle management believes in customer data but the board of directors don't understand or believe in it, they are unlikely to sign off and fund important projects that use it. Everybody needs to be on-board.

At its best, a customer-first approach is executed in such a deep way that customers can feel a difference in their experience. Winning buy-in through the hearts and minds of staff – from the top executive to the employee who stocks the shelves – builds an incredibly powerful army necessary to deliver the strategy. Sadly, most organizations give front-line employees – the faces of their company – very little trust and authority. Customer-first organizations give front-line employees broad authority to resolve customer needs and extend that power to satisfy customers to most members of staff, in some form. They take advantage of their people to deliver what their most loyal customers want. They invest in training to give employees the tools they need and the permission to use them. They share data to make everyone in the company aware of what is important to customers, tailoring the information to be used by people according to their roles. Behaviour change in organizations doesn't happen overnight. Employees have to be engaged via training which teaches examples of good customer judgment. Senior management must be upskilled in leadership behaviours of empathy, dignity and respect for both employees and customers. Aligned behaviours should be rewarded. Everyone in the business should understand they have 'ownership' of the customer.

Show tangible change in-store and online

Customer data may be used to operate loyalty programs but there is less evidence that this data is being used to support changes in the shopping experience. Ranging, assortment, layouts, pricing, promotions, customer service – all these elements that make up the shopping experience should be informed by data from loyal customers to ensure that the retailer is delivering what its best customers seek. And as we said above, after execution, all projects should be measured to find out answers to the important questions the business must ask: 'did it happen? Did it work?' The first question is about compliance: very often decisions are taken at the centre but not implemented properly: the centre, for instance, may recommend a new planogram for a certain category but this may be implemented only in a few stores; new prices rules may be introduced and formalized but category managers may try to bypass some of them to recover margin. Compliance is more automated and more measurable online but very often a real challenge in-store, particularly for cooperative or franchising businesses where the centre has less ownership and control. Measuring compliance is fundamental to confirming that change is happening in-store. Then, of course, there is the measurement of KPIs (sales, customer penetration, items per customer) to understand if it worked for the benefit of customers and of the retailer.

To conclude this chapter, then, it is clear to us that efforts to build customer loyalty and grow sales often fail to produce meaningful results for three key reasons:

1 First, loyalty is not about customers being loyal to the retailer – it's about the retailer acting loyally to its customers.
2 Loyalty is not just a program – it's an approach that puts the customer first in all the decisions a retailer makes.
3 Loyalty is not just about CRM – it's about the store and how the retailer interacts with its customers.

By inviting, listening and responding to customer feedback, retailers can earn the emotional loyalty of their customers. They feel that the retailer cares about them and their needs. Such actions place the customer in the role of a strategic partner. They can share their perspectives and create a two-way conversation. And retailers can embed this idea in their customer interactions to further deepen the relationship.

Acknowledgements

The chapter first appeared in the 2020 edition of this book, contributed by Michela Giacomini and Miriam Panìco, who at that time were with dunnhumby, a distinguished partner of the Loyalty Observatory. Michela is now with PwC and Miriam is with Loyal Guru and we thank them for giving permission to reprint. The reprint and specifically the reproduction of the figures in the chapter has been approved by Marco Metti and Siro Descrovi of dunnhumby.

References

Ciancio, D. (2017) *5 Steps to Becoming a Customer-First Business*. London: dunnhumby.

Ruttenberg, R. (2016) *Re-inventing Category Management: Driving Growth with Category Leadership*. London: dunnhumby.

8

BENCHMARKING LOYALTY MANAGEMENT ACTIVITIES

The Italian market

Giada Salvietti

Loyalty-oriented organizations and advances in Loyalty Management

Customer loyalty is the declared goal of marketing strategies today: corporate presentations and annual reports invariably mention the firm's commitment to retention. However, beyond public declarations, *how does a company change when it truly commits to building loyalty?* We at the Loyalty Observatory have tried for many years to answer this question by analysing a variety of aspects related to a firms' adoption of a customer relationship orientation. Since 2012, we have witnessed several changes that have taken place within companies in Italy which we interpret as signs of an advancing loyalty culture.[1] Our yearly commitment to monitoring the evolution of loyalty culture also allows us to identify major challenges and how they did develop over time. This section describes those changes and offers insights on how company perspectives are shifting when a loyalty orientation is pursued. In order to offer a timely and updated state-of-the-art, results from the studies conducted in the last five years, from 2019 to 2023, are analysed. Companies participating in the survey operate in B2C markets, and include industry brands, retailers, service providers. Also, a separate section of the survey is dedicated to vendors of technologies, services and solutions that populate the market for loyalty management products and services. We believe it is worthwhile discussing these results, and we hope the evidence presented will inspire academic research and feedback from international practitioners.

DOI: 10.4324/9781003400783-8

Dissemination of loyalty programs

Loyalty programs have become increasingly pervasive in the last 5 years: in 2019 and 2020, only about half of companies offered a loyalty program. After the pandemic, the percentage of structured loyalty programs increased to 60% in 2021, and 70% in 2022 and 2023. The majority of loyalty programs is addressed to consumers, although the percentage of B2B programs is slowly increasing as well. The percentage of companies aiming to introduce a loyalty program within the next two years is also growing fast, from 33% in 2022 to 38% in 2023. 44% of companies also claimed they will continue investing in the loyalty program as their major loyalty tool in 2024. Our classification of companies in industry, retail and service providers allows to appreciate between-sectors' differences: the 2022 and 2023 results clearly show that loyalty programs are widely adopted among retailers (85% of companies) and service providers (64%), whereas for many industry brands loyalty programs are not a priority (about 50%).

As what concerns recency of loyalty programs development, more than 20% of interviewed companies has introduced schemes in the last 1–2 years, which is in line with international benchmarks (Comarch & Forrester Consulting, 2022). However, many Italian companies have loyalty programs that have been active for more than 10 years (about 45% as of 2022), whereas international benchmarks report about 6% of programs lasting more than 5 years. Finally, it is to be noticed that most industry brands are introducing their loyalty program for the first time, whereas the majority of retailers can rely on established programs – that, however, are in need of update or renovation. In this respect, we measured when the latest substantial change(s) to the loyalty program occurred: 24% of interviewed companies renovated the program in the last year whereas for 41% of them the program has not been modified in the last 5 to 10 years. 8% even admitted not having renovated the program for more than 10 years. We consider this data alarming, especially considering that customers' behaviours and preferences have undergone deep changes in the last few years, and strongly suggest companies to regularly review their loyalty initiatives.

A final aspect that is revealing of a company's commitment to customer loyalty is whether the top management regards the company's loyalty program as a cost centre or a profit centre. Such radicalization is useful to understand whether management is able to think of the loyalty program as an investment and a source of future profitability, which is in turn a proxy of the company's willingness to increase investments in loyalty strategies. In 2022, according to the Antavo global customer loyalty report, about 60% of international companies considered the loyalty program to be a profit centre, thus recognizing its importance for long-term growth. As what concerns Italian companies, a huge difference was found between companies that had already implemented a loyalty program and those looking forward its introduction. The first mainly considered programs as profit centres, in line with international benchmarks (62% profit centre; 38% cost centre). Positions, however, were completely reversed in companies that were about to introduce a loyalty program, since for 64% of them the top management considered the program as a main source of costs. By analysing sectors, it emerged that FMGC brands express polarized opinions about loyalty programs: extremely positive for those who already had a program (for 75% it is a profit centre) and extremely negative for those who are introducing it (80% consider it a cost centre).

In 2023, the difficult economic conditions (market uncertainty, increase in inflation, contraction in consumption) seem to have further exacerbated management's positions on loyalty programs. On the one hand, in fact, companies about to introduce a loyalty program appear to have understood the strategic advantages it entails, as 62% of them now consider it as a profit centre. This is probably due to the fact that companies investing in times of crisis are deeply convinced of the investment's solidity and profitability, and that many who previously were uncertain about loyalty programs' worth may have just abandoned or delayed their introduction. Notably, industry brands maintain their scepticism (the program is a profit centre only for 33% of them). A contraction is found in companies that already had a loyalty program, as in 2023 51% consider the program a profit centre and 49% a cost centre (Figure 8.1).

This information suggests that, in difficult times, trust in certain loyalty strategies – first and foremost maintaining a loyalty program – may decrease, thus bringing out the need to align all management levels on their benefits. In this sense it is important to invest in evolving the company's culture so as to ensure that strategies are understood and shared at all levels. Moreover, it is also crucial to assess whether management's expectations of loyalty actions' benefits and goals are consistent with their actual potential. Both of these topics will be explored in depth in the next paragraphs.

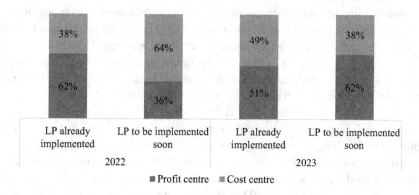

FIGURE 8.1 Loyalty program as a profit or cost centre.

Changes in loyalty program design

Not only loyalty programs have become more pervasive in latest years, but they have also undergone changes so as to adapt to customers' demands as well as offering them distinguished experiences, in line with the journeys designed by companies. Three main changes are identified as follows.

First, as what concerns program structure, most loyalty programs in Italy are based on points accrual (76.9% as of 2022, higher than the aforementioned Comarch and Antavo international benchmarks). Only 33% of companies employ a tier-based structure; nevertheless, tiers are being considered by 12% of companies as a possible evolution of their program in the three years to come. Interestingly, 4% of companies stated considering the introduction of a fee-based tier alongside accrual-based ones (lower with respect to the Comarch and Antavo benchmarks). In fact, also 'pure' subscription loyalty programs are quite rare in Italy. In 2019 only 9% of companies already implemented subscription loyalty programs, and 10% stated they were considering implementing one in the short term. Moreover, 37% of companies were undecided about their eventual implementation, thus indicating an uncertainty about this program structure's fit with their members. This figure has not improved in recent years, since in 2022 only 6% of companies provides an entrance or annual fee. Similarly, coalition-based programs are declining as well (8% in 2023). Italian companies appear more interested in introducing personalized clubs, tailored to specific customer targets. As of 2022, 10% already introduced a club and 17% was considering introducing one in the short term. Such attention towards creating a dedicated space to foster customers is also reflected in the rise of online communities for members only (15% already implemented in 2022 and 16% to be implemented in 3 years). Finally, Italian companies are slowly opening their loyalty programs to other targets than consumers: 29% allows employees to enrol and 3% has started to involve channel partners as well.

A second aspect that is everchanging in loyalty programs are touchpoints that companies are leveraging to communicate with members. Managing loyalty today, in fact, ought to coincide with managing the customer experience through designing and continually renewing touchpoint journeys (Homburg et al., 2017). Firstly, we notice a switch towards online touchpoints, such as the website, mobile app, newsletters and direct mailing, SMS, etc., that have long surpassed physical ones. Such process has significantly accelerated with the Covid-19 pandemic, which has urged many companies to find new ways of maintaining contact with customers that would not involve a physical interaction. Among digital touchpoints, the mobile app dedicated to the loyalty program has received maybe the most significant increase: in 2022, 26% of companies stated they already introduced the app, and another 31% aimed to introduce it or redesign it shortly afterwards. As of 2023, the percentage of companies planning to introduce or upgrade the loyalty program app has risen to 41% in less than one year – figure lower with respect to international benchmarks. Another touch-point that is being swiftly digitalized is the gift catalogue, which in 2019 was still purely physical for 56% of companies. Nowadays, not only it is becoming available on the website and mobile app too, but 25% of companies are introducing digital-only advantages (such as gift cards, coupon codes, etc.). Such digitalization processes also impacted on some traditional touchpoints such as flyers or the loyalty card itself. For example, in 2019 60% of companies still had a physical loyalty card, a percentage that has decreased by 10 per cent in less than 3 years (51% as of 2022). Moreover, in 2023, only 2% and 3% of companies, respectively, have confirmed their willingness to continue investing in printed coupons and communications by post.

Italian companies are therefore demonstrating their intention to encourage online purchases and the use of digital touchpoints by their program members. Despite this, only a few companies are directly acting on payment methods, either by offering their own payment instrument (credit cards or mobile wallets, 11% in 2022), or instalment features such as 'buy now, pay later' (4% in 2023). A rapidly growing trend is instead linked to gamification mechanisms across the physical, digital and mobile channels, such as obtaining badges, challenges, games and competitions. 20% have already introduced these mechanisms within their loyalty program and strategies, and over 30% intend to invest in this direction.

It is to be noted that future investment intentions concerning touchpoints vary greatly between sectors, as displayed in Table 8.1. For example, the mobile app represents a priority for retailers and service providers, but not for

TABLE 8.1 Loyalty program touchpoint investments in the next 12 months

	Industry	Retail	Services	Total
Mobile app	0%	43%	42%	**34%**
Direct email marketing (DEM)	17%	34%	29%	**29%**
Social media pages	50%	19%	25%	**27%**
Digital coupons	17%	34%	21%	**27%**
Events	33%	17%	25%	**23%**
Contests	33%	19%	17%	**21%**
WhatsApp messaging	22%	19%	21%	**20%**
SMS	6%	9%	8%	**8%**
Automatized customer care	0%	2%	17%	**6%**
Metaverse	6%	2%	8%	**5%**
Gift cards	0%	4%	4%	**5%**
Communications by post	0%	2%	8%	**3%**
Printed coupons	0%	4%	0%	**2%**

FMCG brands, that are more committed to investing in social media, events and contests.

A final consideration concerns rewards and benefits offered by the loyalty program. Most programs are still offering exclusively or mainly financial rewards: discounts and rebates, coupons, cashback, etc. Nevertheless, although most benefits offered are of monetary/rational nature (overall, 64%), an increase in non-monetary/experiential rewards is shown over the years, and 40% of companies claim they will introduce more rewards of this kind. This figure is higher with respect to international benchmarks. Experiential rewards include first and foremost advantages for special events in customer life (i.e. anniversaries, holiday, birthday gifts), and access to exclusive events. Companies, however, are also expanding experiential rewards by including offers and benefits tied to values, as programs are being increasingly oriented towards environmental and social sustainability causes. For half of interviewed companies, the loyalty program represents an opportunity to share their CSR/sustainable activities with members, but it is not its main focus; conversely, only 13% of companies aim to fully integrate sustainability within their programs.

In general, loyalty programs worldwide increasingly reward customers for non-shopping behaviours such as: sharing or commenting on brand-related content on social media; referral to friends; taking surveys and/or sharing information that ultimately enables the brand to obtain richer insight. Although Italian loyalty programs have lagged behind in these last features for many years, in recent times the trend has been realigned; in fact, as of 2022:

- 31.5% of companies offer advantages for participation in surveys/questionnaires
- 20% for updating the personal profile/contact details
- 9% for referrals
- 9% for other non-shopping behaviours
- 4% for creating and sharing content on social media.

Loyalty objectives definition and measurement metrics

For loyalty initiatives – primarily the loyalty program – to be effective, it is necessary to define the objectives well and proceed with their measurement before implementing changes or updates. Through our surveys, we therefore try to regularly monitor both the alignment (or misalignment) between the objectives attributed to loyalty initiatives, the metrics used to measure these efforts, and the characteristics of the tools adopted themselves.

Starting with the objectives, we notice that the main goal for companies managing loyalty initiatives is to acquire new customers (38%), followed by customer experience improvement (35%). Both these goals have represented the priority for Italian companies for many years, and still remain stable. Compared to 2022, in the last year, companies have started focusing more on improving customers' data management and insight extraction (35%), which we interpret as a positive trend towards a mature customer relationship management (CRM) orientation. This is especially true for retailers, whose figure is above average (40%). Also, more companies aim to improve purchase frequency (28%) and turnover (25%). We pose that companies have been, therefore, more concerned with short-term outcomes, since other, long-term oriented, goals are pursued by a smaller number of companies: churn prevention/reduction (21%); improving customer satisfaction (20%); improving customer lifetime value (16%). By comparing these results with Open Loyalty's 2022 loyalty trends report, Italian companies display different concerns to their international counterparts. According to this benchmark, in fact, customer lifetime value and churn prevention are top priorities for international companies, although increasing the purchase frequency is becoming more relevant lately.

In 2023, for the first time, due to the pervasiveness of loyalty programs (70% of companies had already introduced a structured program), we investigated objectives specifically assigned to these tools. By comparing (see Table 8.2) objectives defined overall and for the loyalty program, a substantial alignment emerges; this implies that the loyalty program is generally well-integrated within loyalty strategies, with the additional goal of preventing churn and promoting retention.

In relation to these objectives, a variety of metrics emerged. Table 8.3 displays the evolution in the importance of these metrics over the past five years. Redemption rate has long been the most cited performance measure and still remains among most relevant ones. Interestingly, metrics specific to active members in loyalty programs have significantly grown over the years (1st and 4th for importance). Consistently with the main objectives identified, sales/turnover also were largely cited, as well as frequency of visits – which

TABLE 8.2 Top 5 objectives defined overall and for the loyalty program

Objectives: loyalty marketing		*Objectives: loyalty program*	
New customers' acquisition	38%	Maximizing purchase frequency	32%
Improving the customer experience	35%	Churn prevention/retention	29%
Improving customers' data management	35%	Gathering data	20%
Maximizing purchase frequency	28%	Give a preferential treatment to the best customers	20%
Personalization	26%	New customers' acquisition	18%

TABLE 8.3 Ranking of most important KPIs for measuring the effectiveness of loyalty initiatives

	2019	2021	2023
Activity rate of loyalty program members	14°	5°	1°
Redemption rate	1°	1°	2°
Aggregate measures of sales/turnover	3°	2°	3°
Profitability measures (turnover percentage attributable to members and loyalty actions)	10°	7°	4°
Retention rate/churn	7°	8°	5°
Frequency (store or website visit)	5°	6°	6°
Customer satisfaction	6°	10°	7°
Net promoter score	13°	14°	8°
Customer lifetime value	15°	15°	9°
Brand awareness	12°	13°	10°
Open/click rate of DEM campaigns	17°	4°	11°
Percentage of privacy and profiling consents issued	–	–	12°
Other engagement measures	–	17°	13°
Engagement rate on social media	9°	11°	14°
Website/app metrics (conversion, click rates)	4°	3°	15°
Cost measures	11°	9°	16°
Response rate to campaigns	2°	–	–
ROI	8°	12°	–
Share of wallet	16°	16°	–

complement frequency of purchases. Different industries traditionally favour some metrics over others: for example, engagement rate on social media is central for FMCG brands but almost non-existent elsewhere, and the reverse is true of customer satisfaction, which is common in retail and other services. Nevertheless, we notice an overall disregard for measures such as the customer lifetime value, the percentage of privacy consents issued, the acquisition/retention cost ratio, especially if compared to the Antavo 2023 international benchmark.

In this sense, another worrying figure concerns measuring the return on the investment (ROI), which is overall almost absent. Despite the great attention towards the loyalty program displayed by companies, only a few of them calculate a ROI specific to the program (and 60% of those consider the program as a profit centre). This is striking, especially since 21% of interviewed marketers admitted not being satisfied by the loyalty program results in the last year, a figure three times higher in 2023 than in 2022. Antavo's global customer loyalty report 2023 shows a connection between measuring the ROI and positive financial outcomes: 80% of international companies measuring their loyalty program's ROI reported, on average, five times more revenue than their expenses. International benchmarks, therefore, strongly encourage and support tracking financial performances of loyalty schemes.

Among motivations for not calculating such a measure, the most severe refers to the difficulty of accurately allocate costs and revenues (38%). Others complain of not having adequate competencies or tools (19%), question its usefulness (12%), or state that other departments are responsible for measurement tasks (14%). All these pain points also represent directions for future improvement concerning loyalty management, in terms of investing in tools and training and improve internal cross-department coordination.

Commitment to loyalty and future investments

A company's commitment to loyalty can be measured through a variety of aspects, which are expressions of its cultural propensity to embrace retention goals and customer relationship management philosophies. These aspects include: the level of priority assigned to customer retention, the presence of a dedicated function or department for loyalty, how investments are channelled in order to achieve loyalty and retention, and how the company's culture manages to align all levels around loyalty goals.

Dedicated function for loyalty

A first aspect we studied was how companies assign responsibility internally for the deployment of loyalty strategies. Firms may choose to organize either by introducing into their structure a specific function that champions loyalty strategies, or by considering loyalty an overarching goal to be achieved with no specific function in charge. As what concerns Italian companies, the aforementioned wide and systematic use of loyalty metrics is encouraging, as it can be associated with the presence of a loyalty-dedicated function. Other data, gathered in 2023, can contribute to a better definition of this aspect. First, for interviewed companies, the majority of loyalty/CRM teams are under the marketing director's responsibility, whereas only 2% of companies put a loyalty director in charge (which we consider a proxy of a structured department). For 44% of companies the loyalty/CRM team does not report to a marketing function. A second insight concerns the dimension of the loyalty team: most are relatively small; 42% include 1 or maximum 2 people, whereas only 23% of teams involve at least 6 people. This confirms that most loyalty teams are subject to other functions whose main focus is different.

A final remark concerns budget allocation: on average, interviewed companies dedicate 18% of the marketing budget to loyalty and CRM activities. It is also relevant to consider extreme positions: 12% of companies invest in loyalty up to 1% of their marketing budget, 17% invest less than 10%, and only 8% is willing to invest half of their budget or more.

Long-term orientation: investments in loyalty

How far a firm commits in loyalty management is another significant indicator of its commitment to loyalty. Besides the relative weight of loyalty marketing expenditure on the total marketing budget, it is also relevant to identify the company's intentions to invest.

First, our recurrent surveys show a steady progress over the years: Figure 8.2 displays increase and decreases in loyalty investments from 2020 to 2023 and 2024 forecasts. What emerges is that, especially following the Covid-19 pandemic, investments in loyalty and CRM peaked for most companies, or remained unchanged. This is consistent with marketers' perception about loyalty becoming a 'driver for the new start': 79% of them believed loyalty would be crucial to maintain and rebuild their relationships with customers. Interestingly, the pandemic also accelerated omnichannel transition: in 2021 companies investing in both the online and offline loyalty activities at once (and their integration) rose from 38% to 60%.

It is to be noted that the increase in investments is particularly relevant for companies that already had a loyalty program, and for retailers: in 2022 about 80% of them predicted a larger effort in loyalty. Industry brands are most conservative, as 55% decided to keep them unchanged. Moreover, in 2023 we measured investments in acquisitions, since it emerged as the main loyalty marketing goal: 64% of companies claimed they would increase them in 2024, and 34% thought of maintaining their commitment.

Second, we traced the assets and activities attracting future investments from companies. Remarkably, companies confirm strengthening their orientation towards loyalty through CRM. On the one hand, data are used to improve customer relationship beyond the financial dimension: the main activities to which the investments will be allocated in 2024, in fact, are tailored CRM

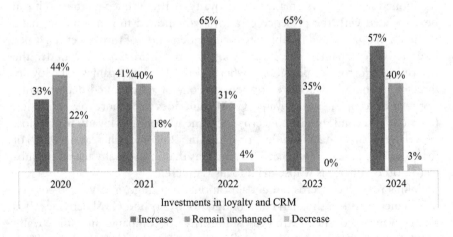

FIGURE 8.2 Trends 2020–2024 for investments in loyalty and CRM.

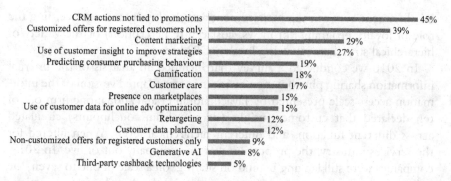

FIGURE 8.3 Main assets and activities to invest in 2024 – forecast.

actions. Similarly, customized actions towards customers present in the database will by far surpass non-customized ones. On the other hand, companies are investing in systematic customer data collection, as well as in improving data usage to generate actionable insights (Figure 8.3). Again, differences are found between sectors, consistently with different future objectives being set: the retail sector is the best evidence of the shift to CRM activities and customized offers (57% and 49% respectively, above the average), followed by service providers. Industry brands, despite a significant interest in retargeting (33%), will focus most of their efforts on content marketing (61%) and expanding their presence on marketplaces (39%).

Figures also support the gradual shift from mass, undifferentiated marketing efforts towards segmented and personalized activities, which is in line with the objective to offer customers more customization (26% of companies in 2023). Personalization ranges from creating dedicated content (65%), to offering customized offers (57%) and rewards (21%), to designing tailored customer experiences (19%). In order to advance personalization, companies must learn how to integrate the wide variety of customer data in their possession. Besides CRM and loyalty program data, which still represent the main information source, companies are increasingly relying on recent complaints, data from social media and from previous interactions.

Embracing a loyalty-driven orientation: the role of culture and employee engagement

For customer information to turn into insight that, in turn, fertilizes loyalty management and CEM, we not only need information collection and integration but also access; that is, dissemination throughout the company to the relevant employees and decision-makers. In this sense, companies must embrace a culture of sharing, leading to all business functions and management levels to be aligned with both short- and long-term objectives. The need for such coordination emerged from many aspects analysed so far, such as misalignment between top management and the loyalty team concerning the role of loyalty programs (profit vs. cost centre perception) or the variety of hierarchical structures involving loyalty/CRM teams.

In 2016 we conducted a survey that included an analysis of the internal information sharing phenomenon by means of an adapted version of the information access scale presented by Jayachandran et al. (2005): one firm out of ten declared that customer insight (derived from touchpoints) circulated across different functions and different hierarchical levels. When filtered for the services industry, the proportion was one company out of five. In 2019, companies were still lagging behind on sharing: on a scale of one to seven, the average score for either sharing customer insights across business functions and top-to-bottom hierarchical levels was 3.5. In 2022, we find a gradual improvement, with both figures rising to 4.6 and 4.3 respectively; in both cases, service providers appear as the most (values above the average), followed by retailers and then manufacturers. Another factor that should further improved concerns the timing of such sharing. As of 2019, only 19% shared customer insights and results of loyalty activities every week; at the same time, many other companies dedicated time and effort to such updates every three months (22%) or even once a year (19%). Companies are therefore required to implement a seamless and regular update schedule, in order to ensure alignment across functions and levels as well as timely interventions on loyalty actions.

Employees are not only a fundamental touchpoint in delivering the customer experience and providing customer care, but also the main reference for enrolling in and engaging with the loyalty program. From the 2023 survey, it emerged in fact that two out of three companies have two or more different types of employees directly involved in the delivery (and perception!) of their loyalty program. Most of these are salespeople (68%) and those responsible for managing emails and social media (52%), followed by employees in charge of the call centre dedicated to members (33%). Only 11% of companies stated that their program does not involve interaction with employees, which gives a measure of their importance in promoting the loyalty program.

Companies themselves admitted to this, as 89% of interviewed marketers stated they were extremely effective in determining the program's success. We further asked to these same respondents which actions are most relevant in rewarding employee loyalty and engagement (Table 8.4). Marketers share consensus on the effectiveness of training employees, insight and results sharing as well as take advantage of their expertise and unique perspective on the program for improvements.

Despite such awareness, and the intention to further invest in customer care (29%), the inclusion of employees in the loyalty strategy and their retention is still in its infancy.

TABLE 8.4 Most effective actions for employee loyalty

Actions	Percentage frequency of responses
Provide specific training on how the program works and customer benefits	90%
Regularly share loyalty program results with employees	80%
Gather employee feedback about the program in a structured way	79%
Assign employees specific goals related to the program	76%
Involve employees in planning moments relating to the program	74%
Provide training on the program to all new hires in the company, regardless of their role/function	74%
Celebrate program outcomes and milestones with employees	72%
Appoint a 'loyalty program contact' employee who acts as a contact between the frontline employees and the headquarters for any issue related to the program	67%
Ensure employees download and use the loyalty program app (if available)	66%
Reward an employee for best results on assigned objectives regarding the program	64%
Make sure employees participate in the program themselves	59%
Have a version of the loyalty program exclusively designed for employees	51%
Introduce gamified quizzes and contexts for employees related to program knowledge	48%
Give employees the autonomy to give certain benefits to customers at their own discretion	30%

In fact, only 3% of companies claims to have a formalized, long-term strategy for employee involvement in the loyalty strategy; about 33% instead admits not having planned precise actions in this sense.

Companies have lagged behind on this aspect for quite a while: as of 2019, 70% of companies were not interested in involving employees in their loyalty strategies. In 2022, only 37% of companies stated regularly measuring and rewarding their loyalty and commitment. As what concerns which benefits are provided, most companies offer flexibility working accommodations (e.g. smart working, 68%), corporate welfare platforms (59%) and a variety of training courses and professional paths (56%). Besides such work-related benefits, companies rely on monetary benefits (meal, shopping and fuel vouchers, 74%; discounts and conventions, 50%). Starting from this, we therefore encourage companies to increase their efforts to involve employees in their loyalty strategies, by adopting structured procedures and by providing experiential benefits as well, thus giving effective value to their contribution.

The market for loyalty management products and services

Loyalty management requires organizations to plan, execute and orchestrate a variety of diverse activities: from designing the loyalty strategy, to translating it into a program with rules and rewards (if a formalized loyalty program), to managing the data flows and data analysis, devising CRM activities, managing communication campaigns across touchpoints, capturing individual customer feedback, and more. Elaborating on a classification suggested by Forrester (see Collins, 2017, p. 4), the business activities required for loyalty management can be classified in three broad groups:

- *Loyalty strategy.* To earn customer loyalty, companies need an approach that's rooted in customer understanding. Loyalty strategy development is defined as the research, planning, and design of loyalty strategies, initiatives, and programs. Specific capabilities include consumer market research, financial modelling, program design, and loyalty measurement and analytics frameworks.
- *Loyalty management (strictly speaking).* To effectively track, recognize, and reward loyal customers, companies need tools and technical expertise to manage the coordination of data, insights, and business rules. Loyalty management strictly speaking is the back-end orchestration of loyalty initiatives and programs. Specific capabilities include currency management, data management, business rules definition and management, integration, call centre management, and rewards fulfilment.
- *Loyalty communication.* To deliver contextually relevant content to loyal customers, companies need flexible and integrated marketing tools. Loyalty communication is the execution of loyalty initiatives across channels. Specific capabilities include campaign management, content creation, and consistent message delivery across channels.

Companies, however, may lack instruments, technologies, or competencies needed to deal with one or more of these business activities, and must therefore turn to highly specialized business providers. It therefore becomes relevant to provide a comprehensive picture of the market for loyalty management products and services (LMPS).

The global market for loyalty management service had a steady growth for the last decade: in 2017 it was estimated at between $1.68 and $1.99 billion (MarketsandMarkets, 2017), was valued at $5.29 billion in 2022 and is projected to grow from $6.47 billion in 2023 to $28.65 billion by 2030 (Fortune Business Insights, 2023).

It is to be stressed that this market also includes a wide variety of providers. Starting in 2018, we created a comprehensive list of sixteen LMPS vendor categories, drawing on analyses by Forrester Research (see Collins, 2016) and Loyalty360[2] of the loyalty management services market and adding businesses

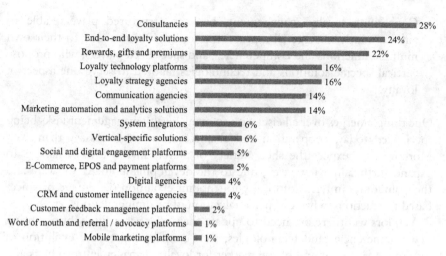

FIGURE 8.4   Types of vendor in the Italian market.

who provide loyalty-related services in Italy, such as suppliers of rewards, premiums and gifts, that are not covered by international reports but play a major role in our country. We tested this list with our survey of vendors, who agreed it accurately represented the market. Figure 8.4 describes the configuration of the Italian LMPS market as of 2023. A first remark concerns the prevalence of vendors able to entirely manage loyalty initiatives, covering all the three activities: strategy, management, and communication, which hints as many companies needing to outsource their loyalty function. 70% of interviewed companies stated they directly manage at least one loyalty program on behalf of their clients.

Some companies, such as consultancy services or communication agencies, indicated that loyalty management activities were only a marginal part of their offer; nevertheless, they remain a significant component of the LMPS market. On the opposite side of the ranking we find highly specialized companies, most of which are technologically advanced and often own of their own platform or solution. An additional information that contributes to the picture concerns the average company size, which is relatively small: as of 2023, 47% of vendors counted less than 20 employees, 30% between 21 and 100 employees and only 23% exceeded 100 employees. According to our recurring surveys, their size has remained substantially unchanged since 2018.

A polarization therefore emerges:

- Concerning loyalty strategy and communications, between consultancies who tend to win jobs requiring the design of a loyalty strategy from scratch and advertising agencies who benefit from their own expertise with brands' other communication activities to expand towards loyalty.

- Concerning loyalty management, between structured players, able to autonomously manage all aspects of a loyalty initiative due to their own multiple functions and competencies, and specialized players, who propose vertical-specific solutions and technologies tailored to serve one aspect of loyalty.

One thing emerges over all else: with so many loyalty management tasks being specialized today, cooperation and alliances are more necessary than ever. Moreover, we expect the sheer variety of players in the LMPS markets to expand further in a few years, due to the developments in AI software and their outcomes in terms of loyalty touchpoint evolution (i.e. image or voice-based interactions, advanced personalization of recommendations, etc.).

Vendors will therefore need to update their offer accordingly by acquiring new competencies and technologies, thus contributing to the evolution of loyalty management and of the market for loyalty management products and services as well.

Notes

1 The Loyalty Observatory yearly conducts online surveys, between the months of June and September, among vendors and brands in Italy. These surveys are aimed at monitoring the state of loyalty practices and culture among Italian companies as well as the evolution of the market for loyalty management products and services. Following the emergence of new issues and challenges, the survey is updated every year with dedicated sections and questions. This chapter presents the results from the surveys conducted from 2019 to 2023. The 2019, 2020 and 2022 surveys are the subject of white papers (in Italian) available at the Observatory website (www.osservatoriofedelta.unipr.it). The 2021 and 2023 surveys have been presented during the Observatory yearly conferences and are now extensively discussed in this book for the first time. Surveys have involved, respectively: 266 valid cases in 2019 (153 companies and 113 vendors); 285 valid cases in 2020 (174 companies and 111 vendors); 248 valid cases (147 companies and 101 vendors) in 2021; 295 valid cases (170 companies and 101 vendors) in 2022; and 231 valid cases (135 companies and 96 vendors) in 2023.
2 We adopted the classification of technologies for loyalty presented in the first Loyalty360 study on the 'State of the Loyalty Industry'. See https://loyalty360.org/content-gallery/loyalty360-research/loyalty-landscape for the 2019 edition of the study. At the time of writing, the previous edition was no longer available online.

References

Antavo (2022) 'Global customer loyalty report – It's time to take action'. Retrieved from https://antavo.com/reports/global-customer-loyalty-report-2022 (accessed 11 January 2024).
Collins, E. (2016) 'The Forrester wave: customer loyalty solutions for midsize organizations, Q1 2016'. Retrieved from https://silo.tips/download/res130081. (accessed 12 March 2019).

Collins, E. (2017) 'Vendor landscape: customer loyalty solutions'. Retrieved from www.forrester.com/report/Vendor-Landscape-Customer-Loyalty-Solutions/ RES58234 (accessed 14 March 2019).

Comarch & Forrester Consulting (2022) 'Loyalty marketing & reward programs – global market report'. Retrieved from www.comarch.com/trade-and-services/ loyalty-marketing/resources/loyalty-programs-digital-marketing-global-market-report-2022/#download (accessed 11 January 2024).

Fortune Business Insights (2023) 'Loyalty management market size, share and Covid-19 impact analysis, 2023–2030'. Retrieved from www.fortunebusinessinsights. com/industry-reports/loyalty-management-market-101166 (accessed 22 January 2024).

Homburg, C., Jozić, D., & Kuehnl, C. (2017) 'Customer experience management: toward implementing an evolving marketing concept'. *Journal of the Academy of Marketing Science*, 45, 377–401.

Jayachandran, S., Sharma, S., Kaufman, P. and Raman, P. (2005) 'The role of relational information processes and technology use in customer relationship management'. *Journal of Marketing*, 69(4), 1771–1792.

MarketsandMarkets (2017) 'Loyalty management market – global forecast to 2021'. January. Retrieved from www.asdreports.com/market-research-report-321174/ loyalty-management-market-global-forecast (accessed 21 January 2019; fee for full access).

Open Loyalty (2022) 'Loyalty trends – discover trends in loyalty marketing for 2021/2022'. Retrieved from www.openloyalty.io/insider/loyalty-program-trends (accessed 17 January 2024).

9

LOYALTY STRATEGIES AND THE TEST OF TIME

Barilla and Starbucks

Cristina Ziliani

Barilla's loyalty strategy: from premium promotions to digital collection schemes

The case we present here is an outstanding example of the strategic use of loyalty promotions to establish a brand and support its leadership over a period of 40 years.[1] Barilla began as a bakery shop founded in Parma in 1877 by Pietro Barilla. The company – now Barilla Group – is still privately owned, by the fourth generation of the family. With a turnover of €3.4 billion and 8,400 employees, it is now the world's leading pasta maker, with 40–45% of the Italian market and 25% of the US market. It is also the leading seller of bakery products in Italy. After several acquisitions beginning in 1973, it now controls the Barilla, Mulino Bianco, Pavesi, Voiello and Academia Barilla (Italy), Harrys (France), Wasabröd (Sweden), Misko (Greece), Filiz (Turkey), Yemina and Vesta (Mexico) and Catelli (Canada) brands. The Barilla Group has several production plants and mills all over the world, including in Italy, Greece, France, Sweden, Turkey, the US and Mexico.

Building brand loyalty: Coccio and Sorpresine

Confronted with a challenging social and economic environment in Italy in the 1970s, Barilla chose a product diversification strategy and identified bakery products as a strategic market. In 1975 it launched the Mulino Bianco (literally 'white mill') brand of cookies, which became an instant success. The brand name and mill logo – chosen to underline the attention paid to the quality of the ingredients – responded to an emergent trend towards rediscovering values linked to nature and tradition. Three years later, in a bakery sector

DOI: 10.4324/9781003400783-9

dominated by two strong leaders (Motta and Ferrero), Barilla introduced its first proof-of-purchase collection scheme. Under the scheme, customers collected 'wheat spikes' and 'wheat sheafs' by cutting out small images of them printed on the product packaging as proof of purchase. Upon mailing them to the company they received a premium – the much-celebrated *coccio*, a terracotta bowl for milk featuring the Mulino mill logo, inspired by the old Italian tradition of soaking bread in milk for breakfast or as a cheap dinner in a bowl. Something that millions of Italians were doing and millions more recalled their grandparents doing – a memory about family and tradition. Between 1978 and 1986 Barilla distributed over twenty million *cocci* as premiums and eight million families collecting six hundred million points (Morosini, 1994).

The strategic goal behind the Coccio Collection was clear from the outset: the Mulino brand was to enter Italian households by means of collectable objects, strongly linked to the brand's values and communication codes, and also accessible to non-heavy users of the brand. It was to be made a daily, familiar presence in Italian households. Mulino Bianco was a young brand on the market at the time. It became a follower in the cookie category thanks to the collection itself, but category handlers were not brand loyal. They enjoyed switching between brands and thus further category share growth seemed difficult to achieve. The collection's main goal was to expand the number of handlers – families consuming the brand – as much as possible in order to quickly gain category share. To support the brand in its march towards category leadership, the collection was to leverage the vast product portfolio, composed of dozens of different types of biscuits, bread substitutes and snacks. As competition mounted, the collection's success stimulated Barilla to advance its thinking behind it in order to engage Italian families even more. It should be said that Barilla was not relying solely on promotions to this purpose but worked on several innovation fronts: for example, it introduced a packaging innovation that greatly impacted upon consumed volumes: Mulino Bianco was the first brand to introduce family packs of snacks, containing individually wrapped snacks in quantities of eight, ten or more. The competing brand Motta was late in introducing the same type of pack, possibly because it had traditionally focused on the consumption of its products in the bar or cafe rather than at home.

Barilla did not stop there. In 1983 it introduced another successful loyalty promotion, this time aimed at children – Sorpresine. Gifts (the Italian *sorpresine* literally means 'little surprises') started to appear inside snack packs, small premiums emerging from a partnership with Graziella Carbone, a specialist in sales promotion. In each snack pack, a matchbox was inserted, with the Mulino Bianco image on it, containing small games and objects that, in the beginning, had the shape of the products themselves: erasers in the shape of Mulino Bianco's pastries and muffins, small items for school, miniature board and card games, stickers and so on. These were destined to become icons of the 1980s and 1990s and Sorpresine represented the continuing success of the original strategy to make the brand a fixture of daily family life in Italy. Between 1983 and 1992, the Coccio Collection and the Sorpresine gift scheme proceeded hand in hand, with equal success. Each Sorpresine premium was produced in at least a million pieces, and the most popular ones reached fifteen million pieces. Some 650 different premiums were designed and produced over the eight years of the promotion. Thirty years later, those children collectors, in their forties, had formed groups that meet to swap, share and celebrate their Mulino Bianco-woven childhood memories! A piece of research conducted in 2023 (Bellavita, 2023) on a sample of 1000 Italian consumers showed that 75% remember collecting Sorpresine, that can still be found in 50% of homes.

Barilla's two premium promotion programs – a collection and a gift scheme – were different but followed the same spirit: any single marketing decision was to remind the customer of the brand, any time of the day. Everything was done in-house at Barilla: new ideas were generated and tested every day, without the support of professional agencies, based on the idea that only the people who live the brand every day can think of premiums that truly express its uniqueness to customers. In 1990 another important branding step was taken: the building of the Mulino itself, a real mill on the hills of Siena, which will become that same year the set for a new TV campaign dedicated to the Mulino family directed by Giuseppe Tornatore with music by his long-time collaborator, the Academy Award winner Ennio Morricone (De Maio and Viola, 2008).

From 1978 to 1995, collection schemes were a strategic part of the Mulino Bianco brand marketing mix. After Coccio, tableware was introduced in the 1980s: sugar bowls, cookie jars, jugs, teapots, plates and trays inspired by Coccio Collection and coordinated with and among it. Terracotta products were sourced with Italian manufacturers only. This was not the first time that a successful premium stimulated an entire industry – it happened in the US with 'depression glass', glass objects employed as rewards to stimulate repeat visits in movie theatres and other outlets (Guenzi, 2015). In the late 1980s, Mulino became embodied in daily objects in children's bedrooms, meaning the brand could 'own' a different dimension of the daily experience: playtime. The new premiums were playful, magic versions of the 'mill', containers for games, pastels, incredible objects full of surprises. In the early 1990s, Mulino Bianco moved back to the kitchen, where it already owned the breakfast moment with its above-mentioned breakfast and teatime tableware. The new premiums were tablecloths, indispensable accessories for everyday family meals in every Italian household. Embroidered with a different, exclusive, Mulino-inspired patterns each year, the tablecloths appealed to mothers, who also did the shopping and chose the brands. To this day, all Italians (or, at least, this book's authors) have at least one relative still using one of these tablecloths.

In the early 1990s, each Mulino Bianco business unit had its own loyalty promotion. Collection schemes peaked between 1992 and 1995 when there were four active schemes running simultaneously: a cross-category one, in which tokens could be accumulated with purchases of any Mulino Bianco product, and three category-specific collection schemes using snacks, cookies and bread substitutes. A significant majority of Italian families (80%) were engaged with two of them – the cross-category collection and one category-specific collection. Customers were rewarded with 'boosters' (i.e. extra points) for 'variety' (sending in proofs of purchases of at least 25 different SKUs across the brand portfolio) and 'velocity' (completing the collection within the first six months of the launch of the yearly collection). In Barilla's marketing department, four to five people worked full-time on the cross-category collection alone.

In those years, half the premiums were shipped directly to households and retailers distributed the other half. Modern chain stores were growing their market share in the traditional and fragmented grocery market of Italy and were only too happy to cooperate with Barilla to deliver premiums because this created traffic in-store. Leveraging a growing network of stores as delivery points made collection operations more efficient for Barilla. Other brands ran collection schemes in those years and employed retail chains to deliver premiums, but Barilla took up most of the time retailers dedicated to the activity. Not only were there four Mulino Bianco collection schemes to run, but another collection related to Barilla pasta and sauces was soon added. However, change was coming. Retail chains were starting to introduce their own card-based loyalty schemes and when, after several years not running them, Barilla reintroduced Mulino Bianco collection schemes in 2006, it quickly discovered that consumers and retailers had changed and were no longer willing to do what the brand wanted them to do.

Monitoring and measuring performance

A crucial part of running a successful loyalty promotion is measuring its performance. Barilla invested in a Nielsen consumer panel and telephone interviews were conducted to monitor closely how its collection schemes was fairing. Such an analytical focus was indispensable if the company was to track progress towards its goal of expanding the number of handling households, and later, in the goal of growing Mulino Bianco's share among handlers. The latter had to be expanded overall and for each product category.

In measuring growth in the number of handling households, Barilla monitored four variables in each collection. First, the number of participants every month was measured and compared with the collection schemes of previous years. At one point, over three million families were involved per scheme. Second, Mulino Bianco's share (measured in volume) in handlers among

Italian families, in general and for specific product categories, was monitored over time and special attention paid to whether that share had risen or fallen after participants had joined a collection and how it compared with previous collection schemes. For some product categories, families who joined the collection increased their share by 20%. A third variable Barilla focused on was the number of different SKUs in the brand portfolio purchased by collection participants, and its trend over time. For example, participants purchased 100% more than the average number of different SKUs purchased. Finally, the ratio of burned and earned points per collection was also taken into account. Such data would allow Barilla to evaluate which products had benefited the most from the collection, especially in the case of SKUs that were not supported by TV advertising. A product that contributed 4% to earned points but 6% to burned points showed a positive 'collection effect'.

Barilla identified separate variables to measure the growth of Mulino Bianco's share among handlers and portfolio coverage: (a) participants in the cross-category collection alone, (b) participants in category-specific collection(s) alone, (c) participants in both types of collection. This made it possible to check for effects specific to product category, and whether each collection worked more towards the number of handling households, the share among handlers, or portfolio coverage. On a methodological point, it must be said that the measure is 'clean' in the year any collection scheme is launched, because the following year handlers comprise both those who carry on from the previous year (or years) and those who join in the current year. In Barilla's case, it was theoretically possible to run analyses with the consumer panel to separate the effects, but it required extra work, and more importantly, increased detail meant less significant data. Accurate monitoring, however, made it clear that participation in both the cross-category and specific collection schemes generated a significant increase in Mulino Bianco's share among handlers, which justified the effort – in terms of the financial and human resources involved – of the multiple 'collection architecture' Barilla had set in place.

Reward redemption was closely monitored too. Monthly reports of consumers' requests and reservations of premiums were produced and compared with previous collection schemes, as well as the concentration curve of reward options (i.e. the few premiums that generated the highest proportion of requests). Moreover, each reward's total requests were decomposed based on the collection that had generated them in order to evaluate if the premiums that had been devised for a specific target group of consumers had appealed to that group in reality. For example, if a Mulino Bianco portable radio had been designed as a premium for customers who regularly ate crackers and similar bread substitutes, it was later checked if that group had contributed more, in percentage, to the redemption of radios when compared with other customer segments.

A change of direction

In February 1996 Barilla discontinued its flagship collection programs. It was a major change of direction made necessary by the new economic climate. The company leadership felt that a strong response was necessary on its part to the rise in retailers' own labels and the discounters, which seemed to be taking the Italian market by storm. The company had lost ground in terms of its value-for-money positioning and decided to regain it, closing the collection schemes and reinvesting funds in a new price positioning. A considerable number of products in the Mulino Bianco portfolio were reduced in price and TV advertising and price promotion were employed to communicate the change to consumers. As well as scrapping its collection schemes, Barilla halted the Sorpresine gift scheme. In the following years, the company lost ground in every product category, especially in snacks, where the widespread appeal to children of gifts in snack packs had probably been underestimated by everyone except Ferrero, who had never abandoned this type of promotion for its own snacks. After just three years, in 1999, Barilla acknowledged this loss to Ferrero and revived the gifts-in-pack model by reintroducing the Sorpresine scheme. Another three years later, in 2002, it launched the Mulino Friends premium, also a gifts-in-pack scheme, which became an immediate hit – so much so that they are still in use today. The Friends are toys in the shape of actual Mulino Bianco products and have become 'heroes' in children's play stories. These products-turned-heroes follow the long-running Barilla tradition of embodying brand in its premium products and speaking to target customers through products themselves. However, it would be a decade before this collection model is reintroduced into the Mulino Bianco marketing mix.

In the years between, Barilla tried new tactics for the Mulino Bianco brand. It worked to engage consumers at the point of sale through in-store events, organized around various themes such as breakfast products, breads, 'holiday pantry', 'back to school', and so forth. Secondary displays were set up in stores and multiple purchases rewarded with direct premiums that were given away by store hostesses. In 2003 the 'collection spirit' was introduced in the events calendar by choosing premiums that were coordinated, complementary and shared a common theme. The complete set of Mulino Bianco direct premiums for the year were presented to customers during the first event in the store. They would receive one 'coordinated item' on their first visit and, if they came back to attend later events, could receive others in the set. Soon stamps, found inside the premiums themselves, were added to the scheme and a stamp booklet provided to customers attending the event. Such a store-based collection scheme was reliant on online media. Being impossible to run in every store, the scheme could only be active in selected retail outlets and offline media advertising would not reach consumers living in areas where no store was participating. The Mulino Bianco website was, therefore, a key tool.

This was, of course, not an *entirely* new direction. Seven years after dropping the more traditional collection schemes, Barilla's new initiative represented a kind of 'visit-driven' collection scheme. The 'collection' technique and the brand philosophy of consistency in values, codes and traditions had simply been extended to the new territory of in-store brand activation promotions.

Three years after the introduction of the in-store collection scheme, market research conducted in 2006 into the Mulino Bianco's brand equity revealed that bread was only a marginal part of it, with consumers thinking little or not at all about bread when mentally representing Mulino Bianco. This was a weakness for Barilla, which was hoping to expand its share in what was a rapidly growing daily consumption category (due to innovations both in the industrial production of soft bread and in advertising). A new strategic goal was set: work on Mulino Bianco's brand equity to develop it in the direction of bread and not exclusively biscuits and cakes as it had been until then. To pursue this goal the collection model was reintroduced exclusively to support the bread category. Given the variety and synergy of different segments and products within the category, such as 'soft' and 'crunchy' products, it was hoped that the collection logic would work as well as it had for the cross-category collection of the previous decade.

Given that the Mulino Bianco brand had entered various soft bread segments (loaves, soft tacos, sandwich breads and so on), a second strategic objective was assigned to the new I Pani del Mulino Bianco ('bread collection') scheme: to push the growth of Mulino Bianco's share among handlers of the various soft bread segments in the category. Mulino Bianco was no longer a challenger and had no need to expand the number of handling households. Therefore, the collection could be aimed at a reduced number of heavy-user households – a marked contrast from the logic of the late 1970s when the collection approach was adopted for the first time by a young brand that needed all users in order to grow share.

The approach worked. During its first year, I Pani del Mulino Bianco impacted handlers' behaviour significantly, driving up volumes as well as the brand's share of category spend, and above all, expanding the number of different Mulino Bianco bread products purchased by handlers and thus subtracted from the sales of competing brands. Just as 10 years before, the number of different SKUs purchased by the average handler family grew by 100%. The collection had the greatest effect on newly launched products, those with the lowest shares in the category, a beneficial effect on the total product portfolio that was first observed during the cross-category collection of the 1970s. The new digital collection schemes that Mulino Bianco has experimented with in recent years have the same objectives. It is the interface that is different – no more physical cutting and pasting but clicks and taps on a smartphone screen – not the goals. The real challenge, however, lies with changes that have taken place in demand and in household habits, not in promotional techniques or technology.

The new face of collecting

Things started to change in the 2000s. The consumers engaging with I Pani del Mulino Bianco in 2006 were different from the members of Barilla's collection schemes of the 1980s and 1990s. As Nielsen data confirms, the number of Italian families willing to engage in a collection scheme in the 1980s and 1990s was much higher. It was between two and three million during the early days of the Mulino Bianco collection schemes, while in 2006 I Pani del Mulino Bianco engaged 800,000 households. There might be two causes at play here: the collection structure and redemption rules and a more general change in the attitude of consumers. We've said already that in the early days of Mulino Bianco, point redemption thresholds were low in order to engage a substantial number of families and expand the number of handlers. In 2006 the goal of targeting heavy users only (the top two deciles of the concentration curve) led to the setting of higher, more challenging thresholds that necessarily reduced the number of participants among category users. Many started collecting points but then gave up when they did not reach targets. On average, 5% of brand users in the category also redeemed in I Pani del Mulino Bianco, as opposed to 30% for the cross-category collection of the 1990s.

The same Nielsen data, however, tells another story. It is the overall phenomenon of 'collectors' that was on a downward slope, not just for Barilla. People's attitude towards clipping, saving, pasting and mailing proofs of purchase had changed. Barilla's competitor Ferrero, which never ceased its use of collection schemes, experienced the same erosion of the number of collecting households. The same happened to the Granarolo and Parmalat collection schemes that had been introduced to the market following Mulino Bianco's success. Collectors had changed: they had gotten used to supermarket point collection schemes, which are easier and don't require brand preference changes, cover the whole grocery shopping, rather than specific brands, and need no cutting or pasting, just a convenient plastic card. Collecting supermarket points is easier and premiums often look similar between supermarket and brand collection schemes – Barilla itself had run a few collection schemes whose rewards were small premium brand electrical appliances for the kitchen. Consumers were happy with the new convenient way of getting something for free, without having to clip proofs from product packaging.

This raises an interesting question for marketers and academics. Today, with digital collection schemes and digital promotions in general, the interface has changed and the gestures associated with participating in promotions too. Will marketers substitute more traditional ways of enrolling and engaging consumers? Will customers self-segment based on their preferences and familiarity with technology? Will memory of the promotion, intention to buy, and actual purchase rate change, compared with plastic cards or stamp collecting? The only way to know is to experiment with the new. That is precisely what Barilla did, and not only with collection schemes. In fact, in 2009, Mulino Bianco launched Nel Mulino che Vorrei ('In the mill, I would like') (www. nelmulinochevorrei.it), an online platform where people can interact with the brand and suggest ideas on the most varied aspects: new products, new packaging, new promotions, recipes and even social and environmental projects. Members can take part in surveys and can personalize product packages and premiums with their own names, photos and traits. Cherry croissants and Focaccelle are two successful new products that have been developed following members' suggestions. The community reached 50,000 members in 2016, largely due to online social networks, and since its inception has generated over 10,000 ideas, 690,000 comments and over 3.5 million votes on members' posts.

To mark Mulino Bianco's fortieth birthday, Barilla decided to launch a new and totally digital collection scheme in 2015 called Mulino in Festa ('Festive mill').[2] The project involved 208 million product packages and 57 SKUs for 38 products in the biscuits, snacks, cakes and bread categories. It aimed to reward both immediate purchase and repeat purchases through point collection and instant wins. Sell out and a higher frequency of purchases were its target metrics. Above all, the scheme, which ran from April to November 2015, aimed to stimulate cross-category purchases to develop medium-user and heavy-user loyalty. The target group was composed of 12.5 million families who could win a prize with any purchased product and participate in a digital collection scheme whose reward threshold was set at 65 points.

In order to take part in the Mulino in Festa promotion, customers entered their receipt data online at the scheme website or via the Mio Mulino mobile app. After registering, they could take part in the daily instant win – entering up to five receipt codes every day – to win a supply of Mulino Bianco products. All users who took part in the instant win by entering at least one receipt code were eligible for the weekly draw for a prize of a weekend for two at the 'real mill' of Chiusdino, in Tuscany, featured in the TV adverts.

Each receipt code entered entitled the customer to a point. Once a user had collected 65 points, she could claim a porcelain cookie jar and customized mugs with her name on them. The style of the jar adapted the design of the historical premium while appealing to contemporary tastes. Extra points could be collected by entering bonus codes which the user could win by taking part in activities related to the collection scheme – many of which took place in-store where promotion cards were handed out to consumers to stimulate engagement. One of the novelties of Mulino in Festa was the opportunity for each user to donate up to a maximum of 10 points or to receive them as a donation. In this way, points that were not redeemed were not lost either because they could be used by another customer to reach the prize threshold.

Of course, other companies and brands in Italy have introduced digital collection schemes. However, Mulino in Festa has distinctive traits as a body of digital promotions for FMCG. Firstly, it allows for multichannel user involvement, via the website and app. Users can connect with the brand while on the move, check their points balance and read about the promotion rules, prizes and premiums. In-app features mean they can take photos of their receipts and receive push notifications and personalized communication, all of which helps sustain engagement and reduce defection. The second innovation was the use of optical character recognition technology to read the images from receipts uploaded by the users and identify data. The system stores each customer's uploads in a customer purchase history that can also be accessed by customer service teams, thus optimizing their operations and costs. Thirdly, the algorithm-based receipt validation system employs two different recognition systems to assign a risk index to each uploaded receipt. All users claiming a reward are ranked according to risk in order to block fraudulent claims and optimize customer service.

Another innovative feature is the MyFanCare customer care tool, which is totally integrated in the promotion so that all requests and communications to customer care from different touchpoints (email, social media, website contact form, phone call with customer service) are consolidated in a single platform where they are classified by topic based on a semantic analysis, receive a priority index and are put through to dedicated operators. Last, but not least, a boosting plan is built into the initiative to offer extra points and different benefits to members in order to reach cross-selling goals and upselling or other sales targets that emerge during the eight-month life span of the promotion. For example, members are offered extra points and incentives to buy cross-category products (generated from analyses of their individual purchase history during the promotion). They can also gain extra points by sharing the promotion with their friends.

In 2023, to mark 40 years since Sopresine's first launch, Mulino Bianco has reintroduced them. Specifically, three sets of six erasers can be claimed for home delivery by using the in-pack codes on the Mulino Bianco website:

> With the new Mulino Bianco Sorpresine collection we want to celebrate the bond with our consumers, rekindle the enthusiasm of all those who have never stopped wanting an iconic object, and arouse the same emotions in today's children … We want to speak to the children of yesterday, rediscovering a beloved game like Sorpresine, and to the children of today, to relive the emotions experienced by their parents, creating new opportunities to meet and play together …
>
> *(Bellavita, 2023, p. 2)*

The launch is accompanied by a treasure hunt on Facebook, an online competition to win a weekend visit to the Mulino Bianco product plant, an interview (available on YouTube) with the Sopresine's creator – Graziella Carbone – limited edition packaging for the snack types involved in the promotion, augmented reality games, a new Tv ad with rearranged Ennio Morricone's music from the1990 campaign, and the involvement of several influencers and content creators.

Looking into the future

The Mulino Bianco case is an outstanding example of the strategic use of loyalty promotions to establish a brand and support its leadership over a sustained period of time, throughout the inevitable ebb and flow of market, economic and social change. What can companies take away from this success story? It seems that there are two things that are critical to the effectiveness of loyalty-building promotion: (a) clear and precise goals need to be defined beforehand, and (b) all elements of the promotion, down to the last detail, must be carefully and methodically designed so that they are consistent with the brand's values and image. Even if the future is full of sophisticated technologies that we cannot even begin to imagine today, we firmly believe that the success of promotional activities going forward will continue to be predicated on these two key factors.

My Starbucks Rewards: from store card to digital loyalty ecosystem

Founded in 1971, Starbucks is the largest coffee house chain in the world. As of 2023, it has more than 36,000 stores in over 80 countries (Starbucks, 2023). Consolidated net revenues have reached $26 billion. 90-day active members in the US have reached 33 million (Beans, 2023) and they generate over 55% of the company's operating revenue. Worldwide, 90-day active digital customers have reached 75 million, and the company is planning to double the figure in five years. Considering potential customers that can be reached and/or activated digitally, Starbucks says they can reach over 200 million individuals worldwide (Pymnts, 2023).

Scott Maw, the executive vice president and chief financial officer, declared that 'over the last couple years, almost all of our same-store sales growth came from those customers that we have digital relationships with and those that are in our My Starbucks Rewards (MSR) program' (Starbucks, 2018, p. 2).

Starbucks' loyalty program achieved an impressive American Customer Satisfaction Index (ACSI) score of 78 in 2022, according to Statista. 21% of Starbucks customers return within three days, with 10% returning within just one day and MSR members are 5.6 times more likely to visit daily. Starbucks excels with a noteworthy customer retention rate of 44%, surpassing the industry average of 25%, according to MJV (2023).

With the above results, MSR is regarded by some as the most successful loyalty program in America and certainly by the company itself as a major source of growth.

Starbucks is regarded today as a great example of a company that has evolved its loyalty strategy by successfully embracing and developing new tools and opportunities as they became available as we describe below.

How the loyalty program has evolved over twenty years

Starbucks launched its first loyalty program in 2001: the Gold card-based scheme had a $25 annual membership fee and provided members with a 10% in-store discount on purchases all year round (Nitin, 2017). However, the company ditched the scheme as sales generated through it stagnated and in 2009 they launched MSR. It was free to enrol in MSR. Customers could load any amount of money on to a gift card and register the card to protect the balance and start collecting 'stars'. Every time a customer made a purchase at Starbucks, they earned one star. The more stars they earned, the bigger the rewards. Customers registering a Starbucks loyalty card were defaulted to the Welcome Level, which included a free birthday beverage (Palnitkar, 2017). Once customers earned five stars, they reached the Green Level. At the Green Level, members got free refills of brewed coffee or tea, free selected syrups and milk when they ordered a beverage off the menu, a free beverage when they bought whole bean coffee, and free trial offers. Customers who accumulated 30 stars over a 12-month period reached the Gold Level. Gold Level members received free refills of ice and brewed coffee and tea, a free drink for every 12 stars, free food and drink offers, a personalized Gold Card that recognized them as preferred customers, and customized coupons.

It is worth comparing the initial fee-based Starbucks program with the MSR launched in 2009. The company shifted away from hard benefits like the 10% discount toward a 'free' card approach that meant no fees for registration and non-monetary rewards: free refills, free drinks for birthdays, free drinks every 12 stars, and so on. This approach changed the customer mindset from thinking in terms of discounts and prices to extras and free gains. Starbucks' decision to reward customers purchasing coffee beans is another telltale detail. It intended to pamper real fans of the product, those customers who love the brew so much so that they take coffee beans home to grind. This way the Starbucks brand and its loyalty initiative entered customers' homes, a loyalty strategy that seeks to own new consumption moments different from the traditional in-store experience. The 'levels' structure stimulates customers to climb the ladder through repeat visits. And removing the fee – even adding the free birthday drink rewarding the simple act of registering for the scheme – played in favour of opening the scheme to a much wider membership base, consisting of not only of heavy spenders but also light spenders, who probably found the previous fee-based program unappealing.

In February 2016 the company announced that it was making changes to the MSR program. The new program went into effect on 12 April that year. Under the new structure, customers earn reward stars based on the amount of money they spend at Starbucks: two stars were earned for every dollar spent on any drink, food, or other item. The more customers spend, the more they earn.

There were also changes made to the program's levels and rewards rate. The Welcome Level had been eliminated and, as they signed up, customers were enrolled into the Green tier: to maintain this status, they needed to earn at least one star per year. Green members still got a free drink on their birthday, free refills in store, and could pay or order in advance through the app (see next section). The accumulated stars, however, were of real value only when the customer reached Gold status. This required 300 stars, in contrast to the 30 stars previously needed, and 300 stars every 12 months (or a spend of $150 per year) were needed to maintain the status. Gold members would need 125 additional stars for a free reward; previously, they needed only 12 (i.e. 12 visits). It had been noted that members often pay for their friends to earn more stars and get closer to their free drink. New monthly 'double-star days' helped Gold members get there faster. Considering that a $62.50 spend was required to earn 125 stars, and a free drink is worth $5, the approximate payback percentage for Gold members was 8% (Palnitkar, 2017). High spenders might like the new program, but rewards for low-spending customers were small.

Starbucks justified the change by saying that some customers had been splitting their orders, asking a cashier to ring up a coffee and muffin separately, to 'game' the system and gain rewards faster; that led to longer queues and customer inconvenience. The other, more substantial reason was that the company wanted more members for MSR: fewer than one in six of Starbucks' 75 million monthly visitors in February 2016 belonged to MSR and with members spending twice as much as non-members (Garcia, 2016a) it was easy to see the reason for the move. Starbucks executives also said the shift to a 'dollars spent' model from a 'number of visits' model was the most requested program change by customers themselves. They cited the US airline industry undergoing a similar conversion, with carriers moving to reward dollars spent rather than miles flown.

The change angered some customers, who perceived that they needed to spend more money to achieve the same benefits they got before, and led to some noise about how the loyalty program wasn't as generous (Snyder, 2016). Some members complained on Twitter (now X), raising awareness of the change among the customer base. To reassure members, Starbucks cited faster in-store queues and argued that the majority of members would earn their stars as fast or even faster than before, due also to promotions and new opportunities both in and outside the store. However, they acknowledged that a 'small minority' would earn rewards at a slower pace (Kilgore, 2016) and admitted that after the change there had been a reduction in traffic. Citing YouGov data, Adweek reported that the company's brand perception slumped by 50% after the MSR change announcement (Kell, 2016).

Deutsche Bank had downgraded Starbucks shares to hold on 12 April over concerns that changes to the loyalty program could have a negative impact on same-store sales, and share prices slumped (Garcia, 2016a). Analysts were also worried about competitors exploiting the situation to poach Starbucks customers: Dunkin' Donuts was said to have plans to target them two days after the MSR program changes to attract them to try its program (Kilgore, 2016). However, a few months after the protests, Starbucks reported that the changes were prompting new customers to join the program, citing 900,000 new members in the second quarter of 2016 (though changes were not effective in the first month). That's an 8% increase on the first quarter of the year, and 16% increase on the second quarter of 2015.

From 2016 to today MSR has seen other changes. In 2019 the Green and Gold levels were removed and substituted with points thresholds. In 2020 the company changed how members earn rewards, that is two points per dollar when using a registered Starbucks card or one point per dollar with other payment options (see next section). Lastly, in February 2023 Starbucks increased the number of stars needed to attain rewards. Currently, there are five redemption tiers and related rewards are as follows:

- 25 stars: Customize a drink with an extra shot of espresso, dairy substitute, syrup or sauce up to $1.
- 100 stars: Brewed hot or iced coffee or tea, a bakery item, packaged snacks and core reusable plastic to-go cups.
- 200 stars: Handcrafted beverages and Cold Brew beverages or hot breakfast.
- 300 stars: Lunch sandwich, protein box, salad and packaged coffee.
- 400 stars: Signature mug, drink tumbler and coffee merchandise up to $20.

Members also get a free birthday reward, a discount for using a reusable cup and free refills of hot or iced coffee or tea in-store. In sum, not counting other opportunities to earn extra stars – such as Double Star Days or games – members using a Starbucks Card will need to spend $100 to earn the 200 points needed to get a Frappuccino, while those using other forms of payment would need to spend $200 to earn 200 points to get it.

The app

The success of MSR is often attributed to its mobile rewards app, launched in 2011. According to a survey conducted by The Manifest business news website in May 2018, almost 50% of US smartphone owners who regularly use restaurant loyalty apps used the Starbucks app (Panko, 2018) with the second most used app in the sector – Domino's – used by only 34%.

The app offers a range of features, such as checking MSR program account information in real time, a store locator, and payment management. Users can set up the payment feature by linking their app to a credit card or PayPal account: they then load money onto the app to use it as a debit card. There is no need to go to the store to load funds, although the option is still available for customers who prefer to do so. The prepaid mechanism acts as a 'lock-in', nudging customers to choose a Starbucks store over competitors since they have already set aside funds for the purpose. They carry their phone with them all the time and as additional purchase occasions arise, they are never out of a means of payment. Moreover, the substitution of cash and credit card can play the trick of making customers feel as if their drinks are practically free.

From the perspective of the company, the prepaid system provides funds that can be reinvested and saves Starbucks fees and commissions that arise when customers pay by credit card. Indeed it has been estimated that Starbucks might pay as much as $0.25 in fees on the sale of a $2.75 cup of coffee (Wathen, 2017). Last but not least, as some customers never use up their credit – this is true of gift cards as well as app-based wallet systems like the MSR app feature – the company earns on the breakage (as unused funds are known in the business). According to a study by *The Wall Street Journal*, in the first quarter of 2016 Starbucks had $1.2 billion in deposits loaded onto plastic cards and the app combined (Ferro, 2016; Meola, 2016). This figure is larger than the amount held at many smaller regional banks or prepaid card firms, and it is almost double the $621 million it had it 2014 (Garcia, 2016b). On breakage income alone – that is, income resulting from lost or unused gift cards – Starbucks earned $39.3 million in 2015 (Ferro, 2016) and $60.5 million in 2016 (Wathen, 2017), or the equivalent to the estimated operating profit of 300 company-owned stores. Bowman (2016) estimates that, with $5 billion in card transactions every year, Starbucks would be able to earn $50 million in interest with a 1% interest rate (assuming it reinvests in high-grade corporate bonds, treasury notes, and certificates of deposit). Combined with the breakage income, that would mean about $90 million in revenue from the loyalty program, or the equivalent of profit from about 700 company-owned stores. And this all without taking into account the increased spending and frequency of MSR members, who are reported to spend three times as much as non-members.

In December 2021 funds loaded on the app and onto gift cards had exceeded 3 billion $, while the average reload per customer had grown from less than 110 $ in 2019 to 122$ in 2022 (Earnest Insights, 2022). Breakage reached $181 million in the same year (up from 145 million in 2000) a figure that amounted to about 1% of its sales and 4.3% of its net income during the year (Patton, 2022).

In the early days the novelty of the app further contributed to the loyalty program's success. When other customers in line see people using their mobile phones to pay, their curiosity is aroused and they may be encouraged to sign up. The app tracks purchase history, stars earned on each purchase, and card reloads. Additionally, it delivers special promotions to users and sends them messages previewing new products before they appear in stores. Geolocation tracking incentivizes users to visit the nearest branch. The Starbucks app has helped greatly to differentiate the program from other standard card-only programs in a market that was fast becoming crowded with loyalty efforts. In fact, the app's payment feature generated over 7 million transactions a week in the first quarter of 2015 in the US, and in the first quarter of 2016 it was used by 11 million people, accounting for 15% of sales and 21% of transactions. That same year it outpaced all other payment apps, including PayPal and Apple Pay. In 2017 it was used by 23.4 million Americans, edging out both Apple (22 million) and Google (11.1 million), according to an eMarketer report that credits Starbucks with having stirred a renaissance in domestic mobile payments in the US (Kats, 2018).

Initially critics were sceptical about the Starbucks app because they thought that it was too complicated for some customers and difficult for baristas to promote at the till. However, Starbucks effectively trained their baristas to talk customers into moving from card to app. Indeed staff play a crucial role in determining loyalty program adoption and success: Starbucks leveraged this by introducing the 'digital tipping' enhancement to the app. This feature gives customers the option to tip the store staff just moments after paying at the till. Customers have a two-hour window to select a tip ranging from 50 cents to $2. Not only does the feature promote a dialogue between staff and customers, and a better service, but it expands the base of customers who actually tip, an activity that might be undermined by a lack of time or small change and distraction.

Another enhancement to the app was the Shake to Pay feature, which simplifies mobile payments. By simply shaking their smartphone, customers can bring the barcode of their Starbucks card front and centre at any time. This gesture, one which links our long-standing gestures in the physical world to new digital devices, not only makes app payment more convenient, but it can surprise the customer and make them feel empowered, and hence positively remember the app experience. The app also offers a 'Gift' tab where users can select a theme – from 'Happy Birthday' to 'Thank You' – and send a digital Starbucks gift card to any email address with just a few taps on their smartphone, a clever feature that serves a customer need, capitalizes on impulse (you can do it anytime, on the go), and contributes to using the customer's preloaded funds, hence ... generating a need to reload. A range of other features of the app enhance the customer experience and engagement. Whenever customers check the app, a brand-new, time-limited bonus offer is created and displayed to reward loyal customers with even more stars. This has the effect of making the program feel fresh all the time (McEachern, 2017). In recent years, the app has also added the 'detailed recipe' feature, describing the nutritional content of each food and drink product in detail, a feature particularly welcome by 'fitness freaks'.

Starbucks were also quick to utilize the power of social media. Anyone with a Twitter account linked to their Starbucks card could buy coffee with a $5 gift card for anyone else on the social platform by tweeting at the handle @tweetacoffee and including the handle of the person receiving the gift (Champagne and Iezzi, 2014).

In 2015 Starbucks added its 'Mobile Order & Pay' order-ahead service. The mobile order-ahead service refers to a consumer-facing mobile payment platform that allows customers to order food remotely, pay for the items on their phone, and pick up their order at a specific restaurant location, without once having to speak to a Starbucks employee (Meola, 2016). Within three months of launching, customers were placing up to 7 million orders per week via this service. Competing quick-service restaurants have been quick to adopt mobile order-ahead services to enhance sales, strengthen customer loyalty, and secure traffic in store. By tapping into each customer purchase history, the Mobile Order & Pay feature encourages cross-selling by suggesting additional items available in store to add to the current order. Taco Bell sees 30% higher average order values on mobile compared to in store, while Starbucks' Mobile Order & Pay represented 10% of total transactions at high-volume stores as early as 2016 (Meola, 2016). In 2018 the company decided to open up Mobile Order & Pay beyond MSR members to any Starbucks customer. This would encourage acquisition to the program indirectly, as users of the service, who give their mobile phone number and email address to gain access to it, are contacted directly via digital marketing and are then exposed to the benefits of the program (Starbucks, 2018). In 2023, mobile order and pay, drive-thru and delivery drove 72% of the US revenue of the company (ConnectPOS, 2023).

Soon after launching the Mobile Order & Pay service, and probably to give it more traction from the start, Starbucks announced that they were going to experiment with different types of delivery service: one that would involve its own employees and also a model that included a third-party service. Members of the loyalty program would be able to request delivery through Mobile Order & Pay. Such a service if rolled out nationwide, it was envisioned, might alter competition and market shares, as time-strapped consumers would switch to Starbucks to take advantage of the delivery service. This raised the bar for the whole quick-service-restaurant industry (Samuely, 2016). Since the early trials of 2016, Starbucks has consolidated a partnership with Postmates and launched a new partnership with Uber Eats in 2019 that made the delivery service available from 2,000 Starbucks stores in the US (Mogg, 2019). In 2022 the company entered in a new partnership with DoorDash to serve all 50 US States by the end of 2023, a signal that delivery is a substantial opportunity for growth. Consumers can place an order for a Starbucks product with the Uber Eats and DoorDash apps, track the order and expect delivery within 30 minutes. Special packaging has been developed to maintain the drinks at the right temperature. The move will acquire new customers to Starbucks among the partner apps' user bases and help expand Starbucks' share of existing customers' wallets since its products will reach customers out of store and fill new spots in their daily habits. In 2023 delivery represent 31% of sales, with a growth of +30% in just one year (Pymnts, 2023). With more Starbucks products available through more than one delivery service in the same city, the company will see growth but will also need to look into price consistency and price perception issues.

Use of customer data

The use of customer data may be a recent phenomenon at Starbucks but it is one that is escalating. Scott Maw declared that Starbucks only started looking into the MSR program data in 2016 (Starbucks, 2019) but now it is leveraging the 100 million transactions a week it records in the US to support personalized offers, equipment maintenance, new product development, store openings and menu adjustments (Rahman, 2020). The company has shared some facts about the use of data for expanding its product lines into grocery stores. For example, data collected in store has shown that 43 percent of tea-drinking customers tend to skip the sugar. To cater to this segment, Starbucks created its lines of unsweetened iced tea. Along the same line, a new line of black iced coffee without milk has been introduced after data revealed that 25 percent of customers don't add milk to their coffee (Rahman, 2020).

Knowing individual customer preferences and buying patterns allows Starbucks to send personalized offers more likely to be relevant: since 2017, with the introduction of its 'Digital Flywheel' program, artificial intelligence algorithms have been applied to determine promotional campaigns. Built around four pillars (rewards, personalization, payment, and order), the program was a major modernization of the company technology stack aimed to replace stand alone, legacy rewards, ordering and other tools, to better organize data and integrate marketing with store-based operating systems, including inventory and production management. The company links this to the goal of merging the physical customer touchpoints with the digital to 'not only drive superior business results in the short term, based on rewards, ordering, and personalization, but we also make it very challenging for digital companies to outmanoeuvre us in the physical world' (Mixson, 2021, p. 1).

Engagement is essential to retain members and this is sustained at Starbucks through personalization and also by employing the principles of gamification. Here are some examples. Starbucks Dash offers customers rewards for visiting a branch multiple times over a certain time period. A Dash incentivizes customers to start a predictable visit routine, awarding them more stars the more times they visit. The app keeps track of how often a member has visited and encourages them to move the video game-like progress bar towards earning their special reward. Bonus Star Combinations work the same way, and require that customers buy (usually) three different items within a certain number of days.

The Starbucks for Life program provides customers with the chance to win free coffee for a year, a month, or a week by completing challenges and earning game plays. With the Summer Game customers can win prizes by completing unique challenges. The Roastery Challenge is a VR and AR experience that encourages customers to explore Starbucks' roasteries, enhancing their knowledge and interest in the company (LoQuiz, 2023). 'Starbucks Pairs' is a digital memory game featuring Starbucks products that can be played on mobile devices. Players earn rewards for completing the game, such as discounts on their next Starbucks purchase. 'Starbucks Bingo' is another popular game where customers fill out virtual bingo cards to earn rewards: this encourages multiple purchases. Finally, the 'Starbucks Nitro Cold Brew Game' requires players to physically shake their phones to create a virtual Nitro Cold Brew drink and rewards players with discounts on their next purchase (LoQuiz, 2023).

The effectiveness of Starbucks' loyalty strategy can be measured by looking at the evolution of spending and customer lifetime value of members as they 'age' in the program. Cohorts (defined by their first year in the program) more than doubled their spend at Starbucks, from $110 in the year prior to joining MSR to over $250 in the year after joining (Earnest Insights, 2022). Cohorts (defined by their first quarter in the program) also nearly doubled their spend from $55 in the quarter prior to joining to about $100 in the quarter after. This, in turn, justifies the spending in the program and its enablers, from the app to the mentioned technology stack.

Expanding the program: from partnerships to digital ecosystem

Over time, loyalty programs strive to expand earning options for their customers and, at the same time, attempt to recruit new members to the program. Starbucks first expanded the scope of its loyalty program when it introduced points for purchases outside of its retail locations. Starbucks coffee beans, tea and ready-to-enjoy drinks can be bought online and in other retail stores. By placing 'star codes' on participating product packs, Starbucks made it possible for customers to earn extra stars while grocery shopping at their local supermarket. For supermarkets, listing Starbucks products means cashing in on the brand popularity as the star codes were an added stimulus for brand-loyal customers to purchase in the categories where the supermarket has enlisted Starbucks products.

In 2015 a multi-year agreement with ride-sharing company Lyft was announced. The deal allowed Lyft users who connect their Lyft account with the MSR account to collect MSR stars for each ride taken. First-time Lyft riders also earn enough stars for a free beverage by linking their accounts and taking a ride within a specified period of time. All Lyft drivers can automatically become Gold members (Harris, 2015; Oragui, 2018). Around the same time, the company revealed that MSR members would soon be able to read select daily news articles from the *New York Times* for free in the Starbucks mobile app. This move went in the direction of adding value to program membership without using discounts and promoting more frequent use of the app. Meanwhile, the *New York Times* gained the opportunity of reaching new audiences while giving away a reasonable amount of content – 15 articles per day (Shah, 2016).

Just as a coffee and a newspaper go well together, Starbucks and music go back a long way. Music can be said to be at the centre of the 'third-place experience'[3] that Starbucks has been successfully building for 40 years. In 1994 a dedicated team began selecting original CDs spanning a variety of musical genres to sell and play Starbucks branches. Seasonal CDs have celebrated Valentine's Day, summer holidays and Christmas, but Starbucks has also become a champion of emerging artists, introducing their music to the public early in their careers (Miller, 2015). As the music industry and consumer habits evolved with the digital revolution, Starbucks began offering Wi-Fi in store in 2002 and in 2007 partnered with Apple to provide free access to iTunes Music (Alba, 2015).

In March 2015 Starbucks ceased sales of CDs in store and announced a new strategy. It partnered with Spotify, the music-streaming service, to use Spotify's mobile app to let music playlists be curated and shared between MSR members, baristas and 60 million Spotify subscribers. The Starbucks app allows users to identify songs being played in store, then download and save those they like to a playlist on Spotify's app. Starbucks employees receive a Spotify Premium subscription so they can help shape in-store music programming using tools provided by Spotify. These partner-influenced playlists are accessible on Spotify via the Starbucks app; thus customers can stream Starbucks music anywhere and anytime from their mobile device and continue enjoying the music of choice even after leaving the store. Moreover, Spotify users can obtain stars in the MSR program (Samuely, 2016).

This was the first time that Starbucks loyalty program stars could be accessed by a third party for the benefit of MSR members and Spotify users. The collaboration goes well beyond providing a substitute for a delisted category in store (music CDs) and offers fresh acquisition opportunities to the loyalty program (Spotify's 60 million subscribers). The fact that Starbucks probably earned a fee from Spotify, which was seeking new subscribers in the US, is only one of many reasons for the strategy. The move adds a service that appeals to the profile of Starbucks' target audience (music lovers and digital users). It counteracts the risk that new digital services could keep customers away from stores (such as order-ahead) by introducing a service that brings them back. An existing but largely dormant digital asset of the company is put to value creation: 20 years of playlists that may be valuable to specific customer segments are made available. Just as when Amazon took the decision to cease reviewing books in-house and open its platform to customer reviews, Starbucks has embraced crowdsourcing for product choices (in this case, music). Involving customers in the co-creation of their store experience creates engagement. Furthermore, it leverages music's connection to human emotions, and the role of positive emotions in purchase and repatronage intentions and behaviour. Moreover, by linking data between the two apps, Starbucks gains insight on their customers' online and social habits. From there, other digital content can be added to what could become a vast digital content platform of the flavour of an Amazon Prime. New revenue streams may open up as Starbucks takes to selling to third parties its audience and targeting capabilities, digital payment expertise, payment services and more.

In 2018 the company announced the launch of the Starbucks Rewards prepaid Visa card, a co-branded credit card in partnership with Chase, the US consumer and commercial banking business of J.P. Morgan. Customers using the card earn stars with every purchase both in Starbucks stores and anywhere in the world Visa is accepted. They receive a physical card within 7 to 10 days of their application, but a digital card is immediately loaded in their Starbucks app so that they can start earning stars right away. Since one star is earned for every dollar that is digitally loaded to the Starbucks app using the Starbucks Rewards Visa Card, the new credit card encourages mobile payment with the Starbuck app (J.P. Morgan, 2018).

In 2022 Starbucks started partnering with Delta airlines to let members earn miles. Linking Delta SkyMiles and Starbucks Rewards accounts opens up earning opportunities and benefits, such as: double stars on Delta travel days, 1 mile per $1 spent at Starbucks and exclusive offers. This alliance allows both companies to tap into each other's customer bases, potentially attracting new customers who are loyal to one brand to become interested in the other, while for customers who already patronize both brands, this partnership reinforces their loyalty and engagement. In 2023 two new partnerships have been announced, in financial services and hospitality. However, there is criticism around the real relevance of the benefits (Pymnts, 2022): when one consider the Delta partnership, one mile per dollar for purchases in Starbucks is a fifth of the accrual for purchases with Delta and, given the price gap between a beverage and an average airline ticket (2 $ for a cappuccino versus 330$ for an average domestic round trip in the US) the accrual of miles is little more than negligible.

However, the partnership moves described above are part – in our opinion – of Starbucks' experimentation with the blockchain, much like the company's foray into NFT's with its Starbucks Odyssey program in the metaverse. The company is exploring how to tokenize Stars and create the ability for other merchants to connect their rewards program to Starbucks Rewards.

Starbucks Odyssey is an extension of the reward program, powered by Web3 technology, that offers users the opportunity to earn digital collectible stamps (NFT's) that will unlock access to benefits and experiences. Stamps can be obtained by purchasing Starbucks goods, engaging with educational activities revolving around the world of coffee and also by playing games. A dedicated marketplace is in place to allow purchasing of some limited-edition stamps too. Stamps have a point value based on their rarity, and the more points, the more exclusive are the experiences they give access to, from a virtual class on how to make coffee-based cocktails to a trip to Starbucks farms in Costa Rica. To make engagement easier and broaden its appeal, Odyssey does not require transferring cryptocurrencies or setting up a crypto wallet: instead NFT's can be purchased with credit cards (Mizerak, 2022). Starbucks says the Odyssey platform will also have features for employees (Borgers, 2022).

In March 2024, Starbucks announced that they are closing Odyssey 'to prepare for what comes next as we continue to evolve the program' (Kubinek, 2024). In fact, the company needs experimenting with Web3 technology to support a more global approach to loyalty, in line with its increasingly global presence. In fact, the presence of different tech stacks, including different POS systems, in the different countries it operates in, prevents a unified managing of the loyalty program, which is instead managed on a per country basis. NFT's and the blockchain could become the new standard, enabling the expansion of the loyalty app footprint across all locations. With new developments inevitably come risks. As Starbucks adds partners to program and payment options to expand the reach of star earning and burning and to monetize program loyalty, it may face the risk of diluting program equity due to excessive stretching or devaluating the 'star' value. Something similar has happened to airlines: fees from partners using air miles for their loyalty programs are a major source of income for many airlines, but this has led to excessive 'minting' and the consequent devaluation of the 'currency'.

A yet more subtle risk is that of fostering loyalty to the app as a means of payment, especially if it becomes an open wallet and is used to pay outside Starbucks too, rather than primarily to Starbucks itself. A third risk is that innovation outpaces capacity. When so many players are engaged (think of delivery apps, partner apps, payment intermediaries, social media, etc. – the

Starbucks app connects with all of them and possibly more in the future) sustaining expectations and service quality may be a daunting task. Service failures and data breach challenges will inevitably multiply, if only due to the escalating number of users.

Notes

1 We wholeheartedly thank Elena Bernardelli, the Global Marketing VP at Barilla, who shared with us both her experience and company data during precious hours of discussion on the success drivers of Barilla's loyalty programs. The history of Barilla presented here draws on various materials provided, some of which are publicly available on the company website'. The data presented in this section, if not otherwise stated, has been made available to the Loyalty Observatory to support the writing of this case study. An earlier version of this section appears (in Italian) in Ziliani (2015), reproduced here with the permission of EGEA. Omissions and mistakes are the responsibility of the author alone.
2 The text that follows is based on an earlier version written by Fulvio Furbatto and has been updated by the author, who is solely responsible for any omissions or mistakes. For more about the scheme, see www.miomulino.it.
3 The 'third place' refers to Starbucks' focus on providing customers with a third option of where to feel comfortable beyond the home and the workplace.

References

Alba, D. (2015) 'Starbucks' grande plan: selling coffee via apps'. *Wired*, 3 November. Retrieved from www.wired.com/2015/11/no-one-is-killing-it-with-retail-store-apps-like-starbucks (accessed 25 February 2019).

Beans (2023) 'Starbucks loyalty program case study'. Retrieved from www.trybeans.com/blog/starbucks-loyalty-program-analysis (accessed 26 December 2023).

Bellavita,J. (2023) 'Nostalgia Anni 80: tornano le Sorpresine'. *io Donna – Corriere della Sera*, 4 September.

Borgers, T. (2022) 'Case study: Starbucks Odyssey'. Retrieved from https://medium.com/3mint/case-study-starbucks-odyssey-5be78d3214d6 (accessed 28 December 2023).

Bowman, J. (2016) '20 million reasons why Starbucks' Rewards program is so powerful'. *The Motley Fool*, 11 June. Retrieved from www.fool.com/investing/2016/06/11/20-million-reasons-why-starbucks-rewards-program-i.aspx (accessed 25 February 2019).

Champagne, C. and Iezzi, T. (2014) 'Dunkin' Donuts and Starbucks: a tale of two coffee marketing giants'. *Fast Company*, 21 August. Retrieved from www.fastcompany.com/3034572/dunkin-donuts-and-starbucks-a-tale-of-two-coffee-marketing-giants (accessed 24 February 2019).

ConnectPOS (2023) 'How Starbucks became #1 in customer loyalty with its rewards program'. Retrieved from www.connectpos.com/learn-from-starbucks-loyalty-program (accessed 28 December 2023).

De Maio, C. and Viola, F. (2008) *Italia 2: Viaggio nel paese che abbiamo inventato*. Rome: Minimum Fax.

Earnest Insights (2022) 'The future of Starbucks: new products and dayparts as breakfast traffic resumes in 2022'. Retrieved from www.earnestanalytics.com/the-future-of-starbucks-new-products-and-dayparts-as-breakfast-traffic-resumes-in-2022 (accessed 28 December 2023).

Ferro, S. (2016) 'Starbucks cards hold so much money the company could be a mid-size bank'. *Huffington Post*, 16 June. Retrieved from www.huffingtonpost.com/entry/starbucks-gift-cards-12-billion_us_5762fab0e4b0df4d586f975b (accessed 24 February 2019).

Garcia, T. (2016a) 'Starbucks loyalty program wins gold stars from most but not all analysts'. *Marketwatch*, 22 April. Retrieved from www.marketwatch.com/story/starbucks-loyalty-program-wins-gold-stars-from-most-but-not-all-analysts-2016-04-22 (accessed 24 February 2019).

Garcia, T. (2016b) 'Starbucks has more customer money on cards than many banks have in deposits'. *Marketwatch*, 9 June. Retrieved from www.marketwatch.com/story/starbucks-has-more-customer-money-on-cards-than-many-banks-have-in-deposits-2016-06-09 (accessed 24 February 2019).

Guenzi, A. (2015) 'Le origini americane delle operazioni a premio'. In C. Ziliani (ed.), *Promotion Revolution*, 251–279. Milan: EGEA.

Harris, R. (2015) 'Why Starbucks is winning at loyalty'. *Marketing Mag*, 28 July. Retrieved from http://marketingmag.ca/brands/why-starbucks-is-winning-at-loyalty-152974 (accessed 25 February 2019).

Kats, R. (2018) 'The mobile payments series: US'. eMarketer, 9 November. Retrieved from www.emarketer.com/content/the-mobile-payments-series-the-us (accessed 15 March 2019).

Kell, J. (2016) 'How a loyalty program change hurt the Starbucks brand'. *Fortune*, 7 March. Retrieved from http://fortune.com/2016/03/07/how-a-loyalty-program-change-hurt-the-starbucks-brand (accessed 15 March 2019).

Kilgore, T. (2016) 'Starbucks' new loyalty program greeted with a stock selloff'. *Marketwatch*, 12 April. Retrieved from www.marketwatch.com/story/starbucks-new-loyalty-program-greeted-with-a-stock-selloff-2016-04-12 (accessed 24 February 2019).

Kubinek, J. (2024) 'Web3 watch: Starbucks shutters its "Odyssey" NFT program'. Retrieved from https://blockworks.co/news/starbucks-terminates-nft-program (accessed 28 June 2024).

LoQuiz (2023) Starbucks: a successful gamification case study, 31 March 2023. Retrieved from https://loquiz.com/2023/03/31/starbucks-gamification (accessed 28 December 2023).

McEachern, A. (2017) 'Loyalty case study: Starbucks Rewards'. *Smile.io*, 24 July. Retrieved from https://blog.smile.io/loyalty-case-study-starbucks-rewards (accessed 24 February 2019).

Meola, A. (2016) 'Starbucks' loyalty program now holds more money than some banks'. *Business Insider*, 13 June. Retrieved from www.businessinsider.com/starbucks-loyalty-program-now-holds-more-money-than-some-banks-2016-6?6?IR=T (accessed 24 February 2019).

Miller, C. (2015) 'Longtime iTunes partner Starbucks goes big with Spotify'. *9to5mac.com*, 18 May. Retrieved from https://9to5mac.com/2015/05/18/spotify-starbucks-partnership (accessed 25 February 2019).

Mixson, E. (2021) 'Starbucks: a masterclass in digital transformation, intelligent automation network'. Retrieved from www.intelligentautomation.network/transformation/articles/starbucks-digital-transformation (accessed 3 January 2024).

Mizerak, J. (2022) 'Starbucks Rewards Program & NFT Experiences review – breaking new grounds with prizes, gamification and Web3'. Retrieved from https://antavo.com/blog/starbucks-rewards-program (accessed 28 December 2023).

MJV (2023) 'Starbucks breakage: discover how unused gift cards are pushing profit forward'. Retrieved from www.mjwinnovation.com/blog/starbucks-breakage-discover-how-unused-gift-cards-are-pushing-profit-forward (accessed 28 June 2024).

Mogg, T. (2019) 'Starbucks coffee delivery lands in 6 more cities via Uber Eats'. *Digital Trends*, 22 January. Retrieved from www.digitaltrends.com/home/starbucks-expands-coffee-delivery-to-6-more-cites-via-uber-eats (accessed 25 February 2019).

Morgan, J.P. (2018) 'Starbucks and Chase launch Starbucks Rewards Visa card'. Chase Media Center (press release), 1 February. Retrieved from https://media.chase.com/news/chase-launches-starbucks-rewards-card (accessed 25 February 2019).

Morosini, I. (1994) 'Virtù dell'oggetto promozionale'. In A. Ivardi Ganapini and G. Gonizzi (eds), *Barilla: Cento anni di pubblicità e comunicazione*, 302–315. Milan: Silvana.

Nitin (2017) 'The science behind Starbucks' massively successful customer loyalty program'.Retrievedfromhttps://zetaglobal.com/blog-posts/starbucks-reward-customer-loyalty-program-study (accessed 24 February 2019).

Oragui, D. (2018) 'The success of Starbucks app: a case study'. *The Manifest*, 12 June. Retrieved from https://medium.com/@the_manifest/the-success-of-starbucks-app-a-case-study-f0af6709004d (accessed 25 February 2019).

Palnitkar, S. (2017) 'Loyalty rewards case study: new Starbucks Rewards program'. Zinrelo, 12 April. Retrieved from https://zinrelo.com/loyalty-rewards-case-study-new-starbucks-rewards-program.html (accessed 24 February 2019).

Panko, R. (2018) 'How customers use food delivery and restaurant loyalty apps'. *The Manifest*, 15 May. Retrieved from https://themanifest.com/app-development/how-customers-use-food-delivery-and-restaurant-loyalty-apps (accessed 24 February 2019).

Patton, L. (2022) 'Starbucks' $181 million in unused gift cards spurs labor group complaint'.Retrievedfromwww.bloomberg.com/news/articles/2022-11-16/starbucks-181m-in-unused-gift-cards-sparks-complaint-to-sec-sbux?sref=zNmRQ0gk (accessed 3 January 2024).

Pymnts (2022) 'How many lattes does a Delta ticket to London cost?'. Retrieved from www.pymnts.com/news/loyalty-and-rewards-news/2022/how-many-lattes-does-a-delta-ticket-to-london-cost (accessed 18 January 2024).

Pymnts (2023) 'Starbucks taps additional rewards partnerships to widen loyalty audience'. Retrieved from www.pymnts.com/news/loyalty-and-rewards-news/2023/starbucks-taps-additional-rewards-partnerships-widen-loyalty-audience (accessed 28 December 2023).

Rahman, W (2020) 'Starbucks isn't a coffee business – it's a data tech company'. Retrieved from https://marker.medium.com/starbucks-isnt-a-coffee-company-its-a-data-technology-business-ddd9b397d83e (accessed 28 December 2023).

Samuely, A. (2016) 'Starbucks whips up mobile ordering with delivery options'. Retrieved from www.retaildive.com/ex/mobilecommercedaily/starbucks-whips-up-mobile-ordering-with-future-delivery-options (accessed 24 February 2019).

Shah, K. (2016) 'Loyalty lessons from Starbucks' *New York Times* Rewards'. Retrieved from www.clutch.com/blog/loyalty/loyalty-lessons-from-starbucks-new-york-times-rewards (accessed 25 February 2019).

Snyder, B. (2016) 'Customers are furious with Starbucks' new rewards program'. Retrieved from http://fortune.com/2016/02/23/starbucks-rewards-program-changes (accessed 15 March 2019).

Starbucks (2018) 'Starbucks at the J.P. Morgan gaming lodging restaurant and leisure management access forum'. Retrieved from https://investor.starbucks.com/events-and-presentations/current-and-past-events/event-details/2018/Starbucks-at-the-JP-Morgan-Gaming-Lodging-Restaurant-and-Leisure-Management-Access-Forum/default.aspx (accessed 24 February 2019).

Starbucks (2019) 'Starbucks reports Q1 fiscal 2019 results'. Press release, 24 January. Retrieved from https://investor.starbucks.com/press-releases/financial-releases/

press-release-details/2019/Starbucks-Reports-Q1-Fiscal-2019-Results/default. aspx (accessed 24 February 2019).

Starbucks (2023) 'Company timeline'. Retrieved from https://stories.starbucks.com/ press/2019/company-timeline (accessed 26 December 2023).

Wathen, J. (2017) 'These 3 companies earned $99 million from unused gift cards last year'. *The Motley Fool*, 15 July. Retrieved from www.fool.com/investing/2017/07/15/ these-3-companies-earned-99-million-from-unused-gi.aspx (accessed 25 February 2019).

Ziliani, C. (2015) *Promotion Revolution: Nuove strategie e nuovi protagonisti della promozione 2.0.* Milan: EGEA.

10

LOYALTY CASE STUDIES FROM AROUND THE WORLD

Cristina Ziliani

When we began discussing a new edition of this book, we wanted to make it relatable and appealing for loyalty marketers in every continent. To do this, it was necessary to reach out and find best in class loyalty stories around the world. Luckily, over the years, our activity with the Loyalty Observatory at the University of Parma has put us in contact with many experts and practitioners worldwide, and we decided to ask for their help. The seven case studies that are presented in this chapter, recounted in their own words by the managers who designed and/or govern them, have been collected from December 2023 to March 2024.

The cases are: Club Matas, Dialog Star Points, Dotz, Picard et Nous, VeryMe Rewards by Vodafone, XPLR Pass and yuu Rewards Club. They come from Brazil, France, Denmark, Singapore, Sri Lanka, United Kingdom and United States. They span from telecommunications to health and beauty retail, apparel and footwear, food, and three are coalition programs.

One program was founded in 2000, others are from 2008–2009, others are as recent as 2022. Member count goes from 1.5 million in Singapore to 2 million in Denmark, 4 million in UK, 10 million in Sri Lanka, 20 million in the US and as much as 50 million in Brazil. They are focused on one country market only, with the exceptions of the French program, Picard et Nous, covering the neghbouring Belgium and Luxembourg too, and the global XPLR Pass program, spanning 12 countries.

The following pages present each case, in alphabetical order, following a blueprint that we proposed to each manager to write the case. First, the main goal of the program is presented, its evolution, and the existence of variations across markets. Then what is special, and most successful, about the program

DOI: 10.4324/9781003400783-10

is highlighted. The top three KPI monitored by the company to measure the program success are discussed. Finally, as one of the benefits of loyalty programs is the insight derived from the analysis of their customer base, one final question is concerned with sharing something that the company did not know and discovered about the customer base thanks to the analysis of the program data.

One last word: if while reading the cases you feel you'd like to see your program featured too, please reach out. We hope to publish online updates to the book in the coming years, and would love to provide a better coverage of the flavours of loyalty worldwide.

Club Matas

Name of program: Club Matas
Year of launch: 2010
Number of members at the present time: 2 million
Country of origin: Denmark
Countries involved to date: Denmark
Parent company(ies): Matas Operations A/S
Industry(ies): Matas is in the retail industry, specifically focusing on health, beauty, and wellness products
Case author: Peter Anders Franch
Program web page: www.matas.dk/club-matas/om-club-matas

The main goal of Club Matas was to create a loyalty program that rewards regular customers and encourages repeat purchases. Over the years, the program has evolved to offer more personalized experiences and benefits, such as tailored product recommendations and exclusive discounts, to better meet the diverse needs and preferences of its members. More than 1.6 million members are active members, meaning that they have had a purchase either online or offline within the last 12 months.

The Club is seen as profit centre. Club Matas members contributed to 80% of the revenue from Matas stores and matas.dk in 2022/2023.

Club Matas also heightens the CLV of Club Matas members and it is a catalyst for our retail media growth. Since 2018 we've realized a growth in our retail media. We cover a wide of services through our Matas Media where brands and vendors can access some of the most efficient, innovative and creative media solutions based upon first party data and analysis: Our Matas Insights, where brands will find the answer to everything, that concerns the vendors' brands and customers in Matas. Lastly, we have our Matas Creative where we deliver the strongest creative team in the business, who can produce high quality, efficient content for their campaigns in Matas. The uniqueness Matas possesses as an insights partner is our access to more than 2 million members through our Club Matas loyalty club. We have our transactional data and our direct communication access, which enables us to exclude any costly third-party companies so that we can offer the strongest possible insights at the best possible prices.

Club Matas is unique in its personalized approach to customer rewards. The program offers tailored product recommendations and exclusive discounts based on individual customer preferences and purchase history. Additionally, it provides members with access to special events and health and beauty advice.

Specifically, Matas get two very important things from the customer club. Firstly, Club Matas is a crucial, direct communication channel to the 2 million members. Secondly, through the customer club, Matas gains access to a myriad of data and thus also knowledge about customers' consumption, preferences, behaviour and the like.

And to provide even more, we have Club Matas PLUS. Club Matas PLUS is the natural extension to Club Matas. For a membership fee (green fee), members gain access to even more benefits. PLUS was introduced to create higher loyalty among our customers, increase share of wallet and frequency. And to withstand competition. The benefits specifically target our strategically prioritized top 25% members. Those who just want more of Matas. Insights show that 500,000 members would specifically save money by joining Club Matas PLUS. The strategy is to bring this insight to customers across all channels. For example, the managers at Point of Sale can see which members Club Matas PLUS is most relevant for, as well as how much they are expected to be able to save with a membership. In this way, the relevance is increased and the dialogue about the concept is qualified.

Our app is award winning. We won GOLD at E-Handelsprisen 2023 with the following statement:

Matas, Matas, Matas. You've done it again. Created a digital success that strengthens sales in physical stores and supports the flow of member benefits. The app is fully integrated into their universe, has been downloaded more than 700,000 times, and has a score of 4.6 in the App Store. It's clear that Matas knows their business, as all new initiatives in the app seem well-considered. A strong focus on personalization and service ensures loyalty and sales. Well done!

We see the app as where it all falls into place and where membership in Club Matas becomes the focal point of the buying journey – both when seeking inspiration and shopping from the comfort of your sofa, or when visiting a Matas store. Quick overview of all member benefits – check how many kr. 'you' have earned that you can use on your purchase – or perhaps 'you' have a bonus gift that can be redeemed. Quick access to and purchase of the entire Matas range – we know 'you' and provide 'you' with a personal shopping experience and with a few clicks, an order is on its way to 'you'. Your companion when 'you' visit a Matas store with what we call IN STORE.

Building upon our app is our e-mail setup. Our e-mail frequency is relatively high (campaign and CRM, and thus excluding receipts and customer service), which sets a high demand for sophisticated segmentation and suppression as well as a need for being relevant, and not overcommunicating.

It also sets the bar quite high from a content perspective as the amount of produced e-mail is high. Thus, consequently, the untapped potential lies in empowering the content team to revolutionize e-mail marketing by saving time spent on mundane tasks, and effectively reach the intended audience. The solution is a reimagination and redesign of the existing work process of e-mail marketing content creation.

The solution, AI Content Automation, aims to significantly reduce time-to-market of e-mails and increase operational efficiency by leveraging available AI in conjunction with Matas's rich first party data. Specifically, the solution will automate mundane and repetitive tasks, liberating the content team to bring additional value to e-mail marketing efforts.

Concretely, Matas will save time that can be used on extra-value adding tasks and money spent on external graphic designers and copy writers.

Furthermore, this will lead to a better customer experience and improved sales.

The AI-driven E-mail Content Tool offers numerous advantages: no direct customer data involvement, inclusion of human validation, well-defined boundaries, high data quality, and scalability opportunities. Most important, it frees up time for the team to work on our Engagement Model in which we communicate relevant content to our users – through e-mail, app, push and web – increase the engagement and subsequent CLV for our members.

The purpose is to increase the individual customer's engagement with Matas regardless of the current level, as increased engagement with Matas in the long term will increase the predicted Customer Lifetime Value (CLV). Engagement is increased through prioritizing the communication that will most increase the customer's engagement – as well as provide the member with content that is most fitting for their level of engagement with Matas – the next time we interact with them.

The insight

Regardless of everything else, the single most important insights are our omni-customers. Turning our members into omni customers enlightened us and our

TABLE 10.1 Club Matas's KPIs

KPIs	Current value	Improvement over time
NPS (net promoter score)	2024 Q1: 39	2021 Q4: 22.3
Club Matas PLUS members	February 2024: 96,125	February 2023: 68,586
Omni members	1 January 2024: 750,244	1 January 2021: 539,297

work around creating omni-experiences and launching Club Matas PLUS. They are more engaged, have higher CLV and is constantly prompting us to create a better and more unified customer experience across channels, both offline and online compared to being solely on- or offline customers.

Dialog Star Points

Name of program: Dialog Star Points
Year of launch: 2008
Number of members at the present time: 10 million
Country of origin: Sri Lanka
Countries involved to date: Sri Lanka
Parent company: Dialog Axiata PLC
Industry: Telecommunications
Case author: Isuru Madhushanka
Program web page: https://dlg.dialog.lk/starpoints

Dialog Star Points is the largest and the most rewarding transaction-based loyalty program in Sri Lanka. The purpose of Dialog Star Points is to provide rewards that are relevant and valued by all retail customer segments. Over the years, Dialog Star Points program has grown to become the #1 loyalty program of the country with the largest rewards members base, widest partner merchant network, charity organizations and nation-wide engagement. It is seen by management as a value creation centre. Below are the points that make it special:

- Most comprehensive: Pay, Top-Up, Transfer, Donate, Exchange/Convert, Gift, and redeem for offers (internal / external).
- 1000+ widest partner merchant network – supermarkets, restaurants, lifestyle, education, travel & leisure, gift vouchers, e-commerce (WOW Mall), Banks (HSBC, Amex), Airlines (Flysmiles).
- Emotional Connect to society – Star Points empowers customers to give back to the society through our Donation partners like UNICEF, Little Hearts, HelpAge, SOS etc.

- Loyalty program that has an element of innovation – Star Points services are enabled in Alexa Voice assistance and Dialog FutureVerse (Dialog's metaverse with Star Points as one of the engagement rewards activities).
- Star Points is linked to VOC and NPS study to identify customer pulse and drive continuous improvements that are relevant to customer needs.
- Star Points is also applicable for non-Dialog customers who transact at partner merchant outlets making it a truly universal loyalty program.
- The only points-based rewards program that is linked to employee engagement in addition to customer engagement – Star Points is a part of Dialog internal employee engagement activities where employees are rewarded with Star Points for achievement milestones i.e. sports events, quiz competition and entertainment events.

We have ensured that both non-smartphone and smartphone users have access to the loyalty program. Non-smartphone users can get the information from the USSD menu. We have given our customers the option of accessing our loyalty program details by dialing the short code #141# from their mobile phones. They can navigate through the menu to get information on their points balance, offers, points transfers etc. So, even the phone users who don't have the access to our app can engage with the program through this method. Smartphone users can log into the Self-care App to access the loyalty platform services.

The insight

We have identified that our customers mostly value the social impact of our loyalty program. Going beyond tangible rewards and creating emotional connect with society by allowing members to contribute to a much larger cause through donations has been one of the most significant highlights of Dialog Star Points loyalty program.

Regarding TOMA (top of mind awareness), we measure the brand recall of Star Points loyalty program through a survey conducted among our customers as its crucial for the business as it can significantly influence consumer behavior, brand loyalty, and market share.

TABLE 10.2 Dialog Star Points's KPIs

KPIs	Current value	Improvement over time
Customer engagement		4 p.p. YoY growth
TOMA (top of mind awareness)		From #3 in 2022 to #1 in 2023
NPS (net promoter score)		Stagnant over the last 2 years

Dotz

Name of program: Dotz
Year of launch: 2000
Number of members at the present time: more than 50 million
Country of origin: Brazil
Countries involved to date: 1
Industry(ies): Coalition Program
Case authors: Leandro Torres and Jonathas Mendes
Program web page: www.dotz.com.br

Dotz is a coalition program in Brazil with more than 20 year leading the loyalty business across the country with diverse retail and bank clients under one brand. The key goal of the program is to provide to sponsors in a coalition and increase their sales and margin, not only for retail but also for banks, telecom, e-commerce.

Over the past years the goal remains the same, what has changed is the way we engage the customer in the purchase journey. We have developed a unique ecosystem that integrates the loyalty business with the customer at Retail POS to a phygital journey from the store to Dotz super app, that enhances customer power of purchase with payments by providing to them credit (BNPL feature) at the cashier. Recently, a sprinted transformation strategy changed the business from a customer transaction process based on point rewards to a complete B2B2C platform based on customer journey by using points, promotions, loyalty, payment and data that enrich the relationship. Dotz POS activation of the customer connected with Dotz Digital Wallet in the company Super APP has proved a successful touchpoint to engage the customer due to the fact that it brings the physical experience to a digital environment in a frictionless journey.

The coalition is a profit centre since it delivers to the sponsors an incremental margin not only because of the customer behavior change but also of the payment method that the customer adopts. As a coalition program we don't have any variations, what changes is the benefits offered to the customers according to the sponsor (mechanics). Dotz is the universal currency used by all of them to approach the customer. It has been successful ever since:

- The ARPU (average revenue per user) can leverage from R$ 20 (Brazilian Reais) to R$ 800 (US$ 4 to US$ 160).
- The wallet app has already reached 3.8 million users (from 1.9 million YoY).
- Cash redemption increased from 28% to 34% YoY – if analysed over 5 years, this redemption did not exist.
- The unique data that Dotz possesses from its users, from demographic and social to credit card and transactional (SKU granularity), has allowed a

credit approval of R$ 210 million in Q3 2023 (43% YoY) and credit risk (Kolmogorov-Smirnov – KS) improvement from 20% to 60% above the market average. It also contributes to the implementation of credit products in retail (BNPL), enhancing both loyalty in retail partners and user's buying power within these partners. All of this is a result of the fact that we know customer behavior in many aspects.

Dotz is a coaltion program with more than 200 employees all involved in the loyalty strategy. On the sponsor's side, the program usually is anchored under Marketing team and CEO/Managing director due to its importance to the company strategy.

The insight

In retail, users who earn points in 2 or more different partners can boost revenue by 20% for both Dotz and partners. On average, it takes 6 months for a user to do its first coalition.

Users with 1 or more transactions within 7 days after registering can enhance app activity, because they can login in a frequency 2x higher and its MAUT is 6 times higher compared to other users. The redemption moment in the journey that can boost engagement and activation best occurs after 2 months. Redemption of points to cash becomes and important trigger for engagement to the customers experience redemption and then turns to create other goals in the program.

TABLE 10.3 Dotz's KPIs

KPIs	Current value	Improvement over time
ARPU	R$ 38,91 (last 12 months)	11% YoY / NA 5y
POS redemption*	1.6 million (last 12 months)	33% 5y
Credit origination**	306 million (last 12 months)	49% YoY / NA 5y
Points to cash***	1.5 million (last 12 months)	9% YoY / NA 5y

* POS redemption: number of transactions in the store when either a reward or a voucher were redeemed.

** Credit origination: total amount of loaned money, in millions of Brazilian Real (R$). Since Dotz also became a TechFin in our ecosystem, they started to give loans to consumers in the coalition program to help them in their daily purchases.

*** Points to cash: number of transactions when Dotz points are converted into money. This transaction is a feature of the Dotz App. It is close to a cashback, but we operate as a redemption. Our customers can use their Dotz Points and redeem to cash/money and use it in their wallet (Dotz Digital Account) to pay bills, to transfer to someone, to make purchases in stores that are not in the coalition, for example.

Picard et Nous

Name of program: Picard & Nous
Year of launch: 2022
Number of members at the present time: 7 million
Country of origin: France
Countries involved to date: Belgium, France, Luxemburg
Parent company(ies): Picard
Industry: Food retail
Case study author: David Gosse
Program web page: www.picard.fr/programme-de-fidelite.html

Picard & Nous's loyalty program aims to be different from traditional programs. Picard did not just want to offer monetary rewards and be innovative (to match the brand's image of constant innovation in the products offered to its customers). Thanks to its loyalty program, the company wants to connect with their customers and not only reward deal prone customers.

In order to build this new program, the company sent out a survey to around 400,000 customers, realized benchmarks, and organized several workgroups with all professions (product marketing, social networks, stores).

The program was built around 4 pillars:

- A loyalty program that must be easy to understand for customers
- A loyalty program that must be easy to explain to frontline employees (staff must make it easy for customers to understand why they need to subscribe and use their card every time they visit the store)
- A loyalty program that must reward customers not only for their purchases, but also for their commitment (for example, downloading the app, giving their phone number)
- A loyalty program that must be customized (customers can choose how they desire to use their loyalty points)

In the loyalty program, there is still a base of monetary rewards because customers expect them (loyalty program members can benefit from discounts on around 70 products per month and benefit from 10% off snacks if they shop at lunchtime) but the program is enriched by other forms of reward such as free products, a cooking class with Atelier des Chefs, a box of wines from Le Petit Ballon, or a personalized appointment with a dietician.

2.7 million gifts were distributed in 2023. The number of partners is deliberately limited so as not to complicate the program for customers, and to create lasting relationships with partners who share similar values to those of the brand.

What is also new is that the program now also rewards other forms of commitment. The idea is to enable customers to quickly obtain their first gift (from 100 points) to encourage them to continue using it. On average, they

TABLE 10.4 Picard & Nous's KPIs

KPIs	Current value	Improvement over time
Share of members using immediate discounts and share of members redeeming points		
Purchase frequency	10–20%	
Share of sales generated by customers who have the loyalty card	87% (+3 points versus 2022)	

get their first gift after two visits. Finally, the loyalty program allows customers to donate their loyalty points to the Food Bank (300,000 products were donated by customers in 2023).

The program is identical in all countries. Only certain rewards vary, such as the name of the partner dieticians.

In 2024, the program should continue to evolve, rewarding other forms of engagement as well as integrating a gamification dimension (awarding points to customers who complete certain challenges).

The most successful touchpoint is the store, and a close relationship with sales staff. The program is digital (downloadable app or account). Sales staff play a key role in encouraging customers not only to subscribe to the program, but also to use it at every checkout.

The top management considers the loyalty program more of a profit centre even if it costs money for the company. Thanks to this new loyalty program, Picard is moving from mass promotion to personalized promotion and the ROI of the loyalty program is higher.

The insight

Picard has noticed a discrepancy between the customers' expectations, as they declared they wanted more relational benefits, and their actual behavior, which is more focused on obtaining free products.

VeryMe Rewards by Vodafone

Name of program: VeryMe Rewards by Vodafone
Year of launch: 2018
Number of members at the present time: 4.1 million
Country of origin: United Kingdom
Countries involved to date: VeryMe is UK only, but the program has set the playbook for loyalty across Vodafone
Parent company: Vodafone

Industry: Telecommunications
Case study author: Michelle Williams
Program web page: www.vodafone.co.uk/my-vodafone-account/vodafone-apps/vodafone-veryme-rewards

VeryMe began as an initiative with three key objectives – the primary to drive customer satisfaction/advocacy and ultimately NPS. Secondary objectives were to protect against GDPR regulations coming in, enabling VF to collect permissions for a fair 'value exchange' with the consumer, and finally to reduce churn from the VF base.

Across multiple VF Group Operating Companies there are variations of VeryMe, called 'Happy'. VeryMe is the most advanced loyalty program across the Vodafone Group and continually sets the trends for other markets to follow in launching innovative features.

The program is unique as it is the only one that uses preferencing, gamified engagement, data, insight and machine learning to understand and give members rewards they really love. Relevance and personalization are key. The program has evolved every year since launch, based on what we learn.

Proposition:

- VeryMe promises its members that the program is built around what they love.
- It gives them rewards that they love, based on their interests and preferences. It learns over time, getting better and even more personal.

Mechanic:

- Digital first, friction free, mobile only app-based mechanic, sitting in the MyVodafone app for brand and data integration and ease of use.
- Since launch there have been numerous new features added every year to optimize member experience; improved preferencing, UX optimization, new game mechanics (e.g. instant win), new Feel Good Fridays promotion where we offer thousands of treats on Fridays, the capability for members to gift their rewards to others (even those not on Vodafone) and charitable donation rewards to name a few.

Rewards:

- Members are offered a curated range of rewards based on what they love – over 30 different rewards are available each month, prioritized and personalized to each member.

- Rewards are personally, seasonally and topically relevant to members and evolved over time. For example, we offer rewards that appeal to the majority, such as a £1 coffee at Costa (48% of VeryMe members are coffee lovers), cinema tickets for £7 from Vue (48% enjoy going to the cinema) and take-away discounts from JustEat (46% regularly get takeaways).
- We also target segments. For example, during the Lions tour we offered rugby fans exclusive discounts on official British & Irish Lions shirts and merchandise (24% are rugby fans) and for the 54% of members who own pets, we offered free pet stockings at Christmas.

The program is fuelled by 6 rich and robust insight and data sources:

1 Weekly YouGov data on VeryMe members (over 190,000 datapoints covering demographics, attitudes, behaviours, interests, media and brands shopped and liked).
2 Robust reward analytics using our unique 'Reward DNA' methodology.
3 Preferencing data 'learned' through member behaviour and questions.
4 Research including tracking, and regular ethnographic, qualitative and quantitative projects.
5 Gamification techniques such as competitions and playable games.
6 Market and trend reviews exploring non telco sectors and markets outside the UK.

Communications:

- A 360 omnichannel approach. The toolkit includes social (Twitter, Instagram, Facebook, Snapchat), TV, email, retail, digital OOH including cinema, radio, display, PR, SMS, MMS and push.

I would say our mechanic is our most successful touchpoint – the primary interaction with our customer is via the MyVodafone App: digital first, friction free, mobile only app-based mechanic, sitting in the MyVodafone app for brand and data integration and ease of use.

Since launch there have been numerous new features added every year to optimize member experience, as menioned above. In addition to this, we also have an incredible supporting CRM and lifecycle journey for customers across the Vodafone base, tailored to the individual and their unique level of participation in the program.

In the first three years the program was a cost centre but in the last two years this has changed to a profit centre – we are on the journey to monetize the program and drive inbound revenue via cross-sell, upsell, reduction of churn and inclusion of affiliate deals within our catalogue of offers.

TABLE 10.5 VeryMe by Vodafone's KPIs

KPIs	Current value	Improvement over time
NPS	+4pts versus control group	
Churn Reduction	3% versus control group	
Onboarded base	>4 million end of 2023	
Permissions (GDPR)	>80% of registered members	

The insight

One of the most surprising learnings from the program to date is the overwhelming interest from customers in participating in competitions. Throughout all of our research it has told us customers visit loyalty programs to get 'freebies' or benefits, however there was little interest in competitions. Despite this insight we chose to include competitions as a way to extend our offers for 'money can't buy experiences' such as tickets to Wimbledon or Glastonbury Festival and these competitions drive significant uplift is new customers joining the program and customers revisiting following lapsed behaviour (having not visited the program in more than 30 days).

XPLR Pass

Name of program: XPLR Pass
Year of launch: 2009
Number of members at the present time: 20 million
Country of origin: United States
Countries involved to date: US, Canada, UK, Germany, France, Ireland, Italy, Netherlands, Spain, Mainland China, Hong Kong, Taiwan
Parent company: VF Corporation
Industries: Apparel, footwear, accessories, retail, equipment
Case study author: Erica Hood
Program web page: www.thenorthface.com/en-us/xplrpass

The purpose of XPLR Pass is to add value to a customer's experience with The North Face so that they choose to come back and purchase again. Due to the nature of the products sold by the brand, our shopper's purchase frequency is consequentially lower and results in a longer time lapse between purchases.

Our loyalty program is built to engage members between purchases and keep The North Face top of mind.

As the program has evolved there has been a shift to focus on experiential benefits in addition to traditional transactional benefits. Experiential benefits aim to build community across our membership and enable access to the outdoors.

TABLE 10.6 XPLR Pass's KPIs

KPIs	Current value	Improvement over time
Membership growth		
CLV – increase in customer lifetime value		
AOV – increase in average order value		
Increase in purchase frequency		
% of DTC (direct to consumer) revenue		

Our program is our channel for connecting to passionate explorers and fans of the brand. We identify our most engaged passionate explorers through surveys, quizzes, and research studies and solicit their participation in product testing, exclusive outdoor experiences with our athletes, and VIP events that give them access to the best of the brand.

Email is our most successful touchpoint for connecting to XPLR Pass members and our member dashboard is the central hub of all our program activities. Between these two touchpoints we focus on delivering inspiration, exclusive offers, relevant product stories, and added value to the member.

The insight

Loyalty program data has given us more insight into the purchase behavior of our most valuable customers. We have been able to identify what product tends to attract new members to the brand for their first purchase and what product categories or brand offers work best to engage and retain those members.

yuu Rewards Club Singapore

Name of program: yuu Rewards Club Singapore
Year of launch: 2022
Number of members at the present time: 1.5 million
Country of origin: Singapore
Countries involved to date: Singapore
Parent company: Minden Singapore Pte Ltd
Industry: Coalition Program
Case study author: Jacky Mak
Program web page: https://yuu.sg/

With an understanding that consumers expect to be seen as individuals with unique preferences and tastes, we utilize cutting-edge machine learning and artificial intelligence to deliver delightful interactions that enrich relationships between brands and their customers. Our goal is simple yet powerful – to enhance engagement, strengthen loyalty, and drive growth.

TABLE 10.7 yuu Rewards Club Singapore's KPIs

KPIs	Current value	Improvement over time
Brand awareness	86%	From 0% to 86% in 1 year; now yuu is the top brand in Singapore loyalty programs based on 3rd party survey
Membership	1.5 million	From 0 to 1.5 million members in ~1 year; highest membership participation in Singapore loyalty program based on 3rd party survey
Sales uplift	n.a.	Uplift of 11–16%, varies by participating brands, based on incremental sales generated based on control group over 9 months study window

We are probably the only true loyalty coalition program in Singapore that cut across all major verticals with significant market share, thus we are able to achieve 1 million members within 100 days after launch. To date, we have 1.5 million members as of end 2023. Besides, we synergize the power of artificial intelligence and loyalty coalition, creating unparalleled value for our partners and consumers. From the consumer perspective, the program is quite similar across markets except the brands in the programs are different. The yuu Rewards Club Singapore is also run independently from the yuu Rewards Club Hong Kong.

Indeed, there is no single channel that stand out, as the different touch-point serves different marketing objectives. However, we found that POSM is one of the most important channels to create awareness of the program when we launch.

The insight

We discovered that there is huge interest to earn same yuu points across brands. 75% earn at cross-partner. Members who have a co-branded credit/debit card are much more engaged with the program.

Acknowledgements

We are deeply grateful to Charlie Hills, Rasmus Houlind, Michael Flacandji, Sarah Richardson, Phil Shelper, Paula Thomas, Leandro Torres and Pooja Venugopal for creating the connections with the case studies authors, and to the authors Peter Anders Franch, David Gosse, Erica Hood, Isuru Madhushanka, Jacky Mak, Jonathas Mendes, Leandro Torres and Michelle Williams for the time and effort they put in writing their own cases along our guidelines and for giving Routledge and the book's authors permission to publish their content.

11

FUTURE CHALLENGES

Marco Ieva

Customer journeys involving old and new touchpoints

The rise of new ICTs such as artificial intelligence (AI) has resulted in customer journeys involving traditional and new touchpoints (Chapter 2). Customer journeys occur in environments where new touchpoints such as ChatGPT, chatbots, virtual and augmented reality share consumer exposure with traditional touchpoints such as email marketing, store flyers and offline word-of-mouth. This poses multiple challenges in terms of data collection and personalization of the customer journeys, harmonization and customer experience.

First, this coexistence of traditional versus new touchpoints leads companies to collect data only on portions of the customer journeys, with the risk of overestimating and posing higher attention on those areas of the journeys that are better measurable thanks to new touchpoints than others.

Second, the personalization of customer journeys is usually possible only for certain touchpoints and for certain customers, leading to dissonance throughout the journey.

Third, we could expect a contrast to emerge between suggestions or solutions provided by human versus AI touchpoints. If we hypothesize that AI will be more and more integrated to assist customers, for example in choosing the perfect ingredients for a recipe, or the perfect item for an outfit, or the best wine for a meal, contrasts between what AI says and what 'human' touchpoints suggest in the store are likely to emerge. The above frictions between AI and humans could be extended to other areas: with the growth of co-pilots, namely suggestions coming from AI on which is the most relevant information or priority to consider, we could expect those contrasts to emerge between a

DOI: 10.4324/9781003400783-11

manager and a co-pilot when it is the time to make a decision on marketing campaigns based on interpreting data. Is AI always right? Should a company trust more AI or 'human' managers? And will the customer trust AI more than humans or vice versa? Moreover, if we focus on customer experiences of customers with physical or mental disabilities, how is AI going to handle interactions? To what extent the AI is going to show empathy?

Fourth, another challenge for managers is the need to re-design traditional touchpoints to deliver an experience that is consistent with the newly added touchpoints. Adding touchpoints to increase engagement with customers should be followed by a re-design of existing touchpoints to make sure to deliver a satisfying customer experience to customers regardless of the touchpoint they interact with.

Measuring and managing the customer experience

In Chapters 1 and 5 of this book we posed that loyalty management has morphed into customer experience management (CEM). Hence, academics and practitioners need to devise and test tools to measure customer experience across a variety of situations: in the store, online and across channels. Given the complexity of customer experience, measuring it is still an issue. We know that the customer experience is subjective and can change over time. Survey based metrics can be of help but they have several issues: short self-reported measures (e.g. NPS) could be collected more easily, but too often they do not provide a reliable and extensive picture, or they are biased by incentives or by how surveys are administered; long self-reported measures, such as those provided by employing multiple-question academic scales, can be very reliable and valid, but they appear to be redundant in the eyes of respondents and it is not rare to find respondents answering quickly without paying attention to questions. Customer experience measures should then be complemented with customer engagement measures that assess engagement behaviours and that could be more reliable as they refer to actual behaviours. In this respect, computing scores such as number of touchpoints used in a given period, number of interactions, number of days since last visit to the website/app, number of website/app visits, email marketing reading behaviour, number of points accrued in a loyalty program, number and type of rewards collected in a loyalty program, could help companies to have a better picture of the overall experience customers are having. The role of measures related to non-purchase behaviours is growing since they shed light on those portions of the customer journey, pre-purchase and post-purchase stage, that have received less attention (especially the post-purchase stage). In this respect, Chapter 6 on engagement and gamification provides guidance and evidence on the increasing importance of involving customers into engagement logics.

Of course, we are well aware of neuroscientific measures that could also complement traditional measures to give a better picture of customer experience. However, neuroscientific measures are complex to capture, analyse and interpret and their external validity is limited, since it is very difficult to implement them in standard shopping contexts. Finally, as far as measures are concerned, we also expect that AI could play a significant role in helping managers to identify relevant KPIs to consider depending on the outcome and goal of interest. In the past certain measures have received high attention from practitioners and academics even though they were not suitable for the objectives they were related to. For instance, number of followers and likes on social media have been considered important for years; nowadays they are relevant only with reference to awareness and their role has been revised also in light of the many fake users that are unfortunately a widespread malpractice on social media.

New data and technologies

When we think about new types of data we think about biometric and spatial data stemming from metaverse devices, or about eye tracking data, or voice data. While the new types of data could be a valuable addition to have a complete picture of customer behaviour, companies are still facing the challenge of integrating 'old' type of data, such as those in the customer database, email marketing database, loyalty program database, website database to achieve a 360 degrees customer view. When thinking about the availability of data, there are several elements to consider: data ownership, data quality and biases. And all three pose challenges to practices in loyalty, CRM and customer experience management.

Data ownership is a key element to consider. Who owns the data? Who is responsible for managing the data collection? Who can have access to the data? In this respect, it is very important to design data flows that allow key managers and analysts to have a direct access to customer data to be able to use the information to gain insights leading to appropriate marketing actions. Nowadays customer data platforms allow this type of access and flexibility, but many companies are struggling to achieve a great level of satisfaction with these platforms. More importantly, data ownership is key to develop important assets for marketing strategies. Companies are developing their own 'walled gardens', namely ecosystems where customers can register to receive offers or news/updates and companies can collect and own data on their customers, building an audience of users and customers that can be leveraged for further actions and can be continuously engaged. Companies are focused not only on attracting new customers and retaining existing customers, but also on acquiring and managing customer data to develop better and more accurate measurement of customer behaviours. The second issue about data companies are facing is related to data quality. Customer data platforms require data sources to be cleaned and complete. 'Garbage in, garbage out' is the well-known expression summarizing the risk if the above is not taken care of. Well-designed tools cannot compensate for poor data. Sometimes data cleaning is not performed properly, with outliers that can significantly influence all the indicators that are displayed on customer data platform dashboards. Moreover, data quality plays a key role: companies are supposed, according to the European GDPR (General Data Protection Regulation), to collect a specific consent not only for marketing activities but also for profiling customers at the individual level. If this consent is not present this represents an issue for companies in using the collected data. It is not rare to find situations where even less than half of customers enrolled in the loyalty program have granted this consent to the program owner. This means having visibility only on a portion of the customer base. Moreover, digitalization has significantly improved data quality when data collection takes place through online forms, but critical situations still exist in B2C and B2B settings where data collection is performed by means of traditional paper forms, thus hampering data quality. Finally, biases are very important to consider when analysing data. The data that is given spontaneously by customers suffer from self-selection bias. Every day, customers enrol in loyalty programs, complete a survey, download a mobile app, register to a website or subscribe to a newsletter: all these actions require a certain and variable degree of effort and involvement. This means that the collected data is not representative of the 'average' customer base. On the contrary, those sharing their data are usually driven by certain motivations or attitudes to provide their personal information to the company. Therefore, the personal characteristics and the behaviours of this group of customers are different from those of customers who did not share their data. This difference leads to the need for carefully evaluating the performance of a loyalty program since loyalty program members usually have different characteristics from those customers who did not subscribe to the program. Self-selection bias should always be considered when assessing the impact of marketing initiatives involving voluntary participation to avoid overestimating its effectiveness.

Re-designing loyalty programs

Loyalty programs have a lifecycle, with different stages. In this respect, companies should constantly monitor the performance of loyalty programs to be ready to fine-tune the program when needed. Re-designing a loyalty program is not small challenge: understanding which aspect of the program requires the re-design and when it is the right time to implement the re-design can be very difficult. There could be multiple reasons for the need to re-design: engagement with the program is declining, the redemption rate for rewards is declining, the penetration of the program on the total turnover is low, the program is not capable of attracting new members, the program does not lead to higher frequency of purchase or higher sales, the program was designed without a touchpoint that is emerging as important for customers and needs incorporation. Therefore, depending on the issue, companies need to face the challenge of a re-design. In this respect, innovating the loyalty program is a very complex task. Usually, the loyalty re-design is related to different areas, for instance the communication and the content strategy of the program, the accrual mechanism, the set of rewards, the visual style, the 'engagement engine'. When thinking about re-design, we can observe several trends taking place nowadays:

- Rewarding pro-social behaviours, to stimulate members to undertake behaviours that are good for the environment or for their well-being.
- Rewarding engagement behaviours, for instance writing a review of products, commenting and sharing content, sharing data or joining a contest.
- Including gamification elements to improve the points accrual system and to increase engagement with the loyalty program.
- Shifting from plastic cards to a fully digital accrual system that encourages the customer adoption of the mobile app of the loyalty program.

Beyond the abovementioned trends, further challenges emerge: how can AI contribute to the loyalty program re-design? Is it possible to achieve a competitive advantage through a loyalty program re-design? Is there a trade-off between renovating the loyalty program and avoiding disruptive changes that could negatively impact members' perception? How can virtual reality and metaverse re-shape gamification features in loyalty programs?

Finally, a generational perspective deserves further attention. Previous generations, such as Baby Boomers, Generation X, Generation Y are quite used to the concept and the mechanics of traditional loyalty programs. Little is known instead about the perceptions of loyalty programs from the new generations, such as Generation Z and Alpha. They have grown up in an era of influencers, streamers, gaming, political and climate uncertainty and a transformation of work-life balance. Our own research, relative to Italians, show clearly that younger generations are less engaged overall with loyalty programs. It is safe to assume that managers cannot take for granted that they will subscribe to loyalty programs as easily as the previous generations, unless they do not see a certain degree of value in that.

Last, but not least, given the surge of loyalty from a marketing tactic to corporate goal, it is fundamental that companies that 'have an issue' with retaining customers look beyond the mere redesign of the loyalty program. On the contrary, they should start questioning how and how much value they are creating for customers, the quality of the customer experience, where are the retention opportunities along the journey and why customers are not taking them. In a word, they should start questioning their loyalty strategy, first, and only subsequently, the redesign of the loyalty program.

Corporate digital responsibility as a new approach to build trust and loyalty

Digital technology, AI, augmented and virtual reality can lead to significant improvements to the customer experience. However, these technologies also bring relevant ethical, fairness, and privacy risks for users (Wirtz et al. 2023). This is especially true if we focus on data and data usage as drivers of customer experience personalization: advances in AI and the power of predictive analytics, automated decision making, and machine learning (ML) raise key ethical concerns.

The abovementioned technologies allow inferences about individuals, connecting data from multiple sources to design a complete overview of each customer. They also employ the past to predict the future, thus carrying all the biases and mistakes related to the past. Moreover, advanced technologies are employed to nudge individuals, predict and assess their behaviours and very often those individuals are not aware of it and do not have knowledge of the permissions they gave to companies to perform those activities (see Chapter 2). In this respect, we could assume that companies should face multiple challenges in how they manage the privacy of their customers, operating in the trade-off between maximizing the potential of new technologies on the one hand and managing in an ethical and safe manner the privacy and security of customers on the other hand. Many companies are thus embracing corporate digital responsibility (CDR) as a paradigm involving firm's ethical, fair, and protective use of data and technology when interacting with customers within their digital service ecosystem. CDR addresses the need for making the company accountable to moral norms and ethical issues as far as all the behaviours and decisions taken when managing customers are concerned. Examples of good CDR practices include, for instance, developing digital technology with a positive effect on the mental and physical health of employees and customers, handling data, privacy and information security in a responsible manner, encouraging the digitally disadvantaged, and offering training for digital responsibility and ethics (PwC, 2023). Why is it relevant to mention CDR as a future challenge in a loyalty management book? CDR could bring positive consequences, not only in terms of mitigating legal and reputational risks (Wirtz et al., 2023), but also in terms of building brand equity and trust with B2B and B2C customers. Companies adopting CDR could position themselves as leading organizations that care for their employees and customers, thus reinforcing the relationship with them and adding a new reason for them to stay loyal. Of course, adopting a CDR strategy is not an easy task: companies should invest money, time, effort and human resources in developing CDR practices that are reliable and credible. However, given the growth of data usage, the number of threats to customer privacy and the possible issues related to misuse of information and data breaches, adopting a CDR strategy represents an important move for the future.

References

PwC (2023) 'Digitization demands value awareness and responsible action'. Retrieved from www.pwc.de/en/sustainability/corporate-digital-responsibility-and-digital-ethics.html (accessed 13 July 2024).

Wirtz, J., Kunz, W. H., Hartley, N. and Tarbit, J. (2023) 'Corporate digital responsibility in service firms and their ecosystems'. *Journal of Service Research*, 26(2), 173–190.

INDEX

Note: **bold** page numbers indicate tables; *italic* page numbers indicate figures; page numbers followed by n refer to notes.

Printed in the United States
by Baker & Taylor Publisher Services